The
Wenner-Gren
Foundation

For Anthropological Research, Inc.

Embedding Ethics

WENNER-GREN INTERNATIONAL SYMPOSIUM SERIES

· ·

Series Editor: Richard G. Fox, President, Wenner-Gren Foundation for Anthropological Research, New York.

ISSN: 1475-536X

Since its inception in 1941, the Wenner-Gren Foundation has convened more than 125 international symposia on pressing issues in anthropology. Wenner-Gren International symposia recognize no boundaries—intellectual, national, or subdisciplinary. These symposia affirm the worth of anthropology and its capacity to address the nature of humankind from a great variety of perspectives. They make new links to related disciplines, such as law, history, and ethnomusicology, and revivify old links, as between archaeology and sociocultural anthropology, for example. Each symposium brings together participants from around the world, for a week-long engagement with a specific issue, but only after intensive planning of the topic and format over the previous 18 months.

In fulfilling its mission to build a world community of anthropologists and to support basic research in anthropology, the Foundation now extends its distinctive and productive pattern of pre-symposium planning to the preparation and publication of the resulting volumes. Never before has the Foundation taken responsibility for publishing the papers from its international symposia. By initiating this series, the Foundation wishes to ensure timely publication, wide distribution, and high production standards. The President of the Foundation serves as the series editor, and the symposium organizers edit the individual volumes.

Some landmark volumes from the past are: *Man's Role in Changing the Face of the Earth* in 1956 (William L. Thomas); *Man the Hunter* in 1968 (Irven DeVore and Richard B. Lee); *Cloth and Human Experience* in 1989 (Jane Schneider and Annette Weiner); and *Tools, Language, and Cognition in Human Evolution* in 1993 (Kathleen Gibson and Tim Ingold). Reports on recent symposia can be found on the foundation's website, *www.wennergren.org*, and inquiries should be addressed to *president@wennergren.org*.

The
Wenner-Gren
Foundation

For Anthropological Research, Inc.

Embedding Ethics

Edited by

Lynn Meskell and Peter Pels

Oxford · New York

English edition
First published in 2005 by
Berg
Editorial offices:
1st Floor, Angel Court, St Clements Street, Oxford OX4 1AW, UK
175 Fifth Avenue, New York, NY 10010, USA

Berg is the imprint of Oxford International Publishers Ltd.

Library of Congress Cataloging-in-Publication Data

Embedding ethics : shifting boundaries of the anthropological profession /
edited by Lynn Meskell and Peter Pels. — English ed.
    p. cm. — (Wenner-Gren international symposium series)
    Includes bibliographical references and index.
    ISBN 1-84520-047-0 (pbk.) — ISBN 1-84520-046-2 (cloth)
  1. Anthropological ethics. 2. Anthropology—Philosophy. 3.
Anthropologists—Attitudes. I. Meskell, Lynn. II. Pels, Peter. III. Series:
Wenner-Gren international series.

    GN33.6.E44 2005
    174'.9301—dc22

                                                                2004028571

British Library Cataloguing-in-Publication Data

A catalogue record for this book is available from the British Library.

ISBN-13 978 1 84520 046 6 (hardback)
         978 1 84520 047 3 (paperback)

ISBN-10 1 84520 046 2 (hardback)
         1 84520 047 0 (paperback)

Typeset by JS Typesetting Ltd, Porthcawl, Mid Glamorgan
Printed in the United Kingdom by Biddles Ltd, King's Lynn.

www.bergpublishers.com

Contents

List of Figures

Participants at the 2002 Wenner-Gren Symposium

Nadia L. Abu El-Haj, Barnard College
Donald Brenneis, University of California, Santa Cruz
Faye Ginsburg, New York University
Martin J. Hall, University of Cape Town
Craig Howe, Rapid City, South Dakota
Pradeep Jeganathan, International Center for Ethnic Studies, Colombo
Rosemary A. Joyce, University of California, Berkeley
Joel S. Kahn, La Trobe University
Marisa Lazzari, Columbia University
Ian Lilley, University of Queensland
Susan Lindee, University of Pennsylvania
Jonathan Marks, University of North Carolina, Charlotte
Lynn Meskell, Columbia University
Peter Pels, University of Leiden
Glenn D. Stone, Washington University
Alison Wylie, Barnard College

In memory of Sarah

Introduction: Embedding Ethics

Lynn Meskell and Peter Pels

This book documents a novel attitude toward ethics in anthropology. Drawing on insights from various disciplines within anthropology—archaeology and ethnography in particular—it proposes a view on ethics that emphasizes the priority of *practical ethical engagement* of the professional self with its audiences and criticizes the dominant tendency to disembed, exteriorize, and alienate ethics from everyday scientific practice. Without dismissing the value of ethical guidelines, the essays in this volume all argue against a conception of the anthropological professional as an ethical adjudicator and emphasize the need for institutionalizing, in research, publication, and public engagement, forms of open-ended negotiation between expert practitioners and their diverse audiences.

The ethical engagement of anthropologists has been a constant source of discussion since the 1960s, typically concentrated on the quasi-legal instrument of the ethical code. In the American Anthropological Association, the first effort at codification arose from discussions among sociocultural anthropologists about the appropriateness of the involvement of anthropologists in imperialist projects of counterinsurgency (Fluehr-Lobban 1991:27). The shift toward new patterns of funding and private employment resulted in critiques of the principles laid down in the early 1970s, and revisions of the American Anthropological Association's code have been under way ever since, most recently because of the scandal around possible violations of research ethics in the ethnographic and medical study of the Yanomami of Venezuela (see Pels 1999:111–112 and this volume). In archaeology, indigenous activism, looting and the illicit trade in antiquities (see Brodie, Doole, and Renfrew 2001; Elia 1995, 1997; Renfrew 2000), and the professionalization of archaeological practice contributed to a discussion about

1

guidelines for conduct. The development of an ethically aware archaeology was further galvanized by the passage of the Native American
Graves Protection and Repatriation Act (1991) in the United States,
discussions of stewardship (see Lynott and Wylie 2000; Scham 1998;
Wylie, this volume), and, most recently, discussions about archaeological "heritage" in the context of the war on terrorism (Colwell-
Chanthaphonh 2002; Meskell 2002b).

Some of these discussions—among European anthropologists in
particular—were skeptical about the value of codification (Amborn
1993; Blok 1972; Ghasarian 1997; Menget 1996; Pels 1994; Strathern
2000a:133–211, 291–295) and even questioned in principle the morality
of drawing up an ethical code (Bauman 1993; van Meijl 2000a). One
American critic described the 1980s proposals to revise the AAA code
as a form of "Reaganethics" that subordinated the interests of people
researched to the interests of private employers (Berreman 1991). At the
same time, however, the development of a principle of stewardship by
the Society for American Archaeology demonstrated the potential value
of a discussion of guidelines for conduct in increasing awareness of the
accountability of experts to others from whom they had previously
pretended to be independent (Wylie, this volume). Among social and
cultural anthropologists, one can discern two different lines of development: a revamping of the ethical code as a form of public relations
aimed at employers and gatekeepers and a use of ethical codes by
representatives of the people studied as a way of holding the researcher
accountable in ways that had not previously been possible (Pels
2000:143–145; see also van Meijl 2000b). Thus, we seem to have arrived
at a fragmentation of views on ethical codification among participants
in the anthropological enterprise.

Zygmunt Bauman argues that the project of codification creates a
situation that is "plagued with relativism, that plague being but a
reflection or a sediment of tribal parochialism of institutional powers
that usurp ethical authority" by means of a code (Bauman 1993:14).
To others this implies that the resort to codes implies the "extinction
of ethics" because codes threaten to replace the autonomous humanity
of the "moral self" (van Meijl 2000a:74, 78). Although, in the conference that led to this book, such concerns about ethical codes were
common, most contributors to this book disagree with this postmodernist argument and, we presume, share our suspicion of the
ethnocentric supposition of the existence of an autonomous "moral
self." Instead, the essays in this book ask for a redefinition of the moral
nature of the work of anthropology that goes beyond the dichotomous

opposition of "scientific" and "moral" aspects of knowledge production (a dichotomy evident, for example, from the debate between D'Andrade [1995] and Scheper-Hughes [1995]). They question the artifice of abstracting ethics from scholarly practice (an abstraction that one may also discern in the postmodernist argument). The dichotomy of science and ethics is to a considerable extent the result of a conception of ethics that anthropologists have adopted from other professions—one that is based on a code of professional conduct and the institution of an ethics committee that monitors this conduct by peer review (for an account, see Pels 1999). This conception turns the ethical code into a kind of "constitution" for the profession and the professional into an adjudicator who, on the basis of this ethical constitution and his mastery of expert information, assumes a position of unquestioned (and often implicit) superiority. The contributors to this volume show that such sovereignty, based on the assumption of expertise and supported by the presumption of the expert's autonomy in ethical matters, is often fictional, usually tenuous, and more often than not out of place. Instead of relying on the sovereign symbol of expertise, they propose that, *if* guidelines for conduct are needed, they should not lay down rules for judging expert sovereignty in an ethical way (for this would assume the value of expertise beforehand, out of context) but facilitate the negotiation of expertise within as well as outside of the profession. Instead of a definition of the ethical duties of scholars on the basis of a (usually implicit) assumption of their sovereign *rights*, ethical guidelines should explicate *responsibilities*—ways in which scholars can respond to those from whom they distinguish themselves as experts and in which they argue that responsibility in front of their peers.

This principle, we maintain, *embeds* ethics in anthropological practice at the same time that it opens up anthropological practice to the negotiation of the interests of the audiences with which it must deal: sponsors, university administrations, governments, the people studied, the media, and the public that needs to be informed or educated. Rethinking ethics in terms of negotiation rather than adjudication therefore implies not just a rethinking of ethics but a redefinition of the location—the proper social, cultural, historical, and epistemological *place*—of anthropological expertise itself. The values of both the symbol of "expertise" and that of "ethics" rely on typically modern attempts at transcendence—on dichotomous purifications of knowledge and morals that customarily dismiss large parts of its everyday working (cf. Latour 1993; Mitchell 2002). A postmodern dismissal of ethical codes fails to challenge this modernism: it tends to reify modernity by

adopting some of its central ideological categories—such as the autonomous "self." Instead, we direct our ethical awareness to certain forms
of ethical institutionalization and practice as a way of beginning to
explore how concrete ethical mediations other than the model of
professionalism may work out.

Thus, although the differences among the contributors to this book
are considerable—not least because of their diverse disciplinary and
professional approaches to anthropological practice—all the essays that
follow rethink ethics in its particular embedded setting; they all suggest
how ethical practice may be profitably relocated in situations that the
model of professional or scientific expertise tends to neglect; and they
all interrogate exemplars of ethical conduct and warnings about their
success or failure. Our grouping of these essays into three sections—
rethinking ethics, relocating ethics, and investigating exemplary
practices—is less a classification of each essay's exclusive focus than a
clarification of its connections with an attitude and a family of arguments about ethics that all of them share and that form the rationale
for the publication of this volume.

Rethinking Ethics

As we have indicated, the embedding of anthropological ethics requires
a rethinking of the practices of producing expert knowledge as well.
As the arguments between conference participants of different disciplinary persuasions showed, ethical practice in the various anthropological
disciplines differs considerably, not just because of different experiences
with codification but because of their different modes of production
of expert knowledge. At the very least, this suggested that we should
examine ethical relationships toward peers, public, and the people
studied in an interdisciplinary way. No one can deny that current discussions about ethics in anthropology have to take account of the recent
proliferation of ethical codes in the field of medicine, the reorientation
of archaeology toward a much more publicly responsible on-site research
practice, the changing nature of museum work, and the critical turn
of ethnography toward issues of representation and globalization. At
the same time, each (sub-)discipline points to defects in the ethical
practice of others. We need to break down the paradigmatic and social
isolation of the expert if we are to rethink ethics in such a way that these
divergent ethical practices begin to speak to and improve each other.

It is, for example, remarkable that the subdiscipline closest to the
medical model, biological anthropology, has not adopted the forms of

ethical codification of sociocultural anthropologists and archaeologists, despite the fact that it is increasingly feeling the impact of the explosion of ethical codification in the health sciences (see, for example, Brenneis in this volume). Jonathan Marks argues in this volume that the history of biological anthropology shows a kind of forcible extraction of "information" (in the form of blood or bones) that may be compared to equally "colonial" practices in ethnography, archaeology, and museum work (addressed by several other essays in this volume) and may find a present-day corollary in the appropriation of genetic information through various forms of patenting of intellectual property.[1] In his recognition of the fact that biological anthropologists have not paid sufficient attention to the ways in which an ethical code may help to hold practitioners accountable, Marks implicitly argues against the postmodernist dismissal of codes: in a situation in which many biological anthropologists do not define their "expert" selves as morally responsible to the people from whom they extract their "information," codes will not inhibit but promote the development of ethical responsibility in the subdiscipline. For the same reason, the adoption of an ethical code by biological anthropologists would redefine their identity as scientific experts. Few may want to go as far as Marks does in arguing that biological anthropologists also need to be responsible (at least in teaching, and without "giving in") to creation scientists, but this principle is at the same time more radical and more mundane when he argues that we need to consider whether people do not have the right to remain "free of science." His argument reveals that we customarily assume that "scientific expertise" is by definition good, and that experts often think that their claim to information is therefore bound to agree with any and all future improvements to be expected for humanity. There is no need to invoke a latter-day Frankenstein or Dr. Moreau (today he would probably be an expert in human genetics [see Verrips 2003]) to see the limits of this assumption.

Marks's profound question—what limits one should put on the expert's right to information—is echoed by others in this volume and has equally profound ethical consequences. Accepting his argument that scientific expertise can militate against society and its ideals, we encounter a crucial reinterpretation of the idea of informed consent.[2] If this argument does away with the modernist illusion that expertise always and everywhere means the progress of knowledge and that scientific research is therefore either harmless or good, it is no longer self-evident that people will accept research provided that they understand what it is about. It is one thing to defend taking blood samples from Yanomami (to take just one example [see Pels, this volume]) with the argument that such samples will lead to better health care for humanity in general (and therefore for Yanomami themselves in the long run) and quite another to make sure that the institutional, practical, historical, and cultural conditions have been met that will ensure that the taking of those blood samples in fact leads to such improvements for those whose consent is being sought. In other words, one needs to distinguish a form of informed consent that may confer a *right* to take blood samples on the basis of transcendent "expertise" from one that institutionalizes the *responsibility* to transform the taking of samples into practical results for the people from whom the samples are taken. The former argument often takes a form similar to the colonial settler doctrine of *terra nullius*: the right to "information" is thought to belong to those who first cultivate its fields, and they therefore can claim both access to it and the right to dispense it as they like if they do so, regardless of what other relationships people may have to this particular piece of "land" or "information." As other essays in this volume testify, the reduction of complex cultural and historical patterns of production and ownership to a Western conception of intellectual "property" can and should be contested, especially in an "information society" in which the capacity to copy and commercialize is so liberalized as to leave larger and larger numbers of people without protection against "free" access to and the virtual theft of their material and cultural resources.

The questioning of the right of "experts" to dictate access to and mastery over information was radicalized by the Society for American Archaeology's seminal initiatives to institute a principle of "stewardship"—part of a movement in which archaeologists reconfigured themselves as "trustees" (Scham 1998) or stewards of the past mediating between divergent interest groups. Alison Wylie uses her experiences as a key participant in the formulation of these ethical principles to develop a particularly enlightening view of the embedding of ethical codification. She demonstrates that, while stewardship was first discussed in a context in which the values of archaeological resource protection were confronted with the tribal values of certain Native American groups, the principles codified on that basis could still be interpreted as safeguarding an archaeological privilege to the past. While agreeing that archaeologists' primary responsibility is to serve as caretakers of and advocates for the archaeological record, ensure its long-term conservation, and promote its use for the benefit of all people, she documents how a "theology of the scientific faithful" tends to turn objects into "information" to be managed by a "conservation ethic." Like some of the biological anthropologists and ethnographers referred to by Marks and Pels (in this volume), the scientific faithful complain about "antiscientific" sentiments that obstruct their access to and mastery over these objects. Wylie suggests that archaeologists should redefine their goal as a search not for a transcendent truth opposed to local or particular interests but for *significant* truths about materials and sites in an open-ended negotiation. This redefinition allows for the recognition of (aesthetic, sentimental, or commercial) values other than the archaeological pursuit of evidence. Both the truths of expertise and the codified guidelines of a stewardship ethics should, therefore, be regarded as *performances* in a particular setting rather than as transcendent information or ethical rules that aspire to go beyond reformulation and public negotiation. Significantly, Wylie highlights that it was a specific performance—the (open-ended, normative but not rulelike) story told by a Native American scholar—that triggered the proclamation of a principle of collaborative stewardship. (We will return to this exemplary moment below.)

Wylie's essay suggests that ethical codification displays a kind of "constitutional modernism" whose "fiction of universalism" makes ethics *exterior* to everyday scientific practice, and this is particularly important for the way we want to rethink ethics. This exteriority, usually unquestioned in both professional and popular discourses on anthropological ethics, is implicit in the reliance of a professional organization like the American Anthropological Association on the model of an ethical code reinforced by a committee of peers. Peter Pels investigates the reverberations of this kind of "constitutionalism" in the recent controversy over Patrick Tierney's *Darkness in El Dorado* (2000), arguing that the attitudes toward ethics of the professional organization, the defenders of "science," and the defenders of the primacy of ethical engagement often obscure the implicit—and rather ethnocentric—assumptions that tend to abstract "scientific fact" from (Western) "values" and vice versa. He argues that we need to interrogate the reliance of professional codes and committees on a form of ethics that enshrines modernist values of individualism, legalism, and nationalism and that bases them on a conception of knowledge as the possession of a kind of "expert" commodity—the "property" of information referred to above. Indeed, this form of "exterior" ethics neglects the moral economy of science itself and its tendency to dismiss other moralities of research (such as trust or public engagement) in favor of the value of scholarly honesty. The historical and contingent event of the El Dorado scandal brings out—despite the conservative gut reaction of many participants to argue from the primacy of either science or ethics—how impossible it is to maintain these modernist abstractions in practice. Pels brings recent arguments about the politics of ethnographic representation and late-twentieth-century globalization to bear on the question whether the El Dorado scandal has irrevocably modified anthropologists' capacity to maintain their scientific or ethical aloofness from other moralities encountered when dealing with the public or with the people studied. Like the archaeologists confronted with a Hopi scholar telling them a story with a moral, ethnographers are bound to acknowledge the moral "duplexity" of research: the fact that engagement with people living in one's field of study requires one to negotiate "other" values instead of implicitly assuming that our principles of ethics and expertise are universal (cf. Pels 1999).

This notion of the moral "duplexity" of ethnographic research can be compared to the central issues raised by Marks and Wylie: at some point or other, researchers meet the people they study (even if only to extract a gene sample) and face someone who may challenge the values on which the practice of research is based. Joel Kahn argues that, when confronted with such a situation—in his case, the deep suspicion of many Malaysians toward an anthropology done by outsiders—we should rethink not just ethics but the nature of anthropology itself and of modernity as well. Reviewing how Kantian, Rortian, or postmodernist philosophy would deal with the problem of Malaysians who argue that their culture or spirituality is too different to be grasped by a Western, colonial science such as anthropology, Kahn finds no solution along these lines and even doubts the possibility of an ethical anthropology on their basis. Instead, he proposes that we need a radically different understanding of modernity—not as a fake universalism emanating from Europe or the West but as embedded in specific histories and cultural circumstances, including those of Malaysia. His rethinking and embedding of modernity points to another possibility for a cross-cultural ethics and a rethinking of the possibility of anthropology as well: an "incomplete" cosmopolitanism that, as the authority of anthropology to represent others is increasingly contested, should aim at listening to these other voices because "only they are capable of really shifting us away from the particularistic presuppositions that inform existing cosmopolitan practices." Thus, we have come full circle: rethinking ethics implies rethinking expertise, and that implies rethinking modernity as well: as something that emanates not from "us" but from interaction.[3] We should locate ethics not in a Kantian, lawlike universal[4] nor in the postmodernist "moral self" whose ethical relation to the elusive other we can only take on trust, but in concrete practices of interaction with others. This is the novel attitude to ethics that we mentioned at the outset.

But what kind of alternative conception of ethics fits such a relocation? What kinds of ethical practices can undo the exteriority of ethics to expertise while preserving the contingent advantages of adopting explicit guidelines for conduct? The remaining essays in this volume work, each in different ways, toward detailed and sophisticated answers to these questions. For a simplified, more abstract and general perspective, however, we may be inspired by Wylie's example of the Native American scholar's attempt to shift the course of an ethical discussion by telling a story. Storytelling exemplifies an ethical practice that ill accords with the legalistic and constitutional model still dominant in anthropological professional associations: despite having "a moral," it lays down no rules and depends for its moral effect on the interpretation of the listener. Storytelling is, in other words, an open-ended practice of moral negotiation (among other things). In fact, it is so open-ended that—one may object—it lacks ethical discipline. A certain kind of discipline—usually known as "theory" and "method"—is precisely what many scholars claim distinguishes their everyday practice from "mere storytelling." Is there an approach to anthropological ethics that maintains the open-endedness of storytelling but still subjects this essential negotiability to a certain discipline and replicability, managing to straddle this contradiction between openness and closure?

Here, the disciplines of archaeology and cultural and social anthropology—as they confronted each other during the conference that led to this book—provide useful insights. Without implying a clear-cut dichotomy (a reification that the contributions to this book would contest in any case), it is fair to say that archaeologists' concern with the presentation, preservation, and contested ownership of the material and the sites they work with tend to make them more accountable to a wide range of interest groups. In contrast, ethnographers are more often wedded to a paradigm of individual work that is still occluded by the mystique of fieldwork (but see, for example, Berreman 1962; Fabian 1983), and their disciplinary awareness of ethical responsibility tends to concentrate on questions of individual advocacy and ethnographic storytelling (but see, for example, Lamphere 2003). In short, ethnographers are less often engaged with an extra-academic public than archaeologists and could be inspired by the latter. Conversely, archaeologists who are aware of the ethical responsibilities to wider audiences that their work entails are making an "ethnographic turn" and adopting more of the critical perspectives on advocacy and storytelling that sociocultural anthropologists have discussed since the 1970s. As we have argued, disciplinary differences may also have produced different attitudes toward the uses and misuses of ethical codification. In other words, different disciplines combine ethics and method in different ways, and ethics and method are both part of these disciplines' technologies of self: the ways in which they attempt to materially produce a desirable subject (Pels 2000).[5] This perspective allows for a focus on the sites and materials, the bodies, the conversations, the charts and writings and committees—in short, the material culture of expert and ethical behavior—that constitute ethical practice at the *core of* rather than exterior to research. It also suggests a way to broaden ethical practice beyond codes and ethical committees.

Relocating Ethics in Current Research

Relocating ethics means first of all focusing on locations of ethical practice other than the constitutional realm of codes and committees. Jonathan Marks brings out how new regimes of intellectual property about genetic patenting turn the laboratory into a place where enormous ethical and political issues are being decided—unfortunately for many, in a way that obscures the ethics or politics of laboratory practice (see also Stone, this volume; Latour and Woolgar 1979). This becomes even more obvious where fieldwork is required. A common thread running through the recent military interventions in Iraq has been a public outcry over the failure to protect the archaeological heritage (Colwell-Chanthaphonh 2002, Meskell 2002b). The Middle East has long been characterized as a locus of precious archaeological resources that require control and management by Western experts and their respective governments. In February 2003, even before full-scale military action was initiated, a group of wealthy collectors and curators met with the U.S. Defense and State Departments to discuss the impending fate of archaeological sites, museums, and collections (Lawler 2003). Some months earlier, U.S. President George W. Bush had discussed the possibility of resuming discussions with UNESCO after a thirty-year silence during which countries including Britain, Germany, Switzerland, and Japan had failed to ratify the 1970 UNESCO convention to prevent the international trade in stolen art and antiquities. The U.S. effort to co-opt United Nations support turned culture into a potent vehicle for these aims, as is shown by the massive media coverage of the so-called looting of the Baghdad museum and the concomitant demonizing of the Iraqi people as destroyers of world prehistory and civilization. These events underscore the intensely political nature of the archaeological enterprise. Global violence affects other fieldworkers as well: one has only to think of the effects of the war in Afghanistan on anthropological experts on Islamism in general and Pashtun-speaking ethnographers in particular or about the extent to which the *intifada* reconfigures the work of scholars who study Palestine. A certain *politics of location* should, therefore, be central to our understanding of anthropological subjects (in all senses of the word) and affect us as practitioners today.

Reembedding ethics implies not only seeking out those locations of ethical practice that the dominant constitutional understanding of ethics neglects but also charting their new configurations "at home" as much as "in the field." The contributions of Marks, Wylie, Pels, and Kahn suggest that these new configurations include changing regimes of intellectual property and bureaucratic management, changing responsibilities (legal or otherwise) toward indigenous groups, shifts in the definition of "home" and "field" under the influence of recent processes of globalization, and the concomitant refiguring of anthropology's heritage of colonial representations, modernist conceptions of expertise, and their perception by "indigenous" intellectuals. These reconfigurations of the places where we work also relocate ethics in new forms of producing a desirable subject: they question who we are as anthropologists and what we are supposed to study—and, more radical, when, where, and how our role as expert becomes or ceases to be relevant to what we do. Here sites of violence are of particular interest in understanding this relocation of ethics. In an earlier incarnation, U.S. anthropologists developed methods for the study of culture "at a distance" to produce a "diagnosis" for the purpose "of facilitating some specific plan or policy" meant to aid the military effort of their country during World War II (Mead and Métraux 1953:397). One does not need to deny the genuine moral convictions that led these anthropologists to support the war effort to see that this position may still make many anthropologists uncomfortable—not only because the moral connotations of cultural relativism are, in this case, made subject to "such nonrelativist purposes as national defense, political propaganda, and outright manipulation and control of other societies" but also because they reinforce the allochronic tendencies—the tendency to locate "them" in a time other than "ours"—inherited from colonial discourse (Fabian 1983:49). Similar questions (with, no doubt, different answers) can now be posed of anthropologists whose field sites have become inaccessible to them because of violence and who therefore fall back on more remote modes of research (such as the Internet). How important to both our expert and our ethical practices is the coevalness of researcher and researched? To what extent do we need to share a location? And to what extent can we maintain the implicit presumption that we possess an ethical or expert stance that allows us to disengage ourselves from violence inflicted on the people studied?

Lynn Meskell and Pradeep Jeganathan both address specific research sites of violence and show that consideration of these sites should lead us to reconfigure the moral economy of research, whether one agrees or disagrees with the World War II anthropologists' activist stance. Both show, as well, that our location of ethics resides not only in the historical and sociocultural makeup of the place in which we find ourselves while doing research but sometimes even more in a feature of research that is too seldom regarded as part of ethical considerations: the epistemology of making an anthropological object (see Fabian 1983). A number of anthropologists of the "literary turn" have taken this as a problem of representation, to be solved by representation (for a critique, see Comaroff and Comaroff 1992; Fabian 1991; Said 1989). Meskell and Jeganathan both show that the ethics of such object making is, instead, part of a history of contest and violence—a history that also comes out in Craig Howe's account in this volume of what happens when one tries to redefine the Native American "tribal" object that a museum can put on display.

Meskell examines these issues in the context of Egypt's "world heritage," where the UNESCO vision of value and archaeological significance is privileged over the needs and concerns of local communities. Interpreting Luxor as a site of violence, she describes the persecution that the community of Gurna has sustained by virtue of its heritage. Government officials, who called on heritage planners, World Bank consultants, tourism investors, and, not least, archaeologists to make recommendations about the future of the Valley of the Nobles in the service of the state, have used real and symbolic violence in attempts at their forced relocation. Moreover, the sites that form the raw materials for the lucrative enterprises of heritage and tourism are violent also in that they provide targets for antigovernment acts of terrorism against archaeological tourists and the revenues they bring to Egypt. Thus, the archaeological site should be recognized as an unbounded geography of difference and contest: it is not merely a piece of "global" cultural heritage exploited by the tourist industry or a site of national imagination (and revenue) and a target of Islamist attacks but also a place where local communities suffer because their history is subsumed by histories classified as more valuable. Taken to its logical conclusion, this implies a radical rethinking of the archaeological object and its ethics: while archaeologists have addressed their wider social responsibilities to diverse communities and stakeholders and rarely assume—as they did in the past—that they are not implicated in the concerns of living peoples,[6] Meskell now suggests that the positivist residue in archaeology derives to a considerable extent from the illusion that the objects of archaeological research are dead and buried (see also Meskell 2002b).

This concern with the allochronic tendency of a discourse about the object to be studied makes archaeology and ethnography much more alike than the idea of their studying either "dead" or "living" people suggests. Pradeep Jeganathan takes up a particularly subtle form of the distanciation that Fabian identified in anthropological definitions of the object of study. He transposes the dilemmas of the expert anthropologist being confronted by an "indigenous" audience (already discussed by Joel Kahn) to a field in which anthropologist and audience are both Tamil and share memories of the violence of the Sri Lankan civil war. Attempting to explain why his lecture about Benedict Anderson's *Imagined Communities* led to friction with his audience of Tamil nationalists, Jeganathan subtly suggests that the way an "anthropology of violence" engages with its object shows that even the scientific definition of the object itself requires a certain moral economy of "disciplined affect." This ethical stance of the anthropologist confronts "other" moral judgments (of the nation but also of violence) in such a way that, like Meskell, he finds himself inescapably caught up in a politics of location. Contrary to the classical positivist notions of science, therefore, which portray the expert as an adjudicator who supposedly stands above the parties in a dispute and ethics as antithetical to politics (see Pels 1999:102), the anthropologist's definition of his own subject and object has ethical consequences that involve him in inherently political negotiations.

It is no coincidence that both these discussions take place in novel locations of ethical activity, where the time-space compression of recent forms of globalization increasingly confronts Eurocentric notions of authority, ownership, and knowledge with alternative conceptions—a confrontation that asks for ethically duplex and therefore inherently political negotiations. Meskell describes a world in which the archaeologists' definition of their object of research is caught up in hegemonic definitions of "world heritage" by which powerful individuals and organizations render particular places valuable, important, beautiful, and meaningful to humanity as a whole and a certain version of the past is essentialized and commodified as a natural resource. Here we again encounter the current problematic of intellectual property, especially where such commodification of the past is contested by Native American (Goldstein 1992; Lilley 2000b; Swidler et al. 1997; Watkins 2000) or Australian Aboriginal groups (Attwood and Arnold 1992; Byrne 1996, 2004; Meehan 1995; Mowaljarlai et al. 1988). For many indigenous groups, the past is not property: it is not to be bought or sold, studied or scientifically tested, or displayed or objectified in ways that Western participants might consider appropriate or unproblematic. As Craig Howe points out in this volume, the necessity to negotiate multiple and sometimes contradictory evaluations of the past, and its consequences for the object studied and displayed to an audience, leads to both hopeful and frustrating confrontations of so-called universal and so-called indigenous values.

In contrast, Jeganathan calls attention to another consequence of recent forms of cultural globalization in which the confrontation of the Tamil anthropological expert with an audience of other Tamil intellectuals raises doubts about the viability and coherence of the notion of "indigenousness" itself. If Yanomami first organize themselves *as Yanomami* in response to a scandal about their scientific exploitation (Pels, this volume) and Malay intellectuals define anthropology as inherently incapable of grasping their culture (Kahn, this volume), how ethical is it, Jeganathan asks, to juxtapose the "expert" awareness of "imagined" communities, cultures, or "indigenous" groups with members' insistence that their culture, nation, and/or indigenousness is a primordial or at least legitimate ground for opposition and defense? We do not claim to provide a final answer to such questions—in fact, an embedded ethics would judge the value of such claims in their specific locations, critical of the attempt to disembed them. The examples show, however, that the negotiation of the ethical position of the expert with competing values is in fact inescapable—that, to use Jon Marks's words, "the right to be free of science" is contested in each case.

Martin Hall provides, in the concluding chapter of this section, an overview of this broader landscape of globalizing change from the perspective of the new South Africa that highlights the necessity to fuse the ethical awareness of the different forms of "disciplined affect" within anthropology—social archaeology, ethnography, and the recent more theoretical critiques of Orientalism and representation associated with "cultural studies." He expresses a view of anthropology as in the process of being relocated in a new landscape of expertise and engagement in which science and ethics are redefined in tandem. Hall relocates archaeological practice in South Africa in the public spaces of the "network society." The exoticization of Africa as the "past" of humanity (as animal paradise, source of human life, or heart of darkness) has always been part of the scientific impetus behind South African archaeology, whether expertise and ethics were based on the civilizing mission (as in colonial archaeology), liberation (as in nationalist archaeology), or science (as in the structuralist archaeology that tried to escape both earlier positions). Now these themes are increasingly incorporated into globalized public spaces: theme parks, game parks, and shopping centers, the famous *Africa: The Art of a Continent* exhibition, even Disney's Animal Kingdom, where postcolonial wildlife conservation has become the core of its morality-as-entertainment. Hall's broad canvas shows particularly well how sociocultural anthropology and archaeology can and should be brought into fruitful interdisciplinary confrontation.

Hall argues that—contrary to the tendency of academic experts to regard past paradigms as superseded and only marginally relevant to the present—these historically different epistemic and ethical systems of South African archaeology persist in the wider, nonacademic realm, raising the question to what extent the academic expert is still responsible for their use and misuse. This point is crucial for our general understanding of how, where, and why anthropological ethics are located, for such genealogies show that the ethical attitudes of anthropologists that emerged at different points in the discipline's history—the morality of "facts," the duplexity of moral engagement, advocacy, ethical codification—cannot safely be relegated to the past and coexist, often in conflict, in the present (Pels 1999:114). A historicizing awareness therefore highlights two ways of relocating our ethics. First, it addresses the possible continuities between present practices and a colonial past of grave-robbing, looting, and ethnographic exploitation. Secondly, it questions whether the attempt to create historical discontinuities—for instance, by drawing up an ethical code that states that we should no longer engage in those practices—can actually absolve anthropologists of the responsibility to disengage their science from a tainted past and engage with the interests of those people who still feel harmed by it. Hall is firmly of the opinion that such public intellectual duties cannot be shirked, even if this means engaging in a politics of location of having to address and accommodate multiple audiences.

Again, our standpoint vis-à-vis practices of heritage and ownership turns out to be central. Richard Wilk and Anne Pyburn have argued that archaeologists cannot regard the archaeological record as their personal possession and, as its stewards, must safeguard public access to materials, documents, and research results without jeopardizing the preservation and protection of archaeological sites (1998:200). Hall's essay suggests that we should go further, extending our awareness of intellectual property issues[7] to questions of the dissemination beyond the discipline of archaeology of images or information for commercial use and profit—taking on, in fact, a much more public role as intellectuals, especially in defense of those subordinate groups that have most to lose and whose position in the network society makes them feel that their culture is under threat (see Coombe 1998; Dowson 1994; Janke 1998; Morris 1997; Smith 1999). If our knowledge products do indeed define the commercial value of gene patents, "aboriginal" art, and displays in a museum or theme park and negotiate the political value of culture (of the "nation," "humanity," the "community," or the "indigenous") in relation to the state's legitimate or illegitimate interventions, the situation in which anthropologists "did not need to resolve conflicts about patent rights and publication priority" (Wildesen 1984:8) is a thing of the past. As a consequence, some of our "expert" values—such as the unequivocal commitment to academic publicity (cf. Brown 1998; Pels 2000:164–165)—are already being renegotiated. As the contributions of Marks, Pels, Stone, and Howe show as well, the conception of ethics we put forward in this book is in accord with recent critical studies of the responsibility of anthropologists to endorse alternative conceptions of cultural property and defend "indigenous" interests in the public sphere, often directed against the increasing velocity with which the past, the land, or material culture are being appropriated by those who dominate the network society. Even if we try to avoid simplistic oppositions of modern exploitation and "indigenous" resistance, we have to take seriously moralities that do not self-evidently mesh with modern academic interests—nonnational sovereignties, different ways of "owning" culture, and spiritual evaluations of the past (see especially Howe, Meskell, and Pels in this volume). Such a relocation of ethics implies not only paying attention to the new sites and places that force us, at times violently, to rethink where we stand or to address the multiple histories (and their multiple layers) that make the present in which we make ethical judgments. It also means rethinking the "moral topography" (Taylor 1989:111) of the academic subject and, in the words of a recent and influential assessment, push anthropologists to reenter the real world and recapture the progressive character of its basic concepts (Fox 1991b:13).

Exemplars and Warnings

It is not, however, self-evident what a relocation of ethics and expertise means in practice. Many experiments take place in which the contours of such a relocation are being drawn, tested, and redrawn as a matter of contesting established power as much as of negotiating new ideas. Just as the essays discussed above are still in the business of rethinking the moral topography of ethics in anthropology, the last set of essays discusses a number of recent experiments in knowledge production and ethical practice. Looking at such experiments, few can escape the conclusion that the pervasive modernist assumptions underlying much of current ethical activity and the power structures in which these assumptions are embedded often stultify promising initiatives for rethinking and relocating ethics. Moreover, certain novel forms of ethical practice—such as the bureaucratic monitoring of ethical performance by internal review boards conceived mostly on the model of biomedical research—are considered suspect by many anthropologists. This section addresses four exemplars of such initiatives and warnings about the extent to which they promise a solution to the problems we have discussed above. Even if they cannot pretend to give an overview of current changes in the field of anthropological ethics, they do portray four widely different attempts to grapple with contemporary demands.

Taken together, the essays by Stone, Howe, Brenneis, and Joyce address the advances and drawbacks of three fields of experimentation in ethnography and archaeology: the problem of renegotiating expertise, the problem of collaboration across divergent interests and antagonistic regimes of value, and the emergence of new forms of governance in global "audit culture." They situate these problems in four locations of scholarly work that have been experiencing radical changes in recent years: the "multisited" ethnographic field, the museum, the academic committee, and the archaeological field site. Each draws on significant advances on previous practices in anthropology, yet each also observes limits to these advances. However, we maintain that it is from such experiments that our rethinking of ethics in anthropology needs to draw sustenance. As we have argued, these improvements are by no means limited to the discussion of ethics: in addition to rethinking expertise, they will also have to face up to problematic manifestations of entrenched and powerful assumptions.

Glenn Stone addresses a situation that, in the redefinition of ethno-graphy that has taken place in the past few decades, has become more and more prevalent. His research on the practices and doctrines of biogenetic corporations such as Monsanto has placed him in an ambiguous position. Endorsing neither the neo-Malthusian ethics of Monsanto (which portrays any opposition to the genetic modification of crops as a contribution to world poverty) nor the crude charges of some environmentalist groups (which argue that genetically modified crops merely serve the interests of corporations such as Monsanto), he finds himself immersed in a "science of the gray"—a contingent redefinition of his own expertise based on a moral commitment to finding out, for example, what kind of crop would be best for Indian peasants. Being caught between such global public relations giants as Monsanto and Greenpeace makes for a rather bleak picture of the possibilities for anthropological research, but it should not be allowed to obscure the radical advances in moral engagement that research like Stone's produces: the more we pursue "multilocale ethnography" that tries to make sense of the global connections between, for instance, Monsanto and an Indian peasantry (see Marcus 1986:171–173), the more we will have to confront the fact that our expertise consists of (re-)negotiating the different and often antagonistic moral complexes that take place in these locales. We now have a situation in which the requirement to "study up" as well as "down" fuses the need to do a more or less distanced ethnography of "local" ethics (such as Mon-santo's "neo-Malthusianism") with the need to commit oneself ethno-graphically to a certain ethical stance. In sharp contrast, an earlier paradigm of ethnography defined the relationship of researcher and researched in dyadic terms (Pels 1999:105,110; Pels and Salemink 1999:3, 40): the moral responsibility of the former—if any—was described in terms of defending the interests of the latter (as in the first clause of the 1971 Principles of Professional Responsibility), and anthropologists who explicitly condemned the morals of the people they studied were treated with suspicion.[8]

Stone's account points to the strengths as well as the weaknesses of such advances in ethnography: whereas their strengths lie in the explicit confrontation of power relationships through multilocale ethnography, the emergence of a scholarly mode of moral engagement, and the critical scrutiny of ethnographic representations vis-à-vis more widely disseminated popular discourses, they remain weak because of the relatively isolated position of the individual ethnographer. Here the contrast with the more collaborative situations discussed by Craig Howe and Rosemary Joyce is extremely useful. Archaeology and museum work are, because of the sites and the material dealt with, more public than most ethnographic work. Howe's account of the collaborative planning of the inaugural exhibition at the National Museum of the American Indian in Washington, D.C., is fascinating both as a model of what can be achieved by negotiating museum displays (both professionally and publicly) and as a warning against the historical inertia that can oppose such experiments in informed consent and collaboration in a morally duplex and highly unequal arena. As does Jonathan Marks, Howe employs the famous case of Ishi's brain (see Kroeber 1961; Marks 1999; Starn 2004) to remind us of the tainted bounty that makes up a large part of the Native American collections in the US museums. The inventory of the artifacts in the possession or control of the Smithsonian Institution that the NMAI was required to undertake in collaboration with tribal representatives resulted in negotiations over definitions of tribal sovereignty, relevant audiences, and the design of the permanent exhibition. Howe shows that these negotiations required a radical confrontation between the notions of the past habitually used by American museums and those (much more "alive," as it were) of the tribal groups themselves—a concrete experiment with the ethics of the location and determination of the object and the concomitant necessity to negotiate antagonistic regimes of value that we have referred to above. Yet, he concludes his essay with an account of how—as in the case documented by Joyce—this emergent methodology of stakeholder negotiation failed, recalling, for Native Americans, a violent history of broken promises.

The broken treaty may, in fact, function as another reminder of the fraught nature of moral codification and its simultaneous necessity and insufficiency. The case of the NMAI shows that moral responsibility—in the widest sense, as aiming at negotiation between morally duplex standards—cannot be fully institutionalized, even when backed by legal force and an impressive experiment in negotiation. Both the content and the methods of codification can, as Alison Wylie also shows, be turned against the intentions that they are supposed to objectify. Don Brenneis demonstrates how the strengths of ethnographic—particularly sociolinguistic—methods can be harnessed to a better understanding of what this means for ethical practice. Adopting the advances made in a relatively new field, the anthropology of policy, documentation, and audit (Harper 1998; Shore and Wright 1997, 1999; Strathern 2000a), he argues that "before we can write culture, we must write money" and that this increasingly involves the ethical documentation required or used by internal review boards. The phrase is crucial, for it points to a further recognition of ethics in locations that once seemed exempt from it. Whereas the analysis of "writing culture" (Clifford and Marcus 1986; Fabian 1983; Said [1978] 1985) criticized ethnographic storytelling for the moral judgments and power inequalities that it concealed, now we should also be critical of what we have to do to "write money"—the filing and discussion of research proposals and their ethical aspects as judged by internal review boards. On the one hand, the bureaucratic institutionalization of ethics exemplified by these boards, predominantly based on biomedical models and involving codes of conduct and committees to monitor them, has forced a greater awareness of ethical issues on practitioners; on the other, many anthropologists complain about the distortions and alien standards that such practices impose on their research. Brenneis's ethnography, however, takes the critique of the bureaucratization of ethics involved to another level. An ethnography of the internal review board's documentation shows not only that it is part of an increase in top-down discipline but also that the framework provided by the "proxy" of documents disembeds ethical guidelines from practice in ways comparable to other forms of audit. Thus, the attempt to educate practitioners in better ethical practice by instituting internal review boards paradoxically takes place in contexts other than those in which ethics is supposed to be learned, serving as a concrete example of the "exteriorization" of ethics that we have discussed.

This becomes particularly clear when the two kinds of committees that are supposed to decide on research practice—funding committees and internal review boards—are compared: whereas the former tend toward a comparative peer review of proposals and hence a negotiation of expertise, the latter try to assess the ethics of proposals individually by including public interests in their proceedings. This division locates the responsibility of the researcher in two different institutions exterior to each other, one dealing with the "interior" of expertise, the other with the "public" of ethical judgment. In practice, however, the intertwining of internal "expert" and "nonspecialist" public judgment is unavoidable, because the internal review board has to make "expert" evaluations of whether a proposal is going to generate "useful data" in order to judge whether it has sufficiently taken account of nonspecialist demands for ethical accountability (compare Joyce's ideas about expert adjudication in this volume). The exteriority of internal review boards to research funding committees first ruptures and then recombines— by proxy, at a distance from research practice—the activity of judging whether a proposal will generate what Wylie calls "significant" truths.

Our rethinking and relocation of ethics suggest that such rupture and recombination can be avoided if expertise and ethics are routinely fused in decisions about funding at whatever level.

In contrast, Rosemary Joyce discusses several practices of archaeological research in Honduras in which such fusions of arguments about money, power, and "significant truth" are being negotiated by different stakeholders in direct confrontation. She ends her contribution with what to her is an exemplar of a successful stakeholders' dialogue about an archaeological site, and we feel that the purpose of this book is best served by ending on this optimistic note. Her vision of "good practice," however, would not be as significant without the contrast to more agonistic negotiations that she experienced during discussions about the famous world heritage site of Copan. Interestingly, the first meetings about Copan resulted in different assessments among the stakeholders present about how the site itself should be interpreted: as information about "the past" (the stake of scientific archaeologists), as a material object to be preserved (the stake of conservationists), and as a "past present" that is of interest, in very different ways, to both tourists, national governments, and indigenous groups. During a second meeting, the globalizing imperatives of the world heritage program added another stake but in the form of a more disembedded feature of global "audit culture"—a "management plan" aimed at turning the Copan site into a "park" to be directed, interestingly enough, by wildlife experts (see Hall, this volume, as well). While the first meeting can be interpreted as an attempt at an ethical practice of collaboration—although with less success and more agony than at Joyce's own research site—the second shows how careful one has to be about endorsing forms of "accountability": forms of governance such as a management plan can, just like the internal review boards discussed by Brenneis, introduce a proxy of moral judgment into ethical practice, shifting the power of decision making away from the actual location where ethical judgment has to be learned in collaboration toward so-called experts whose experience is of something utterly different (in this case, wildlife conservation) and who know little about the discipline's values.

Conclusion: Toward Ethical Methodologies?

Thus, our argument comes full circle. We started out by querying the institutionalization of ethics in codes and committees, a form that we can now identify as a proxy, a distanciation from the ethical practice that practitioners should aim at. Now we see that even practices of collaboration with stakeholders perceived as outsiders to scientific research as such, may be threatened by both the disembedding effects of proxies that try to encode and enforce such collaborations and the social and historical relations of power from which the formulation of such proxies derives. However, we have also seen, in the examples of Stone, Howe, Brenneis, and Joyce in particular, that the stakes of expert academics and their nonspecialist interlocutors may be brought into confrontation. In these examples, the hand and head of science—its method and theory—are intertwined with its heart, with a labor of care that may be passionate but need not take leave of reason and common sense.[9] This invites us to look at ethical guidelines not as constitutions—quasi-contracts determining what it is right to do once one has agreed that academic expertise is the adjudicator of fact and information—but as methodologies: as suggestions about what to do and what to be when engaged in the process of determining what is fact and information and when, where, why, and for whom such work is significant. The fusion of ethics and method—both "technologies of self" (Pels 2000)—seems to promise to constitute the scientific subject as an ethical one immediately, rather than by proxy, even when we realize that "methodology" itself is a proxy that entails a tendency to disembed the expert "self" from the practice of research as such.

To be sure, "methodology is prophylactic in its essence" (Andreski 1973:115) if it is seen as a technology of the self in which researchers aim at becoming totally transparent, impersonal, and apolitical conduits of "objective" sets of facts "out there," pretending to be scientific by denying their social, cultural, and historical personhood. As Max Weber argued long ago, even the most purely scientific of vocations includes hand, head, *and* heart, and in a world of a "polytheism of values" we shall have to "set to work and meet the 'demands of the day', in human relations as well as in our vocation" (1958:156). This intersubjective conception of vocation turns the self-discipline of method from the attempt to isolate a "path over and beyond" (one possible meaning of *meta-hodos*; cf. "meta-physics") into the simpler notion of a "path through" the world that we encounter when engaged in producing expert knowledge—including engagement with people who may not share our valuation of that goal. This would include using our methodology to anticipate where, when, and how we are bound to encounter relations of power that help or frustrate our goals, the goals of the people we move among, and the methods that help us or our potential collaborators to achieve those goals. This, of course, realigns anthropological ethics with the critical discussions of theory and method that anthropologists have conducted throughout the history of their discipline(s). In this history, method was subordinated to expert discipline as well as expert performance—in other words, to demonstrating ourselves, to various audiences, to be responsible (or not) toward "self" as well as "other," in such a way as to show that anthropology is worthwhile. If we have a novel point to make in this book it is, perhaps, simply that anthropology has been made *less* worthwhile by disembedding ethics—through various forms of professionalist ideology—from the everyday practice of anthropological debate about theory and method, the guidance these debates provide about how we relate to people during research, and what these understandings of our vocation tell us about how anthropologists (should) situate themselves in the world.

However, fusing ethics and method in this manner is no simple solution. At best, it opens up the discussion of moral goals to experiments with alternative methodologies of ethical practice, methodologies that, as we have shown, are always embedded in specific social, cultural, and historical relationships of power. No ethical or methodological proxy can escape the force of such relationships. This is particularly evident, for example, in the implicit nationalism of many efforts at drawing up better guidelines for conduct: it is no coincidence that even the ethical practices of the politicized social archaeology and anthropology that we have held up as examples to be emulated in this introduction mostly derive from "settler societies" like the United States, Australia, and South Africa (see, among others, Colwell-Chanthaphonh and Ferguson 2004; Le Fleur 2001; Lilley 2000b; Lynott and Wylie 2000; Skotnes 1996; Wilk and Pyburn 1998; Wolfe 1999)—in short, *in places where researcher and researched occupy the same national public sphere.* The deconstruction of the "field" in sociocultural anthropology, archaeology, and their historiography (Gupta and Ferguson 1997; Fabian 1983; Fotiadis 1993; Hodder 1998; Kuklick and Kohler 1996; Meskell 2001; Politis 2001; Stocking 1983) should also question the nationalist parameters of power implicit in the ethical and methodical abstractions of "home" and "field"—again, proxies that "exteriorize" certain ethical and methodical practices and that rupture the globalized relationships by which they were and are connected (Pels and Salemink 1999). Power relationships in the "field"—the insistently public nature of sites and museums—may help to explain why archaeologists, in particular, have called for the development of methodologies of collaboration (Colwell-Chanthaphonh and Ferguson 2004; Lilley and Williams n.d.). On the other hand, the critique of ethnographic representation reminds us—

as do Pradeep Jeganathan and Joel Kahn in this volume—that there is no self-evident category of people (such as the "indigenous") with whom we should collaborate (see also van Meijl 2000b). As Rosemary Joyce argues, also in this volume, the stakeholders of research emerge in action, and there is, therefore, always a contingent limit to prescribing a method, a discipline, or even a politics for a collaborative and emergent ethics. Here a realistic, perhaps pessimistic note is needed: the claims to sovereignty (that is, of independent decision making) of the different actors-in-negotiation will be translated into performance, where some forms of storytelling will always be interpreted as being more powerful than others and thus decide the course of practical action (as Craig Howe forcefully reminds us). Of course, we do not say that those powerful forms of storytelling will always remain the same. Even more, we have a stake in changing them.

In any case, this does not release us from the duty to try and develop alternative methodologies that map the possibilities and difficulties of moral argument and collaboration. Participants in the conference that led to this book agreed on the idea of developing an outline for a course in anthropological ethics that would stress the importance of ethical practice at every stage of research, from the definition of the object (as discussed by Meskell and Jeganathan) through preliminary framing, proposal writing, funding (as discussed by Brenneis), negotiation of access to the field and fieldwork itself, and writing (as discussed by Clifford and Marcus 1986 and Fabian 1983) and making it available to professional associations, university departments, and other professionals and publics concerned.[10] Such a course could be made integral to the teaching of anthropological theory and method, with the result that ethics would no longer be regarded as external to the discipline. Further exploration of methods of ethical practice in anthropology could be inspired by a discussion of evolutionism with a creationist, by the storytelling of a Hopi scholar, by a willingness to regard both the U.S. press and the Yanomami as relevant audiences for one's ethnographic representations, by seriously considering the arguments of one's unwilling Malaysian interlocutors, by recognizing that Egyptian monuments form a living heritage, by questioning the limits of our discipline's "affect" in the face of violence, by doing a multilocale ethnography of Monsanto, by emulating the planning for a new display of the NMAI's collaborators, by criticizing the ethical proxies of internal review boards, by the practice of jointly interpreting archaeological sites in Honduras, and by the manifold other ethical practices that anthropologists have experimented with both recently and in the past. Like all methods and disciplines, some of these will work better in certain circumstances and others in others, and all will have difficulty in forging a viable future from the position of being subordinated to the social, cultural, and historical power relationships that shape them and their environment together. But if we do not try to ensure that these disciplines of ethical action are embedded in the practices that they are meant to guide us through, they stand much less chance of working at all.

Notes

1. The relation between present-day claims to intellectual property and research ethics is an issue that merits book-length treatment. We cannot do it justice here, although it recurs at several points in this introduction and in the contributions (apart from the essays by Marks, see those by Meskell, Pels, Stone, and Wylie, in particular).

2. One that is not dealt with by Fluehr-Lobban's (1994) otherwise careful essay.

3. The clearest account of "modernity" emerging in the interaction between "Europe" and its "outside" is that of Mitchell (2000).

4. We say this not to dismiss the effort at drawing up nonethnocentric values but because, in *practice,* such efforts tend toward abstraction or the imposition of parochial values.

5. Several participants in the conference related this view of ethics to Foucault's more immanent, processual and historical notion of ethics (see Rabinow 1997:xxvii–xl).

6. Influenced by the voices of indigenous people, a social archaeology has developed that recognizes the role of ethics at all levels of the archaeological enterprise (Cantwell, Friedlander, and Tramm 2000; Green 1984; Lynott and Wylie 2000; Vitelli 1996; Wilk and Pyburn 1998).

7. Wilk and Pyburn refer—usefully and crucially—to the problems of looting, the loss of data, and the vices of the antiquities market under the rubric of "commercialization" but do not take the issue of intellectual property beyond that to others form of commerce with which archaeologists are confronted.

8. As happened with Colin Turnbull's expressions of disgust with the Ik in his *The Mountain People* (1973; see Barth 1974). Barth's critique of Turnbull's lack of moral relativism can be read as a recognition of the endemic conflict of values in ethnographic fieldwork that Pels has called "duplexity" (1999) and that Stone's "multilocale" fieldwork brings out in even more complex ways.

9. Here we adopt terms used by Susan Lindee (who borrowed them from Hilary Rose) during the discussions at the conference.

10. Don Brenneis has agreed to produce a paper on the basis of discussion he had with Lynn Meskell, Faye Ginsburg, and Ian Lilley (see the note to his own contribution in this volume).

Part 1

Rethinking Ethics

Your Body, My Property: The Problem of Colonial Genetics in a Postcolonial World

Jonathan Marks

Until its annual meeting in 2003, the American Association of Physical Anthropologists was the only major professional anthropological organization that lacked a code of ethics. The specifics of its reluctance to adopt such a formal code may be obscure, but there is a considerable extent to which it may be at least understandable. As the anthropological field that self-consciously represents the scientific approach to human studies, biological anthropology would seem to be ideally situated to take the lead in establishing ethical standards to help establish the Baconian promise of better living through science. Yet obviously that is not occurring.

Biological anthropology is not methodologically unified—as archaeology and cultural anthropology are unified by excavation and ethnography, respectively. Rather, it borrows methods from biomedical research and cross-cultural ethnographic, ecological, and historical fields in studying the evolution and natural diversity of our species. Consequently, the development of an ethical code would necessarily reflect the extraordinary methodological diversity practiced under the banner of biological anthropology. But, such a practical matter aside, the field sits in a historical and philosophical trajectory that merits consideration.

Writing in the *American Anthropologist* in 1900, George A. Dorsey reviewed the progress that had been made at his institution, the Field [Columbian] Museum in Chicago, shortly after the Columbian Exposition in 1893:

Naturally much osteological material of great ethnic value was procured, along with many of the collections donated by the Exposition, as well as with many of the collections obtained by purchase. As a result the department was in possession of skulls and skeletons from Alaska, the Northwest coast, and several of the Plains tribes; from Ohio, New Jersey, and Arkansas mounds; from prehistoric graves in Costa Rica, Colombia, Peru, Bolivia, and Chile; and through the Boas and Ward purchases many specimens from America, Europe, Asia, Africa, and the Pacific islands.

A few years later, "From the Blackfeet, Bloods, and Haida was also collected a large amount of osteological material, while a small amount of similar material was obtained from the Kootenay, Tlingit, and Tsimshian." For 1897–98 he reports, "In the division of physical anthropology more than 150 skeletons were accessioned, the most important single collection being one of fifty-two Papuan skulls from Gazelle peninsula, New Britain, received in exchange from Dr Parkinson."

Over a century later, I read these words in conjunction with a project I was undertaking for the American Anthropological Association's Centennial Commission involving the field's history. What jumped out at me was the sterility of the descriptions: the material was "procured," "obtained," "collected," and "accessioned." No description was given of where the bones actually came from or how they were acquired. Of course, it is not hard to figure out. As Franz Boas famously wrote to his sister from the field in 1888, "It is most unpleasant work to steal bones from a grave, but what is the use, someone has to do it" (Freed, Freed, and Williamson 1988; Starn 2004). Boas, it is worth noting, indeed made his initial mark as a collector of skeletal remains, such that his faculty appointment at Columbia in 1897 was as a physical anthropologist.

Thus, the dirty little secret of modern physical anthropology: it began as little better than the metaphorical hunchbacked assistant supplying anthropological science with the gory body parts it used for data. At least this was something of an advance over the premodern version of the field, which was most famously represented by the proslavery polygenism of Samuel George Morton, Josiah Nott, and George Gliddon (Hrdlička 1914; Stanton 1960) and also based on the "collection" of skulls. As science, the field developed a sterile vocabulary to conceal the macabre nature of its work. Following the medical model (whose early founders, such as Vesalius, were dogged by accusations of graverobbing but nevertheless worked ultimately toward the noble goal of healing the sick), physical anthropologists lexically transformed erstwhile people into specimens, materials, and parts of collections. The transformation was sufficiently complete that some contemporary practitioners are able to deny, with an apparently straight face, that their intimate study of dead people's parts is gruesome and rather distasteful to ordinary sensibilities (Killion et al. 1999).

The passage in 1990 of the Native American Graves Protection and Repatriation Act, 25 U.S.C. 3001 *et seq.* (NAGPRA), which deals with both cultural and biological remains, can be seen as the culmination of half a century of progress in biomedical ethics. Although the Hippocratics enjoined each other to "first do no harm," the twentieth century saw the development of a formal concept of responsibility on the part of the scientist to the subject. This of course came in reaction to the excesses of the Nazis in the name of science (the notorious Auschwitz camp doctor Josef Mengele had a doctorate in physical anthropology from Theodor Mollison in addition to his medical degree [Muller-Hill 1988; Robert Proctor, personal communication]) and was formally articulated as the Nuremberg Code in 1947.

The Nuremberg Code assumes that the research in question is medical and invasive and that there is a common cognitive framework shared by the scientist and subject that permits the scientist to assume the responsibility of obtaining the "voluntary consent" of the subject. It assumes further that the only relevant party aside from the scientist is the subject. It is, therefore, and was intended to be, a first step. We now recognize, for example, that a geneticist has a responsibility not just to the patient with a diagnosed genetic disease but also to other family members who are at risk for it. Thus, in the 1990s, successful medical malpractice lawsuits established a "duty to warn" for people whose personal health decisions had been adversely affected by virtue of not having been informed about a close relative's genetic condition (Dolgin 2001).

The recognition of scientific responsibility beyond simply the experimental subject, when combined with the Nuremberg Code's appreciation of "mental suffering and injury" as meriting consideration, implies that NAGPRA is very harmonious with modern biomedical sensibilities when it protects Native Americans from the callous disposition of their dead relatives. Thus, when an archaeologist conservatively objects to the repatriation of Ishi's brain on the grounds that Indian remains "care no more what happens to them than a dead stick off a tree" (Whittaker 2000:4), the point is correct but moot. Other parties do care profoundly what happens to Ishi, and the scientific value of the brain may indeed need to be balanced against their rights. The scientifically valueless brain of the famous California Indian ("the last of his tribe"), long in the possession of the Smithsonian Institution, was ultimately repatriated under the National Museum of the American Indian Act to the Yana-speaking Redding Rancheria and Pit River tribes in August 2000 (Starn 2004).

The Human Genome Diversity Project

My own interest in ethics stems from my involvement with the Human Genome Diversity Project, a consortium of population geneticists who proposed a scheme for collecting genetic material from indigenous people on a grand scale in 1991 (Cavalli-Sforza et al. 1991). One might anticipate that a proposal for establishing a repository of biological materials from indigenous peoples might merit some intense prior ethical reflection about the collection and disposition of such materials, especially coming just a year after the passage of NAGPRA. Yet it did not: virtually all the relevant considerations were reactive, articulated by critics, and only subsequently addressed by the HGDP (Marks 2003).

And yet NAGPRA and the HGDP are obviously linked. The issues that stimulated the passage of NAGPRA—the existence and management of osteological repositories of indigenous peoples—certainly are paralleled in the proposal to establish a DNA repository of indigenous peoples, in the questions of just how such "specimens" are to be "acquired," the discomfort promoted by having strangers take and control powerful, magical, tabooed things, and the ease with which political or economic power can be exercised to obtain and control valuable objects over the reservations of their rightful owners.

An anecdote may serve here: A distinguished senior anthropologist took me aside a few years ago to express his mystification at the ethical issues being raised against the HGDP. He explained that many years ago he had brought blood back from the field for a physical anthropologist to analyze and that it was simply a matter of course. I asked him whether "his people" had taboos about their blood, and he assured me that they did—and how! So how did he manage to get them to give up their blood? Simple, he told me; they traded it to him for penicillin, and if they didn't give him blood they didn't get their antibiotics. Suffice it to say that the blood was acquired in a highly coercive fashion. And while I would not presume to judge this senior colleague's behavior with the aid of several decades of hindsight any more than I would judge Boas's grave-robbing over a century ago, I can certainly speculate that the same sympathies that lay behind NAGPRA would hold sway in a debate over the ownership of the blood.

Indeed, the ties between blood and bones for physical anthropologists are very intimate. Both are studied as markers of ancestry, and both are—or have been—considered as causes or at least physical manifestations of behavioral tendencies. Earnest Hooton, for example, carried out the skeletal analysis of Pecos Pueblo (recently repatriated from Harvard's Peabody Museum) in 1930, and less than a decade later he published the extraordinary work *The American Criminal* (Hooton 1939), purporting to discover physical differences between criminals and volunteer firemen that he believed underlay the development of the criminalistic tendency. Hooton believed that he was discerning a constitutionally inferior human type that could only be dealt with eugenically, through segregation or extirpation.

While Hooton's work sold so poorly (because of its statistical naïveté, among other things) that Harvard University Press declined to publish its successor volumes, there is remarkable intellectual continuity between his work and modern investigations into the neurobiology or genetics of criminality (Allen 1999). The technology changes and the methods change, but the basic questions, assumptions, and approaches remain: studying the body in one era was a means of probing deeper constitutional pathologies, as in another era studying the genes is.

In other words, the bones and the blood are connected by scientific epistemologies stretching across the decades. And although the architects of the HGDP were not themselves concerned with behavioral genetics, one need hardly look far to find its relevance. Dean Hamer, discoverer of the (apparently nonexistent) homosexuality gene on Xq28 (Hamer et al. 1993; Rice et al.1999) tells us that "since the discovery of the gay gene, my lab has gone on to find genes for two other personality traits: novelty seeking and worry" (Hamer and Copeland 1998:11). And naturally "there is still such great variation in the [novelty-seeking] gene in modern day humans. . . . Different ethnic and racial groups, who evolved under different environmental circumstances, have noticeably different frequencies of the different variations" (Hamer and Copeland 1998:49).

The point is simply that the accumulation of genetic material at the turn of the twenty-first century entails a research program similar to the accumulation of osteological material at the turn of the twentieth century—biobehavior and biohistory—that was judged inadequate to justify the human rights violations now perceived in the collection of the bones. (To these research programs we may add the medical knowledge that grew as a result of these skeletal collections, which is paralleled in the genetic research as well, even though in both cases that is not what the materials were principally collected for.)

The offspring of human genetics and anthropology, anthropological genetics exists in the shadow of the eugenic legacy of one parent and the colonial legacy of the other. For all its muddled and inflammatory allegations, *Darkness in El Dorado* raises a key issue about the control of biological remains of a sacred nature when it observes (Tierney 2000:51):

> [James Neel, for the Atomic Energy Commission] purchased twelve thousand Yanomami blood samples, dispensing a steel gift for each vial of blood. . . . Today, those vials are located in an old refrigerator at Penn State University, where Chagnon once taught, and are the property of the Human Genome Diversity Project of the U.S. government.

They are actually in the custody of a former protégé of Neel's at Penn State who was involved in trying to start up the HGDP—which is itself of questionable status and in any event is certainly not a part of the federal government. But there are indeed vials of blood collected years ago under circumstances that would not pass bioethical muster today, and if one wishes to do a genetic study of the Yanomami one need not contact any Yanomami or any representative of the Yanomami. Somehow that just doesn't seem right.

The HGDP became aware of these issues shortly after it coalesced, and it attempted to deal with them by developing an idea of "group consent" (Greely 1997). Since the project was formulated as population genetics, it was interested in people specifically as group members. The idea of requiring the consent of the group as well as that of the individual would serve both to create the appearance of a heightened concern for ethics and to reify the group as a natural, bounded unit. Juengst (1998) challenges the value of group consent on the basis of the fluid and hierarchical structure of human populations. Additionally one may well ask whether the consent of the group undermines the ability of the individual to give consent voluntarily.

The most critical issue faced by the diversity project, however, is one that osteologists were spared: the value of the biological object itself as a commodity (Cunningham 1997). (Here, of course, pothunters and other looters of cultural artifacts would have a common ground with the geneticists.) Patent law in biotechnology strongly favors scientists, as the unsuccessful cases of John Moore (Greely 1998) and the descendants of Henrietta Lacks (Jackson 2000) showed (these plaintiffs were denied the right to share in the profits made from cell lines derived from their bodies). In the case of the blood of indigenous people, the National

Institutes of Health applied for patents for cell lines derived ultimately
from the blood of a Hagahai (New Guinea), a Solomon Islander, and a
Guaymí (Panama).

When confronted with possible financial issues arising from the
ownership of indigenous people' blood, the HGDP replied meekly that
it was interested in the blood solely for science's sake ("The Project
is not a commercial enterprise" [http://www.stanford.edu/group/
morrinst/hgdp/faq.html]). And yet, the people to whom they were
avowing this were well aware of the development of "bio-colonialism"
on the part of agribusiness (see Stone, this volume). Availing themselves
of indigenous people's knowledge freely given, large agricultural
corporations were making considerable profits in which the people
whose knowledge they needed were not sharing. If there is economic
value in the blood of indigenous people (why else would biotechnology
companies be so acutely interested in it?), then what is a fair price?

I suggest that the same guidelines as govern the disposition of
osteological specimens should govern genetic specimens as well. If
bones belong to people rather than to science, then blood and its
derivative products should as well. The collection and use of genetic
samples have been flying under the radar for a long time, but the same
principles of dignity and respect for indigenous rights should govern
them. The market value of blood or DNA makes it even more crucial
to recognize ownership and control of these materials.

Four Concerns of Human Genetic Research

Contemporary ethical concerns in human genetics generally focus on
four issues: autonomy, beneficence, nonmaleficence, and justice (from
the WHO Meeting on Ethical Issues in Medical Genetics, Geneva,
December 15–16, 1997). These are directly applicable to anthropological
genetics and raise significant issues about whether and how they can
be met in a cross-cultural context.

Respect for the autonomy of persons centers on the ability of an
individual to make a free and informed decision about participating.
In particular, it is a safeguard for those with diminished autonomy,
notably children and impaired adults. The spirit of this guideline surely
extends to people whose diminished autonomy is a result of their
isolation from the communities of modern science and business.

Beneficence is a requirement to ensure that scientific research delivers
some good to the people participating. While there are theoretical
benefits that may accrue as a result of population genetic research—a

cure for diabetes in Native Americans is sometimes brandished in this context (e.g., Kidd, Kidd, and Weiss 1993)—it is a far-fetched proposition given the way in which the project was designed. Its objective was to collect samples for microevolutionary studies—hence the desire to include some Hopis, some Navajos, some Inuit, and so on. In order to utilize the genetic sample, a researcher interested in, say, diabetes among the Navajos would have to be able to correlate the phenotype, the trait, with the genetic variant. In other words, the researcher would have to know which samples came from people with diabetes. Further, if the samples had in fact been collected by a researcher who recorded whether they came from diabetics or not, making it possible to use them to study the possible genetic etiology of diabetes, they would be of use to the next researcher, who might be interested in the genetic etiology of gallstones, only if there was a record of which samples came from people with gallstones. Thus, these samples would be of only exceedingly minor benefit to the people they came from unless they were accompanied by comprehensive medical histories. Benefit to the communities of interest was never a goal of the project or even a sidelight; it was always for the benefit of the scientists themselves. Indeed, other people's blood has commonly become a commodity among genetic researchers, a medium of exchange and a locus of reciprocal obligation (Anderson 2000).

The third concern, nonmaleficence, is the safeguard against the callous or cruel scientist. There is certainly no doubt that the architects of the HGDP had no intention of inflicting harm or pain on others. And yet of course harm and pain come in many forms. In a "puff piece" for *Time* on the project we learn the following (Subramanian 1995:54):

> On one occasion, when Cavalli-Sforza was taking blood from school-children in a rural region of the Central African Republic, he was confronted by an angry farmer brandishing an ax. Recalls the scientist, "I remember him saying, 'If you take the blood of the children, I'll take yours.' He was worried that we might want to do some magic with the blood.

Ignoring the problem of the diminished autonomy of the school-children-subjects, we are still faced with the geneticist's causing obvious distress to the local people. And while this anecdote seems to invite us to ridicule the ignorance of the ax-wielding savage, we might look at it instead as exemplifying two other problems about the scientist. First, the fact that the farmer is concerned about the possible magic indicates that the scientist has not fulfilled his responsibility to explain the research to the subjects so as to obtain their full consent. Second, obviously the scientist is the source of some emotional unease; whether the farmer was a lone pathological actor or simply articulated a more widespread feeling we cannot say. However, there was clearly the feeling of harm and pain—spiritual, perhaps, but clearly no less real to the farmer—of which the scientist was the source.

Finally, by justice is intended the fair distribution of whatever benefits may accrue as a result of the research. There is little to add to the preceding discussion of the way in which contemporary patent law favors scientists. The issue with respect to indigenous people came to a head in 1996 with the filing of a patent claim on the cell line originating from the blood of the Hagahai man mentioned above. The sample had been collected by a medical anthropologist not affiliated with the HGDP who had actually attempted to broker an agreement that would have had the Hagahai comprehending what they were participating in and sharing in any financial benefits. In the wake of protests, the National Institutes of Health withdrew its patent application. But the story does not end there (Harry and Marks 1999:304):

> Dr. Pauline Lane . . . has been working with the Hagahai to find out about their impressions of being subjects of a genetic patent. She tells us that there have been no long-term benefits to the community. . . .There have been no additional medical services or supplies provided to the Hagahai. With regard to community understanding, Lane further tells us, "The community members I spoke to were confused. They feel that Jenkins had helped their community, but they also felt that maybe they had been cheated out of some money for their blood. They did give informed consent for blood to be taken for diagnosis but NOT to be taken out of the country for research. They suggested that they would NOT trust researchers again."
>
> Who could fault them for concluding that once researchers had what they wanted (HTLV-1 sample), then the Hagahai were no longer of interest? The Hagahai cell line is now available to the public at the American Type Culture Collection as ATCC Number: CRL-10528 Organism: Homo Sapiens (human) for $216.

The HGDP fared exceedingly poorly using the ethical criteria generally in place for medical genetics. It is hardly a surprise, then, that a blue-ribbon panel concluded that while "a global assessment of the extent of human genetic variability has substantial merit and warrants support" it nevertheless "foresees numerous ethical, legal, and human-rights challenges in the prosecution of a global effort" (National Research Council 1997:1–2).

The Rights of Scientists?

The HGDP was designed by and for the scientific community. Its subject was one that the scientists were interested in: microevolution. The same panel acknowledged up front that the merit of the project was specifically that "the insight the data collected could provide into the origin and evolution of the human species" (National Research Council 1997:2). Or, as one of its advocates gushed during a meeting in 1996, "We're going to tell these people who they really are!" I am still stunned by the presumption that nonscientists do not know who they are and that whatever ideas they may have about their own identity and descent are somehow trivial and irrelevant.

This exposes another paradox in the HGDP. In order to muster initial support for the project, its proponents wrapped themselves in the liberal humanism of "no-race" rhetoric. In their summary document of 1993 (http://www.stanford.edu/group/morrrinst/hgdp/summary93.html) they tell us:

> The HGD Project will also provide the scientific data to confirm and support what is already clear from population studies—that, in biological terms, there is no such thing as a clearly defined race. . . . Most importantly, therefore, the results of the Project are expected to undermine the popular belief that there are clearly defined races.

This goal was very quickly criticized in two ways: first, if we already knew this (and we did), it was hardly a compelling justification for undertaking such a large-scale project; and second, the proponents' own work was often presented sloppily, lending itself to an interpretation that there were indeed real races, which could even be color-coded: Africans yellow, Australians red, Mongoloids blue, and Caucasoids green (Cavalli-Sforza, Menozzi, and Piazza 1995; Marks 2002).

More recently, the issue has been revitalized with the publication by the remaining participants in the HGDP, now working with a genetic repository based in France, of a paper in *Science* on the computerized genetic clustering of human populations (Rosenberg et al. 2002). When asked to divide the human genetic samples into two groups, the computer program dutifully did so, and likewise with three and four groups. When asked to divide the world into five, it came out with Africa, Eurasia, East Asia, Oceania, and America, and when asked to divide the world into six, it separated out from those five the Kalash of Pakistan. On the face of it, this would seem to lend no support to popular ideas about race: the Kalash are hardly equivalent to the Africans, and there is nothing racially commonsensical about juxtaposing Eurasia–Africa with East Asia–Oceania–America. And yet, the take-home lesson of the *New York Times* was "Gene Study Identifies 5 Main Human Populations," and the HGDP's spokesman, Marcus Feldman, "said the finding essentially confirmed the popular conception of race" (Wade 2002).

Given that the "popular conception of race" has been disconfirmed many times over (Montagu 1963; Marks 1995) and that the article in question did not actually purport to confirm it, what is going on here? Perhaps it needs to be understood in the context of another widely publicized study, one claiming that race is genetically real and biomedically useful (Risch et al. 2002) and that the previous half-century or so of the study of human diversity is just so much fluffy political correctness. And yet, epidemiology seems to be roundly rejecting the genetic hypothesis for racial differences in health (Goodman 2000; Kaufman and Hall 2003). A cynical (realistic?) look at these geneticists' attempt to revitalize race might take note of the desire to rationalize target markets for the pharmaceutical industry (Duster 2003) now that federal funds seem to have dried up for the HGDP.

Once again, though, putting aside the question of whether human population geneticists have an inside track to truth or a good track record pursuing it (and I don't think they do), there is a more fundamental question underneath the scientistic arrogance. Anthropology is a unique field in that it relies fundamentally on the goodwill of the subject matter toward the scientist. A chemist does not have to worry what about boron thinks of him. Without the goodwill of the people involved, however, there can be no anthropology, whether it consists of having people agree to be measured or bled, to have their ancestors excavated, or to be visited.

One of the most extraordinary suggestions to emerge from the Kennewick Man fiasco of the past few years (in which physical anthropologists took legal action to prevent repatriation of a ninety-five-hundred-year-old skeleton in Washington that they claimed was not the ancestor of Native Americans because they are Mongoloid and he was Caucasian [Preston 1997; Chatters 2001]) is the notion that the rights of scientists were thereby being violated. The Kennewick skeleton was taken out of the hands of the scientists only after they had made plans to transport it from Washington, where it was the subject of a NAGPRA claim, to the Smithsonian, where it would be easier to retain control. Anthropologists at the Smithsonian had purchased airline tickets for the transportation of the bones away from the tribes claiming them and from the Army Corps of Engineers (Chatters 2001:74)—a point virtually never noted in popular renditions of the story. When that plan was thwarted, however, the scientists filed suit, arguing that "their civil rights were being violated" (Thomas 2000:xxi). In an opinion issued June 27, 1997, U.S. Magistrate John Jelderks noted that "the . . . plaintiffs filed suit . . . to enforce what they contend is a legal right to study the remains." I certainly cannot blame the Native American groups who wished to bury Kennewick Man without letting science study him, when the scientists' initial plans were to transport him to the Smithsonian without any permission so that he could be studied in comfort and repatriated with difficulty.

This is the issue on which the HGDP and Kennewick Man converged for me: Do scientists have the right to study whatever they want, without regard to the wishes or sensibilities of the relevant people? That question has, of course, been answered for all time in the wake of World War II. They do not. The advancement of science is important, but it must be weighed against the encroachment upon basic human rights. And today there is a fundamental human right under constant threat: *the right not to be a scientist.*

Science in the modern world can be a ruthlessly ethnocentric and intolerant ideology, many of whose most prominent representatives believe that they have a Victorian destiny to supplant religion. But being a scientist or doing science does not necessarily entail evangelism for science. After all, teaching or doing art history does not involve intellectually cloning art historians; it simply involves instilling an appreciation for what art historians have done and for the way they think.

A Smithsonian anthropologist defended the lawsuit on *Nova* ("Mystery of the First Americans," February 15, 2000) with the thought that "a clear and accurate understanding of the ancient past is something that the American public has a right to know about," as if he had it to offer! What links the HGDP to Kennewick Man is the cavalier fashion in which scientists and, in both cases, self-righteous, self-interested, self-proclaimed, and slightly paranoid advocates for science could rewrite origin narratives and identities of other peoples on the basis of partial, ambiguous, or dubiously interpreted evidence. In both cases, skeletal and genetic anthropology, the current generation faces a different social and political landscape for the production of scientific knowledge from its predecessors'.

In the case of the HGDP one could legitimately ask why people would wish to participate in a project designed to denigrate and contradict their own ideas of who they are and where they came from. It is significant in this context to note that the peopling of the New World is now known, on the basis of genetic studies, to have occurred from Asia in *one* migration (Merriwether, Rothhammer, and Ferrell 1995; Kolman, Sambuughin, and Bermingham 1996), *two* migrations (Karafet et al. 1999), *three* migrations (Greenberg, Turner, and Zegura 1986), and *more than three* migrations (Szathmary 1993; Torroni et al. 1994).

Neither the HGDP nor the Kennewick Man battle casts science in a particularly favorable light. Both call attention to scientists' belief they have a right—perhaps even a duty!—to delegitimize other people's ideas about who they are and where they came from. There is, in fact, no compelling reason to think that Kennewick Man and his contemporaries are any other than ancient Native Americans and the ancestors of modern Native Americans (Eshleman, Malhi, and Smith 2003).

This is not to say that science should not be interested in such things. Bio-history is a patently approachable question scientifically and an entirely legitimate venue of scientific inquiry. As does any scientific program, it advances unsteadily and makes several errors for every achievement (one may recall the many wrong DNA structures, including Linus Pauling's three-stranded model, before Watson and Crick's publication, and the reluctance of many early molecular geneticists even to accept DNA as the genetic material when proteins were so ubiquitous and so diverse).

The question is: How, then, does one honestly secure the participation of the people whose ancestors, relics, relations, or blood one wishes to study when the research agenda is constructed to undermine their beliefs? Who would want to participate in such a study, if its purpose were as candidly disclosed to them as it was to the scholarly audience— telling these people who they "really" are?

Presumably securing the participation of people in such a microevolutionary study requires either risking the withdrawal of its most valued subjects by explaining the hegemonic goal of discerning who they "really" are and where they "really" came from, or else simply not disclosing it fully. This is of course a problem, for there is a recognition of some degree of tolerance of and respect for other beliefs and lifeways in this work, but whether it is operationalized in any way or is merely lip service is unclear.

Thus, the HGDP's 1993 "Summary Document" notes under "Field work issues" that "customs and traditions of participating communities must be respected at all times." But this is noted only in the context of procurement. After the substance changes hands and becomes a laboratory specimen, there is no acknowledgment of the need for such respect. The laboratory is a privileged site, it would seem, where the concern for biochemical toxicity and radiation may need to be acknowledged but otherwise the science is unfettered by the apprehensions and ideological conflicts that it might be causing.

Creationism and the Right Not to Be an Evolutionist

Another area in which biological anthropology interacts with public sentiments, often with hostility and authority, is the general presentation of human origins. Obviously the scientific origin narrative, evolution, more accurately represents "how we got here" than other origin narratives. And yet one finds repeatedly in creationist rhetoric a theme that should be familiar to anyone knowledgeable about the anthropology of myths—that there is more to them than simply the details of the story (Numbers 1992; Toumey 1994).

Once again, genetics is at the center of the storm: bodies are built clonally from a single zygote; the zygote contains all the information necessary for the process of development; genes constitute that information; different genes build different organisms; alternative forms of genes (alleles) differ from one another in specific and knowable ways; alleles spread through a population over generations by a small number of fundamental processes; and these processes work to transform a population over long periods of time. All of these are parts of the scientific canon, and all are unimpeachable except in very narrow and highly exceptional senses. With a basic understanding of the processes, of course, we try to reconstruct the details of our evolutionary history— limited by the fossil record and our creativity in making sense of it (Landau 1991).

Yet creationists, by and large, do not want to argue about the stochasticity of genetic drift or the six-million-year-old biped *Orrorin tugenensis*. They are, for the most part, interested in more fundamental issues of whether the universe is governed by a benevolent hand, morality, ultimate justice, good and evil, happiness, and what lies beyond death. These are issues to which science and especially evolution have little to contribute, and yet they are the very issues that all origin myths deal with to some extent. Origin myths are culturally integrated to a far greater extent than science is. Science's standard operating procedure is to take some aspect of new knowledge and to substitute it for whatever alternative existed before it—generally without looking for or dealing with the broader implications or cultural and symbolic connections (but, for an important exception, see Simpson 1949).

With respect to evolution, there seem to be three responses to this. Some seek spirituality through evolution (Teilhard de Chardin 1959; de Duve 2002); others invoke evolution specifically to reject spirituality as illusory (Dawkins 1995; Avise 1998; Wilson 1998), and still others respond by denying evolution and seeking to undermine it as reliable knowledge (Behe 1996; Johnson 1998; Dembski 2002). It is in this latter group that we generally find the "creationists," who strive to introduce some version of biblical literalism into public school science curricula.

Suffice it to say that introducing creationism into the science curriculum as an equivalent or even relevant alternative to evolution is quite simply fraudulent. And yet there is a different side to this coin—namely, that the comparative study of worldviews and origin narratives is a traditional focus of anthropology. Further, an application of some of anthropology's classic relativistic humanism should imply a modicum of respect or at least tolerance for creationism—*not, of course, as a representation of the content of field of biology* but as part of the anthropology curriculum, whose very reason for existence is the ultimate wisdom that comes from encountering or experiencing the breadth of ideas that people have and the cultural logic that guides them. And if we agree that creationism should be acknowledged and engaged (rather than accepted or combated), then what better locus for it than biological anthropology, a field that self-consciously constitutes the boundary between natural science and systems of thought?

Conclusions

I once flew home from the physical anthropology meetings on a puddle-jumper next to a distinguished senior colleague. I had just given a paper critical of the Canadian psychologist J. Philippe Rushton (e.g., 1995), who argues that black people have small brains and large penises, which he freely translates to mean stupidity and licentiousness; that yellow people are the opposite; and that white people have evolved a happy medium. The physical anthropologist with whom I sat took the liberty of upbraiding me for my paper. He said, "You see, you're too critical, you're too contentious."

I said, "Don't we as scholars and as anthropologists have a moral obligation to combat racism?"

He said, "I don't believe in morality."

Was I sitting next to Darth Vader? I asked whether we could begin by at least agreeing on the proposition that racism is evil.

He said, "I don't believe in good and evil. Those are constructions"—quickly becoming a relativist of convenience.

I said, "I agree they are constructions, but that doesn't mean they're the same thing."

He said, "You see, that's your problem, Jon. You're causing trouble by criticizing that work."

I replied, "You've got it backwards. The racist is the one causing the trouble; the problem is racism—not the critique of racism."

He told me I just didn't understand, and at least he was right about that. But there is one thing I do understand: I certainly would not want my children to study with him.

Obviously, a field in which one can have such a conversation with a senior representative is probably unlikely to be a leader in ethical practice. Physical anthropology's finest hour arguably came in 1963, when the field (led at the time by Sherry Washburn) coalesced against the racism inherent in Carleton Coon's (1962) interpretation of the origin of races, which was being invoked by segregationists with the author's blessing (Marks 2000; Jackson 2002). While some of the issues linger, it faces new moral and ethical challenges today.

One of the major recent ethical triumphs in this area has been the repatriation of Sarah Baartman, "The Hottentot Venus," whose genitalia had been dissected by the leading anatomist in Europe and whose body parts had remained for nearly two hundred years in the Musée de l'Homme in Paris. The "old" South Africa was not interested in the remains of Sarah Baartman, but the "new" South Africa was—she constituted both a complex national/racial/political symbol and a real-life person with descendants, relatives, and newly empowered co-ethnics. This was obviously not covered by NAGPRA, nor did it sit well with museum people generally—certainly the Louvre would not want to set a precedent that could result in the Mona Lisa's being returned to Italy. And yet her remains were of no scientific or aesthetic value, nor were they on display—why keep her? Ultimately it required a personal appeal from Nelson Mandela, years of political maneuvering between the parliaments of France and South Africa, and a series of negotiations between the South African physical anthropologist Phillip Tobias and his French counterpart, Henri de Lumley (Tobias 2002). She was repatriated in May 2002.

It seems to me that there has to be more to the relationship between geneticists and indigenous peoples than simply trying to talk them out of their precious bodily fluids (the phrase is from the film *Dr. Strangelove* and curiously appropriate here). Any operative idea of full disclosure should entail not only the scientific issues involved but as well the possible financial benefits to the scientist. And, more to the point, there should be some exchange between the people and the scientist to clarify the value to them of the research question to which they are contributing.

The many physical anthropologists who work in an atmosphere of respect and amity with indigenous groups have been given a black eye by the arrogance and belligerence of the few who re-create exploitative or insensitive relations with local communities. Modern research in human population genetics certainly does little to mitigate the widespread fear among traditional and impoverished people that Americans want their blood or body parts (Scheper-Hughes 1996). For a field that began as little more than simple grave-robbing, this is perhaps not unexpected. But an anthropology that treats people contemptuously—as represented by the high-profile HGDP and the Kennewick Man combatants—will make it hard for the rest of the field to survive honorably into the current century.

The Promise and Perils of an Ethic of Stewardship

Alison Wylie

The 1970s were a turning point for Americanist/anthropological archaeology in many respects. The emergence of the New Archaeology is usually cited as instituting an optimistic age of self-consciously scientific practice, dedicated to the pursuit of internally defined, anthropological goals the significance of which was marked by their generality: the understanding of long-term cultural processes operating on a scale well beyond the lifeworld interests of individual agents and localized cultural traditions. Understood in these terms, archaeology may have seemed a safe haven from the pressures then transforming sociocultural anthropology, and, in fact, in my second year of graduate school in the late 1970s a classmate who had been passionate about ethnography made the switch to archaeology for just this reason.[1] He had come to the conclusion that he would rather work with subjects who were safely dead; the live ones, he said, were just too much trouble, demanding that you account for yourself, for your interest in their lives, for what you were going to do with anything you learned about them. The dead ones didn't talk back.

This view was by no means without precedent. No less a statesman and archaeological forebear than Thomas Jefferson held that "the dead have no rights" (as quoted by Thomas 2000:52, 209), and certainly a great deal of archaeological research has proceeded on this assumption (for overviews of this history see Thomas 2000; Watkins 2000). A currently practicing bioanthropologist quoted by David Hurst Thomas makes the underlying principle explicit: "Ancient skeletons belong to everyone"; they are "the remnants of unduplicable evolutionary events which all living and future peoples have the right to know about and understand" (2000:209–210). The extension of this principle to all prehistoric and historic remains affirms the conclusion that, absent the subjects themselves, no contemporary community-specific interests can trump the interests of humanity or society as a whole. More to the point, no "living culture, religion, or interest groups, or biological population" (as quoted by Thomas 2000:209) can justify restricting the research mandate of scientific experts who have the necessary skills and knowledge to make the best use of surviving "remnants" as evidence. In this spirit, my classmate saw archaeology as one area of anthropology in which one could (still) proceed on the assumption that the chief value of the cultural material under study lies in its evidential significance; the more general the problem on which it bears, the greater the significance.

By sharp and, in the view of my classmate, worrying contrast, cultural anthropologists were facing the complexities of a double life, as Pels later described the ethical tensions inherent in ethnographic practice (2000:146). The rights of human subjects were taking center stage: federal funding agencies were requiring institutional research board reviews for all research involving human subjects, nonmedical as well as medical, and even fields that did not deal with human subjects were under pressure to take seriously the human, social implications of their work and establish effective mechanisms of self-regulation. The Committee on Scientific Freedom and Responsibility established by the American Association for the Advancement of Science (AAAS) in the late 1970s concluded, after reviewing the ethics standards of its affiliated societies, that scientists in a range of fields could not continue business as usual; if they did not develop detailed codes of conduct backed by mechanisms of enforcement, they could expect the imposition of highly restrictive external regulations (Chalk, Frankel, and Chafer 1980:101; Wylie 1999). By 1980, when the AAAS report appeared, the American Anthropological Association (AAA) had had a code of ethics in place for nearly a decade. Galvanized into action by concern about allegations that anthropologists had played a role in mission-oriented (counterinsurgency) activities in South America and Southeast Asia (Berreman 1991:39–42), the AAA had adopted principles of professional conduct that made respect for research subjects and their well-being a paramount responsibility for anthropologists. No matter whom my classmate chose to study he understood that, as an ethnographer, he would have to negotiate his research agenda—his practice, his publications, his professional identity—not only with the sponsors of his research and his professional colleagues but also with an expanding array of nonacademic interests and with research subjects who were increasingly prepared to return the ethnographic gaze. This was unacceptable to him. As he understood the mission of scientific inquiry, whether physics or anthropology, it should be uncompromised by parochial interests, values, and demands external to science. In this he embraced the tenets central to science policy in the United States after World War II; pure science had to be insulated from practical concerns even though its costs (in a number of senses) were ultimately justified by its anticipated social benefits.[2]

In retrospect, however, it is a profound irony that my classmate should have seen archaeology as safe from controversy.The 1970s were pivotal for archaeology not only because they marked the zenith of enthusiasm for scientific goals and disciplinary identity but also because the conditions of archaeological practice were beginning to change dramatically and in directions that required just the kinds of external accountability he had hoped to escape. Native Americans were mobilizing, and one target of their activism was the desecration of sacred sites and burials by archaeologists; American Indian Movement (AIM) activists, tribal leaders, and traditionalists all made it clear that the nameless ancients were, in fact, their ancestors and the archaeological record their cultural heritage. In 1971 AIM shut down excavations in Welch, Minnesota, and took over a Colorado State University anthropology lab (Thomas 2000:198–199; Watkins 2000:7–8); through the 1970s tribal groups began to use historic preservation legislation to assert legal control over archaeological resources on their lands (Ferguson 1990), and expansive analyses of Native American heritage rights were appearing in Native American journals and in legal reviews (Watkins 2000:9–13). By the late 1970s several archaeologists had published assessments of the situation, calling on colleagues to take seriously the "protest themes" voiced by First Nations activists (Johnson 1973). Relations with Native Americans had been identified as one of a half-dozen pressing issues that defined the agenda of a special conference entitled "The Future Direction of Archaeology" sponsored by the Society for American Archaeology (SAA) (McGimsey and Davis 1977; Watkins 2000:11). Although the direct subjects of archaeological research might be dead, descendant communities with an interest in these subjects were very much alive.

In the same period conservation issues took on particular urgency for archaeologists; the destruction of archaeological sites and material had escalated at an alarming rate in the postwar era, not just as a consequence of exponentially increasing land development, especially in affluent nations like the United States (for example, resource extraction and the construction of highways and subdivisions, power lines and pipelines), but also as a result of the dramatic expansion in the 1970s of an antiquities market hungry for material that, for the most part, could only be supplied by systematic looting (Vitelli 1984). In 1974 William Lipe argued that, "if our field is to last more than a few more decades," archaeologists would have to make the conservation of archaeological resources their primary responsibility (1974:214); he urged a reorientation of research practice away from an "exploitative model of utilization of archaeological resources." In this spirit, there has been strong emphasis on the development of nondestructive investigative techniques and on public outreach; a great many archaeologists have made it a priority to do all they can, through public education and advocacy, to raise awareness of the significance of archaeological sites and materials and to counteract systematic looting and the commercial trade in antiquities.

The 1970s was also a decade in which patterns of funding and employment in North American archaeology were fundamentally reconfigured. Federal legislation protecting archaeological resources had existed in the United States since the early twentieth century; the 1906 Antiquities Act designated the archaeological record a national trust, prohibiting looting on federal lands and establishing a mandate for ongoing archaeological research (Thomas 2000:xxxi). But in response to the destruction described by Lipe and others, a spate of new federal legislation was instituted that substantially strengthened these protections—the 1966 Historic Sites Preservation Act, the 1969 National Environmental Policy Act, and the 1974 Archaeological and Historic Preservation Act (the Moss-Bennett bill)—and created a regulatory environment that required the systematic assessment and mitigation of any archaeological sites that might be affected by land development on federal property (Thomas 2000:142–144; Vitelli 1996:269–271; Watkins 2000:38–44). Within a decade the federal government and private industry would become the major employers of archaeologists in the United States, with budgets for contract archaeology that vastly outstripped anything available for research.

In short, by the late 1970s many archaeologists were acutely aware that increasingly, and in virtually all aspects of their work, they would be required to negotiate conflicts with and among living peoples who were staking a variety of claims to the archaeological record. When Mark Lynott and I were asked to convene a new ad hoc SAA ethics committee in 1992, the magnitude of this sea change was clearly evident. Two key developments are emblematic of how deeply the conditions of archaeological practice had changed. Accountability to Native American interests had been legislated in 1991 with the passage of the Native American Graves Protection and Repatriation Act (NAGPRA); this meant that few archaeologists could avoid dealing with descendant communities. And by 1992 the dominance of the cultural resource management industry had been established. "Over 20 times as much money [was being] allotted to CRM as to institutional or academic research" (Stark 1992: 49), and, as a consequence, a majority of practicing archaeologists found themselves rendering professional services that were (for some) highly lucrative in a structurally adversarial environment; they were multiply accountable to employers, clients, employees, and a range of publics, as well as to the discipline and the internally defined research goals of archaeology. As Miriam Stark described the situation, "archaeology [was] no longer the exclusive domain of the scholar" (1992:53). The decision by the executive board of the SAA to set up a committee that would review its existing statements on ethics issues and chart a course forward reflected an appreciation that, like it or not, these legal and economic realities were forcing archaeologists to redefine their priorities at a fundamental level.

Stewardship in Formation

Despite these pressures for change, there has been stiff resistance in some quarters to any reassessment of the values and commitments that have traditionally defined archaeology as a research discipline—a science and a subfield of anthropology. Brian Fagan addressed this issue directly in a column he published in *Archaeology* in 1993. Although "basic research is important to the vitality of our discipline," he said, he was dismayed by the extent to which archaeologists continued to regard anything but narrowly specialized academic research—anything to do with "teaching, conservation . . . resource management, and the administering of the archaeological record" (1993:15)—as a marginal secondary interest. The vision of archaeology that was so compelling for my graduate classmate—a research discipline driven by its own internal cognitive values, uncompromised by the demands of accountability to external interest groups—was still (and continues to be) a powerful force in the archaeological community. Lynott and I encountered just the kinds of resistance Fagan described when we applied to the National Science Foundation (NSF) for support for a meeting of the

SAA committee and its advisers. Although the Ethics, Values, and Society panel endorsed our proposal and ultimately secured funding for it, the Archaeology Division declined to cosponsor it on the grounds that its funds should not be diverted from primary research to secondary concerns such as disciplinary ethics. As one member of the Archaeology Division panel later told us, he did not see how a project concerned with issues of external accountability could be relevant to the substantive, scientific interests of archaeology.

When this meeting of the SAA ethics committee was convened in November 1993, it had the support not only of NSF but also of the National Parks Service and the Policy Institute for Cultural Resources at the University of Nevada–Reno, where the meeting was held, and it included not only members of the SAA ethics committee but also a number of advisers to the committee: Native American representatives, an archaeologist who worked with commercial salvors, archaeologists active on ethics issues in diverse subfields and parts of the world (for example, classical and European archaeology, Mesoamerican and Australian archaeology, underwater and historical archaeology), and representatives of other archaeological societies (among them the Archaeological Institute of America [AIA], the Society for Historical Archaeology [SHA], and the Society of Professional Archaeologists [SOPA]). The aim of this meeting was to set an agenda for future work on ethics issues within the SAA. Although the point of departure for discussion was an assessment of existing SAA ethics policies and statements, it was not our aim to formulate new ethical principles; indeed, we took it to be an open question whether this was a useful initiative under the circumstances. In the event, however, it was at this meeting that the proposal for an ethic of stewardship was drafted. It emerged, initially, in the context of a discussion of how archaeologists should respond to looters, collectors, and a range of commercial interests in the archaeological record. Midway through this first session of the workshop Leigh Jenkins (Kuwanwisiwma), then the director of the Hopi Nation Cultural Preservation Office, identified a number of ways in which the issue of resource protection, as we had conceived it, was fundamentally at odds with tribal values. For example, if the Hopi wanted to receive restitution for damaged sites or repatriate stolen objects, they were required to attach a monetary value to sacred objects and places, which might violate conventions of secrecy and imposed a system of valuation that fundamentally misrepresented what was at issue. He described a case in which a sacred Hopi kachina had been repatriated from a collector who had bought it from a member of the

Hopi tribe. The basis for the Hopi's case against the collector was that no individual had the right to alienate this kachina; it was the common property of all the members of a secret society to which the seller belonged.

Jenkins drew no particular lesson from this account; he left it to the assembled archaeologists to think through its implications for the issues they had been discussing. After a pause Christopher Chippindale observed that, as director of an anthropological museum in the United Kingdom, he was deeply frustrated by pressures to assign a commercial value to its collections for insurance purposes; like the Hopi, if for very different reasons, he regarded them as priceless. By requiring curators to assign monetary value to this material, the legal and economic framework in which they worked betrayed its real significance and obscured their responsibility as stewards holding it on behalf of the larger society. Several other museum-affiliated archaeologists concurred with reference to collections held in the Americas. Other participants reflected on ways in which archaeologists had succumbed to the imperatives of a collecting mentality, and still others expanded on this point, insisting that the scope of stewardship extended not just to extant collections but to all the records associated with archaeological research and to in situ archaeological resources. We broke for lunch, and that afternoon several participants returned with the draft of a statement on what an ethic of stewardship involved and the recommendation that we break into working groups to consider the implications of stewardship ideals for various of the issues we had been discussing. When I later had occasion to read James Tully's account of constitutional pluralism (on which I draw, below, for an analysis of stewardship), I was struck by the parallels between Jenkins's intervention and the description Tully gave of a story told by the Haida artist Bill Reid about his sculpture *The Spirit of Haida Gwaii* (Tully 1995:33):

> Like all great Aboriginal storytellers [Bill Reid] refuses to provide answers to the questions raised by his story. This would defeat the didactic purpose of storytelling, which is not to set out categorical imperatives but to develop the listeners' ability to think for themselves. Elders tell stories in a manner that encourages and guides listeners to reflect independently on the great problems of life that the story presents to them. . . . The test of understanding is . . . how they go on in various circumstances to conduct their life in light of what they have learned from reflection on the story. . . . There are a multitude of ways of being guided.

I do not know if we went on in any of the ways Jenkins might have hoped, but go on we did. His story about repatriation was a pivotal intervention, changing the tone and certainly the direction of what had begun as a quite diffuse discussion. Where there had been much skirmishing around tightly circumscribed points of disagreement—who counts as a looter; what distinguishes legitimate from illegitimate collecting practices, the entanglement of museums with the antiquities trade—his reflection on a deeper conflict of values focused attention on issues that everyone knew we had to address but no one knew how to approach.

As adopted by the SAA in 1996, the stewardship principle, the first of eight "principles of archaeological ethics," specifies that the primary responsibility archaeologists have is "to serve as caretakers of and advocates for the archaeological record," to ensure its long-term conservation, and to promote uses of the record "for the benefit of all people" (SAA 1996:451). The next two principles set out a requirement of accountability, according to which archaeologists must actively consult and if possible collaborate with all groups affected by their research (principle 2), and a broad responsibility to avoid activities that contribute to the commercialization of the archaeological record (principle 3). Subsequent principles affirm commitments to public education and outreach, responsible training and practice, timely public reporting of archaeological findings, and the preservation of archaeological records and materials (1996:452).

Reactions to these principles took roughly three forms.[3] Many welcomed them as a promising response to the rapidly changing conditions under which archaeologists were then working; they saw the principles as a new departure that, at its most ambitious, began to articulate a new, substantially broader vision of the goals and responsibilities of archaeology. Others rejected them out of hand for essentially the same reason. By explicitly acknowledging and, indeed, putting primary emphasis on *public* accountability, these critics objected, the SAA ethics committee had capitulated to external pressures that would deeply compromise the integrity and autonomy of archaeology as a research enterprise. At just the moment when we should have staunchly defended the core ideals of scientific, anthropological archaeology, we had drafted a set of principles that mentioned "scientific study" just once (as an interest compromised by commercialization [principle 3]), that required archaeologists to negotiate their research interests with "all parties" who might be said to have an interest in the archaeological record (principle 2), and that enjoined archaeologists to put their "specialized knowledge" about "human behavior and culture" at the service of these diverse publics (principles 1 and 4).

To my mind, however, the most challenging criticisms took quite a different tack. In an invited commentary on the draft principles Larry Zimmerman voiced a concern that a number of others had expressed privately: that these ideals of stewardship represented no significant break with the entrenched values that underpinned conventional practice (1995:65). They simply reaffirmed, in different language, the very assumptions of privilege—of access to and control over archaeological sites and materials—that we should have been questioning. By unilaterally declaring themselves stewards of the archaeological record, archaeologists were essentially foxes setting themselves up to guard the chicken coop (Wylie 1996:181). Clearly, then, the concept of stewardship as presented in the 1996 SAA principles was at least systematically ambiguous if not also, as Zimmerman suggested, strategically contradictory.

It is not surprising that the SAA principles should have embodied such internal tensions. One lesson reinforced by our review of existing statements on archaeological ethics was that they were always responses to specific problems; however much they were intended to reach beyond the particularities of current practice, they were deeply structured by the conditions of their production. For this reason we emphasized the point—in discussion and in print, and in urging the SAA to establish a standing rather than an ad hoc committee on ethics—that the principles we proposed should be treated as provisional: not just open to but requiring continuous reassessment and revision as conditions of practice evolved.[4] It is in this spirit that I revisit them. I first consider in more detail the background against which these principles were formulated and then close with a critical assessment of competing conceptions of stewardship.

Significant Truths, Conservation, and Professionalism

Archaeologists have established their professional, disciplinary identity by exploiting a series of contrasts with nonanthropological, nonscientific interests in the archaeological record (Denning 1999): initially nineteenth-century antiquarian and twentieth-century commercial interests and subsequently a range of (merely) descriptive, particularistic interests. The common denominator here is that the excluded or contested practices are characterized by a preoccupation with the object. The archaeology that was being institutionalized in North American museums and universities at the beginning of the twentieth century was distinguished, above all else, by a commitment to approaching archaeological material as a record of the cultural past whose significance lay in its informational content (as evidence), not its aesthetic or sentimental or commercial value. Writing in 1908, Edgar Hewett made the case that archaeological research required much more than "the [mere] recovery and study of material"; indeed, it required practitioners to go beyond the "recital of events" and undertake an investigation of "their genesis" (1908:595). By 1913 Roland Dixon felt confident in declaring that "the time is past when our major interest was in the specimen"; archaeologists were chiefly concerned "with the relations of things, with the whens and the whys and the hows" (1913:565). A few years later Clark Wissler endorsed, as the "real, new archaeology," a form of practice characterized by the "reasoned formulation of definite problems" and the application to them of systematic, explicitly scientific methods of investigation (1917:101). Its hallmark was its pursuit of evidence specifically relevant to the questions central to anthropology, "the science of man" (1917:100).[5]

It is striking that, in this early, formative literature and in virtually every subsequent North American debate about disciplinary goals and identity, the distinctive anthropological and scientific mandate of archaeology is defined in terms of what Philip Kitcher describes as "significant truths" and in opposition to a shifting gallery of others (within and outside the discipline) who fail to pursue or to realize significant understanding. As Kitcher puts this point, "there are vast oceans of truth that aren't worth exploring" (2001:148). Commonsense appeals to the ideal that the sciences search for truth are not enough, on their own, to define what it is to be a science; "the sciences are surely directed at finding *significant* truths" (2001:65), and the difficult question is what counts as significance. If there is any consensus of principle in anthropological archaeology it is that knowledge of the contents of the archaeological record is not, in itself, significant, however rich or appreciative it may be; what *archaeologists* seek is an understanding of the cultural past that produced this record. The themes evident in arguments for the first "new archaeology" of 1908–17 are reiterated by successive generations of North American archaeologists who repudiate not only outsiders who continue the tradition of nineteenth-century antiquarians—looters, dealers, and collectors who destroy potential evidence in the pursuit of profit or personal satisfaction—but also a range of insiders: not-fully-anthropological or scientific archaeologists for whom the description and systematization of archaeological data has become an end in itself (see, for example, Kluckhohn's [1939] critique of "narrow empiricism") or whose culture-historical reconstructions are little more than redescriptions of temporal and spatial patterning in the record (see, for example, the New Archaeologists' critiques of traditional archaeology in the 1960s and 1970s [Wylie 2002:61–66]).

These commitments are explicit in the first position statement on ethics developed by the SAA, the "Four Statements for Archaeology" published by the Committee on Conduct and Standards in 1961 (Champe et al. 1961:137). The authors begin with a definition of archaeology: "Archaeology is a branch of the science of anthropology . . . [a scholarly discipline] concerned with the reconstruction of past human life and culture . . . Its primary data lie in material objects and their relationships [systematically collected and documented]. Value attaches to objects so collected because of their status as documents, and is not intrinsic."

They go on to specify, in general terms, what archaeologists must do to make effective use of their data as a record, and they condemn any practice that compromises the evidential value of archaeological data, especially practices such as the buying and selling of artifacts that "usually result in the loss of context and cultural associations" (1961: 137). The by-laws of the SAA, drafted in 1977 and revised in 1997, define the objectives of the society more generally: the first stated objective is "to promote and to stimulate interest and research in the archaeology of the American Continents" ([1977] 1995:17). Although these objectives set out no explicit definition of what counts as archaeological research, it is clear in several subsequent clauses that the mandate of SAA archaeologists is to do *scientific*, anthropological research defined, as in 1961, oppositionally. They are to "operate exclusively for scientific and educational purposes," to counteract any nonarchaeological interests that threaten the destruction of archaeological resources or, indeed, any "loss of scientific knowledge and access," and to "aid in directing the . . . efforts [of all those interested in American Archaeology] into scientific channels" (objectives 4, 8, and Postscript [SAA (1977) 1995]). One key difference from the 1961 statements is the appearance of a new professional and ethical obligation: the second objective is to "advocate and to aid in the conservation of archaeological resources," a clause that appears (in one form or another) in virtually every archaeological statement of objectives or ethical code drafted after the early 1970s.

The centrality of a commitment to "significant research" is particularly striking when one considers what these SAA statements do not do. The committee that drafted the 1961 statements had been formed in response to growing concern that, with the dramatic postwar expansion of archaeology, informal mechanisms of self-regulation were no longer effective; it was becoming necessary to codify professional standards, to define "who an archaeologist was and what that person was qualified to do," as McGimsey put it in retrospective discussion (1995:11). In the event, this committee chose not to develop a code of conduct or any very specific mechanisms for enforcing the principles it set out; in particular, it chose not to establish requirements for professional standing. It acknowledged that many of the most conscientious, productive members of the SAA were committed avocationals who had never been formally trained or professionally employed as archaeologists; there was a strong predisposition to avoid any guildlike rules that might draw a line between professionals and nonprofessionals. Archaeology was thus conceived as a calling, not only or necessarily a profession, and the SAA as a scholarly society, not primarily a professional association. The later objectives make this commitment to inclusiveness explicit; the fourth is to "serve as a bond among those interested in American Archaeology, both as professionals and nonprofessionals" (SAA [1977] 1995).

The SAA revisited the question of professional standards in the mid-1970s, under pressure from a number of members who, taking stock of the impact on the field of cultural resource management, forcefully argued the need to institute a register of professional archaeologists, a formal code of conduct governing their practice, and grievance procedures to enforce this code. A committee on codes and standards was set up to do this, but the SAA executive board declined to act on its recommendations, citing the threat of legal and financial ruin if self-regulation went awry and a concern that any systematic distinction between professional and nonprofessional members would change the character of the society. In 1978 members of this committee founded an independent society for professional archaeologists, SOPA, which has been reconstituted, twenty years later, as the Register of Professional Archaeologists (RPA), jointly supported by the SAA, the SHA, and the AIA (McGimsey, Lipe, and Seifert 1995). For many the motivating concern was that, with big money at stake and a regulative structure that puts archaeologists on the front line in ensuring compliance with heritage legislation, both contract archaeologists and their employers need clearly specified, collectively endorsed guidelines that set out what professional archaeologists can and cannot do. Although the ultimate goal of cultural resource management is to serve a broadly conceived (social, human) interest in understanding the cultural past, in practice it applies the tools of archaeological investigation instrumentally, as a technology of recovery and documentation that is to varying degrees disconnected from the anthropological and historical problems they were designed to address. Good archaeology of the kind envisioned by generations of "real, new archaeologists" is expensive, and, in a competitive lowest-bidder environment, the economic realities of cultural resource management practice often mean that there is not even adequate funding for storage and preservation, let alone for analysis and publication that goes beyond the requirements of descriptive reporting on the contents of the endangered archaeological record.

The SOPA code, now implemented by the RPA, makes these tensions explicit. Archaeology is defined, first and foremost, as a profession: "The privilege of professional practice requires professional morality and professional responsibility, as well as professional competence, on the part of each practitioner" (SOPA 1991:7). The goals of science figure chiefly in the clauses that specify standards for research performance. Professional archaeologists have a responsibility to "design and conduct projects that will add to our understanding of past cultures," and effective design is understood to require a "scientific plan of research" (9). They are also expected to keep up with developments in their field and to report the results of their work to "colleagues and other interested persons" (10). Although SOPA clearly endorses an overarching commitment to seek significant truth about the cultural past, this defining disciplinary goal is embedded in a complicated network of competing responsibilities to a range of stakeholders: clients and employers, employees, colleagues, students, and the public at large, as well as the field of archaeology itself (7–8).

When Lipe (1974) proposed that archaeologists should embrace a "conservation ethic," he was responding to the situation created by the compliance industry as much as to the widespread destruction of archaeological resources that gave rise to cultural resource management. He argued that salvage archaeology should be conducted only as a last resort and that when it was unavoidable, those engaged in such work should strenuously resist pressures that might compromise the research value of their work: "piling up data for its own sake, proving the obvious, archaeology by rote—are all pathways to stagnation" (1974: 243). "Salvage archaeologist[s]," he said, should be mindful that they were "also working for the whole profession" (234); the challenge was to find ways to "make a research contribution on the basis of a site or set of sites selected . . . by circumstance" and to recover data that would be relevant to future research problems without knowing clearly what these would be (231). If cultural resource management was practiced with a "strong primary problem orientation," Lipe was confident that the demands of compliance could be reconciled with (and even be made to serve) the scientific goals of the discipline. But his chief emphasis was on the need for all archaeologists to embrace a conservation ethic—to take "responsibility for the whole resource base" (214)—and to recognize that this would require them to forgo the excavation of sites that were not threatened if there was any possibility of meeting "the data needs of a problem" through the use of existing collections or the excavation of sites within "the available pool of [those] requiring salvage" (213). The rationale for circumscribing the pursuit of significant truth in this way was not, however, a concern that archaeological interests must be weighted against other interests in the record; it was to ensure that future archaeologists would have a database with which to work. Lipe reinforced this primary commitment to the goals of scientific archaeology in a later article, "In Defense of Digging" (1996), in which he argued that he had never intended to foreclose all "consumptive uses" of the resource base; "an archaeology without excavation is one that cannot fully achieve its potential social contributions" (1996:24), which he characterized as "the production and dissemination of new information about the past based on the systematic study of the archaeological record" (23). The trade-off imposed by Lipe's conservation ethic is not between archaeological and nonarchaeological interests but between the long- and short-term research interests of the archaeological community.

Divergent Models of Stewardship

Considered against this background, the stewardship principles drafted in 1993 (adopted in 1996) clearly build upon the conservation ethic that had already taken shape in North American archaeology. At the same time, however, a commitment to stewardship requires archaeologists to be accountable not just to the current and future interests of archaeological research but to "the full range of publics and stakeholders whose heritage this record is" (Lynott and Wylie 1995); in this it represents a significant expansion upon and, on some construals, a break with the principles of conservation and the paramount commitment to the research goals of archaeology articulated by previous statements. Just how radical a shift this is and what it entails was the focus of much discussion at the Reno meeting. The position paper on stewardship reflects the tenor of this discussion, noting that a (self-ascribed) mandate to serve as stewards "do[es] not establish any presumption of ownership or control over archaeological resources"; appeals to the goals of science should not be assumed to displace all other interests, and when archaeologists do pursue their disciplinary interests "they have a responsibility to ensure that their research benefits the public(s) in whose trust archaeological material is held, documented, preserved and sometimes exploited" (Lynott and Wylie 1995). As Zimmerman observes, however, there remains an implicit presumption that archaeological expertise establishes a privilege of oversight (1995:65–66); the language of public trust, which archaeological research is assumed to serve, is juxtaposed with an acknowledgment that the interests of the publics in question are by no means congruent with one another nor convergent on any common, transcendent set of values where archaeological sites and material are concerned. The range of responses provoked by these principles testifies to this transitional instability; they embody the contradictions they were meant to address.

These contradictions are inherent not just in principles of *archaeological* stewardship but also in the complicated legacy of thinking about stewardship as a guide for action more generally. In the context of environmental ethics, the idea of an ethic of stewardship originated in religious doctrine that represents man as "God's deputy," a kind of farm manager, Passmore suggests, responsible for protecting the divine creation and perfecting its "beauty, usefulness, and fruitfulness" (1974:30, 31). The challenge has been to determine how a secular ethic of human responsibility for nonhuman nature can be motivated and authorized. If we cannot confidently appeal to a divine authority, do we then invoke some presumed universal interest of all humanity? Or perhaps the more concrete but speculative interests of future generations of humans? Or some more prosaic combination of anthropocentric interests and virtues, for example, loyalty and benevolence, as Welchman (1999) has suggested? The impulse inherent in the concept of stewardship is to seek some reference point, some foundation that transcends local, individual interests on which to base its claims. In an archaeological context this impulse, reinforced by the legacy of a deeply entrenched commitment to significant inquiry, is to appeal to a distinctively rational, panhuman interest in a particular kind of knowledge about cultural past: the kind of knowledge that scientific, anthropological archaeology is best fitted to provide. This presupposes the theology of the scientific faithful, as Kitcher (2001:3, 9) describes it: that the sciences at their best provide accurate, authoritative knowledge that transcends practical values and localized interests, knowledge that has intrinsic value for all people, whether it directly benefits them or not, and that "represents the apogee of human achievement."

Deployed in the context of intra- and intercultural conflict between fundamentally different ways of valuing archaeological material/ cultural heritage, the appeal to a transcendent public interest in scientific knowledge of the past shares many elements of the "residual imperialism" inherent in modernist conceptions of constitutional negotiation (Tully 1995:43). On Tully's account, constitutional modern-ists assume that there must be some unique, universal standard of rationality, often modeled on scientific rationality (185), that is strictly neutral with respect to contesting cultures, a standard that all parties will embrace if only they free themselves from the bonds of parochial custom and establish themselves as the proper subjects of universal principles of formal equality, undifferentiated with respect to need or interest (60). Tully objects that this fiction of universalism—this "imperial fable" about the "universality of the guardians and the institutions they guard" (93)—is itself specific to a particular colonial, imperialist context and is founded on highly questionable assumptions about the evolutionary superiority of those cultures that embrace, incompletely as it turns out, just the ideals of rationality that are presumed to be necessary for forming modern constitutions and running modern democracies. Appeals to a public interest made within the framework of this fiction are appeals to the interests that all citizens would have, counterfactually, if they were to transcend the dogmatic conventions of lesser cultural forms.

As stark a caricature as this may seem, claims along just these lines have been made in opposition to NAGPRA and, indeed, to any assertion that archaeologists should be prepared to compromise the pursuit of scientific, anthropological goals out of respect for the interests of stakeholders who understand the cultural past and value archaeological sites and material in fundamentally different ways. Consider Geoff Clark's sharp opposition to the claims of "various pseudo- and anti-science constituencies" (1998:22) that challenge the scientific world-view he embraces and that, he says, threaten to undermine all the accomplishments of Enlightenment rationality, science having been instrumental in "achieving the modern world" (22). "We all lose," he argues, "if for reasons of political expediency, Indians rebury their past" (24); to accede to repatriation—to accept that the ethnic and religious beliefs of Native Americans should be considered "on an equal footing with science" (24)—is to capitulate to a "demon haunted world" (1996), a family of worldviews characterized by religiosity, obscurantism, and ignorance that are "curious survivals of earlier cognitive evolution" (1998:22). A commitment to "reasoned inquiry," to the antidogmatic, self-correcting practice of scientific inquiry, is a commitment to the pursuit of systematic, empirically grounded knowledge of a "generalized human past . . . part of a universal heritage not circumscribed by ethnic or cultural boundaries" (24).

Virtually every element of this argument is open to question if not patently unsustainable, from the assumptions about cultural evolution to the claims about the transcendent status of scientific knowledge. I make these arguments as an epistemological conservative; I endorse a modest realism (Wylie 2002:97–195), and I have argued for a moderate pragmatic objectivism in archaeological contexts (Wylie 2000). In other words, I believe that systematic empirical inquiry can and frequently does establish reliable, precise, explanatorily probative knowledge of an independently existing reality, social and historical as well as physical and natural. In Kitcher's language (Kitcher 2001:11–28), science establishes truths about the world, albeit truths that are understood always to be open to reassessment and revision. In this the diverse and evolving methodologies of critical scientific inquiry are immensely valuable, but I see no reason to conclude that this insulates the scientific enterprise or its products from political, moral, and social scrutiny, much less establishes that scientific interests have a transcendent value that takes precedence over all other interests. As suggested earlier, the key point here is that scientific inquiry is a search not for truth as such (or, more modestly, for empirically credible knowledge as such) but for *significant* truth (or knowledge). And the assessment of significance is inherently project- and practice-specific: "objective explanation goes on in the sciences, but only against the background of our questions and interests" (Kitcher 2001:75), which are diverse and shifting, conditioned by a wide range of factors. The contextual factors that constitute significance include everything from the internal intellectual dynamics of the research tradition itself, through changes in the conceptual and technical resources available for inquiry that are both internal and external to the research tradition in question, to more strictly external factors such as the practical considerations mediated by funding initiatives, the hegemonic interests of a dominant elite, or the transient Zeitgeist of an era. In this sense "moral and social values [are] intrinsic to the practice of science" (Kitcher 2001:66; see also Longino 2002:124–144).

I also see no reason to assume that, even if the goals of science did transcend local (culturally specific) interests, they should take precedence over (all) other values and interests. We acknowledge that scientific inquiry must be constrained by respect for the rights and interests of human subjects and by concern with more indirect consequences for those who are affected by but are not the subjects of inquiry. In this it is recognized that (scientific) knowledge is not categorically good (or bad); even the most obviously beneficial knowledge comes at a cost. Kitcher makes this case with reference to biomedical research (the Human Genome Diversity Project) and argues that the issue is not whether scientific knowledge is a good (or bad) thing *as such* but whether its costs and benefits are equitably distributed (2001:181–197), an issue that is especially salient in the case of archaeological and anthropological inquiry that concerns Native Americans.

Finally, I see no reason to accept the claims about cultural evolution central to Clark's argument or the conclusions he draws from them. Why should we assume that communities or cultures that do not grant priority to scientific interests are inherently inferior to those that do? Centrally at issue here is the most all-encompassing of questions: what makes for a high-quality life. Surely such lives can take a great many different forms, only some of which (or some aspects of which) are well served by the pursuit of scientific goals. Perhaps more to the point, why should we assume that the unevolved, parochial values rejected by Clark will disappear with proper education as those who embrace them realize fully modern rationality and assimilate an idealized set of universal human values? As the constitutional pluralist Tully observes, the cultural and social diversity that obtains both within and between modern states has by no means withered away, despite no end of efforts in this direction. Native Americans are just one among many examples that subvert modernist ambitions and expectations; they sustain distinctive cultural traditions and forms of self-government that are internally complex, dynamic, and shaped both in interaction with and in opposition to dominant Euro-American cultures that have done everything in their power to dispossess and annihilate or, alternatively, assimilate them. This resilient and proliferating pluralism throws into relief the parochial nature of modernist ideals; as Tully argues, these are anything but transcendent, emerging in and sustained by highly specific conditions of cultural dominance and opposition. But such pluralism does not necessarily undermine the viability of constitutional negotiation; Tully delineates a rich historical tradition of intercultural negotiation that has thrived on the margins of constitutional modernism and that takes the recognition of cultural difference as its point of departure (1995:99–140).

Taking these various lines of argument into consideration, I see no brief for according professional archaeologists the status of stewards responsible for the archaeological record in any sense that presumes that they have unique standing in the service of a generalized social, human interest in knowledge of the cultural past that conforms to their identity-defining, scientific and anthropological goals. This is not to say that what archaeological inquiry offers is trivial, of only marginal interest. Archaeologists have a developed tradition of skill and knowledge, a commitment to systematic empirical research that contributes enormously valuable understanding of the cultural past and, by extension, of our diverse contemporary selves. Archaeology is the only basis for learning about the vast majority of human ancestors who are lost to memory and history or, indeed, about many aspects of the lives that are otherwise remembered and recorded (Wylie 2002:205). And, in the way of anthropology generally, archaeological insights can very effectively make strange what we take for granted, recovering alternatives to and contingencies in the history of dominant cultural and social forms that we tend to reify, to naturalize. Of course, archaeology is not always used for these purposes, as nationalist appropriations make plain (Kohl and Fawcett 1995; Trigger 1984, 1989). What is at issue in cases such as these is often not so much deliberate misrepresentation as "epistemic asymmetries" (Kitcher 2001:97): the risk that ambiguities of evidence and interpretation will systematically favor those reconstructions that reinforce existing social and political inequities. Nonetheless, archaeology is one of the technologies of inquiry that can cultivate the kind of intercultural vision that Tully recommends as an essential condition for effective intercultural negotiation.

Collaborative Stewardship

If the concept of stewardship is to play any useful role in navigating the conditions of practice that are reshaping archaeology, it must be construed not as a matter of wise management on behalf of an abstract higher interest (that of science and, by extension, society or humanity) but as a matter of collaborative, negotiated co-management among divergent interests (including archaeological interests) none of which can be presumed, at the outset, to take precedence over the others. This is by no means a novel suggestion; the recommendation that stewardship be considered a joint venture was prominent in the Reno discussions and has been advocated by a great many others, albeit in quite different senses (for example, Ferguson 1990, 1996; Forsman 1997; Goldstein 1992; Nicholas 2000; Spector 2000). A common theme in these recommendations is that archaeologists must be prepared to make a case for pursuing their goals as co-participants in an open-ended process of negotiation in which all the questions that Clark forecloses—who should be involved, what interests are legitimate, how these interests should be weighed—are on the table. To specify what is entailed by stewardship in this spirit, I draw inspiration from Tully's account of intercultural constitutional negotiation, which in many key respects converges on the practices instituted by archaeologists and Native Americans who have established productive collaborations.

The first of three requirements set out by Tully (1995:116) is that negotiation should begin with a recognition of difference, not the presumption that difference obscures an underlying (rational, universal) framework that is neutral with respect to diverse cultural values. As Tully describes this requirement of mutual recognition, it is a matter of ensuring that all parties to the dialog "speak in their own language and customary ways," that "each listens to the voices of the others in their own terms" (24), that they "participate in their diverse cultural forms [and develop] a form of intercultural understanding that does not presuppose a comprehensive [neutral] language" (57). The ability to do this effectively, "to change perspectives—to see and understand aperspectivally," is something participants acquire "through participation in the intercultural dialogue itself" (25). The need for this kind of communication—for the kind of sustained engagement necessary to build trust and understanding, sometimes across acrimonious differences—is pivotal to virtually every recommendation for collaboration that has been made by Native Americans and archaeologists alike. Beyond this, Tully outlines a process by which negotiating parties articulate for one another just what identity-significant values are at stake in the conflict under negotiation; he characterizes this as a matter of establishing "continuity." This many Native Americans do as a matter of course when entering negotiations with archaeologists, and it is, in essence, what archaeologists recommend when they insist on the need to communicate clearly and publicly exactly what their goals are as archaeologists—what their interests are in archaeological sites and material.

Mutual recognition and arguments of continuity provide a framework in which to negotiate accommodations that take account of, if they do not fully satisfy, the interests of all involved, subject to the principle that "what touches all should be agreed to by all" (Tully 1995:122). Any closer specification of what joint stewardship involves—of the conditions under which it thrives and of practical guidelines for its implementation—will require the analysis of cases that illustrate the various forms that "best-practice" stewardship can take. This is a strategy for moving beyond the polarized debate over repatriation and the control of cultural resources that is already evident in much recent literature on the prospects for fruitful collaboration between Native Americans and archaeologists (for example, Swidler et al. 1997; Dongoske, Aldenderfer, and Doehner 2000; Watkins 1999, 2000).

Archaeologists may worry that, without the anchor of universal values—without the possibility of appeal to values that trump all other interests—they stand to lose all access to archaeological sites and materials. Certainly the cost of doing business in the way it has been done will be the loss to archaeologists of some important research opportunities. But the growing literature on what becomes possible when archaeologists "make every reasonable effort, in good faith," to develop ongoing working relationships with "affected groups" (SAA 1996:451) suggests that there is much more to be gained than lost. What my graduate classmate failed to realize was just how much a research tradition can be enriched by sustained interchange with values and interests that lie outside its insular boundaries.

Notes

1. This was 1977–78 at the State University of New York in Binghamton.

2. I draw here on Kitcher's assessment of the arguments developed by Vannevar Bush in a report on science policy published in 1944. With a primary focus on defending the idea of pure science and no detailed account of the value of such inquiry for society, "the institutional framework of the report is one in which scientists are left free to pursue their own curiosity but simultaneously saddled with the task of advertising their research as potentially satisfying the untutored preferences of the public" (2001:141).

3. Forums for debate and discussion of these principles were organized at a number of regional and national meetings of archaeologists in the two and a half years before they were adopted by the SAA. One of these, a plenary session at the 1994 annual meetings of the SAA, resulted in a widely circulated special

report of the SAA that included papers by participants in the 1993 Reno meeting explaining the rationale for each of the original six principles as well as a number of critical assessments and commentaries by contributors who had not been involved in drafting the principles (Lynott and Wylie 1995).

4. Our point, in emphasizing the need for continuous and systematic reassessment of these principles, was not just that their conditional nature should be recognized but that their elaboration and refinement cannot be treated as an end in itself. The importance of clearly articulated statements of disciplinary goals, standards, and guidelines should not be trivialized; the authors of the AAAS report of 1980 (Chalk, Frankel, and Chafer) give a clear account of the functions they serve and the liabilities faced by professional groups that lack them. But, as they also point out, the formulation of such statements is not an adequate response, on its own, to the problems they address. There is no guarantee that instituting explicit statements of principle or even a formal code of conduct will be a force for positive change. Moreover, once codified, such principles are always vulnerable to manipulation, cynical application, and subversion; they are no proof against unethical, exploitative, self-serving behavior. To be effective, ethical principles and guidelines must be embedded in a broad network of institutions and practices—a disciplinary culture—that reinforces robustly responsive, accountable forms of professional practice.

That said, codification can be an important locus for disciplinary change in some contexts, at some junctures; the development of principles of stewardship in the SAA may be such a case. We were acutely aware, however, that the process of debate—the public articulation of issues and ideals occasioned by the proposal of an ethic of stewardship—was at least as important as the product of our deliberations. And we were concerned that, if this impetus was not to stall, much more would be required than the writing (or updating) of codes and principles. In this spirit, the standing committee on ethics that the SAA executive board established in 1996 has put a great deal of energy into developing conference sessions, workshops, publications, curricula, and educational materials that keep these issues alive and expand their reach within the discipline and beyond. See, for example, the ethics textbook recently assembled by the SAA Ethics Committee (Zimmerman, Vitelli, and Hollowell-Zimmer 2003:xi–xii) and the proposal put forward by the SAA's Task Force on Curriculum that an ethic of stewardship and related principles of professional ethics should be the defining core of the archaeological curriculum at both the graduate and the undergraduate level (Davis et al. 1999:18–9; Bender and Smith 2000).

5. These historical antecedents are discussed in more detail in the first section of *Thinking from Things* (Wylie 2002:25–40).

"Where There Aren't No Ten Commandments": Redefining Ethics during the *Darkness in El Dorado* Scandal

Peter Pels

Ship me somewheres east of Suez, where the best is like the worst,
Where there aren't no Ten Commandments, an' a man can raise a thirst.

(Rudyard Kipling, *Mandalay*)

When, in September 2000, a confidential e-mail by Leslie Sponsel and Terence Turner to the president and president-elect of the American Anthropological Association was leaked to the public, anthropologists were suddenly confronted by a colonial specter. The e-mail, warning the AAA chiefs of the scandal about to be caused by the publication of Patrick Tierney's *Darkness in El Dorado: How Scientists and Journalists Devastated the Amazon* (2000b), suggested that the Amazon had become, once more, a colonial place "where there aren't no Ten Commandments" and where "the best is like the worst," that is, where, in research among Yanomami of the Orinoco region, the lofty ideals of science and civilization had been corrupted by misrepresentation, greed, and cruelty. Soon thereafter, critics of the e-mail message were suggesting that morality was being violated in the best of places—"at home"—by "irresponsible journalism," "conspiracy thinking," and unscientific "vendettas." The cross fire of accusations became so acrimonious and public that, to the horror of the average practitioner, anthropologists were being described as "the most bellicose tribe on earth" and "the academic equivalent of the Jerry Springer show" (Zalewski 2000)—east of Suez, right in our midst.[1]

For many anthropologists this was a "public-relations disaster" (as the former AAA president Jane Hill [2000] put it): a regrettable, disorderly deviation from what were supposed to be the real and regular routines of anthropological conduct. As a result, many reactions to the scandal were written in a defensive mode: in the words of one commentator, by "circling the wagons,"[2] in particular, around accepted conventions of "science" and "ethics." In this essay, however, I would like to read the *El Dorado* controversy as a form of anthropological ethics in its own right and to take the scandal as a form of acrimonious and violent negotiation over the meaning of these conventions. These negotiations subvert common assumptions about the ethics of anthropology and identify situations that prevent anthropological practitioners from dictating "commandments" to anyone—whether on the basis of ethical standards or of "scientific" expertise. The *El Dorado* scandal not only displays how anthropologists commonly draw the boundaries between ethics and scientific expertise but also uncovers, through its discursive excesses, the common and rather ethnocentric assumptions on which these boundaries are based. Consequently, it questions the adequacy of the ways in which anthropological professionals define themselves. Thus, the scandal raised a thirst for rethinking the ethics and the profession of anthropology, and it eventually did so in ways that sometimes radically differed from the initial, conservative gut reactions to it. I will first present a brief outline of the scandal to bring out some of its more controversial negotiations.[3] In two subsequent sections I will try to distill, from these features of the controversy, some of the less conspicuous assumptions on which our common institutionalization of ethics and professional expertise is based and show how these ethnocentric assumptions routinely *exteriorize* ethics from professional practice. In the last two sections I hope to show how other features of the controversy—its media effects and its global relationships, in particular—undo this exteriorization and reembed ethical argument in anthropological work. In conclusion, I return to the question of how the *El Dorado* scandal may redefine the anthropological profession and its ethics.

Darkness in Anthropologyland: A Chronology of Scandal

The *El Dorado* scandal was launched by the global "leaking" of Turner and Sponsel's August 31, 2000, e-mail announcing Tierney's upcoming "revelations" (described as "convincing" and "well-documented"), which were alleged to show that Neel and Chagnon—whom the authors dubbed "corrupt," "depraved," and even "genocidal"—had fostered a measles epidemic among Yanomami and subordinated research findings and human life to the proving of pet theories. Moreover, Chagnon was said to have violated research ethics in his Yanomami fieldwork and harmed Yanomami interests by his dealings with corrupt members of the Venezuelan elite. Chagnon (Neel died in 2000) immediately announced legal retaliation, while the AAA cautiously publicized its awareness of a possible violation of its code of ethics and emphasized its public commitment to the cause of indigenous peoples. The *Chronicle of Higher Education* of September 20, however, noted doubts about the AAA's ability to investigate or discipline scholars who violated its code of ethics and quoted Joe Watkins, chair of the AAA Committee on Ethics, to the effect that since 1998 the AAA had restricted itself to educating members about ethics and stopped "going out and censuring anthropologists." In this case, however, Watkins said, the possibility of "trouble with foreign governments" over research permits might require the association to reconsider (quoted in Miller 2000). The AAA's president, Louise Lamphere, also emphasized the difficulty by saying that, while they would have to do something about it, "it's not like anthropologists are doctors or attorneys who can have their licenses revoked" (quoted in Wilford and Romero 2000).

Hysteria mounted as Turner and Sponsel's accusations ballooned in the press and supporters of Neel and Chagnon came to the latter's defense. Most rebuttals concentrated on James Neel and the impossibility that his research team had intentionally spread a measles epidemic or violated the Hippocratic oath when confronted with it, and some of the evidence led Turner to retract the accusations of spreading measles and genocide.[4] Turner, Sponsel, and Tierney were accused of "witchcraft accusations," "McCarthyism," "character assassination," sensationalism, "feuding," and deliberate dishonesty. On October 8, President Lamphere announced that the AAA would withhold judgment until it had conducted a fair and impartial review of all the accusations, but anthropology's public stature plummeted to a particularly low point with Zalewski's column in the *New York Times* ("bellicose tribe," "Jerry Springer Show"), in which a Chagnon supporter criticized present-day anthropology's supposed tendency to put "ideology" before "evidence" and opposed Chagnon's "great empiricism" to his opponents' "postmodern lunacy." The article implicitly identified such lunatics when Paul Rabinow allowed himself to be quoted as saying that, today, nobody took Chagnon seriously and that "the idea of someone going to the most technologically simple societies and trying to learn lessons about human nature by studying them, that's been refuted." Readers were left to conclude that simply observing a threatened culture was now seen as "irresponsible" and had given way to activism. Given that "empiricism" sounds good and familiar and that the article did not give the reasons for the activists' "refutation" of the idea of learning by observing simple societies, Nancy Scheper-Hughes's assertion that a "beautiful" ethnography on a Sierra Leonean village had had to be rewritten because some of her colleagues thought it did not help the people "in getting their arms chopped off" cannot have helped dispel the impression of academic lunacy (Zalewski 2000).

Despite the first publication of Tierney's own words in *The New Yorker* of October 9—considerably more moderate in tone than the Turner/ Sponsel e-mail (Tierney 2000a)—the supporters of Neel and Chagnon seem to have had the floor during the rest of October and a large part of November. On October 20 a so-called official statement from the University of Michigan (where the Yanomami expedition of Neel and Chagnon had originated) marshaled evidence against Tierney, Turner, and Sponsel in an attempt to show that both Neel and Chagnon had been unfairly accused and that, more important, the accusations made by Tierney, Turner, and Sponsel could be mirrored by arguing that the latter were conspiring with Salesian missionaries among the Yanomami and that they were driven by a theoretical interest: a "Moral Agenda" that opposed "Science" to "Anti-Science" and Chagnon's objectivism to the ideas of Nancy Scheper-Hughes (see Scheper-Hughes 1995). On the Internet, too, the majority of reactions to John Tooby's "unmasking" of Tierney's book as "fiction" rather than fact reinforced popular anti-intellectual images of academia (favoring the Neel/Chagnon position) even after *The New Yorker* posted a refutation on October 27 (see Tooby 2000a). At this time the controversy was, indeed, a "public-relations disaster" for anthropology (Hill 2000).

By the time that anthropologists first openly debated the issue at the AAA meetings in San Francisco on November 16 (*Darkness in El Dorado* finally appeared on the same day, too late for most to ascertain its actual contents) the tide seems to have turned again. While descriptions of anthropology as "the world's most fractious tribe" still abounded, the critique of Tierney and his "conspiracy theory" was balanced by equally passionate denunciations of the "colonial arrogance" of Chagnon and his supporters. While one of the worst effects predicted actually occurred (a moratorium on research among indigenous peoples was proclaimed by the Venezuelan government), Tierney himself admitted some of his mistakes about Neel's work and redirected attention to "the other 90%" of his book that dealt with Chagnon and others (Dalton 2000; Vergano 2000). A much more balanced account in *Newsweek* concluded that the "effect of scientists on their subjects" may still be "anthropology's heart of darkness" (Begley 2000). The AAA Executive decided, after the November meetings, to appoint a task force led by former president James Peacock to examine the allegations, to charge the ethics committee with drafting new guidelines for researchers faced with health emergencies, questions of remuneration for and material assistance to people studied, the social impact of the publication of factual data, and informed consent, and to establish a task force to investigate the plight of South American indigenous populations.

In February 2001 the (confidential) report of the Peacock task force advised further investigation of the allegations, a task that was taken up by the El Dorado Task Force, chaired by Jane Hill. Its interim report of May 2001 made clear that, whereas the charge of spreading a measles epidemic could be rejected, the other allegations by Tierney needed careful consideration. Another interim report was laid before an AAA audience during its meetings in November 2001, but members of the audience and a minority of the task force asked that it be withdrawn because its incompleteness might slant it toward selective reporting. Another interesting development was the result of the horrified reaction of a majority of University of Michigan anthropologists to the so-called official departmental statement of October 2000: on the basis of the Spring 2001 seminars of the doctoral program in Anthropology and History, a statement from the Office of the Provost of May 29 acknowledged that despite the limitations of Tierney's book it also raised "fundamental, general questions about the ethics, methods, and effects of scientific research" that should be resolved "through regular academic channels" (University of Michigan 2001). Robert Borofsky's Public Anthropology also brought opponents together, and this resulted in a joint open letter to anthropologists on August 30, followed by several joint motions during the November 30 AAA business meeting in Washington. Together with the activities of the ethics committee, which solicited reactions to briefings on the new guidelines requested a year before and formulated a new statement about the nature of "informed consent" in anthropology, and the appearance of the El Dorado Task Force report in the course of 2002, these events signal a new, more productive cycle of the scandal's social life—but one that, unfortunately, was no longer as interesting to the media (EDTF 2003). Last but certainly not least, the controversy also triggered a new cycle of developments in Latin America, resulting, first, in a meeting of Yanomami at Shakita on November 20–23, 2001, that may well prove a landmark in the transformation of their political and ethnic consciousness and, secondly, in bringing to the fore initiatives by Brazilian and Venezuelan researchers that had gone largely unheeded before the scandal (see Albert 2001).

In other words, in the course of 2001, the controversy seemed to shift from the acrimonious "public-relations disaster" of the fall of 2000 toward a more constructive and less antagonistic phase during 2001 (although anyone who witnessed the November 2001 AAA business meeting in Washington could note the suspicion, emanating from both sides, of some of the AAA Executive's initiatives).[5] While hysteria mounted, many participants in the controversy tended toward a predominantly conservative gut reaction, the "circling of the wagons" mentioned earlier, and this was probably exacerbated by the sound bites that such bickering provided to the press. The cover-up of anthropology's "heart of darkness"—the tendency not to examine publicly how scientific research affects the people studied—is part of that gut feeling, and it remains a dominant trend in dealing with the *El Dorado* issues, not so much because there is a heart of darkness that needs to be covered up as because ethics and expertise are often institutionalized in such a way that "ethics" becomes exterior to the production of expertise—and thus something that can be "unmasked" as not integral to the latter. However, when media attention died down and tempers subsided, ways toward a more creative exploration of the questions raised by the controversy opened up. Given the trenches dug during the first part of the controversy, I was personally surprised to find that the boundaries that protect the profession's public image were allowed to shift, especially after November 2001. I will first turn to what the conservative reaction tells us about the institutionalization of ethics and professional expertise and then deal with the possible new openings— the "rethinking" of ethics—that the scandal provoked.

The Profession and its Ethics

One of the more interesting features of the initial reaction to the Turner/ Sponsel memo was the AAA's profession of weakness with regard to censuring colleagues who might have violated its ethical code. To some, at least, this may seem unprofessional, especially in comparison with the immediate legal consequences that would arise from a similar case among medical or legal professionals.[6] Others associate this ambiguity with the feeling that ethics is invoked "less for the defence of those for whom unethical behaviour has real consequences than for the defence of the associations themselves" (Nugent 2001:13). To understand the AAA's initial stance in the *El Dorado* controversy one needs to historicize its ethics and embed its code's precepts in its common institutional practice. The AAA's ethical code, implicitly adopted from Western professionalist models, was embedded within an ideal technology of the self: a quasi-legal mode of producing a morally responsible subject by the example of explicit guidelines of conduct and a committee of peers that could warn or sanction those who departed from them (cf. Foucault 1988; Pels 2000:137–138). However, the voluntary membership of the association made any professional sanction impossible and soon reduced the ethics committee to an arbitrator of squabbles between colleagues (Levy 1993). Any pretense at being able to adjudicate professional disputes was abandoned in the course of the 1980s and, as Joe Watkins has indicated, more or less officially abolished by 1998; what remained of the ethical code's functions was a commitment to the fostering of ethics education. Another function, latent in the 1971 Principles of Professional Responsibility, came more to the fore when the ban on secret or clandestine research for some powerful sponsor— echoing fears of the late 1960s of being co-opted into U.S. counter- insurgency research—was watered down or deleted during the rewriting of the code since the mid-1980s (Pels 2000:143–144). Some feared that this shift indicated that the public relations of the profession rather than the welfare of people studied had become paramount (Berreman 1991; Pels 2000:143–144; cf. Nugent 2001:13). This trend seemed to be confirmed by Jane Hill's having called the *El Dorado* scandal a "public- relations disaster" while failing to mention the plight of Yanomami, thus implicitly suggesting that what had happened to them was not "the real story" (Hill 2000; Pels 2001a).[7]

The weakness of the AAA's ethical routines—without sanctioning force but still focused on the ethical code and on a committee of peers responsible for making the code operative in research practice—can be partly understood by acknowledging that many anthropologists work in "what are almost by definition ethically ambiguous or dubious situations" (Nugent 2001:13), doing fieldwork characterized by what I have elsewhere called moral "duplexity," or the simultaneous applic- ability of several different moral complexes (see Pels 1999 and below). Here I would like to underscore the ethical code's complications by using the *El Dorado* controversy to show that the weakness of the AAA's technology of ethical conduct also seems to lie in the current ethical code's reliance on certain typically modern, ethnocentric, and deeply buried assumptions—assumptions that often contradict other ethical standards of anthropological activity, especially those that obtain during fieldwork.[8]

The first of these is the implicit assumption (explicated during the controversy by Biella [2000]) that ethical codes are written for the guidance of *individual* practitioners and spell out their individual accountability to sponsors or the people studied. During the controversy this individualist habitus focused debate on the individual intentions and biographies of persons such as Neel, Chagnon, Tierney, and Turner. However, one should discard the assumption if one wants to rise above the simple conclusion that neither Tierney nor Chagnon "will have an easy time with their next human subjects review panel" (Stoll 2001) and address the question whether "the effects of scientists on their subjects" is not the more important darkness at the heart of anthropology (Begley 2000:75). As the focus on the potential individual misdeeds of Tierney, Chagnon, or Turner shows, the assumption is particularly effective in an ideological sense by implicitly allocating blame to individuals. Thus it hampers the development of a more *social scientific* perspective on the structural features of suspected violations of ethical guidelines or the situations in which they are discussed. I hope to show that, since November 2001, the *El Dorado* controversy has triggered significant departures from this assumption within and outside of the association.

Secondly, ethical codes have so far tended to promote trust in the future *legalistic* resolution of conflict. Rule-governed transcendence usually motivates the drawing up of new and ideally universal guidelines for research conduct. It bypasses the recognition that "in matters of knowledge, as in real estate, location is decisive" (Coroñil 2001a:266). It thereby contravenes common anthropological opinions about the role that "rules" play in social life (see, for instance, Bourdieu 1977 or Comaroff and Roberts 1981) and ignores alternative modes of redress that systematically acknowledge and relive a history of injustice (for example, in the South African Truth and Reconciliation Commission). Legalism informs a number of reactions to the *El Dorado* scandal and is closely linked to the individualist conception of ethics; both are apparent in Louise Lamphere's statement that anthropologists cannot have "their licenses revoked," in Joe Watkins's suggestion that a neutral institution be asked to adjudicate the accusations, and in the general sense among both the officials of the association and its members that some form of "judgment" was necessary.[9] Legalistic expectations also inform the ethics committee's response to the scandal: the formulation of new abstract guidelines displays—in the words of Don Brenneis (in this volume)—a trust in the formulation of "proxies" that are distant from the practice to be reformed. This is not to deny the value of codification as such but to suggest that alternative assumptions about ethical action may inform it—a point to which I will return in the discussion of the ethics committee's new guidelines below.

Thirdly, the institutionalization of ethics in codes, committees, and associations is usually *national*—or, better, it implicitly accepts citizenship in a certain nation-state as the framing assumption of the negotiation of identity during research. This becomes apparent not only from the identity of the *American* Anthropological Association and its initial concern with the public image of anthropology in the United States but also from the relative neglect of Tierney's charges against the French anthropologist Jacques Lizot.[10] Moreover, it is reinforced by the recognition that earlier critiques and protests by foreign colleagues—(from Brazil and Venezuela, in particular)—of the work of Chagnon had not been taken as seriously as an American journalist's sensationalist accusations (EDTF 2003, 1:9; 2003, 2:1), and by Joe Watkins's justified fear that the controversy might prejudice "foreign governments" against American researchers. (The latter fear has a history in the sense that the AAA's 1971 strictures against secret and clandestine research were partly meant to warn anthropologists against being co-opted for counterinsurgency research by their own national government, not least to prevent them from being barred from research by Third World governments.) This ethnic claim—always problematic, because many anthropologists are citizens of nation-states other than those they study—becomes the more visible and debatable now that globalization is increasingly transforming the nature of the hyphen between nation and state—a point forcefully made by Kahn and Jeganathan (in this volume) and one to which I will return.

Last but by no means least, codes of ethics usually presuppose the distinction between an expert and a lay audience on the basis of the capacity to identify, produce and possess *commodified knowledge* (or "information"). This may seem self-evident but is in fact strange because it leads to the paradoxical situation that ethical codes rarely discuss explicitly what seems to be the primary value of the profession: the aim to produce propositions about humanity that are more reliable than those used by laypeople.[11] If codes prioritize responsibilities toward the people studied, they rarely grant them the role in the *production* of such propositions that they occupy (see ASA 1987 and the codes collected in Fluehr-Lobban 1991:248, 274). But without the unstated assumption that professionals interact with "others" in order to produce or disseminate more reliable information, ethical codes, which stipulate how to avoid harming people while gathering that information or how to relate to the public, the discipline, its students, and its sponsors as someone who possesses such information, make no sense. This means, first, that this assumption positions ethics as *external to* (the production of) scientific expertise. A second implication is that this assumption is violated by the concrete experience of empirical research—as anyone who has ever done fieldwork knows. However, before examining this externality and supplementarity of ethics and expertise further, I would like to discuss another, related issue: that this assumption underlies the dichotomy of a "scientific" as opposed to a "moral" camp in the *El Dorado* controversy, a dichotomy that is contradictory and paradoxical because it ignores the moral economy of scientific research.

"Science" and Its Moralities

"Science" is an ideological notion just as much as it is a label for the production of knowledge that is more stable or reliable than that on which lay audiences can rely. On the one hand, anthropologists have long tried to imitate scientistic methodology and theory to conform to an ideological "scientific" subject that, through the mastery of certain routines for establishing truth, becomes a neutral channel of value-free information. On the other hand, they have never been comfortable with the implicit transcendentalism of positivist "science." In anthropological theory, a critique of the dominant values that informed so-called value-free social science has been a staple of its discourse since Boas and Malinowski. In the area of method, anthropology's reliance on qualitative research has, despite the scientistic rhetoric of Boas, Malinowski, and many of their descendants, inhibited its entry into the world of "hard science" (because the latter is dominated by the quantifications of statistics [see Asad 1994]). Yet, as does any other academic endeavor, anthropology has forms of discipline that earn it a place in the field of "expertise"—however this is conceived. Academic disciplines are what Foucault called "technologies of the self" (1988), and as such they carry explicit or implicit moral arguments—arguments about what it is "good to be" that encompass and ground an ethical code's arguments about what it is "right to do."[12] Whether these technologies of the self take place in the "field," the laboratory, the museum, or the armchair, they imply a moral economy of research—of the good practice expected from a researcher—that disrupts any scientistic expectation of value-free research (Daston 1995; Scholte [1989] 1974). To understand such an alternative conception of methodology, "value-rich" rather than "value-free," I want to investigate the moral complexities of the assumption of a so-called value-free science—what, during the *El Dorado* scandal, was referred to by "scientists" as the honest endeavor of "telling it like it is." One can understand this complexity by locating this scientistic position in some of the institutions from which some of the *El Dorado* debate was conducted.[13]

My prime examples of this disciplinary complexity are the widely different official reactions to the controversy produced by different members of the University of Michigan's anthropology department, Neel and Chagnon's home base for their first Yanomami expeditions. The document released on the World Wide Web as "The University of Michigan Report" on October 20, 2000, consisted of three parts: the first denounced the allegations against James Neel (which had, at that time, been largely refuted by public discussion on the Internet and in the press); the second countered the critique of Chagnon's ethnography and tried, instead, to blame it on a conspiracy of Tierney, Turner, Sponsel, and the Salesian missionaries on the Orinoco; and the third turned the latter accusation into a battle between those who "believe in a scientific paradigm" and those whose "antiscience" was "subjective, qualitative, personalized, moralistic, and based on individual authority with no accommodation of contrary views" (University of Michigan 2000:9). Echoing this, the more extreme representations of the anti-scientific enemies associated them with "witch-hunts," "feuds," or "vendettas" (all terms referring to classical anthropological notions of premodern, Third World politics), while others classified them as "the academic left," "ideology," or "McCarthyism" (terms echoing cold war and Second World politics). This was a rhetoric that presented the true scientist as someone who did not shirk from saying that the empirical evidence proved Yanomami to be a "fierce people" and that this evidence on aggression implied some unpleasant conclusions about the evolutionary functionality of gender inequality and male violence—the sociobiological program of Chagnon's later research, much denounced by his critics.

Such scientism usually positions ethics in a subordinate or negative role. In the presentation of theory, ethics becomes the source of "ideology." In the presentation of empirical evidence, more than one error of critique warrants the suspicion that the individual author's moralism has systematically "distorted" evidence (University of Michigan 2000:17; see also Chagnon 2000; De Munck 2001; Tooby 2000a, 2000b). The scientific naturalist temper's gut reaction to ethical argument is that *all* description should be honest "information"—that is, free of the contest of values. Paradoxically, it thereby adopts a culturally particular moral standpoint, for it trusts the *honesty* of the individual scientist to keep ulterior motives out of the propositions he claims to make. Those who say that scientific language is not restricted to providing propositions about the world—because they think that this language *makes* the world just as much as it reflects it—are branded "conspiracy theorists."

The second set of statements about the controversy to come from the University of Michigan (collected in Coroñil 2001b) radically departed from the individualistic "conspiracy" thinking that characterized both the Tierney and the Chagnon camp. Seriously disturbed by the earlier "Michigan" statements, its authors dropped the rhetoric of conspiracy altogether and explicitly reversed the first document's suggestion that none of the accusations in Tierney's book merited further examination. Moreover, the series of debates organized by the Michigan doctoral program in Anthropology and History did much to criticize the "propositional" conception of knowledge as "information," and this perspective also came to inform the final report of the El Dorado Task Force (see the discussion below).

The freeing of statements about what is from what ought to be has, of course, been central to claims to scientific authority since Thomas Huxley led the Victorian scientists' fight against clerical domination. Huxley was sharp enough to see that objectivism required that the "foundation of morality is to have done, once and for all, with lying" (1892:235), thereby echoing early modern scientists' morality of trust (Shapin 1994). However, another strand of objectivist thought, brought out by the pro-Chagnon "Michigan statement," thoroughly *mistrusts* honesty in its suspicion of "subjective, qualitative, personalized" reporting based on "individual authority." This shows that objectivism requires a complex social construction of moral injunctions to make good its claim of maximizing "the degree to which an account gives information about the object being described" (D'Andrade 1995:399–400). Even if it draws a line between morality and knowledge by trying to produce "information"—a type of knowledge that is sufficiently commodified to be passed on from expert to audience without contest or loss of content—it relies on the social acceptance of the factory model of commodified knowledge once popularized by Huxley (see Desmond

1997). Understandably, a modern university, being a disciplinary institution, is loath to publicize an occasion on which "science" fails to live up to this image of the value-neutral production of commodified knowledge, especially since a scandal like this reinforces anti-intellectual tendencies in society (see the majority of reactions to Tooby 2000a).

In anthropological fieldwork, however, a morality of trust is the necessary condition for the production of whatever "information" an "expert" can disseminate, since without intersubjectivity and "rapport" one cannot realize the methodological requirement of fieldwork to be disciplined by the knowledge acquired from the people studied. If the objectivist morality of honesty and trust is applied only to besmirch the character of the individual scientist (as the "scientists" in the El Dorado controversy implicitly did), objectivism and honesty work, along with the code of ethics, as yet other ways of avoiding the discussion of actual research conduct (just as Chagnon's professions of rapport with Yanomami contradict his published accounts of violating their moral injunctions [see Sahlins 2000; cf. Begley 2000]). Such individualist and objectivist assumptions contribute, therefore, to the venerable tradition in anthropology of mystifying field methodology exemplified by Laura Nader's preparation for fieldwork by her tutor, Alfred Kroeber, who handed her a fat ethnography and said, "Go forth and do likewise" (Nader 1970:98). Objectivism and its resistance to trust, ethical behavior, intersubjectivity, and personally mediated and individually authorized knowledge are an important reason that the methodology of describing what actually takes place in the field—in other words, what conditions anthropological knowledge to become more reliable than that of the average layperson—has not been more extensively investigated and described. A major factor in this is the resistance, in the public perception of scientific knowledge, to ambiguous, that is, value-rich, knowledge. Public scientism declares that expertise should be, at least for the time being, a certified and sure commodity, not a process of expertly weighing different values against each other. Public scientism uses a fundamentally flawed conception of social-scientific expertise that reduces the moral complexity of doing research and makes ethics exterior and supplementary to the actual process of producing expertise.

Ethics as Supplement and as Practice

As long as the professional ethics of anthropology is dominated by the four assumptions discussed above, it will remain largely exterior to actual anthropological practice. Individual responsibility personalizes and obscures the structural social inequalities that condition the relationship between researcher and researched and thus removes ethics from research practice. Legalism shifts the emphasis of ethics away from research practice to the practice of rule making. The national location of most ethical codes and committees confines our attention within the boundaries of a particular nation-state when most anthropological research has been and still is transnational in some way or other. Finally, the reification and commodification of expert knowledge make ethics external to the production of expertise and replace productive relationships with the people studied, sponsors, and the public with methodology or, worse, ideology. This, I feel, is the major reason that many of my colleagues show signs of boredom when discussion shifts to the ethics of codes and committees: anthropologists are usually confronted with ethics as an afterthought or reminder, a set of guidelines or clauses that one should check in order to ward off accusations of having poorly executed what one had already decided to do anyway. Ethics can easily appear as burdensome moralism if it tends to come in from the outside, from spheres of moral regulation beyond those in which one does one's regular work. In such a situation, ethical review may create *more* rather than less unethical behavior (Klockars 1979; Reiss 1979).

Rather than dismissing the work of ethical codification (as certain postmodernists do [Bauman 1993:14; van Meijl 2000]), we should become more aware of the ways in which we institutionalize ethical codes, especially those that turn ethics into a *supplement* rather than an integral part of our work. The notion of ethics as a quasi-legal set of injunctions that fills a gap or adjudicates a dimension left open by the usually amoral activity of producing truth is based on a typically modern set of abstractions and contradictions. As a supplement, ethics adds to as well as replaces what it is intended to reform or regulate. It is added to anthropological research in an attempt to enrich it with the fullest measure of moral responsibility, but it also replaces the contingent ethical engagements of anthropological research with an abstract set of guidelines. Ethics as a supplement is therefore "*exterior*, outside of the positivity to which it is super-added, alien to that which, in order to be replaced by it, must be other than it" (Derrida 1976:144–145). But the positivity that such an ethics supplements is not actual research but an already reified expertise, one that assumes that it will inevitably lead to the expert's having a certain amount of commodified "true" knowledge about the world. When governed by this double abstraction, ethics comes to indicate the moral inadequacy of the scientific objectivity it supplements, just as objectivity signifies the factual inadequacy of ethics.

This contradiction is typically modern. It relies on the dominant "acultural" theory of modernity that assumes that humanity will universally shed the blinkers of tradition, religion, and external authority and free itself through the individual understanding and possession of objective or natural truth (see Taylor 2001). If the acultural theory of modernity acquires its starkest outline in the various forms of positivism, it is also fundamental to a more romantic strain of modern thought that argues that positivist materialism obscures a higher, ethical and spiritual but equally acultural and universal realm in which we will find a better future for humanity. Both forms rely on the modern denial of the aporia of life by temporal rupture and on the concomitant fantasy that at some revolutionary moment in the past, present, or future, ignorance and moral contradiction have been or will be resolved in a comprehensive, unitary set of rules that all human beings can accept (Bauman 1993:6, 8). However, moral philosophy has consistently failed in the utilitarian or functionalist attempt to ground ethics in objective fact and human nature (MacIntyre 1984:47–48; Taylor 1989:22–23). Modern ethics is always under threat of being "unmasked" as being in someone's particular, objective interest by the forms of "emotivist" moral theory that deny that ethics can be rationally founded (MacIntyre 1984:11–12; Taylor 1989:9, 22). Because modern autonomous individuals have no self-evident function or "framework" (Taylor 1989:16), they cannot define a moral telos of humanity that can be made to measure the "facts" of human imperfection, for this ethical goal may itself be just a means to a particular, self-interested end (MacIntyre 1984:passim). Thus, modernist thinking creates an endless oscillation between ethical standards, on the one hand, and objective facts, on the other.

The *El Dorado* scandal provides an interesting twist to these strings of oscillations, if one that is rarely remarked upon publicly. The main aim of Tierney, Turner, and Sponsel was *to unmask the objectivity* of certain researchers among the Yanomami—James Neel and Napoleon Chagnon in particular—as a cover for selfish and destructive interests. Their opponents countered with a reaffirmation of the language of scientific objectivity: the duty to "tell it like it is" and to provide "empirical evidence," often coupled with a classical "emotivist" critique of the moral accusations of Tierney and his supporters as themselves based on partisan interests in the Orinoco region. Thus, the oscillation between ethics and scientific objectivity was often reduced to a debate between two essentialized positions: the "scientists" versus the "moralists" (as the supporters of the former often put it). But this public oscillation should not be permitted to obscure the fact that what Turner, Tierney, and Sponsel suggested was not only that scientific objectivity was morally deficient because of its value-free factuality but, much more profound, that value-free factuality was itself a moral choice. This argument, derived from the critical anthropology of the late 1960s (Scholte [1969] 1974:433) and reinforced by recent science studies (Daston 1995), indicates that much of the discussion between "scientists" and "moralists" (the terms are the former's) was based on a typically modern reduction and abstraction of ethics.[14]

When we broaden our conception of ethics in this way and think about what (and who and how) a large number of anthropologists who do fieldwork think it is "good to be," it becomes obvious that anthropological ethics includes the (positive) value of *becoming someone else*— temporarily adopting, for both "home" and "field" audiences, another identity that both enriches and destabilizes one's "self" (Pels 1999: 107).[15] This means that anthropologists take up a peculiar position toward the constitution of self and other—that is, toward what Bauman (1993) and Taylor (1989) regard as the foundation of morality. This position is neither marginal nor extraordinary: a "doubling" of identities and ethical standards is necessary for all human beings who immerse themselves in what is for them a new form of social interaction. What distinguishes many anthropologists is that they ask themselves to remain conscious of the contradictions of this epistemological doubling in factual and methodological as well as ethical terms— that is, that they try to turn a common and all too human necessity into a form of academic discipline. What is truly remarkable is *not* that modern people have tried to systematize this practice of epistemological and ethical uncertainty but that even brilliant philosophers feel that they need to *deny* that ethnography and fieldwork are ethical—on the basis of the otherworldly fantasy that ethics is based in an unambiguous, singular community (see, for example, MacIntyre 1993).

In contrast, I have argued elsewhere that anthropological fieldwork— along with most of the forms of human migration that followed in its wake and that now proliferate under globalization—minimally requires double standards and double identities. Anthropologists' negotiations of those multiple standards are "duplex" rather than duplicitous, because they are based not on bad faith but on necessity (Pels 1999:102). This redefinition of anthropological ethics implies, first, that the distinction between "field" and "home" is problematic because anthropologists' disciplinary awareness of duplexity positions them both in the field and at home at the same time—at least when engaged in professional pursuits. Secondly, it implies that "the anthropological good" outlined above completely crosscuts the distinction between ethics and scientific objectivity. And, thirdly, it suggests that we need to interrogate the desire for an ethical code, for it may seek to replace the ethics of research by the illusion that the professional anthropologist adheres to a *single* moral complex—the one adopted by the professional community. In my view, the *El Dorado* scandal was a scandal precisely because it exposed this illusion: it exposed the AAA ethical code as a simulacrum, "a truth that hides the fact that there is none" (Baudrillard 1994:1; see MacIntyre 1984:2), a "truth" that supplemented rather than inhered in the relationships that produce anthropology as a discipline and a profession. However, the scandal also produced a less obvious political effect. If anthropologists, similarly to the people they study, often mistake their precepts for what actually occurs in practice (see Malinowski [1926] 1972), the practice of scandal may also force them—sometimes surreptitiously, at other times with full awareness—to shift their precepts. I want to suggest that such a shift is taking place both at home and in the field and that this becomes especially visible once we study how the *El Dorado* scandal forced anthropology to open up to the media as well as to a more differentiated conception of the "field."

The Other at Home: "The Public"

The exteriority of ethics to anthropological research practice is paralleled by the boundary between "the public" and anthropology's "interior" expertise. The *El Dorado* scandal shows that this boundary no longer shields anthropology's expert operations from the public—if it ever did. *Darkness in El Dorado* forced anthropology into a "battle for truth and visibility in the press" (Briggs and Mantini-Briggs 2001:270) and can be said to have caused the first anthropological "electronic panic" (Ramos 2001a:274). Panic reactions to the scandal by both supporters and critics of Tierney's book often stressed the moral depravity of mass communications and the evil effects of hyberbole and rhetoric, thus trying to reinforce the boundary. However, there are clear signs that the controversy has helped to push through a different understanding of "the public" among anthropologists, at least at the level of their professional association.

In the initial stages of the controversy, however, conservative condemnations of evil laypeople—journalists in particular—abounded.

When a Dutch journalist asked Chagnon why Tierney wrote *Darkness*, he said, "For money, of course" (van der Hoeven 2000). While this is obviously true, it also implicitly contrasted the loftier ideals of academia with the journalist's base motives (thus erasing the fact that many journalists do not lack ideals and many academics are driven by financial motives). "Sensationalist journalism" was one of the most frequently heard condemnations of Tierney's work by Chagnon's supporters, and some of these commentators deplored the moral downfall of *The New Yorker* in comparison with the news on the Internet (see the reactions to Tooby 2000a). But such alienation from the media was not restricted to a single camp: Louise Lamphere refers to anthropologists' "horror stories" of their complex analyses being misquoted in the single sound bites required by the press (2003:154 n. 2). Alcida Ramos lamented that a "second-rate piece of journalism" such as Tierney's had succeeded in jolting U.S. anthropologists out of their ethical apathy where their colleagues had failed (2001b). The "media-naivety" of the AAA at the time of the outbreak of the scandal (Lamphere 2003:154) is exceeded by Turner's and Sponsel's laments about the immorality of "leaking" their message on the Internet (more about this below). There is, of course, some reason for anthropologists' suspicions: even a "quality" European newspaper was particularly quick to reproduce the juicier bits of rumor and hearsay generated by the leaked message (Brown 2000; see Lamphere 2003:154). But suspicions of playing to an audience could be reciprocated, for instance, by the *Forbes* writer who thought that moral activism in anthropology was a ploy to attract graduate students by pushing "political hot buttons" (quoted in Nugent 2001:12).

Playing to an audience can be suspicious only when skill in addressing the public is not conceived as being a normal part of professional practice. Despite the widespread recognition since Said ([1978] 1985), Fabian (1983), and Clifford and Marcus (1986) that anthropologists' rhetorical skills are both professionally necessary and politically significant, the controversy displayed perhaps even more suspicion of rhetoric than suspicion of the media. I have already recorded above that Chagnon's supporters defended objectivism and "science" with the claim of "telling it like it is." Turner and Sponsel, too, pretended to be merely "describing" or "summarizing" Tierney's arguments, conveniently forgetting that they used epithets like "convincing" and "well-documented" for Tierney's work and "fascistic," "perverted," and "depraved" for that of Neel and Chagnon (see Sponsel 2002:149; Turner 2000). Tierney's opponents correctly identified a form of rhetoric by labeling his work "conspiracy theory." Indeed, *Darkness in El Dorado* often conforms to this genre, which characteristically amasses detail while tending to leave the jumping to conclusions to readers (many lamenting the "textual display" of Tierney's 1,599 footnotes: Hames 2001; Lindee 2001; Ritchie 2001; see Pels 2001b). But for Tierney's opponents this was meant to identify rhetoric as Tierney's sin and to throw suspicion on his truthfulness rather than to recognize that conspiracy theory is also a *learned* genre (Hofstadter 1967:38). In fact, Tierney's opponents eagerly employed the genre themselves (see, especially, University of Michigan 2000). Unmasking conspiracies lurking behind the moralism of public rhetoric has, of course, been a staple of folk moralism at least since E. D. Morel and Roger Casement unmasked King Leopold's "protection of the natives" in Congo as violent expropriation and inspired Joseph Conrad's *Heart of Darkness* (Hochschild 1999). Today terms like "heart of darkness" and "colonialism" have themselves become part of the vocabulary of accusatory rhetoric, doing the controversy's labor of "othering" together with other notions such as "witch-hunts," "feuding," and "McCarthyism." Even Stephen Nugent's balanced lament that the scandal shows that in anthropology "weight of argument would seem to count for less than plausibility of hyberbole" and that the rhetoric of "bumper stickers" replaces a more genuine argumentative practice (2001:11) derives, in the end, from Thomas Huxley's rejection of rhetoric, "that pestilent cosmetic" (1892:219).

However, anthropologists' moral condemnation of a mercenary press and their dislike of rhetoric now seem as naïve as the stress on value-free honesty characteristic of objectivism. If we often "tend to be, or pretend to be, babes in the woods about . . . the nature of the world we live in" (Schepers 2001), several developments that emerged in the wake of the *El Dorado* scandal suggest that such naivety can no longer be maintained. Among other things, anthropology is caught up in movements toward increasing "public trust" by state-driven "human research participant protection programs" (AAA 2001b). This new governmentality of "visibility" and "monitoring" has huge problems: it may produce new rhetorics of the avoidance of ethical responsibility (Reiss 1979), it can victimize scholars in the process of protecting research subjects (Shea 2000), and it probably reinforces the performance of commodified knowledge that exteriorizes ethics from research (Brenneis, this volume; Shore and Wright 2000:85). The aftereffects of the controversy are more likely to increase than to prevent anthropologists' subjection to such forms of accountability. They serve to show that we would do wrong in concentrating our awareness of anthropology's public image on the media: the public comes to us—has done so throughout the history of the discipline—in many less spectacular and mundane guises, such as funding committees, philanthropic foundations, or internal review boards. Nor should we pay much attention to the argument that anthropology "normally" stays out of the media spotlight, because in the sense just described it remains public even when moving in relative obscurity.

Nevertheless, it is in relation to the media that one can note some of the more conspicuous effects of the controversy. Louise Lamphere has recorded how, since the shock of the first media contacts, the AAA has tried to remedy its media-naivety by seeking professional help in dealing with the press and trying to put across a different, more up-to-date image of what anthropology is like (2003:154). Anthropologists have something to learn from James Neel, who, when hearing of Tierney's publication plans shortly before his death, was acute enough to "plant" some of his field notes in an archive so that the charges against him could be more easily refuted (Lindee 2000), or from Susan Lindee's careful consideration of how one should write to avoid tendentious misquotation in what is already a hyberbolic environment (2001:273). Such a redefinition of professional competence so as to include rather than reject anthropology's media presence may not prevent anthropologists like Paul Rabinow and Nancy Scheper-Hughes from being turned into the authors of damaging quotes by a single-minded and tendentious journalist, but it may convince us of the importance of clear and repetitive one-liners that convey the core of what we want to put across to laypeople. Moreover, if such media-consciousness includes the Internet, it may help to prevent such astonishing political innocence as led Turner and Sponsel to expect that their bombshell e-mail and its inflammatory rhetoric would remain confidential (and, perhaps, persuade them to pick up a telephone instead). The gut reactions of anthropologists to the media—as outside of and a threat to their competence—may in fact be changing under the influence of a sophisticated anthropological study of what it means to live in a mass-mediated world and what this suggests about anthropological responsibilities (see, for example, Hannerz 2003). The final report of the El Dorado Task Force, in any case, argues that promoting insight into the media effects of the representations that anthropologists produce should be a major goal of any introductory course in anthropology and that anthropologists should learn to deal with the simplifying and essentializing tendencies of publishers and journalists by media training (EDTF 2003, 1:39–40).

The task force's final report indicates, in the same context, a change in attitude toward rhetoric. It exhorts anthropologists to be aware of the adverse effects on a broader audience of their representations, citing the example of the Brazilian army's use of journalistic renderings of Chagnon's work as an excuse for further genocidal measures against Yanomami. In this context, the report refers to Johannes Fabian's critique of the "denial of coevalness" in anthropological constructions of the other—the most profound political critique of anthropological rhetoric after Edward Said's *Orientalism* (Fabian 1983; Said [1978] 1985). Such critiques have gradually moved beyond a rarefied postmodernism toward a widespread recognition of the evaluative dimension of *any* way of "telling it like it is" in ethnography (for an early application to the ethnography of Yanomami, see Ramos 1987). The El Dorado Task Force's acceptance of rhetoric as skill and politics rather than as an invidious use of hyperbole or verbal cosmetic has important consequences for anthropological ethics: it shifts ethical argument away from the individualist intentionality that is assumed in the objectivist's suspicion of rhetoric (and in anthropological ethics in general) toward the recognition that the choices of language that we make in our descriptions and theories always involve ethical judgments—beyond individual good or bad intentions and relative to larger sociocultural relationships of inequality. Similarly, a motion to withdraw the interim report of the task force at the AAA's November 2001 business meeting was motivated by recognition of the "performativity" of knowledge—the possibility that publishing factual but provisional statements might prejudice the public toward selective conclusions—and this also indicates the growing consciousness that "information" is not a politically innocent commodity.

Thus, we see that awareness of "the other at home" is already undercutting the individualist and commodifying assumptions underlying much anthropological ethics. This is not a development without its own dangers: in a world in which public accountability often shades into corporate merchandising, such consciousness may easily degenerate into mere public relations and, even if that is avoided, may wedge the anthropological practitioner between the sometimes incompatible claims of different stakeholders—such as sponsors and the people studied (Pels 2000:164). However, it suggests that we always have to try to understand how anthropological thinking simultaneously intervenes in and interprets this increasingly media-dominated world— and that, to recapture anthropology's progressive promise, we have to try to understand how it has done so ever since the discipline emerged from global trade and colonialism.

The Other Elsewhere: Toward a Global Anthropology

Anthropology has always been characterized by contradictions of a global nature because its locus of authority rarely coincided with the locus of research and the latter was, more often than not, situated outside the sovereign jurisdiction of the researcher's nation-state. The friction between the two is evident from one of the first ethical scandals of the AAA, Franz Boas's 1919 denunciation of anthropologists spying for their own, U.S., government during World War I (Fluehr-Lobban 1991:16–17; Price 2000a, 2000b), in which what in other views would have been regarded as good citizenship was now condemned as unethical. It is, however, also evident from Joe Watkins's early statement during the controversy that "trouble with foreign governments" might lead the AAA to reconsider its policy of not censuring members whose ethical conduct could be criticized or the moratorium on research among the "indigenous" peoples of Venezuela declared by the Venezuelan government after the scandal broke (Dalton 2000).

If these statements show that anthropology is and always has been globalized, they also remain within the orbit of internationalism—of relations between sovereign nation-states and their views about the jurisdiction of legal systems. Thus they do not produce a critique of the nationalist and legalist assumptions underlying anthropology's ethical frameworks. But if some argue that that the *El Dorado* scandal might help us to think through the nature of the "global university" by questioning national and disciplinary cultural politics (Kennedy 2001), we can also suggest that a "global anthropology" should criticize and overcome the limits that national sovereignty imposes on the ethical practice of an anthropological association. This argument runs parallel to globalization theorists' (more confident than accurate) prediction of the end of the era of the nation-state (Appadurai 1996:19; Featherstone and Lash 1995:1–2) but is motivated by the opposite observation: that the continuing hegemony of nationalist and legalist doctrines of sovereignty over other modes of association demands that anthropologists learn to recognize, practice, and propagate available alternative ethical practices. I will restrict myself to two transnational (and by implication, translegal) forms: the global responsibilities that arise from the solidarity between anthropological practitioners beyond national citizenship and those that arise from the negotiation of multiple values characteristic of fieldwork. The discussion on human rights triggered by the *El Dorado* controversy will bridge the two topics.

If two national associations of anthropologists were to collaborate in criticizing the military elite of one of the two nations, we would have an example of a truly transnational ethical practice of anthropology. The history of anthropological dealings with Yanomami, however, shows transnational frustration rather than collaboration. When the AAA's Brazilian sister association complained that Brazilian newspaper reports of how Chagnon represented the Yanomami directly authorized the Brazilian military to act against the tribe genocidally, the letter was carelessly handled by the AAA's secretariat, and when it was finally published in the *AAA Newsletter* in 1989 Chagnon himself and American colleagues defending him got more and easier opportunities to do so than their Brazilian colleagues (Carneiro da Cunha 1989; Chagnon 1989). A resolution at the AAA's 2001 business meeting by Robert Borofsky and the final report of the El Dorado Task Force tried to redress the imbalance (EDTF 2003, 2:11). North American condescension also characterizes—at least in Brazilian eyes—the fact that most of the critiques of Chagnon's work that Tierney collected had already been published by colleagues from Brazil and Venezuela but that it required a "second-rate piece of journalism" like Tierney's book to succeed where these had been ignored (Ramos 2001b; see also EDTF 2003,1:9). Nevertheless, the existence of such frustrations should not be allowed to obscure the fact that, practically speaking, the two associations already have a relationship—that, in other words, a *national* association of anthropologists is a contradiction in terms once we recognize that the history of the discipline makes it a transnational one. Chagnon's dealings with corrupt members of the Venezuelan elite—Tierney's most damning accusation, upheld by the El Dorado Task Force report as a breach of the Principles of Professional Responsibility (EDTF 2003,1:31, 41, 44; Tierney 2000b: chap.11)—is in itself a sad reminder of this inescapable fact and shows that the transnational ethics of anthropology should not stop at the point where the different jurisdictions of two nation-states have been negotiated in a formally legal way, since in any country the law may act against the interests of the people studied.

Discourses on human rights already extend beyond narrowly legal jurisdictions toward a transnational or global ethics, and they are increasingly being incorporated into the AAA's view of research responsibilities. The task force that investigated the status of indigenous peoples in South America concluded that the problems these communities face "are not simply local or national in origin, and that US-based anthropologists share a common responsibility for fostering structural changes in collaboration with their colleagues in the region" (AAA 2001b:13). This further popularizes an argument coined in the late 1960s: that, because global inequalities are an inescapable condition for anthropological research, anthropologists cannot disengage their ethics from this situation. Therefore, a radical *social* critique of the individualist presuppositions underlying most forms of ethical codification is needed. Of course, that recognition does not imply that "human rights" or, for that matter, "development" are by definition good: their invocation does not absolve anthropologists from the task of critically examining whether and when "human rights" and "development" themselves contribute to fostering global inequalities. One cannot, for example, simply proclaim a human right to health care when that standpoint is part and parcel of the suspicion of the "antiscience" anthropology of Chagnon and his supporters and when it exports this suspicion to Peru without attempting to understand why indigenous peoples and "local" anthropologists express hostility toward scientific research (see the discussion between Hurtado, Kaplan, and Lancaster [2001] and Tatomir [2001]). We need the ideals of Yanomami improvement and human rights for their sake (see First Interim Report El Dorado Task Force, e-mail message to members of AAA, May 25, 2001), but we have to accept that their understanding of improvement and right may legitimately differ from ours.

This brings us back to the core work of anthropology itself and to the remarkable fact that anthropological codes of ethics have so rarely been built around what seems to me to be the basic ethic of anthropological research: "to grasp the native's point of view, his relation to life, to realize *his* vision of *his* world" (Malinowski 1922:25), and (realizing that "native" is neither a self-evident nor a masculine category) to use it to measure one's own (of course, without reifying, à la Durkheim, a society's precepts at the expense of studying its practice [Malinowski (1926) 1972]). In more practical terms, this translates into the injunction not to intervene in any society without using the standards and experiences of that society's people to criticize and reform the hegemonic and usually Western moralities of development that determine those interventions. This lands us squarely in the middle of moral duplexity. If, indeed, many Yanomami want the blood samples taken by the Neel/Chagnon expedition back because they think that body parts need to be destroyed on the death of the person, this conflicts with the scientific ideal of using the samples for research that is directed at improving Yanomami (or any other people's) health. However, the recognition of such conflict is already a first step in a process of ethical negotiation. Some Yanomami seem to want to negotiate collective health benefits in order to compensate for the taking of their blood samples without informed consent. Similarly, some American scientists have agreed to open up discussion about the repatriation of Yanomami blood samples. This may well lead to further use for research of these samples but with Yanomami participating in the process as full decision makers—this, at least, is the direction in which the El Dorado Task Force's final report points (EDTF 2003, 1:14, 30, 49).

Such negotiations should continue in directions that may seem less self-evident. Some Yanomami, at least, seem to think that Chagnon brought *xawara*, a pestilential smoke that causes illness and is associated with sorcerers, *gringos*, and their goods (Tierney 2000b:183). If such "informed lack of consent" is widespread and was caused by the Western impact on Yanomami, one is again faced with duplexity. On the one hand, one could say that under these conditions a renegotiation of research access with Yanomami is required; on the other, renegotiation on these terms may seem to stand in the way of outside help in the legal defense of the Yanomami biosphere or much-needed health care (since most researchers would honestly admit that they do not believe that *xawara* exists). Along the lines of the previous discussion of Yanomami blood samples, one could suggest that this is, among people who can think of asking for collective health benefits, a partial view at best and that negotiation would indeed modify access. However, one should remain as anthropologically realistic as possible and concede that, if the controversy also helped to trigger the first all-Yanomami meeting on the Upper Orinoco in November 2001, negotiation is modifying not only the terms of exchange but also the identity of those who are doing the exchanging. The emergence of new groups, middlemen, and spokespersons is changing the power relationships that partly define the categories of "Yanomami" and, perhaps, the "indigenous" peoples of Venezuela more generally. At present, one can only hope that, now that the scandal's reverberations have died down, they will continue to affect the power relationships and identity of Western scientists as well.

Both of the above examples show that fieldwork provides an ethical template that is radically different from that from which ethical codes have usually been formulated. "The Other Elsewhere"—even when the anthropological object has been changing for some time, anthropologists are increasingly as native as their natives, and the inequality between researchers and researched cannot be taken as given—reminds us that the primary moral engagement of fieldwork is the negotiation of different moral complexes with each other. The necessity of living with double standards—in duplexity—signifies a moral topography of differences that pertains everywhere—not only among Yanomami but also when we study a biogenetics company, participate in the definition of an archaeological site, or try to get used to the linguistic conventions of an internal review board (to take a few examples from the other essays in this book). Such a conception of ethics is prelegal rather than quasi-legal, transnational, social rather than individual, and concerned with knowledge production and performance rather than being added as a supplement to already commodified information.

As I have indicated, there are many signs that ethics is indeed being redefined in this way: the call for a nonlegalistic notion of "informed consent" (Fluehr-Lobban 1994), the trend toward collaborative research (Lamphere 2003:156; EDTF 2003, 1:45–46), and the increase in sensitivity about the "denial of coevalness" in an unequal world (EDTF 2003, 1:38–39) are cases in point. But the lure of codification still takes the radical sting out of many good intentions: some of the briefings on new ethical guidelines prepared by the AAA's ethics committee in the wake of the *El Dorado* controversy have difficulty breaking out of the mold and avoiding the professions of weakness and ethnocentrism that have often accompanied anthropologists' ethical codification. The issue of proper remuneration of informants, for example, should ideally bring forward the questions to what extent a community or society has monetized labor and time, for what purposes, which types of prestation cannot be remunerated (such as hospitality) and which can, and how such circumstances may affect the process of remuneration. Instead, the briefing on remuneration is awash with ethnocentric terms ("equal pay for equal work," "intellectual property," "heritage") that are high in moralistic content (what is "right to do") but low in answers to the question whether one can impose these terms on the sociocultural relationships under study. It also fails to mention the inequalities that still pervade many relationships between researchers and researched and whether their intended reciprocity should include a historical consciousness of how global inequality affects research and the researcher's responsibility to help redress it (as displayed by the third AAA Task Force [see AAA 2001a]). The section ends up with the profession of weakness that fair remuneration needs to be "individually negotiated" in each case.[16] Similarly, the briefing on informed consent fails to put this requirement in the context of the inequalities that can characterize research and of social science's history of contributing to the violent disciplining of populations. It appears unconscious of the basic contradiction that one should get informed consent before research has started, while research is often the only way to find out how to achieve informed consent, and therefore leaves several contradictory statements (that informed consent is a process as against the idea that informed consent has to be officially acquired before one starts gathering data) happily confronting each other.[17]

At the same time, Joe Watkins has recently produced an interesting typology of forms of informed consent that places them in a history of colonial and postcolonial relationships of inequality and envisages a shift from colonial to more collaborative forms (quoted in EDTF 2003, 1:45). Likewise, in his briefings on the ethics of sexual relationships in the field Watkins also explicitly addresses the power difference between researcher and researched and stresses the differing cultural valuations— the duplexities—of the relationships in question. Lastly, he has briefed AAA members on the possible negative impact of their ethnographic representations (although he is more concerned with avoiding "sensationalism" than with clarifying the difficulty of distinguishing "information" from "performance" in a relationship of inequality).[18] This shows that it is not so much the problem of codification as the kind of interpretation of a written set of guidelines that it invites that influences the extent to which ethics remains exterior to research. A written statement that says that it is in the nature of anthropological knowledge production to be implicated in unequal, transnational power relationships with the public and the people studied and that the methods of producing anthropological knowledge are themselves statements of ethics has already bridged the divide between the production of information and the production of ethical statements. Thus the spirit and the letter of the guidelines themselves help to determine whether they are guidelines—that is, advice about what to do in situations in which one finds oneself as a professional and, as such, indistinguishable from methodological guidelines—or whether they are a "code." The latter term invokes the desire for rule-governed transcendence—the Kantian imperative—that, as anthropologists have known since Malinowski criticized Durkheim for his legalist reifications (Malinowski [1926] 1972), complicate and distort professional self-conceptions instead of helping them to reach an ethically more consistent discipline.

Conclusion

"Where there aren't no Ten Commandments" serves as an epigraph for this chapter partly to remind us of anthropology's colonial past. The intertextualities at the heart of *Darkness in El Dorado* are not mere "pestilent cosmetic": there are, indeed, correspondences between the silence of present-day anthropology about research procedure and the darknesses at the heart of modern colonial history, as some of the conclusions provoked by Tierney's book show. But Kipling's ballad may have to be interpreted in a more democratic way, in which Mandalay is a place where the best (the elite) is like the worst (the poor soldier) and the latter can escape the straitjacket of the Christian Ten Command-ments and have his drink and his Burmese sweetheart too. Thus, the place "where there aren't no Ten Commandments" becomes one of desire and liberation (although its sexism and colonialism, hardly a problem for Kipling, remind us of its moral dangers). Taking a hard look at anthropological research may, indeed, uncover a dark recess in which anthropologists have tried to hide their pursuit of Western academic or political interests, their lack of impersonal method, their forms of impression management, or their inventions of tradition and culture—all features of fieldwork with colonial genealogies. However, one will also find a storehouse of experience and empirical knowledge about how people negotiate double standards and identities, a practice of moral negotiation that, with all its flaws, has been institutionalized in fieldwork even if it has never found explicit expression in our ethical codes.

Therefore, one may also interpret "a place without commandments" as an ethical model rather than as an anomaly and regard anthropo-logical research as one of the few (and increasingly popular) forms of scholarly discipline in which it is practiced. But to do so we still need to radicalize some ongoing reinventions of our discipline. First, an anthropology that merely takes "other cultures" as its subject matter has become impossible: instead, the proper object of anthropology is the study of the social, cultural, and historical dimensions of the contacts and clashes between "us" and "them" (of which the "other cultures" we used to study were and are the historical result). Second, when thus positioning ourselves historically, we inevitably have to adopt a value-rich conception of theory and method, for we may want to defend—on good historical or empirical grounds—a theory or method that has its roots in colonial inequalities or attack it precisely for that reason. Third, this means that our ethics become (as, to some extent, they always have been) internal to our research rather than added on later as quasi-universal rules of conduct. Fourth, it means that we identify anthropology as transnational, prelegal, social rather than individual, and concerned with the how of the production of knowledge rather than the commodity of what is true. This does not mean that we do away with universal standards altogether—we need those, at least, to straighten out the bad guys. It just means that we embed the desire for transcendence of certain universal rules in the equally universal observation that all humans beings can and must negotiate moral duplexity and that this negotiation keeps—even more, *protects*—our universal standards from becoming absolute.

As I have tried to show, many initiatives along these lines have been taken, despite first appearances and early gut reactions, by protagonists in the *El Dorado* scandal and, most notably, a number of people working for the American Anthropological Association. This is not to say that the AAA has now suddenly become a different organization and its ethical practice has been reformed or that other effects of the scandal may not be damaging to the discipline in the long run. But we have here a clear example of a political event that has brought about a shift in the precepts on which the profession was based. This shift may not yet have become fully conscious. Moreover, anthropologists should remember that precepts are not practice. But there is reason to think that what Raymond Williams has called a "structure of feeling" of a critical and reflexive anthropology—one that has been developing in anthropology since the 1960s and that consists of a number of very different critical layers—has resulted in important resolutions and documents of the professional association (1977:128–135). As yet, this new sense of embedded ethics has yet to materialize in more "finished products"—changes in our curricula, different presentations of our ethical status before internal review boards, a more accurate presence in the media, and, most important, consistently different relationships with the people studied. But the current moment is enough to identify the *El Dorado* scandal itself as an important form of ethical action in anthropology, whether one likes it or not.

Notes

1. Many friends and colleagues have helped me with gathering material and thinking about the *El Dorado* controversy. I especially thank Ben Orlove and Dick Fox for much information and invitations to contribute to the debate and Fernando Coroñil and Webb Keane for sharing their thoughts on the University

of Michigan contributions and the El Dorado Task Force. The participants in the conference on which this book is based and my former colleagues at the Research Centre Religion and Society at the University of Amsterdam provided invaluable corrections to my sometimes flippant remarks on anthropological ethics. None of them is, of course, responsible for the statements and opinions I express in this chapter.

2. This phrase was used by a colleague commenting upon the atmosphere surrounding the discussion about Tierney's accusations during the AAA meetings in San Francisco in November 2000.

3. It is not my task or intention to judge the standpoints in the controversy—that is a task well performed by the El Dorado Task Force (EDTG 2003)—although I cannot refrain from stating some of my personal views. My aim is to use the sometimes violent negotiations between these standpoints to bring out alternative ways of practicing anthropological ethics.

4. See the data provided on the web site of Chagnon's former department, http://www.ucsb.edu/chagnon.html (accessed September 25, 2000).

5. I could not attend the San Francisco meetings but was present at the presentation of the El Dorado Task Force interim report in Washington on November 30, 2001.

6. This, I suggest, is what made the statements by Watkins and Lamphere quoted above "newsworthy." Lamphere has since recorded her regret about the AAA's media-naivety in this situation (2003:154)—see below.

7. However, Jane Hill went on to contribute in much more positive and important ways to the controversy, notably by chairing the El Dorado Task Force.

8. This, to some extent, limits my argument to the work of those anthropologists who can identify themselves with fieldwork (others may derive more authority from laboratory research or armchair work; for a discussion of the field sciences, see Kuklick and Kohler 1996); also, I acknowledge the differences between linguistic, primatological, archaeological, and ethnographic fieldwork within anthropology—my model has obviously been the latter. However, I think that my arguments about the moral complexity of fieldwork and the ethnocentricity of the assumptions about ethics associated with current uses of ethical codes are relevant to all forms of fieldwork.

9. Quoted in Miller (2000) and Wilford and Romero (2000). This is not to deny the need for judgment (for a balanced view, see EDTF 2003) but to emphasize that there are alternative ethics beyond the legalistic and adjudicatory framework.

10. The possible exception being an interesting briefing paper on fieldwork and sexuality by Joe Watkins that, however, does not refer to Lizot explicitly (see below).

11. The interesting exception is the 1976 ethical code of the Society for Professional Archaeologists, which, unlike the AAA codes, spells out "standards of research performance" (see Fluehr-Lobban 1991:259–62). One explanation for this could be that, as discussed in the introduction to this volume, archaeologists' sites of research and representation are more "public" and therefore they are more often held accountable for their claims to expertise than those in other anthropological fields (see also Wylie, this volume).

12. I borrow this phrasing from Charles Taylor, whose inquiry into the "moral topography" of the Western self has inspired many of my thoughts about the embedding of ethics in contemporary anthropology (1989:111–14).

13. This paragraph builds on a philosophy, history, and sociology of science that, since Kuhn and Feyerabend, has demonstrated the impossibility of demarcating a transcendental scientific "method." In particular, it draws inspiration from the challenge to the transcendent claims of methodology of linguistic and cultural anthropologists arguing that the production of knowledge is necessarily intersubjective and knowledge is always co-produced by scientists and their research subjects (Hymes 1964; Fabian 1981, 1979, 1983; Scholte [1969] 1974)—an argument echoed by ethnographies of laboratory work arguing that the objectivity of "hard science" equally depends on intersubjectivity (Latour and Woolgar 1979).

14. A reduction summarized, as noted above, by Taylor's (1989:3) thought that ethics is usually seen as something that is *right* to *do* rather than the much broader question of what (or how or who) it is *good* to *be*.

15. See n. 8.

16. See http://www.aaanet.org/committees/ethics/bp2.htm (accessed January 11, 2002).

17. See http://www.aaanet.org/committees/ethics/bp5.htm (accessed January 11, 2002).

18. See http://www.aaanet.org/committees/ethics/bp6.htm and http://www.aaanet.org/committees/ethics/bp4/htm (accessed January 11, 2002).

Anthropology's Malaysian Interlocutors: Toward a Cosmopolitan Ethics of Anthropological Practice

Joel S. Kahn

As Peter Pels has observed, in the late 1960s anthropologists in North America, Europe and, one should add, places like Australia began to show a renewed concern with the problem of professional ethics. Further, while such concerns in earlier periods in the history of the discipline were primarily with the ethics of the anthropologist as public servant, the focus now shifted to "the ideal professional anthropologist [as] someone whose first and paramount responsibility is to 'protect the physical, social, and psychological welfare and to honour the dignity and privacy of those studied'" (Pels 2000:138). Without questioning the importance of establishing ethical relationships with those previously thought of mainly as objects of study, however, I want to argue here that this hardly exhausts the ethical dilemmas faced by contemporary anthropology. For better or worse, the project of anthropology—insofar as it now comes to constitute itself as an anthropology of modernity (see Kahn 2001b)—now faces a set of ethically fraught relations with individuals and groups that do not fit easily into either the category of the discipline's more traditional publics (fellow academics, funding bodies, publishers, academic employers, and others) or that of "those studied." And while these individuals and groups may in the past have been ignored or treated as a nuisance to be dealt with in a purely instrumental fashion, I will suggest in this chapter that we are now compelled to broaden what we mean by ethical practice to include the way we negotiate such relations.

Ethical codes designed to govern the relations between ethnographers and their subjects are not adequate, for example, to handle the issues that emerge when an anthropologist seeks to create the conditions necessary for carrying out even more or less "traditional" ethnography[1] in faraway places—obtaining visas and official permission to carry out research, seeking the assistance of government officials as well as others in making satisfactory living arrangements, collecting official and unofficial statistics and publications, consulting the work of local researchers and academics, and negotiating access to a variety of "primary informants." In so doing the ethnographer encounters a series of agents neither simply "professional" nor part of that earlier class of ethnographic "informant." Similarly, in seeking to disseminate the results of such research (which includes the social processes through which these results are circulated, read, evaluated, and interpreted), anthropologists increasingly have to negotiate with a range of interlocutors who are neither academic colleagues from "home" nor themselves the subjects of research as classically conceived. Sociocultural anthropologists have been slow to acknowledge that these are anything more than practical matters to be negotiated, circumvented, or even ignored when possible when it comes to fulfilling our "real" obligations to the people we study. But is such a response adequate now that the boundaries between the "us" and the "them" of classical anthropological discourse are seen as increasingly porous? Or do the relations between anthropologists and these other kinds of "interlocutors" require us to go beyond the ethical considerations inherent in most existing codes of professional conduct?

I will propose no simple resolution of these problems, if only because I do not have one to offer. As a result, this chapter might be better included among those "agonistic confessions" documenting an ethnographer's "personal failures" of which Pels (2000) has written. But it may be worth asking at the outset whether there can or should be a resolution at all, at least at the level of the discipline. Anthropologists will and do obviously react in different ways to the kinds of challenges described here. And there is no reason to expect otherwise, since, as the situation so clearly reminds us, the universality of any ethical system may always be contested. "Anthropology," moreover, in no way defines, nor should it be made to define, a unitary moral community. All that can be offered here, then, is a discussion of options that might be explored in response to the ethical dilemmas posed by these new challenges to ethnographic authority.

Contesting the "Anthropology of the Malays"

As an anthropologist who has been engaged over some twenty-five years in on-again/off-again research in Malaysia,[2] I would contend that Westerners involved in "Malay ethnography" face a series of especially acute ethical dilemmas at all stages of the research process, dilemmas that ethical codes designed to protect "those studied" do not appear to recognize. Although these arise in the doing of ethnographic research in Malay rural communities, they both preexist and persist well beyond the period of ethnographic research. These include, of course, dilemmas that emerge in the relations between ethnographer and "those studied," but they are by no means restricted to such relations. Indeed, the impression of an outside ethnographer with at least initially a more traditionally conceived—that is, village-based[3]—research agenda has been that it is relationships with Malays who reside outside villages but in different ways exercise a degree of control over access to villages and over the way Malay village culture is represented that are the most fraught.

The ethical dilemmas are acutely felt particularly because the anthropology of the contemporary Malays is a field in which outsider ethnographers have come in for a great deal of critical scrutiny. This comes not so much from professional colleagues "back home" in the West—where, significantly, the general reaction to "Malay ethnography" is frequently that it is boring, presumably because it takes place in a locale considered insufficiently "exotic"[4]—as from a broad range of Malaysians many of whom are in a position to make such research difficult. What is suggested, then, is that many of the obstacles placed in the paths of Western anthropologists seeking to carry out research in Malaysia are generated by what might be described as at best a profound ambivalence toward foreigners and especially Westerners among government officials, academics, and others upon whom such visitors must rely to carry out their research. These range from stringent restrictions on the type of work one may carry out and the topics one may investigate (work on "race relations," "religion," and "class" has almost always been forbidden), extensive vetting of research proposals by government departments and local academics with whom one must make links in order to obtain official research permission, and, even when that is granted, significant difficulties in obtaining information from official and nonofficial sources.

Although, for example, I was granted government permission to carry out my first piece of research on aspects of peasant economic organization in Malay villages in the state of Negeri Sembilan (a project that with hindsight I can recognize as being framed by many of the assumptions of classical anthropology [cf. Kahn 2001b]), a senior academic at the University of Malaya closely monitored my work. I was required to meet with him at regular intervals, and he never failed to lecture me at length about what I should and should not say about Malay village life. The status of his advice was never entirely clear. It may not have been legally binding in itself, and he had no immediate sanctions at his disposal to back up his warnings. But my central concern here is with the ethical constraints his involvement should or should not place on my research and writing. Did I owe him the same rights of full disclosure, anonymity, etc., that, according to existing ethical codes meant to guide the conduct of ethnographic research, I owed the "real" subjects of that research?

Such obstacles to my "freedom" to carry out research as I and my subjects saw fit did not end with my academic sponsor. I have over the years, for example, found it almost impossible to obtain government reports or even a map of my research area. When one visits government offices at the federal and state level to request even public documents, one is almost inevitably told that legislation such as the Official Secrets Act forbids access to them. While in certain cases such legislation may indeed cover this material, it is quite clear that government office staff maintains a more or less blanket ban on granting access to foreign researchers even to the most innocuous materials. It is quite standard in Malaysia to get around such obstinacy with the help of inside contacts. Most Malaysian academics will have a range of such contacts, very often former students now working in relevant departments and ministries. Outside researchers rarely have such personal contacts, and it is the rare Malaysian academic who will assist a foreigner by providing introductions to his/her own inside sources. Indeed, we are pretty certain of one instance of a local colleague's actually having asked the staff in a certain government office not to cooperate with us at all.

Lack of interest, skepticism, and even hostility to outsiders is widespread in Malaysia and comes from a diversity of groups and individuals outside Malay villages. What constitutes ethical behavior in such instances? The hostility is particularly marked among Malaysian academics and intellectuals. Skepticism among nonacademics about the value of social research is perhaps not altogether surprising, but fellow academics might be expected to at least show a certain interest in it. While this was the case in some instances, particularly among non-Malays, many especially in the Malay academic community either showed little interest in our work or were downright hostile to it. More often than not this hostility was not openly expressed but manifested itself in endless broken appointments, suggesting strongly that the "hidden" forms of resistance described by James Scott (1985) as part of the strategies of poor Malay peasants are alive and well among the Malay middle classes as well. I distinctly remember on an early visit approaching a Malaysian-Chinese academic, one of the most astute observers of modern Malaysian culture and society, who had offered to share his insights with us on a diversity of topics. When he arranged to meet us on a university campus, he deliberately located an out-of-the-way meeting place so that, as he told us, he would not be observed by his Malay colleagues talking to foreign researchers.

When academics do attempt to explain their reluctance to provide assistance, they frequently regale one with what are clearly intended to be cautionary tales about the naïveté of outside researchers and recitations of long lists of foreign academics who have purportedly stolen the work of local researchers and passed it off as their own. Only once have I ever been asked to present a seminar discussing my research findings at a Malaysian university, and an audience that reminded me that as a non-Malay I could hardly expect ever to understand Malay culture received that seminar with considerable hostility. And, although this is more difficult to discuss, even to document, there were times when we suspected that there had been what we then saw as deliberate sabotage of our attempts to gather information.

Reaction to the published work of foreign researchers on Malay matters is tinged with similar sensitivities. More often than not the work is ignored, and those Malay scholars who do choose to engage with it tend to be highly critical of and antagonistic toward it. Again, this does not on its own stop one from working on and writing about the Malays, even if the almost inevitably hostile reviews of such work inside Malaysia tend to be discouraging. It would also be a mistake these days to assume that especially Malay academics have no power to control what is written about Malaysia. Academic publishers in the West increasingly seek the advice of "native" anthropologists and, perhaps in reaction to a generation of postcolonial critics of Western knowledge about Asia, are sensitive when they produce hostile reviews of manuscripts submitted for publication. But again, the question that concerns me here is not so much whether it is possible to carry on anthropological work on the Malays under such circumstances as whether we need to pay closer attention to the ethics of carrying on such work in the face of such opposition from Malaysians who do not seem to be members of the category of "ethnographic subject" as that category is classically conceived.

Nor do all these issues disappear after one finally turns to the "real" business at hand—the doing of village ethnography. Few were willing to assist us finding a research site, and, perhaps having absorbed these sensitivities from others, ordinary villagers with whom we interacted were often very reluctant to answer our doubtless annoying questions. Indeed, as has been already suggested, precisely because Malay villages are in no real sense the kind of self-contained cultural universes of classical ethnographic discourse, there is no reason to suppose that the close concern with insiderhood and outsiderhood experienced by aspiring ethnographers in the cities will disappear once one crosses the boundary between city and *kampung*.

Many villagers simply refused to cooperate, just as later did the members of the new Malay middle class on housing estates we interviewed in Seremban, Penang, and Kuala Lumpur. Some in the villages and many more of our middle class "informants" expressed much the same sort of skepticism as to the value of outsider researchers' attempting to understand their lives as did government officials, academics, and intellectuals more generally. This was generally embedded in a highly developed discourse on insiderhood and outsiderhood, West and non-West.

To paraphrase the responses of urban, suburban, and even some rural Malays to our questions about their views of the West and the role and value of Malay culture and Islam in their everyday lives: "You in the West may be good at the application of scientific knowledge or at making money, but in your blind pursuit of technological advance, money and power you neglect moral values, spirituality, and meaning." "Asians (or Muslims, or Malaysians) can be just as good as you Westerners at development, but we can develop and not neglect our families, our personal obligations or our religion." "Without in-depth knowledge of the Malay language, available only to native speakers, how could you, as outsiders, ever understand Malay culture?" Or, alternatively and less frequently, "Life in the West is better than it is in Malaysia, because individuals there are free of meaningless traditions and traditional obligations." These contrasts between "East" and "West" are an inevitable part of ethnographic interaction at all levels of Malay society, and all are characterized in one way or another by the framing of the relationship between Malays and Westerners as an intercultural one, one that brings together people from radically different cultures, even cultures irreducible one to another. Of course existing professional codes of conduct urge us to be sensitive to the attitudes of the subjects of our ethnographic enquiries. But what about those of others who claim, among other things, the right to speak on behalf of those subjects and are sometimes in a position to influence the attitudes of those same subjects? Do we need to behave ethically toward them? And if so, what would constitute ethical conduct?

The Malaysian example is important to the question of professional anthropological ethics precisely because this challenge to the outside ethnographer is deeply embedded in Malaysian culture and society— among "subalterns," "the middle classes," and elites alike. In other words, a very broad range of Malaysians, well beyond those constituted as the subjects of classical Malay ethnography, at least see themselves as "stakeholders" in the research enterprise in one way or another. Interestingly, this takes place in a nation in a position of at least relative strength in the contemporary world. Whatever its people or political leadership may feel about the huge gulf in wealth and power that divides Malaysia and the United States in particular and however much Malay intellectuals may decry Western neocolonial aspirations in the Third World, Malaysia is no more a Third World country these days than are most small Western states. Its record of economic growth and "development" would be the envy of all but a handful of world economic superpowers. Indeed, although economic nationalism runs high on occasion, for example, in the aftermath of the 1997 financial crisis, there is remarkably little opposition in Malaysia to direct foreign investment in the country by (Western-based) multinational companies (economic nationalism being mainly directed against foreign currency speculators and investors of so-called hot money).

It is important to acknowledge that the Malaysian case is not unique. Similar challenges have been and are being mounted to "outsider" anthropology in other contexts both at home and abroad. These issues, for example, are quite clearly at play in Australia, particularly when it comes to the ethnography of indigenous Australia. And of course the challenge to "Western" thought has become particularly acute throughout the Muslim world, even more so in the aftermath of September 11. Moreover, as suggested above, it would be misleading to argue that even in the heyday of modernism anthropologists in European and American academies had a monopoly on the production of anthropological knowledge. Far from being a case of a recent leaking out of the culture concept into the world, as is implied by a number of recent writers, the formation of the modern discipline was as much informed by outside intellectual and artistic influences as vice versa (cf. Kahn 1995).

Nor am I suggesting that these negative reactions to foreign researchers in Malaysia are unjustified. Anthropologists, with their classical concern to avoid "ethnocentrism" at all costs, to say nothing of their sensitivity to more recent postcolonial and other critiques of the discipline, are probably already predisposed to be hypersensitive to problems of outsiderhood in their research. Based, as they often are, on relatively short research visits, how can the accounts of foreign scholars ever be as detailed, informative, and sophisticated as those of local scholars? Why should an outsider's accounts of Malay culture and society ever be thought superior to those of Malays themselves?

Ethnographers are of course familiar with the argument that to privilege the accounts of Western observers amounts to a form of cultural imperialism whereby the truth claims of the anthropologist are made possible only because of the disparity in power between ethnographer and "informant." Is it really possible ever to separate anthropological knowledge from its colonial roots? Many Malays would suggest that it is not. More often than not the resistance to their constitution as objects of ethical judgment or of ethnographic investigation prompts Malay "interlocutors" to point to the colonialist, even racist implications of all Western representations of Malays/Malaysians/Asians/Muslims, anthropological or other. Malaysians may well implicate all such attempts at knowledge production in what are widely described as the neocolonial aspirations of the United States or the West more generally.

Anthropologists from less powerful Western states such as Australia are not spared such criticism. Indeed, at least in the case of Australia the challenge may be even more vociferous as a result of the long history of Australia-bashing in the Malaysian media. Can the relations between Western ethnographers and their Malay "interlocutors" be distilled from the network of (neocolonial) economic and geopolitical relations between Malaysians and Westerners that has emerged in the post-colonial, post-cold war, post-September 11 world in which the power of particularly the United States and American economic interests reigns supreme (Said 1989)? Does the fact that such objections to the practice of anthropology in and on Malaysia are raised, if not by "those studied," then by Malay academics, intellectuals, theologians, and journalists impose new ethical burdens on Western ethnographers?

The point at issue here is not so much whether such objections to Western anthropology are understandable as whether they demand a new kind of professional ethics. And what makes the Malaysian case so appropriate to such a discussion is that, however understandable such challenges to anthropological knowledge making may be, they are not inevitable. At least in my own experience of working in both Malaysia and Indonesia, for example, the role of "outsiders" is far more acutely contested in the former. By contrast, foreign researchers in Indonesia are more likely to be received enthusiastically, one might even suggest overenthusiastically, by villagers and local colleagues alike. Rarely, for example, is quite the same challenge posed to Western anthropologists in Indonesia, even when there may be a clear case of conflict between Indonesia and the anthropologist's home country as occurred recently during the crisis in Australia-Indonesia relations provoked by the conflict in and over East Timor. During this time life was uncomfortable for many Australians, including academic researchers, in Indonesia, but from what I can tell this rarely involved a radical othering of Australia or the West or a defense based on some notion of uniquely Indonesian values.

What makes the Malaysian example relevant to a consideration of ethical issues in contemporary anthropology, then, is not so much that contesting the intrusion of Western anthropology is seen as justified or unjustified as that the challenges generated by the doing of anthropology of the Malays can be used as a kind of test case for considering the ethical implications of doing anthropology in a world in which anthropological authority is in doubt.

One may, of course, choose to react in different ways to the challenge to the doing of an anthropology of the Malays. One reaction—one that might in fact flow from a reading of many codes of professional conduct—would be to maintain that since one's primary responsibility is to "those studied," most challenges emanating from individuals and groups in Malaysia not directly under ethnographic scrutiny are in some sense irrelevant—if not to be ignored, then to be negotiated according to some kind of instrumental rationality. Another reaction would be to take such criticisms to mean the inevitable end of anthropological practice altogether, leaving the field of speaking "for" or "on behalf of" the Malays entirely in the hands of, variously, Malays, Malaysians, Asians, or Muslims (depending on how those traditional subjects of ethnography are predominantly identified).

But unlike those who would return to the days when we could get on with the business of anthropological science by ignoring or discrediting the motives of those interlocutors described above (treating them merely as difficulties to be overcome in purely instrumental fashion, along with the weather or tropical parasites), I want here to consider what it might mean to take the ethical implications of such challenges seriously. And as someone who has continued, however unsuccessfully, to practice an anthropology of the Malays, it would be disingenuous of me now suddenly to claim that such a project is ethically impossible. I will therefore proceed in the "agonistic confession of failure" mode recommended by Pels.

Ethics: From Universalism to Particularism

A discussion of the ethics of any Western intellectual practice such as anthropology leads one implicitly or explicitly to engage with the foundations of both ethical and scientific thinking within the modern intellectual tradition, a task for which an anthropologist may not be particularly well trained or equipped if only because in the classical formulation of the anthropological problematic it was conceived as a means of escaping from that tradition. It is my impression that until relatively recently, unless they sought it out, budding anthropologists have not had much exposure in their training to courses on the history of Western philosophy or social theory, perhaps because it was not thought to be directly relevant to anthropological theorizing.

Be that as it may, one could hardly begin to consider the ethical dimensions of anthropological practice—at least once it is recognized that anthropology stands firmly inside rather than outside the traditions of modern thought—without at least considering the ways in which modern thinking (ethical, "scientific," and political) is grounded in a form of secular universalism.

Although there is an argument that these interconnections are approximated in earlier periods of European intellectual history, it is the eighteenth century that is most widely accepted as marking the beginnings of modern forms of universalist thought. Indeed, the recent perception that postmodernism and multiculturalism have led to ethical negligence and political apathy has prompted some to call for a return to the ethical and methodological absolutisms of natural law or the attempts by Enlightenment philosophers in particular to ground their ethics in the science of a universal human nature.[5]

While certainly not typical of the period, Immanuel Kant's is probably the most sophisticated of such Enlightenment philosophies in which a modern ethics is grounded in a "science of man." In his famous formulation of the categorical imperative, the basic form of the moral principle, Kant enjoins us to "act according to that maxim which you can at the same time will that it should become a universal law" (cited in Wood 1999:79). What for Kant makes morality possible is precisely its universality across humanity considered as a unified category of beings. And what makes this category both unitary and distinctively human is the human capacity for reason. Moral principles are therefore universal to the extent that they are the uniform outcome of the a priori of human reason acting on sensory experience (see Wood 1999). The very possibility of modern ethical conduct for Kant, then, is secured because it can be grounded in science, here the science of human nature (what Kant meant by the term "anthropology"). And such a "science of human nature is again universalizing at least in aspiration" (an aspiration that Kant terms the "cosmopolitan ideal"). Anthropology for Kant therefore "cannot content itself with the study of what makes each people different but must be oriented from the start to what they have in common" (Wood 1999:99).

Of course, a philosophical system such as Kant's, should we choose to resurrect it, provides an obvious solution to the dilemmas thrown up by the project of anthropology in places like Malaysia. It enjoins us both to aspire to universal principles of ethical conduct and to pursue universalizing forms of anthropological investigation. Indeed, to the extent that our aims are precisely to investigate what it is that "we" and "they" have in common, it can be said that the practice of anthropology, being "cosmopolitan," is itself ethical practice. And presumably the practice of those who would oppose it thereby becomes unethical at a stroke.[6] But a significant objection to a simple resurrection of the Enlightenment project in this way (a way, incidentally, that does grave injustice to Kant himself) is that it is problematic because, with the benefit of hindsight provided by at least twenty years of intellectual critique, to say nothing of the challenges mounted by our new interlocutors outside the Western academy, it is apparent that at least in *content* it is not universal at all but highly particularistic and thereby exclusionary (see Kahn 2001a).

A case in point is the British "emancipatory" narrative analyzed by the political scientist Uday Mehta, who, assessing the links between liberalism, with its ideas about universal freedom and emancipation, on the one hand, and the denial of freedom to colonial subjects by liberal regimes, on the other, maintains that modern "anthropological" narratives (in the Kantian sense) are, in spite of their pretension to universality, so inflected by particular cultural assumptions about the nature of mature human reason that they inevitably become exclusionary. Examining, for example, the underlying conceptualization of human reason present in the works of classical British liberals, Mehta finds it so imbued with the very particular values of middle-class, white, and, one might add, male Englishmen of the time that it would have inevitably found Britain's colonial subjects in India incompletely rational, hence justifying their exclusion from processes of political emancipation perhaps indefinitely ([1990] 1997). The very same critique of the Kantian system can also be made on the grounds of Kant's stated views on the superiority of Europeans and the white race more generally.[7]

The implications for a universal ethics of the particularistic, racist, patriarchal and/or Eurocentric assumptions lurking behind the pretense of universalism have of course been the subject of some twenty years of feminist, postmodern, multicultural, and postcolonial critique affecting the social sciences and humanities very broadly. This is not the place to rehearse such long-standing debates. It is, however, helpful to consider how certain twentieth-century philosophers have, as a consequence, been led to a substantial reformulation of the problem of ethics. Many have come to the view that there can be no universal ethics in a world characterized by what they call a plurality of "comprehensive doctrines of the good," a plurality that they see manifest in the fact of cultural diversity whether within the nation or beyond. Instead, liberals such as Rawls (1971) sought grounding for what they now described as a cross-cultural ethics not in a universal human condition but in the existence of an "overlapping consensus." In the case of Malaysia it is clear that a case for such a consensus could be made, since there certainly are Malaysians and Malays who reject the relativizing assumptions that lie behind the discourse on Asian cultural uniqueness, advocating instead some version of a universalizing liberal discourse. This overcomes the problem of insiderhood and outsiderhood at the level of the nation. But, as Apel (1999) has pointed out, it does not solve the problem finally, since the consensus would include only those Malaysians whose views do in fact overlap with those prevailing within the "Westernized" consensus. And since we have no foundation for taking their views rather than those of their critics as a basis for formulating an ethics applicable to Malaysia as a whole, then all we have done is expose a problem in nationalist rhetoric that embeds *a* culture within *a* territory, not the rhetoric of the "irreducibility" of competing doctrines of the good.

Such criticisms of the "overlapping consensus" approach lead to the view that a universally applicable ethics across competing doctrines of the good is impossible. The upshot of Rorty's (1991) arguments, for example, seems to be that competing visions of the good are irreducible one to another, and all we can do is proclaim our own and seek to persuade others of its superior worth. A related outcome, one that also rejects a priori ethical judgments across cultural boundaries, is entailed in the arguments of deconstructionists. Rejecting any grounding for ethics in a universal human nature because of what he calls the impossibility of an "acontextual human being," Derrida (1999) follows Levinas in arguing for a continual opening out to the other as the only genuinely ethical stance.

The idea of competing doctrines of the good embedded in irreducibly different "cultures" is one with certain persuasiveness. It is especially appealing when the less palatable dimensions of universalism and universalizing social, economic, and political projects—racism, exclusion, and cultural imperialism—are exposed. Its persuasiveness is brought home, for example, in a place like Indonesia when exaggerated respect is paid to outside researchers because of their association with prestigious Western nations/universities. Nor is it consistent to discredit postcolonial intellectuals and others who draw our attention to such exclusions by pointing to their instrumental motives if we do not at the same time reflect on and acknowledge the real rewards that come to Western anthropologists who carry out "successful" research in the postcolonies.

This in any case provides us with reasons to take seriously the ethical as well as the more purely practical implications of the Malay challenge to the project of an anthropology of the Malays. It means engaging precisely with the terms in which that challenge is posed; to the extent that anthropology is understood as a "Western" practice, the assertion of the radical alterity of Malay culture clearly raises significant ethical barriers to the doing of anthropology among the Malays. In short, the problem, at least as it first presents itself, is precisely a problem in cross-cultural ethics and, indeed, of "cross-cultural communication" more broadly.

Yet whatever the merits of these various attempts to come to grips with the philosophical problems that flow from an acknowledgment of the presence of competing doctrines of the good, and each of course has its critics as well as its defenders, it is difficult to see how any of them provide anthropologists engaged in cross-cultural research with answers to questions about what constitutes ethical behavior, especially when they are faced with arguments about the irreducibility of the cultural gulf between East and West like those of anthropology's new Malay interlocutors. Indeed, to the extent that philosophers such as Rorty and Derrida draw attention to the intimate connections between the problem of cross-cultural ethics and that of cross-cultural understanding *tout court*, it may be suggested that they compound the problems for aspiring anthropologists in places like Malaysia. It is difficult to envisage how any kind of "cross-cultural" interaction is possible if Malays are presumed to be unutterably alien to at least some of their non-Malay interlocutors, including anthropologists from Western academic institutions. It is impossible to see how granting some kind of "stakeholder" status to such Malay interlocutors or granting them an ethical independence that stems from their adherence to a doctrine of the good that is radically different from our own actually gets around what is now not just an ethical problem but also one of methodological particularism. It is impossible to see how such fuzzy notions as "strategic" or "situational" ethics can be defended without any philosophical grounding. In the absence of some form of Kant's "cosmopolitan" ideal, the very idea of an ethical anthropology strikes me as a contradiction in terms.

Conclusion: Anthropology as Cosmopolitan Practice?

To the extent that we take seriously what anthropology's Malay critics are saying, we must question whether the only means of responding to their challenge is either to treat them as an inconvenience to be dealt with in instrumental fashion or alternatively to abandon the possibility of an anthropology of the Malays altogether. It is one thing to recognize that the "other" operates according to a doctrine of the good that differs radically from our own or to acknowledge (and somehow remain "open" to) that radical alterity and quite another to claim to know exactly in what that alterity consists. But while there is no prima facie reason that anthropology should survive either as a distinctive discipline or as a body of theories and concepts, we do need to ask about the relevance of such philosophical arguments to the world within which anthropologists now operate. Is it best described as a world characterized by a multiplicity of competing doctrines of the good, each anchored in a discrete and distinctive "culture"? There is a distinct and growing body of opinion both inside and outside the discipline, itself a reaction to the perceived shortcomings of postmodern, postcolonial, and multicultural currents in the humanities and social sciences, that it is not and that processes within which cultural difference is constituted in the modern world are systematically misrepresented when they are subsumed to a model of the world as cultural mosaic (cf. Kahn 1995). This is not to suggest that any simple return to the universalism of the Enlightenment is either possible or desirable. Instead, a rather different understanding of both modern universalism and the project of anthropology may be called for.

The problem with the universalistic aspiration of Enlightenment social philosophy has been exposed as the problem of its inflection by particularistic and by definition therefore exclusionary cultural presuppositions. In conclusion, I want to argue that an alternative needs to rest on two rather different assumptions. Reorienting our search for cross-cultural understanding in these ways produces an unexpectedly pivotal role for anthropology's Malay interlocutors and therefore imposes an ethical obligation on outside anthropologists both to engage directly with their claims and to give serious attention to the ethical dimensions of relationships among all of those who would, in cooperation or in competition with Western anthropologists, claim to "speak" the authentic culture of the Malay *kampung*.

First it may be necessary to accept that all universalistic projects are inevitably also particularistic and that, rather than attempting to construct new forms of universalism free of cultural presuppositions, the way forward in seeking a grounding for a cross-cultural ethics may be to accept that all such attempts to seek the universal in the human condition will inevitably be "contaminated" by the historically, culturally, and socially particular. A great deal of the discussion of modern universalism rests on the basic if often implicit assumption that there is such a thing as a pure modernity "uncontaminated," to borrow Peter Wagner's (1999) term, by the facts of culture and history. Such a view probably stems in part from the tendency to conflate (high) modernism and the modern condition more broadly conceived, a conflation that almost inevitably renders modernity in highly abstract aesthetic or philosophical terms. Note the way in which the problem of the encounter between modernist narratives and ethnographic experience is expressed at the outset. Places like Malaysia are different because there modern institutions, behavior, culture are in some sense "contaminated" by culturally and historically specific relations, ideologies, sets of social relations. Western modernity is thus represented as the original/pure form that becomes "indigenized," hence contaminated when it is exported to other parts of the world (see Kahn 2001b). If, in contrast, we recognize that there is no such thing as a "pure" modernity, then it will be seen that processes, institutions, ideologies, and cultural projects deemed modern, including ethical universalism, are *always and everywhere* embedded in particular histories, institutional traditions, cultures, religions, etc. This is just as much the case in the "West" as it is in the "East."

A major problem in the "application" of universalizing narratives such as Kant's, then, is that it is mistakenly assumed that a pure, abstract universalism is ultimately possible, whereas in fact if we were to turn the problem on its head and examine concrete "Western" universalizing projects through the modernist metanarratives inherited from exemplary modernists such as Kant, Hegel, Marx, Weber, and Baudelaire the problems we would encounter would be exactly the same as those encountered in places like Malaysia. This is not to resurrect some notion of modernist homogeneity—only to draw attention to the faultiness of a starting point that aspires to "decontaminate" universalism in modern contexts.

Second, it may be possible to seek a new understanding of the anthropological project, a redefinition of anthropology as a form of practice that is cosmopolitan in aspiration but never in fact. We have seen how critics of Western modernist narratives have pointed to the particularistic assumptions underpinning them. At the same time anthropological narratives have been scrutinized on precisely the opposite grounds, namely, that they are more "modernist" than has conventionally been assumed. We have come to recognize, in other words, that anthropological knowledge does not consist solely of unmediated accounts of the other-to-the-modern subjectivities of nonmodern peoples that somehow precede the ethnographic encounters that produce them. Instead we are compelled to acknowledge that it emerges only out of concrete ethnographic encounters and, more broadly, out of the long history of encounters between Westerners and non-Westerners. Therefore, in spite of the promise of an escape from ethnocentrism and the claims of cultural relativism, anthropology is at least as much a product of the modern Western imagination as it is of the (supposedly non-Western, nonmodern) imaginations of its "objects." In this sense, then, ethnography can be seen to be embedded in a broader body of representations, images, symbols, beliefs, and languages that have developed for the purpose of expressing and regulating the relations, interactions, and conflicts between and among groups which, of course, given the history of such encounters, certainly include those we would want to characterize as imperial. Moreover, to the extent that such knowledge is shaped by and circulates and is evaluated and consumed entirely within modern nations, empires, and the global system, there is no reason to assume that it has an epistemological status any different from modern knowledge more generally. The simplistic assumption that anthropologists could shed all (ethnocentric) presuppositions in order to immerse themselves in alien beliefs (then to report them back to the modern world) has been thoroughly and rightly discredited.

How, then, should we conceive of the doing of anthropology in the modern world when all universalizing narratives are at the same time particularist and all particularizing ones equally universalistic? The key, it seems to me, lies in the ways in which a cosmopolitan practice may seek or, better, be forced to seek to become more inclusive. It is evident that all forms of cosmopolitan thought—those that, following Kant, aspire to treat diverse human beings for "what they have in common"— will inevitably begin with culturally inflected presuppositions about what it is that constitutes that common humanity (a human essence, whether defined biologically or otherwise). At the same time, in practice cosmopolitan ideas will also inevitably generate notions of radical alterity, as those presuppositions come under the challenge of human diversity. Perhaps unchallenged, there is no reason for would-be cosmopolitans to revise their notion of the human essence, no reason not to proceed on the assumption that diversity is evidence of "perversity" in one form or another—as evidence that the bearers of difference are either redeemably or irredeemably not, or not yet, fully capable of human reason.

Yet precisely because all such universalist ideals are informed by particular, culturally inflected notions of human essence, they are not in principle immutable. There is, in other words, no logical reason that they should take the form that they do. A colonial narrative that constitutes Malays as perverse forms of humanity incapable (or not yet capable) of reason, hard work, and responsibility could be transformed into a more inclusive narrative in which Malays are possessors of fully mature human rational powers. The question is how such changes come about, how an exclusionary narrative becomes more inclusive (while doubtless now in turn defining new exclusions). And it seems equally clear that the answer does not lie at the level of will. The resolution, in other words, is not a philosophical one. Nor, no matter how attentive one is to the "dialogical" character of ethnography, is the resolution likely to come at the level of the individual act of ethnographic research, at least in classical settings, where the differences in the power-to-represent between ethnographer and subject are likely to be too great for even the best-intentioned ethnographer to overcome.[8]

But for reasons that deserve more careful scrutiny then they normally receive, there are increasingly those who would challenge the authority of Western academic anthropologists to represent otherness and thereby to appropriate other rationalities to their own. "How can anthropologists work in and write about the world at present?" asked Richard Fox in his introduction to a collection of essays seeking to "recapture" the anthropological project in the aftermath of the fragmentation of the discipline that began as early as the 1960s (Fox 1991; see also Stocking 1995). A significant feature of this "world at present," one that lurks on the horizons of most contributions to this volume, is the growing challenge to the authority of anthropologists to represent other cultures. The more recent decline in the persuasiveness of anthropological representation is most frequently attributed to the wave of postmodern, postcolonial, feminist, and multicultural attacks on the work of anthropology alluded to frequently by Fox and his contributors. But these intellectual developments might be seen as symptoms of the same global shifts in the configuration of power relations in the cultural sphere that give rise to the crisis of anthropological authority. These include, among other things, a decline in the rhetorical effectiveness that derives from membership in the Western academy (particularly of membership in those parts of the modern university dedicated to teaching and research in the humanities and social sciences)—the development of classical anthropology in Europe and North America in the interwar years being intimately bound up in the development of the modern/Western university—along with a corresponding proliferation of both nonacademic and non-Western "voices" competing with academic anthropologists for the right to speak for or on behalf of groups that had been constituted as objects of classical ethnography.

Given this shift in the balance of the power to represent other cultures and societies, it is precisely these other voices to which we must now listen. Whether we like what they are telling us or not, only they are capable of really shifting us away from the particularistic presuppositions than inform existing cosmopolitan practices. Finding ways, therefore, of establishing ethical modes of interacting with our new interlocutors—no matter how fraught, difficult, even conflictual such relations may be—therefore seems to be the only way in which anthropology can genuinely recapture its claim to be a cosmopolitan practice in the modern world.

Notes

1. My own project as it was originally conceived very much fits this description. It has been transformed over the years, partly because of the encounters described in this paper.

2. American by birth, British-trained, professionally employed in Australia, I have been carrying out research mainly among Malays in Malaysia since the mid-1970s, usually in collaboration with my partner, Maila Stivens, whose interests and ideas have in many ways shaped what is discussed in this paper. Financial support for the research has been provided at different times by the (then) Social Science Research Council in the United Kingdom and the Australian Research Council, and I gratefully acknowledge their support here.

3. In both the classical anthropological tradition and the distinctive discipline of "Malay studies," the Malay village or *kampung* has always been considered the *locus classicus* of "pure" Malay culture (see Kahn 2001a:esp. chap. 4).

4. The comment by an academic in London that our fieldwork locale was somehow inauthentic because the houses had electricity is one manifestation of this attitude; the questioning of our motives for working in Malaysia when a far more interesting place (Indonesia) is so close is another.

5. A succinct statement and critique of the ways in which Enlightenment philosophers grounded a universal ethics in a "science" of human nature is provided by Hawthorn (1976:13) For a recent version of what is still essentially the Enlightenment argument see Rushdie (1998).

6. This is the spirit of the argument that the sorts of challenges mounted to anthropological practice described above can essentially be ignored because of the instrumental motives of those who mount them and, more generally, of those who argue that universalism, by overriding cultural differences, amounts to a form of cultural imperialism. Certainly one of the most vocal critics of the ways in which Malaysia is represented in the West is none other than Malaysia's former prime minister, Dr. Mahathir Mohamad. And his interest in deflecting Western criticism of the authoritarian style of his regime and the misdeeds of his "crony" capitalists is well known. Some have argued that the challenge of so-called postcolonial intellectuals is equally discredited by their desire to use the postcolonial critique to obtain comfortable academic sinecures. And similarly, those interested in recapturing the Enlightenment notion of universal human rights accuse those who would deflect the human rights agenda using discredited "essentialized" notions of cultural difference of bad faith or unethical conduct. Finally, there are those who argue that concerns with the "right to difference" have derailed antiracist movements. (For a few examples of such critiques see Taguieff 1992; Stolcke 1995; Robison 1996; Guillaumin 1991; Turner 1997; Wolf 1994.) Recently attempts such as these simply to dismiss all culturally relativizing rhetoric in favor of universalism have been effectively criticized (see, for example, Brown 1999 and Woodiwiss 1998. for examples of such arguments that are particularly pertinent to the Asian context).

7. Even as strong a defender of Kant as Allan Wood has accepted that Kant was "undeniably" racist and Eurocentric (see Wood 1999; see also Pagden 1995, 1998). See also Harvey's critique of attempts to resurrect Kant because of the underlying contradictions between Kant's cosmopolitanism and ethics and "the awkward and intractable particularities of his geography" (2000a:535)

8. Ethnographers, especially of poor rural communities in the Third World, are in my view naïve if they think that they can treat their "informants" as "interlocutors" in any real sense, even presuming that such informants had any real interest in how they are portrayed in academic texts.

Part 2

Relocating Ethics in Current Research

Sites of Violence: Terrorism, Tourism, and Heritage in the Archaeological Present

Lynn Meskell

L ocating and materializing ethics in archaeology remains a relatively recent undertaking in part because of the illusion that the subjects of our research are dead and buried and our research goals are paramount. Archaeologists have traditionally operated on the assumption that they are not implicated in the representation and struggles of living peoples and that all such political engagement is negatively charged. Field praxis and the production of heritage sites and their ramifications have only recently come to be considered serious research loci (Fotiadis 1993; Meskell 1998, 2002b; Politis 2001; Scham and Yahya 2003). It has also taken time to persuade archaeologists that ours is a subjective and political enterprise that is far from agenda-free. The primacy of positivist archaeology, particularly in North America, has postponed a sustained disciplinary engagement with ethical discourse (Meskell 2002a). But a new generation of archaeologists is increasingly aware of both the centrality and the embedded nature of ethics (Blundell 1998; Byrne 2003b; Colwell-Chanthaphonh 2003a, 2003b; Shepherd 2003; Watkins 2001). We are also witnessing a greater convergence between archaeological and ethnographic practices—field projects in which the two disciplines are combined and practitioners with interests in all dimensions of cultural heritage, past and present.

This chapter explores the entwined politics of archaeology in Egypt, specifically around the village of Gurna (West Bank, Luxor), where the preservation of ancient monuments has taken precedence over the needs of the living. It charts political developments over the past decade

123

including government directives for the creation of an open-air archaeological museum and the local community's resistance to its forced
relocation. Tensions between the archaeological community, the
government, and locals about ethical issues of looting and preservation
have been juxtaposed with the use of state-sanctioned violence toward
the Gurnawis. As a result, the community has mobilized to create its
own museum, which celebrates Gurna's recent past and architectural
traditions rather then focusing on its pharaonic heritage. This alternative construction of heritage de-privileges the famous New Kingdom
tombs upon which the modern community is situated and expresses
concern for the villagers' economic livelihood and traditions. This
effectively inverts the prioritizing of past over present that is dominant
in the nation-state's vision of heritage and modernity. The chapter also
examines a key episode in the ongoing violence surrounding Luxor, the
massacre at the Temple of Hatshepsut in 1997. Since tourism and
terrorism have come to be inextricably linked in recent years, the
discussion foregrounds the tensions surrounding presentation of the
pharaonic past at the expense of later periods in Egyptian history,
specifically that of Islamic Egypt. In examining the Egyptian tourist
industry and its role in national development, one can see how
performing the past has proven a necessary, albeit fraught, endeavor
in the context of Islamic nationhood.

More generally, I hope to expose the ramifications of an unthinking
attitude toward archaeological heritage, especially for archaeologists
working outside their own countries, and its implications for local
communities that may fall outside the boundaries of the national
imaginary. Archaeologists have been eager to tackle issues of politics
and nationalism in the past decade but less inclined to venture onto
the slippery terrain of intranational struggles and the connections
between diverse groups and constructions of heritage. The latter have
local and global impacts upon the practices of tourism, another critical
area that has been neglected by archaeologists (see Blundell 1998; Logan
and Leone 1997; Meskell 2001; Odermatt 1996), remaining the purview
of anthropologists and sociologists (see, for example, Boniface and
Fowler 1993; Castañeda 1996; Chambers 1997; Edensor 1998, 2001;
Franklin and Crang 2001; Herbert 1995; Kirshenblatt-Gimblett 1998;
MacCannell 1992, 2000, 2001; Rojek and Urry 1997; Urry 1990). An
emergent literature in tourist studies foregrounds the importance of
archaeological places as the sites around which narratives of heritage
and identity fuse. Drawing on examples from Egypt, specifically the
village of Gurna, I attempt to show the interconnectedness between

heritage, tourism, and violence at both the real and the symbolic level, suggesting that archaeologists must become more cognizant of their roles in broader political spatialities. An emergent ethics in archaeology must tackle archaeology, heritage, tourism, and national modernity as they coalesce in the countries in which we work and live.

Heritage and Modernity in Ethical Context

A concern with ethics should ideally inflect all modes of archaeological praxis, including fieldwork, publication, education, stewardship, preservation, and, axiomatically, all archaeological engagements with the historical legacies of other communities. One way to ensure responsible archaeology at home and, to some degree, abroad is by crafting codes or guidelines for good practice. Ethical codes and programmatic statements have traditionally been developed under the auspices of national bodies such as the Society for American Archaeology (SAA) in the United States and the Australian Archaeological Association (AAA) in Australia, where local issues of indigeneity are paramount (Lilley 2000a; Lynott and Wylie 2000). Yet a genealogy of ethics highlights the dearth of writing on the conduct of archaeology in foreign countries, where practitioners and situational interests take on more complex layerings. How are issues of representation reconciled when archaeologists are separated but not disentangled from the construction and effects of national heritage? I have noted elsewhere that problems inhere in the global legislation and classificatory regulations surrounding the notion of "world heritage" (Meskell 2002b). One consistent theme emerges throughout: all engagements surrounding archaeological heritage must be examined in context.

Archaeologists are gradually starting to interrogate the discipline's public face, specifically our responsibilities to many different constituencies. At issue are the discursive technologies of the self as academician and fieldworker in a variety of contexts—most notably in foreign domains. Archaeologists have rather different concerns from ethnographers, who have long been instrumental in the service of the state, particularly in times of war and counterinsurgency (Pels 1999:110–111). Although the latter have always maintained a higher profile, archaeologists have been similarly involved in politics through negotiations with governments, World Bank consultants, tourist agencies, heritage brokers, local communities, and myriad individuals. It is no longer possible to speak simply of the dual relationship between the researcher and the data—the "dead subjects" of an archaeological past. In an archaeological present we confront influential third parties with authoritative values and protocols. Whether we are involved to the same degree as our anthropological colleagues is difficult to determine, since so little historiographical critique has emerged. Under the influence of postprocessualism the older vision of "pure" academic research has been occluded by political realities including the indigenization of archaeology, the passage of the Native American Graves Protection and Repatriation Act, the Balkan crisis, and he Gulf War (Meskell 2002a). Within the disciplinary context of anthropology, Pels (2000:163) has identified the possibility of an emergent ethics no longer tied to a specific community but entangled in a much larger, more pervasive network. Strathern (2000b:280) takes this farther, arguing that while "anthropological models of society and culture once provided a cue to the conduct of encounters, now such encounters are to be governed by professional protocols which create altogether different kinds of interacting subjects."

Ethics is essentially a theory of social relations rather than a transcendent entity or body of facts. What we see in heritage legislation is a utilitarian ethic that operates as a standard for judging public action, aiming to satisfy the majority's preferences (Goodin 1991:241, 245). Individual utilities are aggregated into an overall measure of social utility that has obvious shortcomings, among them an assumed comparability of individuals. This assumption gives rise to problems when cultural difference is interpolated, as it is in the heritage sphere. This has serious consequences for the production of ethical codes, because such codification can represent inert knowledge rather than knowledge produced in response to the context of application (Pels 1999:113). We must acknowledge the shifting nature of global political contexts, most recently demonstrated in the deployment of archaeological sites and materials for political purposes in Afghanistan and Iraq. Numerous attempts to regulate archaeology and archaeologists have been made by the Society for American Archaeology (SAA), the International Committee on Archaeological Heritage Management (ICAHM), the Society of Professional Archaeologists (SOPA), and others (Scham 1998:304). These codes or guidelines are not redundant; rather, they constitute a locus for further interrogation—texts produced at specific times and places that signify certain practices and mentalities. Ethics and politics are inseparable, and therein lies the danger; they are peculiarly local. When we consider legislating internationally or creating mandates that would have an impact on living communities in other cultural contexts, dialogue and negotiation are key (for an excellent example, see Colwell-Chanthaphonh and Ferguson 2004). Essentially we need to be vigilant in self-monitoring, self-evaluation, and the sharpening of our moral sense.

In the field of heritage there has been considerable debate over the moral and political implications of the words "property," "patrimony," "heritage," "resources," and "treasures," and while the term "cultural heritage" is objectionable to some because of its implicit moral claims, it may be expedient when discussing the ethics of studying, owning, and preserving the past (Messenger 1999:254). In uncritically subscribing to certain dominant ethical perspectives surrounding the heritage of other cultures we are espousing *ethical absolutism*—imposing a single system on local moral values. An alternative position could be described as *moral relativism*, which acknowledges cultural difference and context and opposes interference with other cultures' moralities: different societies legitimately follow different rules (Buckle 1991:173). Relinquishing our power to intervene in the affairs of others may have uncomfortable repercussions, and some of our aesthetic determinations will inevitably be compromised. The most recent example of this conflict can be seen in the Taliban's destruction of the Bamiyan Buddhas and the resulting outcry from Western commentators (Colwell-Chanthaphonh 2003a; Gamboni 2001; Meskell 2002b)

International charters concerning heritage coalesce around three constructs: rights of ownership, rights of access, and rights of inheritance. The notion of rights was ostensibly propounded by the likes of Grotius and Locke, but whereas the eighteenth-century notion was protective and negative, attempting to limit the power of governments over their subjects, the modern concept includes rights to various forms of welfare. The latter actually justifies the extension of government in the pursuit of social wealth, comfort, or economic advantage (Almond 1991:260). Legal rights and moral rights are not necessarily coterminous, and some purely legal rights can be deleterious to the individual. And what of the rights of others, especially those with whom we disagree? If a right can be linked to prohibiting interference by others, rights can be read as benefits that are open to many, among them diverse communities with variant beliefs and perspectives.

The creation of heritage is a culturally generative act that is intrinsically political. Heritage consultants and archaeologists could be said to invent culture and, in the process, constitute heritage (Hufford 1994:5). Heritage itself has a history and mirrors the divisions of the world formulated by academies and other cultural and scientific institutions. Legislative measures from the 1960s and 1970s designated three arenas:

(1) nature (natural species and ecosystems), (2) the built environment (artifacts, buildings, sites, and districts), and (3) folk life/culture (living artistic expressions and traditional communities). Each sphere had its professionals, legislative mandates, public and private supporters, and assorted goals and visions (Hufford 1994:2). However, some forms of heritage take precedence over others, some types of folk life or culture are deemed undesirable, and particular sites are privileged over communities with their own living cultures. Heritage is iterated and enforced by the multinational bodies with which archaeologists frequently interact. The most powerful organizations, such as UNESCO, the International Council on Monuments and Sites (ICOMOS), or the World Bank, are multinational in structure, but Western member states are usually responsible for establishing procedures. Nawal El Saadawi (1997:56) insists that the wave of violence surrounding tourism in Egypt can be linked to the neocolonialist operations of United Nations organizations and development agencies including the General Agreement on Tariffs and Trade, the World Bank, and the International Monetary Fund. Decision making may be orchestrated at the national or the global level, while the serious consequences are most often experienced at the local level.

It could be argued that the construct of "global world heritage" is, in part, a remnant of colonialism. Intimately tied to an Enlightenment project of exploration and knowledge, preserving and showcasing global heritage is always construed as serving a "common good" that purportedly fulfills universal aims. Archaeology is deeply imbued with colonialist residues. Benedict Anderson demonstrated decades ago that while colonial regimes in South Asia sought to link monumental archaeology and tourism, promoting an image of the state as guardian of local tradition, ultimately archaeological spaces operated as performative regalia for the colonizers (Anderson 1983:181–182). Colonizing the monumentality of the past—a process that has its roots in bygone centuries—has served to separate countries such as India and Egypt from their past glories and future potentials in the service of the ruling empire. Egypt and its riches are still seen as a global resource and hence responsibility, involving heritage managers, conservators, planners, funding bodies, and international organizations. However, archaeologists today occupy the positions of facilitator and manager, this time in the service of Egypt as a modern nation. Some might claim that we also facilitate our academic ventures; none of us should forget that we are making a living from archaeology (Pyburn and Wilk 2000:79).

Foundational to colonial imperatives was the notion that subject cultures required management and regimes for articulating, mapping, and controlling resources such as their monumental past. Following these directives, individuals and organizations still insist that modern Egyptians are incapable of managing these resources, that they must be effectively administered and controlled by the West. Although ultimate decision making resides with the Egyptian antiquities service, it relies heavily on international archaeological investment for both fieldwork and preservation. One example is the effort of UNESCO and German engineers to relocate Abu Simbel after the construction of the Aswan High Dam. UNESCO's funding of the Nubia Museum in Aswan is another high-profile initiative that has become embroiled in controversy over questions of ethnicity, citizenship, and transnational culture (Smith 1999). Organizations such as UNESCO and the World Bank make recommendations and implement schemes that assign patrimony to certain groups and situate the extant traditions of groups, whether Nubians or Gurnawis, in new relationships that produce new notions of humanity's "common cultural foundation." This removes the local and undermines difference in the service of the global. Heritage sites act as markers that signify the identity of the place and its rank within the scheme of world heritage. And the prime mover for these designations is commonly international tourism, which ultimately universalizes culture and society within an implicitly Western framework (Lanfant, Allcock, and Bruner 1995). As archaeologists and heritage practitioners, we are entering a new era of accountability in which we are increasingly answerable to an ever-expanding web of institutions and individuals (Strathern 2000c), not least the foreign communities in which we work.

Touring Places and the Spaces of Resistance

In 1991 Egypt reformed its economic system to embrace liberalization and privatization, including deregulation and financial stimuli to attract private-sector interest. The Egyptian minister for tourism and civil aviation claimed that the government's pricing policy reflected market forces, and, with the floating of the Egyptian pound, the country has been able to keep prices low, making travel to Egypt for foreigners attractive (Jenner and Smith 1993:134). The early 1990s also witnessed major changes in the operations of the Egyptian state tourism organization. A tourism development unit was created with funding from UN agencies, the World Bank, private banks, and the Ministry of Tourism.

The World Bank and the Egyptian government undertook a joint project to develop a US$300 million fund to preserve the environment in the face of tourist development (Jenner and Smith 1993:140–141). Despite its accounting for only 1.2 percent of the gross domestic product, tourism remains Egypt's largest single source of foreign exchange earnings (approximately 23 percent), generating around US$3 billion annually in 1998–2000 and employing 145,000 people (Huband 2001:134). Since the political instability and violence of the early 1990s the market has been inclined toward specific sectors: the young budget traveler, the diver, and the domestic traveler.

The tourist industry combines services, culture, and ethnicity and results in a product that unifies and packages society, culture, and identity. It exploits cultural heritage as a resource to be maximized (Lanfant, Allcock, and Bruner 1995:98–99). In numerous tourism publications, economists seek to quantify these elusive sociocultural factors in their cost-benefit analyses, but economic changes are commonly imputed to be positive and sociocultural ones negative, thereby widening the gap between the two (Lanfant, Allcock, and Bruner 1995:109). For the people of Egypt, the economic benefits of tourism are often less than anticipated. North American and Western European companies are responsible for the majority of the tourist investment in the developing world, and this is by no means a charitable venture; the transnationals involved retain the bulk of this tourist expenditure, only 22–25 percent of the retail price remaining in the host country (Urry 1990:64–65). Thus we have to ask whether many developing countries have alternatives to tourism as a development strategy. While there are serious economic as well as social costs, in the absence of alternatives developing countries have little choice but to develop their attractiveness as objects of the gaze of tourists from North America, Western Europe, and Japan. According to Urry (1990:132), the sovereignty of the consumer and trends in popular taste combine to transform the museum's social role. As we will see in the case of the planned open-air museum at Gurna, the overwhelming mass of the population will inevitably be excluded, and this exclusion is linked to a transformation of the nature of citizenship. People who live in a particular place have enjoyed certain rights and duties by virtue of that residence; citizenship has been not just a matter of national rights and duties but also a matter of locality (Urry 1995:220). While heritage politics generally concerns the local, the specificities of place, it is by no means removed from broader spatialities. Sanctioned heritage becomes part of national imaginings (Jacobs 1996:36), and local sites are heavily involved in global processes of commodification. The politics of identity is undeniably also a politics of place and thus an unbounded geography of difference and contest.

There are real tensions in the state's attempts to embrace Western tourism on a grand scale—to reap the rewards of its revenues and provide an experience for foreigners that neither detracts from the glories of the past nor subjects visitors to the harsh realities of Egypt's socioeconomic deprivations and the anti-Western sentiments of a militant minority. Thus, in situating archaeology and its relationship to the modern Egyptian state in global terms, several themes emerge. First, the concept of touring modern Egypt is constructed primarily around a privileging of its Pharaonic and, to a lesser degree, its Classical antecedents. Pharaonic Egypt is reified more than its later hybrid counterparts. The state and many archaeologists who have worked within its boundaries tend to describe Egypt not in terms of a historical continuum but as a series of unrelated parts forming a chain of "decline." Periods later than the Pharaonic are underappreciated and understudied. This reductive strategy affects archaeologists and their research agendas as well as tourists and governmental tourist authorities. As Fahim (2001:10–11) puts it, modern Egypt is still represented as

> two contrasting cultures that co-existed side by side: one was ancient and great while the modern way of life was still medieval and backward. It is ironic to observe that this dual presentation of Egypt's cultural image that dominated the writings of most nineteenth-century European travellers is still used by both European and Egyptian travel agencies to promote tourism and attract individuals and groups to visit Egypt today. I view this practice as alarmingly counter-productive because of the potential conflict of interest between the local and foreign tourist industries and the country's aspirations and efforts to present its image in the eyes and minds of its own people and the outside world as an integrated culture, rather than a polarised one with its potentially serious social and political implications.

As have many developing countries, Egypt has employed cultural tourism as a means to modernization, transforming its heritage into a tourist product and profit-making capital. This entails a cultural involution in which it must construct its future by clinging to its unique past. Thus modern Egypt has to return to its Pharaonic heritage in order to construct a suite of tourist-recognized symbols of identity (Lanfant,

Allcock, and Bruner 1995:105). What can archaeologists do in this situation? They can focus their work on the full spectrum of Egyptian history, including all its disparate and divergent groups through time, and they can work more closely with various communities and become more proactive in the tourist sphere. Caroline Simpson (2000, 2001), for example, a sometime resident of Gurna, has helped to promote a new vision of the Gurnawis' modern history through the establishment of a heritage center called Gurna Discovery. It seems to me an embarrassment to the discipline that it was left to a nonarchaeologist to facilitate the positive presentation of this previously disenfranchised group.

Archaeology can be productively used in the service of indigenous groups by reconstructing heritage that has been lost through conquest and deprivation, and, as Pyburn and Wilk (2000:79) submit, "archaeologists can also offer real support for developing tourism, jobs, crafts industries, self-respect, education, and public awareness. . . . Educational outreach must go beyond attempts to instill a preservation ethic in school-age children." Here again we see that heritage, tourism, and local politics are inseparable. In Egypt as in many places, tourists' desire for authenticity induces them to compromise the physical stability of heritage sites, eroding their symbolic value in the process. Tourist authorities should be educated to consider travel not simply in commercial terms but as an opportunity to initiate a cultural dialogue between residents and visitors; learning how to be a responsible tourist should be integral to learning how to be a tourist (El-Din 1999:1). Moreover, the tourism industry exploits archaeology for commercial gain and should therefore promote better direct communication with professional archaeologists, and archaeologists must become willing to enter into such dialogue (Herscher and McManamon 2000:50). All stakeholders must communicate more with each other, whether they participate in government, tourist, heritage, or archaeological spheres or happen to dwell among the ancients.

Dead Subjects and Living Communities

Within the archaeological community it has long been said that, because of the impact of Islam, the Egyptian people have no special relationship with antiquity and are largely uninterested in knowing about their past, much less in preserving it. This suggestion assumes a single, normative set of relationships with the past and allows Western scholars to continue their current practices in Egypt in time-honored ways. Gurna is a case in point (Meskell 2001; van der Spek 1998).

Timothy Mitchell (2002:chap. 6) has explored the complex machina-
tions between the Egyptian government and one local community
involving the forced relocation of the Gurnawis, the tourist trade, and
the development of an open-air museum. He focuses upon the desperate
attempts of the local people to reclaim their homes and their only
source of income. This struggle involves diverse local groups and top-
down global pressures stemming from notions of shared world heritage.
Having excavated in the Valley of the Nobles for several field seasons,
I understand the threat of destruction, the escalating pressures of
tourism, and the fractious relationships between archaeologists, tourists,
and Gurnawis. As archaeologists we become part of the tourist spectacle.
Groups of visitors trekking to the famed tomb of Sennefer would see
us working in the courtyard of an adjacent tomb and begin photo-
graphing us, asking us questions (typically "Have you found any gold?")
or breaching the security cordon to enter the excavation area. We too
became part of a tour that they had paid for, and many felt that they
had a right to see archaeology performed.

Archaeologists are an important part of the political mix. The
professional Egyptologists of Luxor have been instrumental in offering
human-impact assessments at Gurna. Not surprisingly, they have
opposed the "deleterious impact of the village upon the stability and
preservation of the tombs [due to] theft, erosion, building, and vandal-
ism," arguing that the presence of a community here is "disastrous to
the survival of the tombs" (van der Spek 1998). Both Egyptologists and
tourism officials continue to describe Gurna as an ancient Egyptian
landscape, devoid of its living community and its own unique heritage,
again reiterating the fantasy that *our subjects are dead*. Privileging the
ancients has been further reinforced by several ICOMOS recommendations released in June 2001: that the plan for the site should identify
(1) the archaeological areas that must be explored and protected, (2)
the houses that should be conserved and the conditions (building
materials, management of water, etc.) required to allow some residents
to continue living in the village, (3) visiting trails and the use of those
constructions that would be left vacant pending the assessment of the
potential for important archaeological strata, and (4) the appropriate
location of functions and activities that are not compatible with the
safeguarding of the site (commerce, etc.).

The situation at Gurna has not been resolved. We are being asked to
prioritize the dead over the living, and this has uncomfortable repercussions. Western intervention has a long, complex and unpleasant history.
"Archaeology cleared the way for excavation and tourism by evicting

villagers from homes in the temples of Luxor and Edfu. . . . The uneven personal and regional benefits and costs of tourism, the tensions between insensitive tourists and conservative villagers, folk-beliefs about the fertility-inducing power of antiquities, and the antipharaonism of Islamist purists are all pieces of an as yet little-known puzzle" (Reid 1985:139–140).

Relocating the people of Gurna has been a governmental imperative for decades. In the past ten years state authorities have deployed bulldozers, armed police officials, tourism investors, and U.S. and World Bank consultants, and the heritage industry has made use of violence in pursuit of its goals. In one attempt at relocation four people were killed and another twenty-five or more were injured. In 1998 the head of the Luxor City Council was quoted in *Al-Ahram* as saying that the shantytown of Old Gurna would have to be depopulated because "you can't afford to have this heritage wasted because of informal houses being built in an uncivilized manner" (see also Mitchell 2002:196). Yet Gurna is not an isolated instance. The Egyptian government has also tried to move families away from the pyramid at Meidum, the temples in Esna and Edfu, and the Great Pyramids in Giza. Some years ago officials succeeded in removing from Gurna some thirteen hundred families who lived in traditional mud-brick houses directly on top of the four hundred Tombs of the Nobles, a major tourist attraction. Many of these Gurnawis are now housed in newly built concrete buildings in a nearby village set up largely by Egypt's armed forces. While some may see this as a step toward modernization, the concrete constructions are less well-suited to the Egyptian climate than traditional ones and could be perceived as alienating in specific context. It is clear that violence, both real and symbolic, has been done to the Gurnawis, ironically in the name of their own national heritage. The global remains privileged territory.

It has long been held that for Luxor to reach its full heritage (read tourist) potential, the village of Gurna would have to be depopulated. In 1982 the World Bank hired U.S. consultants to devise plans for enhancing tourist revenues; the same group had been hired for the same purpose in 1953. This revenue was to be derived from the promotion of high-end tourism: the development of luxury hotels and Nile cruise ships. The government then spent US$60 million, more than half of it borrowed from the World Bank to pay for foreign expertise, on certain improvements (Mitchell 2002:196). The preferred visitor management scheme aimed to promote the physical separation of tourists from the local community by means of separate transportation, restaurants, and shops. For instance, one of the plans included an enclosed visitor center, complete with restaurant and shops, that shielded tourists from any unnecessary engagement with the Gurnawis. Another plan involved an elevated walkway over one village, allowing visitors to move from their luxury coaches to adjacent archaeological sites while avoiding the village. The tourists would literally walk above the villagers, making concrete the perceived hierarchical distinction between foreigners and locals. To date, neither of these plans has come to fruition.

A striking parallel is the forced relocation of the Bidul Bedouin, who once lived in caves at the site of Petra, Jordan. The Jordanian government positioned the Bedouin as remnants of a premodern era whose lifeways were at odds with a new vision of modernity. In Fabian's terms, any discourse that marks the "primitive" is one that already precludes observation or study: it is a temporal concept employed as a distancing device between observer and observed. While the Bidul (similarly to the Gurnawi) could be marketed as a tourist attraction, they embodied troubling temporal notions concerning "progress," "evolution," and "modernity" (Massad 2001:73–79). The image of the nation is often apprehended through the tourist gaze. Cultural tourism relies on the existence of difference, and while modern nation-states suppress cultural difference within their borders they are eager to market their ethnic minorities for tourism revenue (Crick 1994:6). Ultimately, however, the government's plan had always involved their permanent removal. Strategies for relocating the Bidul since the 1960s have included ideas about returning them to farming (again, similarly to the Gurnawi situation) so that Petra could become an open-air tourist museum free from the incursions of its native inhabitants. In the 1970s there was armed resistance against the government's initiatives, and in the 1980s a permanent settlement was built for the Bidul (Massad 2001:79). Both Luxor and Petra were deemed too central to their nations' identity and heritage to have these indices of modernity undermined by an undesirable group and its particular lifeways.

While problems abound, ethical solutions remain scarce on the ground. One tactical shift that might alleviate tensions between communities would focus on conserving "history" rather than simply historic sites. The tendency of conventional conservation approaches to naturalize historic resources (Hufford 1994:6–7) reflects a purist notion of the past that also serves to dehistoricize them, divorcing them from their other histories and contemporary interpolations. Heritage is not the same as history: "Heritage is history processed through mythology, ideology, nationalism, local pride, romantic ideas, or just plain marketing into commodity" (Schouten 1995:21). By shifting attention from *sites* and *structures* to a more dynamic conception of the past, including its multiple manifestations and uses through time, we might more fully appreciate and accommodate living communities. Since touring historic sites involves a particular experience of the materiality of the past, it might similarly encompass contemporary spheres of interaction that could include local residents, archaeologists, and other interest groups. On the one hand, this is more akin to an "archaeology within anthropology" approach. Such an approach should find special support from North American archaeology, since it is already housed within anthropology departments. On the other hand, this perspective finds resonance in innovative trends in tourism research that demarcate heterogeneous tourist space as a multipurpose space in which boundaries are blurred and a wide range of activities and people may coexist. Such a space provides stages where transitional identities may be performed alongside the everyday actions of residents, passersby, and workers (Edensor 2001:64), what might be deemed a "heterotopia" in Foucauldian terms. In sum, conserving multiple histories rather than simply the site, including many lines of heritage rather than privileging a singular story line, is one way of ameliorating the contention inherent in situations such as those described in Egypt and Jordan (see also Scham and Yahya 2003 on Palestine). Adopting a more inclusive, more anthropological approach to the archaeological past in which past and present act productively for a greater number of stakeholders and audiences will accommodate contemporary concerns and communities within an inclusive framework of cultural and temporal difference.

Tourism and Terrorism on the West Bank

Gurna was a major tourist center until an attack on the Temple of Hatshepsut by Muslim extremists in November 1997 took the lives of fifty-eight foreigners and four Egyptians. Local people are reported to have chased the gunmen armed only with sticks and then spat at their bodies as they were brought down from the surrounding hills. Some are said to have wanted to burn the militants' bodies in their disgust: "They were so ugly. They were not from here. They were not Egyptians. They were mad, evil, not God's people. . . . They were others, alien, not like us" (interviews conducted with Caroline Simpson, November 19, 1997). Many Egyptians who were interviewed by the foreign press distanced themselves from the terrorist attack, declaring that it did not represent Muslim sentiments and could never be condoned. The attack severely damaged Egypt's lucrative tourism industry. Figures from Egypt's tourist authority show a drop of 12.8 percent, equating to a decline of 56.8 percent in numbers of tourist nights spent in Egypt. From 1997 to 1998 revenue fell from US$3.7 billion to $2.5 billion (Travel Industry World Yearbook 1998–1999:131). While a few Egyptologists reported the news on various web sites, the topic did not fuel further discussion; it was considered an extreme instance in an escalating series of attacks on tourists over the past few years. This silence is part of a wider malaise in Egyptology as a discipline. Egyptologists have convinced themselves that they have little to do with the lived experience of people like the Gurnawis. They remain outside the processes at work, processes that they are deeply involved in by the nature of their work and the very subject matter of archaeology.

The 1997 massacre is a nodal point in political, religious, economic, social, and spatial terms. This violent assault on one of the most iconic monuments of the pharaonic past was directed primarily against tourists. The visual spectacle of the temple's space has long been recognized and it is similarly celebrated as a performance space: the opera *Aïda* is often performed there, and in fact President Hosni Mubarak himself had attended a performance there a month before the attack. The temple's history became part of the media coverage, as Swain (1997) reports: "Some of the worst savagery took place at the sanctuary of Anubis, the ancient god of embalming and the dead who is represented by the heads of a jackal. Blood and pieces of human flesh stuck to the walls and high ceiling as the terrorists shot and slashed at their victims with knives, making the chamber with its beautiful bas-reliefs look like a primitive slaughterhouse." Ancient grandeur and modern savagery is a common bifurcation in the media's construction of Egypt, with the decline of civilization due to the impact of Islam alluded to throughout.

The Temple of Hatshepsut is a major tourist site and a popular stopping point on the journey to Luxor (Fig. 5.1). Reports from the Egyptian authorities suggested that the attack was primarily aimed at the police and security forces, but this was generally assumed to be a government strategy to allay fears and minimize damage to the tourist industry. There had been similar attacks in April 1997, when militants shot nineteen Greek tourists, believing them to be Israelis, outside their hotel near the Giza pyramids. Another terrorist assault occurred in Cairo in September of that year. Gunmen ambushed another tourist bus in front of the Cairo Museum, killing nine tourists and wounding another nineteen. This famous place, which houses the treasures of Tutankhamun

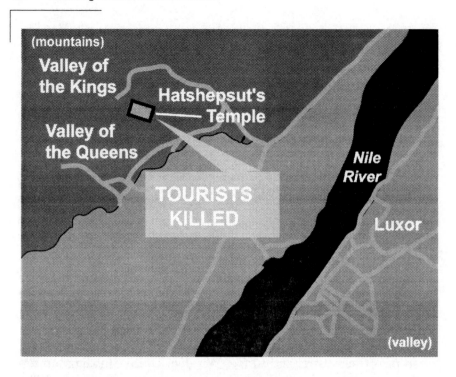

Figure 5.1. The Luxor area, showing the location of the 1997 attack.

and thousands of other archaeological masterpieces, is a key tourist site for almost every visitor to Egypt. Clearly tourists were the prime targets, ensuring global coverage for the militant cause and maximum damage to the national economy and worldwide profile. A leaflet found in the fatal stomach wound of one Japanese tourist at Hatshepsut's temple read *No Tourists in Egypt—Omar Abdel-Rahman's Squadron of Havoc and Destruction* (Sennott 1997). The Gemaa Islamiya's leader, Talaat Fuad Qasim, interviewed in 1995, called tourism "an abomination, a means by which prostitution and AIDS are spread by Jewish women tourists" (*Economist* 1997). It has been claimed that between 1992 and 1997 some one thousand Egyptians—police, officials, Coptic Christians, and left-wing intellectuals—were also killed.

The press coverage in Britain and the United States in 1997 focused heavily on two themes: tourism and terrorism. The first is couched in terms of Egypt's financial decline as a result of damage to its second-largest source of foreign economic injection. British newspapers used the Luxor incident to brand the Middle East as the locus of political violence and terrorism, and some writers demonized Islam in a manner that could only be described as racist and Orientalist. Walter Ellis (1997) of the *Sunday Times* declared that "right from the beginning Islam was associated with violence." These are sentiments that resurfaced after the events of September 11 in a wave of retaliations against Muslims in the United States and also in Europe and Australia. Islam as a religion has no specific agenda against touring or tourists. On the contrary, there is much in Islam that implicitly and explicitly accepts the notion of travel and encourages it; an obvious example is the pilgrimage to the holy sites of Mecca and Medina. Why, then, have tourists become such a attractive target? Heba Aziz (1995:93) argues that in Upper Egypt there is an enormous gap between tourism development (such as Nile cruises) and the development in the area itself and that the tourist industry actively promotes this phenomenon as an attraction. In many developing countries the socioeconomic inequalities between hosts and guests are extreme, and the atmosphere of relaxation and indulgence is set against poverty and desperation without any obvious benefits in terms of local development or employment opportunities. In such inflamed contexts tourism introduces the behavior of a wasteful society into the midst of the society of want (Aziz 1995:93). Tourists in their luxury ghettos are the most visible signifiers of Western domination; the wealth and comfort of the "have" societies is juxtaposed with all the moral, religious, and social values of the "want" society. Perhaps unsurprisingly, a large percentage of the Muslim activists are clustered in Upper Egypt, where tourism proliferates; 83.5 percent of the particularly militant activists are younger than twenty-five years old, and the majority belong to a low socioeconomic group (Aziz 1995:94). This disenfranchised group has targeted tourism as a symbol of the new global economy and their exclusion from its benefits while similarly wounding Mubarak's government in terms of its international profile.

Apart from blatant anti-Muslim sentiment, colonial incursions into Egypt were also foregrounded in the subsequent media frenzy. Britain's most conservative newspaper, the *Times,* reported that "Britain has a special relationship with the Valley of the Kings, where almost exactly 75 years ago—on November 30, 1922—*The Times* was first to tell the world of the discovery of the tomb of Tutankhamen by Howard Carter and the Earl of Carnarvon" (Murphy 1997:3). In the same issue an article entitled "Blood on the Nile" proclaimed the "shame of ordinary Egyptians that a country that was the cradle of civilisation should now be associated with such barbarity." The invocation of this familiar trope—the cradle of civilization—highlights the paternalistic and colonialist implications of considering the nation's infancy its crowning achievement. In Orientalist fashion, this suggests that these countries of the Middle East have never surpassed their early glories and that the torch of civilization has since passed to Europe. The most offensive coverage of the massacre in the *Times*, by Simon Jenkins (1997), drew heavily on stereotypes of Oriental despotism and violence:

> When the Assyrian warrior Ashurbanipal descended on Thebes in the 7th century BC, he razed it to the ground. This first great terrorist boasted that he took the entire city. . . . Monday's massacre on the site of that city saw a new Assyrian terror, from fanatical opponents of Islamic reform. But whereas Ashurbanipal terrorised by laying waste to an entire city, the death squads of al-Gamaa al-Islamiya needed only to machine-gun a busload of Western tourists: A dead Westerner is a media ticket to ride.

He went on to appropriate Egypt as an extension of the known world of England: "We know these places. The path to the Sphinx, the Corniche at Luxor, the drive to the Valley of the Kings are corners of a foreign field that have become forever England. Machine gun us there and you machine gun us in our own backyard, surrounded by cultural family and friends." This sentiment was transferred to Egypt's monuments, too, in the language of global world heritage. Jenkins argues that the Temple of Hatshepsut "no longer 'belongs' to Egypt, but to the world. It is being restored by European archaeologists with UNESCO money. To the fundamentalist, Luxor is a cultural colony, occupied by the armies of world tourism." Foreign intervention in the form of USAID, the World Bank, UNESCO, and so on, is seen as a means of appropriating, controlling, and owning Egypt's cultural resources as part of a shared global property (Meskell 2002b). Inevitably this property is wrested from Egypt and incorporated into Western heritage. Jenkins's article was illustrated by a cartoon depicting two pyramids composed entirely of the bodies of slain tourists that was both insensitive and insightful, combining national heritage, archaeology, tourism, and violence before the colonialist gaze.

Performing Ancient Egypt

Severing ties with antiquity underscores all narratives about a contemporary lack of interest in the past and inflects both tourist and heritage practice in Egypt. It serves as an implicit acknowledgment that modern and ancient Egyptians share no lineage whatsoever and that the former are simply the recalcitrant caretakers of the latter's legacy,

Figure 5.2. Ancient agricultural enactment from the Pharaonic Village, Cairo.

"minding the store" in metaphoric and literal terms—explicitly cashing in on a past that has little relevance within a predominantly Muslim Egypt. All of these tensions come to the fore in the shape of one very famous tourist locale in Egypt, Cairo's premier theme park, the Pharaonic Village (Fig. 5.2). Here tensions over religion, nation, authenticity, and performance of the past by both "colonized" and "colonizer" are enunciated. As a heritage locus for the *longue durée* of Egyptian history, the Pharaonic Village evinces the latent problems in attracting tourists to later periods, undoubtedly because they do not traditionally tour Christian and Islamic sites and are therefore lack the knowledge and interest required to make history heritage.

Dr. Hassan Ragab spent ten years and over US$6 million creating the Pharaonic Village, which was opened in 1984. The official web site for the village claims that ancient Egypt is "brought to life by an incredible group of actors and actresses, faithful and exact reproductions of buildings, clothing, and lifestyles . . . to create the most precise *living* recreation of the golden days of Pharaonic Egypt" (http://touregypt.net/village). The village covers 150,000 square meters at Ya'aqoob Island, Giza, close to downtown Cairo. It is claimed that some three hundred people supposedly live in an "ancient Egyptian atmosphere and practice various agricultural and industrial activities with the same tools and implements used in antiquity." Claims with regard to authenticity are paramount. Official web sites declare that while "the city of Cairo surrounds the island, not a trace of it penetrates the thick wall of trees planted around the island," thus screening the vestiges of modern life and making visitors feel as if they had gone back five thousand years in history.

Tourists usually visit the site as part of organized package tours and are transported through the island village on barges moving along canals, accompanied by a fixed soundtrack in a specific language. Since groups are confined to their boats, their movements and sightlines are deliberately restricted. The tourist gaze is directed solely toward the costumed actors as they perform their repetitive roles. Visitors are screened from viewing the mundane objects of modern life in Cairo: brick walls, construction zones, and other scenes of everyday life such as young men fishing on the Nile. Timing is also tightly controlled; the staged vignettes of life, such as the threshing of grain or boat building, are performed in quick succession. Many of the workers look complacent or dejected at the futility of the repetitive simulacra (Slyomovics 1989). Perhaps even more disruptive are the moments when actors, breaking out of their designated roles, wave back at the tourists or ask them if they want additional photos. There is something wonderful about these resistances, which offer relief from the monotony of the staged acts. The uncomfortable modalities of power are suddenly thrown into sharp relief or perhaps even inverted as the objects of the gaze disrupt the aura and distance that the tourist desires. As Urry (1990:66–67) argues,

> The tourist gaze is structured by culturally specific notions of what is extraordinary and therefore worth viewing. This means that the services provided, which may of course be incidental to the gaze itself, must take a form which does not contradict or undermine the quality of the gaze, and ideally should enhance it. This in turn poses, as we shall see, immense problems of management of such industries, to ensure that the service provided by the often relatively poor paid service workers is appropriate to the almost sacred quality of the visitors' gaze on some longed-for and remarkable tourist site.

Tourists are also asked to perform at the Pharaonic Village, but they do not assume the roles of "ordinary people" as do their local counterparts. Rather, they are dressed and photographed as ancient pharaohs and queens, fulfilling additional colonial desires about power, beauty, and otherness. The absurdity of middle-aged European and Japanese tourists' living out their fantasies of being Rameses or Cleopatra needs little explication. Such forms of cultural tourism are strongly influenced by

Figure 5.3. Tour guide with tourists and performer at the Pharaonic Village, Cairo.

the longing to experience otherness, a desire that developed during the colonial era (Edensor 1998:22). Being photographed in luxurious, quasi-royal settings provides another means of purchasing and consuming visual property and specific cultural histories: no one dresses up as an agricultural laborer or a weaver. And there are additional difficulties over authenticity with regard to the pharaonic clothing worn by the participants, particularly for women. The representation of pharaonic life is restricted by the confines of Islamic protocols, with the result that the actors' garments form a strange hybrid of modern styles and ancient motifs (Fig. 5.3). The coherence of most tourist (and host) performances depends on their being performed in such specific "theaters."

Several years ago it was decided to integrate Islamic history into the narrative experience of the Pharaonic Village. After visiting the United States, Abdel-Salam Ragab felt that Westerners did not have a clear picture of Islam. One employee stated that "Islamic culture is part of Egypt's history, and therefore we found it suitable to have it included alongside the pharaonic." Another argued that "the aim of this museum is to educate everybody about this great civilization. The image of Islam abroad is that of fundamentalists and terrorists. People should know that this is not correct, and that Islam has a glorious history and civilization, and that it produced great philosophers and scientists" (http://www.ahram.org.eg/weekly/1998/393/tr1.htm). Here again tourism and terrorism are conjoined in the specter of Islamic fundamentalism, again an inflamed association in the aftermath of September

11. But, sadly, few Western tourists are interested in the Muslim museum or, for that matter, the Coptic museum, and most choose to skip those parts of the tour. Visitors want to see how the pyramids were built or what a nobleman's house was like; they do not care to see how more recent (perhaps, oddly, less familiar) Egyptian histories are articulated and presented. Given that both appear very late on the tour, it is not surprising that many feel exhausted and overwhelmed by another history lesson with which they feel unconnected. While many visitors may have been exposed to pharaonic Egyptian materials in the Metropolitan, the Louvre, and the British Museum, few may have been educated about Late Antique or Muslim culture and history. These periods certainly lack the essential exoticism that marks ancient Egypt as the quintessential *other*.

Conclusions

The terrain covered in this chapter is necessarily messy. Archaeology cannot remain inviolate, since it inhabits a number of domains— landscapes, ethnoscapes, finanscapes, mediascapes, and ideoscapes, to use Appadurai's (1990:296) familiar taxonomy. Archaeological materials and practitioners are instrumental in the production and marketing of heritage sites, working with diverse governments and communities and ultimately providing the raw materials for a burgeoning global tourist economy. The past is also instrumental in political debates, from local-level community tensions as witnessed at Gurna to the more insidious agendas at the global level evidenced by the media coverage of the 1997 attacks. While phrases such as "global village" may seem appropriate, given that expansionary industrial capitalism and modern communications technology have unified the world and set in train various processes of cultural homogenization, they mask the continued inequitable reality of localism—of cultural and ethnic particularism—in the contemporary world (Crick 1994:6). Tourists and archaeologists both participate in colonialist and Orientalist fantasies while touring Egypt. And, while it may appear to be an excessive claim, El Saadawi (1997: 168–169) suggests that "Egyptology is an example of cultural genocide or terrorism, in which a whole nation and its civilization and philosophy are violently reduced to a few stones or ruins . . . [to be] looked at by tourists." In developing nations such as Egypt, specialized archaeological and conservation expertise may be wanting, but we must question whether the advantages of Western technology give us *rights* (legal or moral) to the heritage of others. With future funds and training, indigenous Egyptology may attain additional control over its own past and thereby challenge the West's ideological monopoly (Wood 1998: 192). The impossibility is extricating archaeology from the dense web of consequences that it inspires. Archaeologists are both products and producers of the political, and herein lies the primary reason for our engagement with ethics.

Archaeologists are arbiters of the past for myriad stakeholders and communities, and by virtue of the discipline's ventriloquism we occupy the important and responsible role of translator for past cultures and individuals. Yet how that role is defined and performed is negotiable. Traditionally, archaeologists have presented themselves as "trustees" of the past, albeit without explicit acknowledgment, in both legal and practical arenas, but their role is more akin to the contractor's. As Scham (1998:302–303) proposes, there is much to be derived from the notion of the archaeologist as trustee—someone required to defend property from adverse interests. By the nature of our destructive work, we are placed in the unique position of informed interpreters with access to the past in the present. This confers upon us a particular burden different from that of historians, who can repeatedly reconstitute past events. Our position diverges from that of ethnographers, too, since their interpretive constructions are changeable (premised on theoretical positionality) and rarely susceptible to the popular deployment of archaeology's materiality. Beyond heuristics, archaeological remains are more than objects of memory: they are instantiated in the present and in present-day politics.

Politics and ethics are two sides of the same coin: both are constructed and need to be understood contextually. Ethics is neither neutral nor value-free, although it retains a deceptively positive aura. Ethical discourse has only recently reached archaeology, and, while national codes have been a topic of growing interest in the United States, Canada, Australia, England, and elsewhere, they cannot simply be extrapolated to archaeological practice in foreign contexts. Few have even considered this a salient issue, particularly those who work in the shadow of empire, as in Egypt. Archaeologists cannot uncritically impose Western liberal, economic rationalist, or preservationist values upon all other cultural milieus. Moreover, ethics should properly occupy a shifting terrain, one that is under constant negotiation with divergent interest groups. This promises to make field practice more complex, since archaeologists will need to be more cognizant and considerate of other parties, specifically local governments and communities (Moser et al. 2002). We will have to consult, collaborate, negotiate, incorporate,

and be willing to forgo our own research agendas—something archaeologists have been reluctant to do. Undoubtedly, archaeological practice
will be fraught—more complex and conflictual—and attuned to a
critical, postmodern vision of ethics. Constructions of heritage may
then emerge as more networked and developmental. Heritage as a
disciplinary locus may then be redefined, giving serious weight to living
communities and shared histories rather than merely the physical sites
that have traditionally been prioritized. Through this convergence we
can address our ethical responsibility in the contemporary world,
helping archaeology to move beyond the paradigm of dead subjects
toward a new vision of lived histories.

Pain, Politics, and the Epistemological Ethics of Anthropological Disciplinarity

Pradeep Jeganathan

On February 14, 2002, I stood in a packed seminar room at the Eastern University in Chenkaladi, a few miles north of the town of Batticoloa in the Eastern Province of Sri Lanka, preparing to spend an hour with the second-year undergraduate sociology concentrators, who were taking a course on nationalism with my friend and colleague Suresh Sivaraman.[1] As we were driving up to the campus on the road of stunning beauty that leads north of the city—the still, almost gray waters of the lagoon on one side, yellow-green fields on the other—I had suggested a lecture on Anderson's (1984) *Imagined Communities*. "It is so canonical, maybe I should do it?" I had asked, and he had kept driving, smiling to himself. I had wondered to myself why he did not teach it.

It was my fifth day in Batticoloa on this trip, my first since 1987. Then as well as now, what I saw and felt as I moved around the district was a scene of devastation so awesome as to defy description: a world turned inside out, both stunned and animated by its grotesqueness. In 1987 Batticoloa had begun to experience the authority of the Special Task Force, a newly formed commando unit of the government of Sri Lanka that had tortured and massacred, arrested and disappeared thousands in an attempt at pacification. By 2002 the Liberation Tigers of Tamil Eelam (LTTE), the militant face of Tamil nationalism, had responded with great force, pushing back the government forces with their own. Now there was a stalemate. In the months before my arrival a new

147

regime had been elected in the South on a platform of peace, and a de facto cease-fire was in place. Soon a formal memorandum of understanding between the LTTE and the Sri Lankan government, audited by the Norwegian government, was to be signed. Militant Tamil nationalism was triumphant, finally claiming the land that it had fought for with parliamentary, extraparliamentary, and militant means for over fifty years. As we drove, Suresh would point to places at the edge of a road or on the banks of the lagoon and explain the logic of the massacres that marked them. I listened, trying to remember every detail.

The campus of the Eastern University, which was founded in 1987, is imposing and well kept. Its library is rather good and faculty offices well supplied; I had spent time on the campus two days before, when I gave a faculty seminar on subaltern studies. It had gone well, and a stimulating discussion had ensued. My lecture today was different, for it was for students, rather more pedagogic than a seminar. Suresh was to provide a simultaneous translation, because I knew that my academic Tamil, unlike my Sinhala, would not hold up to sociology, which in this university as in others in Sri Lanka would parallel anthropology in an American one. I proceeded with questions and answers, marker weaving on the whiteboard, to set up what I took to be a lecture that I was fluent in and had given several times, at the University of Chicago and University of Minnesota, where I have taught. The simple point of this twenty-minute presentation was to delineate and amplify Anderson's concept of the "imagined" and go on to contrast it with others. Ten minutes into the presentation I could see that questions had arisen. I consulted with Suresh, noting that "imagined" needed to be translated carefully. He agreed, noting in turn that the Tamil word lacked the nuance I was trying to convey. I agreed but wanted my elaboration to be spelled out, and he went to a good deal of effort to do so. "Imagined," he explained carefully, in Anderson's usage did not amount to "made-up." Not at all.

When several junior lecturers who were sitting in—for by this time the event had taken on the tenor and style of a public lecture—rose to speak in English, it was clear to me that our disagreement was not a product of a mistranslation or misunderstanding but something far deeper. "Why do we need this theory at all?" one philosopher asked, and another literary critic urged me to abandon Anderson for Fanon and Cabral. The point, at one level, was that I was suggesting that nationalism and therefore Tamil nationalism was imaginary, and that was unacceptable. Yes, it was understood that "imaginary" was not the same as "made-up," but why even conceptualize "imagined communities?" I replied that the "imagined" and "imaginary" were powerful, flexible ideas that could do important analytical work and, furthermore—the professor in me asserting itself—Anderson's work was canonical in the study of nationalism and we needed to understand it before we set it aside, as I was happy to do, for Fanon or Cabral.

As the discussion grew more intense, I recalled that some of the students and several of the junior lecturers had photocopies of and had read in a discussion group the previous night a short essay of mine published in the Sri Lankan journal *Pravada* in 1998. In that essay I had argued for the importance of a particular kind of Tamil, the dissenting Tamil, who seemed to have disappeared from our landscape. Such a Tamil, I had argued, would be one who did not, in the current context, see the Liberation Tigers of Tamil Eelam, as his or her sole representative. In fact, I had written plainly and clearly, as a Tamil, that the LTTE did not represent me. I had sought to dissent as a Tamil. It struck me as I faced the question of the "imagined" qualities of nationalism that I was being viewed here not just as a visiting professor from Minnesota taking a position on nationalism but as the very same fellow who had written "Who Are the Tamils?"

There flashed through my mind as I spoke—breathing deeply to keep my composure in face of the force of the responses, listening carefully to the opposing arguments, insisting with all the effort that I could muster on the merit of my own position—passages from two essays that I find I carry with me, Noam Chomsky's "The Responsibility of Intellectuals" (1967) and Partha Chatterjee's "Talking about Our Modernity in Two Languages" (1997). Chomsky's injunction, which I read one cold January evening in Cambridge after having heard him speak for the first time, is simple and hard: "The responsibility of an intellectual is to speak the truth and expose lies" (1967:325). The charge at least is clear, if the terms are always open to clarification.

What I remembered on this occasion about Chatterjee's essay was not his important argument about modernity but his unusual account of what I would call "dual location." Considering the power of hybridity as a concept but then setting it aside, Chatterjee wrote:

> But perhaps there is another figure that is far more ubiquitous in the history of non-Western modernities: that of the bilingual intellectual who is sometimes on one discursive terrain, sometimes on another, but never in between. He or she does not necessarily feel commanded to choose. When he is in the Western academy, he abides by the institutional rules of that academy. But he brings to it a set of intellectual concerns that

have emerged somewhere else. Those concerns put him or her in an uneasy and intensely contestatory position in relation to the prevailing disciplinary norms of those institutions. There is no comfortable normalized position for the bilingual intellectual in the Western academy.

On the other hand, when the same person is a participant in an intellectual arena shaped by a modern non-European language, he or she is conscious of being an active agent in the forming of the disciplines in that arena, far more so than would be the case with him or her in the Western academy. But this role in the non-Western intellectual field is, paradoxically, premised on one's membership in the Western academy. Whichever way one looks at it, therefore, the relation between the intellectual and the academy in the two cases is not symmetrical.

I had begun the lecture in the first mode, with a sense of my location in the Western or what I might call the metropolitan academy, where canons matter and traditions of scholarship are maintained within well-known rules and protocols. There are, of course, institutions in which such rules and protocols matter outside the metropole, in Delhi or Peradeniya,but the Eastern University at Chenkaladi is not of that mold. The arguments in that room were, in a word, militantly political, and I found myself wanting to shift from a metropolitan location that valued canons and disciplines and particular epistemological architectures to another in which I too could make militant political arguments within Tamil nationalism, a location I inhabit comfortably if very critically.

But to do so I would have had to abandon the former location, that of a disciplinary anthropologist, and move to a location in an oppositional political field of high stakes, a field where positions matter a great deal beyond their own articulation. Such a position, I suggest, is antithetical to what I will call the "epistemological ethics" of a disciplinary anthropologist. The rest of this chapter is offered as a careful attempt to clarify that line. But before I proceed into the thicket of that argument, let me elaborate a little, for I realize that I have prized apart here what is not supposed to be divided. Some will argue that Marx conjoined epistemology and politics in his theses on Feuerbach, but many others, not all that serious about Marx, will insist that they are both anthropologists and "always already" political.

In this chapter, I seek to raise a cautionary flag over this view. While, on the one hand, it may be readily conceded that all anthropological activity is political, as many would claim, it is easy to see that such a claim signifies little. Its significance must rest, then, on what counts as "politics" in relation to a given activity. As a first pass, it is useful to visit Carl Schmitt's ([1932] 1996) distinction between "politics" and "the political." For him "the political" is that space of activity in which the writ of the state does not hold with ease; it can be an arena of oppositional work. One does not have to be a Nazi to see that most claims about the politics of anthropological work depend on an argument about a location in what Schmitt would call "the political." My argument, counterintuitive and strange as it may be, is that such a location does not sit easily with the epistemological ethics of disciplinary anthropology.

An overview of what I mean by the epistemological ethics of anthropology may be helpful here. At the heart of my argument is an analogy between early modern European experimental science and anthropological fieldwork involving both the figure of the investigator and the protocols of securing evidence. The analogy depends not upon the collapsing of the social context between experimental science and anthropology or laboratory and field but rather on reflection at an epistemological level on the production of truth claims. My argument, in brief, is that securing anthropological knowledge requires a epistemological ethic of *disciplined affect.*

My journey to that core argument passes through the anthropological problem of the "tortured person," a move that at first glance may appear circuitous. While my argument about epistemological ethics in anthropology seeks to be a general one, I find it helpful to rehearse it in relation to the "tortured person" and the associated problem of pain. These problems throw my general arguments into sharp relief and may serve to clarify them.

Person, Pain, and Punishment

There is etched in my mind a moment in which I heard the sound of torture. I had thought of it before, thought through it before—but then I heard it: it sounded like a sharp breaking, like the snapping of a twig. I was in Colombo at the time—the late summer of 1987, during a lull in the fighting between the government of Sri Lanka and Tamil militant groups. I was working as a research assistant at the International Center for Ethnic Studies, and a colleague was describing a visit to the east of the country, which had been inaccessible to scholars and activists from Colombo because of government restrictions predicated on the ongoing war up until the cease-fire. In his presentation my colleague, Jeevan Thiyagaraja, described a routine practice of arrest, imprisonment, and interrogation then prevalent in the Batticoloa area. In particular, he described an interrogation practice of the Special Task Force that was known as the "helicopter" and consisted of a person's being hung by his thumbs, arms stretched and twisted, until they broke.[2] After this, I visited Batticoloa. Suresh had just started teaching at the university.

Let me say at the outset that I have no stable definition of "torture" to offer; in fact, Talal Asad (1997) has recently argued that the phrase, in the language of the United Nations, "cruel, inhuman, and degrading punishment," is quite "unstable" upon reflection. I do not take issue with his formulation; rather, I am most sympathetic to it. But here, instead of reiterating the argument concerning the instability of the category, I wish to map out the terrain of those instabilities in an effort to make them productive of knowledge about anthropology itself.

As a way into the problem, let me begin with the person. In his much-discussed essay on this question, Mauss (1985) draws a distinction between "persona," which can be seen as a "role," a "mask," or a "face," and "person," ultimately a moral, that is, a Christian being, an individuated part of Christ. Mauss then traces the "transformation" of this notion of the person into the notion of the self, which is tied to ideas of self-knowledge and consciousness—what might be called "interiority." This is not very far from Charles Taylor's notion of an interior self embedded within a person taken as moral being.[3] This Taylorian person is not simply calculating like a clock or a computer and, again, not simply agentive like the geyser Old Faithful, which does something in the world, such as spouting hot water regularly, but a respondent who thinks, knows, considers, judges, and acts guided by a capacity to make moral sense of the world.

Such a notion of the person, which undergirds, it seems, the very liberal social and political order upon which many things rest, is that of a person who can learn—be educated and cultivated externally and internally—but also, crucially, a re-formable person. In other words, in this scheme, a person who has acted transgressively in the moral order he is embedded in can be acted upon through a routine procedure so that his inner core—his self—can resignify the prior act in a new frame and attain the realization of remorse.

In fact, from a rather different perspective it is possible to argue, I think, that the very idea of the linkage of "remorse" and "re-form" was produced in eighteenth- and nineteenth-century European prisons—taken to be penitentiaries, inhabited by penitents.

Michael Ignatieff, in *A Just Measure of Pain* (1978), documents the emergence of these practices in early-nineteenth-century England and their institutionalization in Pentonville, a penitentiary—a key site of reform. And reform was predicated on the application of particular kinds of pain to the body of the person. Not only was the inner self of the person available for reform—incarceration was rare in the 1770s, exile being far more common—and not only was that inner self made available to authority through the regimenting of the body and the interrogation of the soul through protocols of confession but also these practices were, by their own logic, *applications* of measured, just pain. Nothing it seems to me, demonstrates this better than Bentham's whipping machine, which was designed to whip with a controlled, measured stroke, at regular intervals and in private, producing just enough pain for penitence and then reform. Considering it this way—critically, against the grain, as it were—it may be possible to reconfigure the Maussian person or the Taylorian person as a person whose very condition of possibility is tied to the application of regulated pain.

I will take this relationship between person, pain, and the practice of punishment as our way into the problem of torture. Let us treat the practices of torture, initially at least, as a practice that produces pain in relation to a person as a form of punishment. Now, that is not to say a great deal, undoubtedly, but if we grant the well-described relationship between person, pain, and punishment in the particular place and time—Pentonville, England, in the 1840s—then perhaps we can map out distinctions between the cluster of those three poles there and similar clusters in other spatio-temporal locations and thus think as specifically as possible about the tortured person and the anthropology of that person.

Immediately, I argue, the move is useful to me, for it helps draw a distinction between the penitent inmate at Pentonville and the tortured person. They are quite clearly not the same. So we make progress negatively—the relationship between person, pain, and punishment in the one is not what we might expect in the other. Another classic essay is most helpful here. In explicating this distinction in a first approximation, pain and truth in medieval Christian ritual, Talal Asad has argued, are dependent upon each other, and in fact the practices of judicial torture depend upon just such a relationship. The contrast he draws between "ordeals," "duels," and "trials," on the one hand, and "judicial torture," on the other, is most instructive, and I will rehearse it here. Encounters of the first order are ones between social equals, Asad argues, and the "truth" of the matter is decided given the winner of the encounter; the social details of the matter being decided are already well known to the parties involved and to the judge, whose participation is nominal. In the logic of judicial torture, "pain," so conceived of, is applied in well-delineated ways that control and regulate such application in aid of the production of a confession. This confession is, then, not the sum total but a crucial part of the *judgment* of a given matter, which is, of course, the truth produced here. I note, following Asad, that pain does not really arise as a category in "trials" or "ordeals" but does in judicial torture. I note furthermore that this pain is thought to be applied to the body, physically, and it is because of its application that the confession is thought to emerge. This confession itself, Asad shows, must be in some way valid outside the application of pain: the tortured must produce the confession in court, while not subject to pain, or is led away for more torture. The theory of the matter, then, is this: pain applied to the body reconstitutes the person in some way allowing for a confession. This reconstitution must persist after the moment of the application of pain; it cannot be simply contingently available at that moment. And yet, clearly, this reconstitution is not the reform that we visited earlier in Pentonville and that appears, of course, many centuries after the period under consideration by Asad. The tortured person is not a reformed person; he or she undergoes what may well be a just measure of pain not to enter into a new permanent state but rather to speak truthfully about the past and after that is of no use to the apparatus of power.

Having sketched out in this way what may be another relationship of person, pain, and punishment at another moment and, importantly, under the sign of torture, let me stop here to consolidate and underline the larger claim on which this account rests. The tortured person, I have been assuming, is an "anthropological object." This assumption, I want to underline now, depends on a set of assumptions about anthropological disciplinarity. The central assumption is that the anthropologist does not have transparent access to the world of empirical particulars that he seeks to describe; the idea of an object indicates an epistemological posture allied to a conception of prior anthropological knowledge that constitutes this object in prior fields of knowledge and may be conceptualized, in turn, as a set of discursive statements that are archivally arranged and that produce, through that arrangement, inclusions and exclusions from "the true" (Foucault 1982). Alternatively, one can argue, following White (1978), that discourses are about the "tropes" that govern them and are so structured.

Such a view has, it seems to me, much to offer to the kind of internal description of anthropology I am attempting in this project, and its strong influence upon me has guided me thus far in this preliminary account of "the tortured person" as an anthropological object. I do not wish to suggest that I have here offered a full account of the discursive production of the "tortured person" or the allied triangulation, person, pain, and punishment in anthropological discourse, but I do suggest that I have sketched the bare outlines of such an account and signaled its possibility. There are, however, several prior sophisticated and comprehensive accounts of anthropological disciplinarity that do just that, in general: I shall take David Scott's (1994) *Formations of Ritual* as exemplary of such an account.[4] What I wish to do now is describe what emerges as "anthropology" in his important book and work out my own account of "anthropology" in relation to it, attempting to build my own account in the epistemological space made possible by its power. Scott writes, "So long as anthropology presumes that the objects of its discourse are not only self-evident but entirely outside the genealogical network of discourses within which it [anthropology] participates [which he then illustrates with a wonderful image] and are in fact simply waiting there at the dusty edge of a village to be approached," it will be not theoretical but ideological and more often than not colonial (1994:135). He also distances this account of the internal logic of anthropological disciplinarity from another well-known critical description, "anthropology as a form of writing," which is, of course, identified with the work of James Clifford, George Marcus, and Michael M. J. Fischer (Clifford and Marcus 1986; Marcus and Fischer 1986). In this view it is not simply ethnography, which is undoubtedly a form of writing, now a post-Barthian "text," but anthropology itself that is a form of writing. I am as skeptical as Scott is about this account of anthropology as text, but I am not myself certain that the description of anthropology as discourse is a complete one.

The effort that produces violence as an object in disciplinary anthropological practice has focused my attention on a particular absence in this description of anthropology as discourse—the absence of the anthropologist. This is not some simple oversight, Scott will protest. There are good, no, *necessary* theoretical reasons for this omission. This argument can be located in relation to his critique of Geertz's concepts of "experience-near" and "experience-far," which are, of course, the *locus classicus* of the interpretative capstone of contemporary American anthropology. Scott's point is simply this: Regardless of any dialectical tracking that might be attempted between experience-near concepts and experience-far ones on the way to the holy grail of the "native's point of view" (which is of course Geertz's epistemological stance), each and every one of those concepts is discursively produced, a priori, in archives of anthropological knowledge. Ritual is an anthropological object, and no amount of tracking will make it Sinhala Buddhist; the idea that Yaktovil is a ritual is an anthropological one, not a Sinhala Buddhist one. And so this matter of discursive construction "[has] little to do with the political or moral attitudes of this or that individual anthropologist." Again, I am in agreement, but now it is time to unpack some of the specificities of Scott's anthropological project so that I may build on his work.

Scott's concern is with something called Yaktovil, and while he correctly problematizes both its relation to "demonism," "exorcism," and "ritual" itself, he seems to consider it a *discourse* in its own terms. A discourse is an already explicit, well-formed, even, perhaps, coherent set of statements. What if one's anthropological project were an effort to describe what Malinowski ([1922] 1972:18) might have called "imponderabilia"? The anthropology of pain, which wishes to configure the tortured person as an anthropological object, may, I submit, be so challenged; in the paragraphs that follow I will elaborate on this problem before returning to Scott and questions of anthropology as such.

The Anthropology of Pain

I turn to Valentine Daniel's (1996) *Charred Lullabies* and a specific chapter within it, "Embodied Terror," taking at its word that it seeks not to make a specific point about a specific spatio-temporal moment, Sri Lanka in the middle 1980s, but rather to work with those specific materials to make much larger claims about "violence" and "culture" theoretically. Daniel accounts for two men whom he constitutes as tortured persons in his methodological field. The first is Benedict, a young Tamil man arrested by the Sri Lankan armed forces in eastern Sri Lanka in November 1983. He is subjected to a practice that seems logically akin to judicial torture, although Daniel does not call it that. Benedict is beaten with plastic pipes filled with sand in ways and places upon his body that will not leave marks, in ways that are controlled and ultimately, within their own logic, designed to lead to a confession. The process is unsuccessful, but later, in a different facility, given an even more intricate and controlled process of self-induced torture—in which Benedict is made to swallow his own saliva every six seconds for fifteen minutes at a time—he agrees to answer questions, yes or no, and so, by extension, produces a confession.

The second is another Tamil man, Guhanesan, who is a "torture victim" of the other side, as it were. Guhanesan joins a Tamil militant group after the great riot of 1983, and 1984 finds him in a training camp in South India. His simple request is for a few days' home leave to see his newborn child. He is denied this by the camp commander, but he decides to proceed anyway, back to family and back again to the camp, returning in the length of time specified in his original request. He is punished for this transgression by the camp commander. A nail is driven into the sole of his foot, pounded in, and left there until it festers and the foot becomes infected. It is then removed and his back and then legs are broken, and he is made to remain in the camp, legs numb and immovable, pulling himself about on an old tire and living on the charity of his fellow militants (Daniel 1996:139–142).

Let me consider the logic of Daniel's anthropological account here, underlining, of course, that I am not myself offering a kind of ethnographic reconstruction here but confining myself to the implications of this prior account. To me it would seem that the two logics of punishment that Daniel attends to are quite different, since the second does not depend upon interrogation and confession at all. Rather, it seems, it parallels the kinds of spectacular punishments that have yet another logic of pain, person, and practices embedded in them: those of public examples that serve as deterrents. Daniel, as I have remarked, does not seek to draw such a distinction; for him both persons have been "tortured." From his analytical vantage point, perhaps the distinction does not matter, for his point is about "pain." He argues, suturing Pierce to Scarry, that pain is a "sinsign" that is exhausted by its "singularity." Pain in this view is characterized by its "particularity," "unshareability," and "incommunicability"—it is precultural, it would seem: "At this level of experiencing pain it appears that one is unlikely to find any significant effect of culture." Daniel's point about both Benedict's account of his own torture and pain and accounts of Guhanesan's (Guhanesan is unavailable to him) is that the very mapping of pain upon the surfaces of the body is racked by social doubt. Not only do others like him disbelieve Benedict but he disbelieves others who claim torture and subsequent pain. Guhanesan's pain, localized in the sole of his foot, is disbelieved by other militants in the camp, who know that his legs are numb because his back is broken. He is in fact, Daniel learns from informants, a figure of fun in the camp as he pulls himself around on his tire, begging for acknowledgment of his pain.

This, Daniel qualifies, is an account of particular kinds of pain, not "socialized pain" such as a headache, a toothache, and a backache but a privatized pain that is produced by the practice of torture itself. It is, if I have read him right, the very extremity of this particular kind of pain that makes it precultural. This point, for Daniel, is underscored ethnographically by repeated silence in the face of his probing questions. "The newly freed victims did talk. But in interview after interview I found these individuals willing to talk about their capture, their cells, their meals . . . but of torture they ventured little" (1996:143). Nor did these silences fill over time. The reticence continued, Daniel notes, in settings of "greater acquaintance and trust" in later years of fieldwork (1996:143 n. 6, 224). One can, perhaps, question Daniel's method here, and he himself notes that any interlocutor becomes the torturer for the tortured, given in particular the form of the questions that he reports using, but my move is not to delegitimize this work by setting up such a set of concerns. Rather, what I wish to dwell on is the formulation of the anthropological problem of the tortured person. In the example of Daniel, the anthropology of the tortured person turns on the accessibility to the investigator of the "pain" of the "tortured person." And it is upon this accessibility, this intelligibility, that the analysis hinges. There is then, here, an investigator, an anthropologist, who is analytically visible to us. The problem of the intelligibility of pain makes him visible to us; the reticence of the tortured makes him visible to us, just as in the classic account of the Nuer the reluctance of an informant to speak his name makes E. E. Evans-Pritchard as an anthropologist, as an interrogator, visible to us (1940:18–19).

Having offered what may seem a curious analogy, let me qualify and mediate precisely what may seem inflammatory about it: Daniel is not an outsider to his "field"; he was born and grew up there, speaks the language with extraordinary fluency, and surely, by any measure of "social" or "cultural" identity—that is to say, any measure of the "nativity" of the "native" anthropologist in its many accounts[5]—he is an insider. Such identities undoubtedly matter in many ways, but my point is that the epistemological importance of those identities is subordinate to that of another identity that is not "social" in that way— that of the anthropologist. This is a crucial point, it seems to me, that I would underline, for in another, rather more commonplace view the anthropologist becomes his sociality. Daniel's account, I am trying to suggest, would call such a view into question. He is not "other" in a social or cultural sense and yet does encounter reticence.

Daniel and Evans-Pritchard, it seems to me, are best described not as Tamil man and white man but rather as anthropologists engaged in disciplinary practice, and there is, I want to claim, an analytical visibility of this self in relation to the reticent informant. The problem of pain— to return fully to Daniel's account—gives rise to this reticence.

Now, for Daniel this reticence, detected and underlined by him, becomes in *his* analytical account a property of pain itself. Pain is such that it cannot enter into culture—it enters culture, in Daniel's terms, only as terror and beauty. I am struck also by the way pain, in this view of it, cannot do constitutive work, either, upon the personhood of the tortured, on the one hand, or in relation to the investigating anthropologist, on the other. I have not fully understood this gap in Daniel, for it would seem at least from his own discussion that the application of "pain" has constitutive effects in both examples. In the first it produces a confession, as it might under the conditions Asad has described, and in the second it produces an effect of deterrence through its very apparent unshareability. Thought of this way, personal pain, that is to say, pain that inheres in a person, does work in the world. And furthermore, the person is constituted in myriad ways by the application of pain. I offer these remarks not as an attempt to lesson the importance of Daniel's pioneering work but rather as a way of underlining the worth of the particular account of anthropological disciplinarity that I have delineated earlier. An account of the relation of pain and person as prior anthropological objects that are constituted in the archives of post-Enlightenment thought speaks to the larger point I have learned from Asad and Scott—that our anthropological objects do not authorize transparent access to the world, that thinking them through an archive leads to theoretical gain. But, having argued that, I do not want to lose what I want to take away from this reading of Daniel: the anthropology of the tortured person may hinge on the intelligibility of the pain of the tortured to the investigator, taken as an anthropologist.

A Moral Economy of Anthropological Knowledge

To delve deeper into this question, I bring to my aid or, perhaps better put, comfort here an essay that traverses this terrain of the anthropology of pain with extraordinary analytical weight and affective fortitude, Veena Das's (1997) "Language and Body: Transactions in the Construction of Pain." It is not an essay that simply stands alone but rather is both cumulative and reflective of sustained labors in the field that are brought together with palpable integrity. And, yet, it is in the light of these labors that Das begins: "In repeated trying to write the meaning of violence against women in Indian Society, I find the languages of pain through which the social sciences could gaze at touch or become *textual bodies* on which this pain is written often elude me" (67). And she concludes: "It worries me that I have been unable to name that which died when the autonomous citizens of India were simultaneously born as monsters" (88).

There is, then, an echo here of a question we encountered earlier, the enunciation of pain within the logic of disciplinary anthropological practice. Das, fascinatingly, broadens her field of vision to the social sciences, and in mapping out that disciplinary epistemology her essay produces an "I," an investigative self, that I missed in Scott's account of anthropological discourse. This "I" does, in my reading, crucial work in Das's essay, and I want to think with it. To do so, I will place this "I" in what I will call a moral economy of anthropological knowledge, hoping that this will illuminate both the problem of pain and anthropology itself.

I take the idea of a moral economy not in its well-known Thompsonian sense—as in the moral economy of the English crowd—but rather in its less well-known but nevertheless flourishing usage pioneered recently in critical histories of the early modern European experimental sciences. Key here is Lorraine Daston's (1995) essay "The Moral Economy of Science," which maps out the concept, building on her own fascinating work (see Daston and Park 1998), as well as that of Steven Shapin (1998), Simon Shaffer (1994), and Peter Dear (1995), in particular. "Moral" here stands for a "web of affect-saturated values" that link, in well-defined relation to each other (hence "economy"), the particulars of a post-Baconian world to the investigative self. Thus the investigative self is linked by these relations to the particulars that surround it, and it is given these "moral" relations that those very particulars and, therefore, "science" can be made available to the self in a secure way. In Daston's understanding, as in my own, to say that science has a "moral economy" is not simply to say that its conclusions are value-laden, its investigators are interested, or its practices are partial, nor is it to argue that there are other social, economic, or political forces behind science. Rather, it is to suggest that modes of knowing such as quantification and empiricism are secured *by moral economies,* particular relations of affect between investigator and field, on the one hand, and investigator and critical audience, on the other. For example, in Daston's argument the empirical is secured by three modes of knowing, or three moral economies—testimony, facticity, and novelty—and, in brief, testimony works through trust, facticity through civility, and novelty through transformation of curiosity into a virtue. Daston can build here on the work of Steven Shapin, who has demonstrated, for example, that Robert Boyle's truth claims were so authoritative in the early years of the Royal Society precisely because his testimonies were thought to be trustworthy and society itself was constituted by the virtue of civility. Central to all three is a transformed notion of experience that emerges and develops in scientific practice in the seventeenth century. This new form of experience is distinct from and opposed to an Aristotelian notion of *common* experience, a known experience and taken as such, but is intimately tied to the notion of the experiment itself, being infinitely repeated and repeatable but very specific and particular, staged, if you like—an act that secures an argument, given the facts it produces, as in Robert Boyle's celebrated air pump, described by Shapin, or the kind of either/or event-based experiment authoritatively practiced by Isaac Newton that has been described by Peter Dear. Crucial here is that these emerging forms of experience are coded as disciplinary—that is, governed by rules and protocols producing inclusions and exclusions that form them and thus make them secure and authoritative.

Two of these concepts, disciplined curiosity and particular, disciplined experience, can perhaps be captured in a single classic quotation from Isaac Newton, purportedly his first response to seeing light shine through a prism:

> It was at first a pleasing divertissement to view the vivid and intense colours produced thereby; but after a while applying myself to consider them more circumspectly, I became surprised to see them in an oblong form; which, according to the received laws of refraction, I expected should have been circular. . . . Comparing the length of this coloured spectrum with its breadth, I found it about five times greater, a disproportion so extravagant that it excited me to a more than ordinary curiosity of examining from whence it might proceed.

This is the opening passage of Newton's "New Theory of Light and Colours" which he wrote to Henry Oldenburg, secretary of the Royal Society of London, on February 6, 1672. In their insightful analysis of this quotation, Daston and Park (1998:303–304) caution their readers that this is a fictionalized reconstruction of this moment, but caution underlines the importance of the rhetorical moves made in this paragraph: here is a self-description of disciplined curiosity and disciplined experience by a great performer of the practice. Note how the first mention of "divertissement" is leavened by "circumspection," then surprise, then a more careful observation of shape, of length, measured comparatively, which then leads to "excitement," which produces just a slight excess of curiosity, which opens the way for more experiment. This, to put it simply, is a moral economy. The investigative self here is governed, disciplined, by a web of controlled affect. This is what makes Newton a scientist and secures his claims to truth.

What, one may well ask, does early modern experimental science have to do with contemporary anthropological practice? Not very much, if we are to think in conventional modes of historicity or sociality. But my suggestion is this: If we let these accounts stand on an analytical plane different from the socio-historical, perhaps that plane will allow for the illumination of the epistemological architecture of the discipline.

Put another way, I make no claim that early modern experimental experience is in any straightforward way similar to our experiences in the field. Rather, all I wish to suggest is that the category of disciplinary experience itself may be helpful in describing anthropology. The worth of this argument depends upon the practiced anthropologist's recognizing its usefulness.[6]

Transactions between Personal and Disciplinary Experience

If I gaze on the landscape of Sri Lanka as a disciplinary anthropologist, I face a "scene of devastation" that, if I may paraphrase Das's unbearably true words, has become strange and desolate through violence and loss. The scene of violence is a scene, it seems to me, of unremitting, unending grotesqueness—scenes and sights and persons that are in their very terms grotesque. The pain of Daniel's tortured persons is such pain because it cannot be acknowledged, it cannot be heard, and its very unintelligibility becomes a source of enjoyment. The power of Das's essay for me lies in its refusal to flinch in the face of the monstrous grotesqueness around her, not foreclosing her argument in view of the feeling of horror but moving forward thinking of herself as constituted by her inability to enunciate her own pain.

But in so doing Das fails, she suggests, and I have tried time and time again to elaborate on that failure for myself. And I myself have failed, many times, at this seemingly simple task of reading a short essay, but I have taken comfort that each time I have reentered its words I have felt the texture of its body. This, I think finally, is a better sense of her point. Words, voice, language are here "bodied forth" in the Wittgensteinian sense of a language game that by its very operation calls fundamentally into question the boundaries of mind and body, person and skin, that we live with (see, for example, 1958:103–122). Language and body are transacted. Das's voice, she tells us, is pawned to Tagore,

Manto, and Wittgenstein, and it is that pawned voice that bodies forth in language.

And yet, that body of language does not, for Das, represent disciplinary experience. There is a moment, deep in the essay, when she remarks, "In my own experience, the question of how good death and bad death is to be defined by the act of witnessing is a more complicated one" (1997:81). She goes on to describe how good deaths are worked through in the world, drawing on what is clearly disciplinary experience, and ultimately says that she will now offer an amplification that she has constructed, "for it was never possible for me to get an exegesis of such statements from the women themselves" (82). There is here, in the last quotation—even though unmarked semantically—recourse to the kind of experience that I have been trying to identify as disciplinary experience, which contrasts, perhaps, with the kind of experience invoked in the first quotation. It is between these two passages that Das wrestles with the silence of pain.

In his subtle remarks on Das's essay, Stanley Cavell (1997:97) pauses at her use of the notion of "experience," noting that it is the ground upon which she writes and that this concept of experience parts company with Wittgenstein's, but he has also noted earlier that what is being invoked is not Indianness in some straightforward way—that is, experience as being "inside or outside a culture," which has become, perhaps, commonplace, at least implicitly, in some anthropological quarters. But I think he is correct in pointing to the importance of the concept in undergirding the essay—in my terms, both as disciplinary experience and what may be its excess, which might be called personal experience. These double invocations of experience are perhaps also transacted, just as language and the body are, and there is in that transaction a crucial production of anthropological knowledge. Recall Renato Rosaldo's (1993) well-known meditation on the head-hunter's rage—that the juxtaposition of rage with grief was unintelligible to him for years until, given an extraordinary confluence of personal experience and disciplinary experience, it became, through that transaction, intelligible to his anthropological self and thus took its place among the formations of anthropological knowledge.

"Indeed," I can imagine a not hostile interlocutor remarking," such transactions may be the hallmark of particular, subtly textured anthropological knowledge. Is it your conclusion that violence, taken as an anthropological object, emerges in the discipline through such transactions between personal and disciplinary experience?" My reply would visit a tautology: I would argue that disciplinary knowledge can be fashioned only by disciplinary experience, and therefore extradisciplinary experience must be subsumed in some way into the disciplinary. Visiting tautologies isn't hard; what I am trying to do is to describe the bounds of what counts as disciplinary experience.

Let me map this boundary with a contemporary example of cross-disciplinary reflection. Consider what Stephen Greenblatt (1999) worries over in his recent reflections on Clifford Geertz's work many years after his discovery of it. For Greenblatt, as one might expect, his appreciation has to do with interpretation as a method—the thrill of discovering the cross-disciplinary provenance of a "tool kit." There is a place, then, to consider the ethnographic in relation to the imaginary: "What should we make of Geertz's claim that an anecdote from a field journal is 'not all that different,' as an imaginative reconstruction, from *Madame Bovary*" (Greenblatt 1999:21) as far as interpretative method goes? But, if Geertz had invented any of his field encounters, it would not work for Greenblatt, however much he might share in the interpretative method: "If . . . it turned out that Geertz had made up Cohen [an informant], I at least would have concluded that as an ethnographer Geertz was not to be trusted, and his work would have immediately lost much of its value"(1999:21).

I note how easily trust appears here as the virtue upon which the security of Geertz's anthropological claims rests. Trust—if I may return to Daston—is an aspect of a moral economy, and here, as I revisit it, what I wish to underline is its doubleness as both affect and virtue. In other words, I wish to note the concatenation of both an affective economy and an economy of virtues in the invocation of trust here. Geertz's disciplinary self is invoked throughout the essay in a double sense, on the one hand his sensibility is fine and textured, and his interpretations reflect this, for they are acts of the imagination—but on the other hand, simply, he doesn't lie. The two economies move smoothly through each other, even though they are not the same, but finally they make up, as they do for Greenblatt, a whole.

This, in this double sense, is what I would call a moral economy of anthropological knowledge. This is an extension or amplification of Daston's argument; she holds back from underlining the second idea of the moral. This is as it should be, for the epistemological practices I am trying to describe are distinct, in a sense, from the ones she describes. The post-Baconian particularities of an experimental world are indeed different from those in a world of participant observation; they are imbued with meaning in a different way. Questions of interpretation and imagination are different, and therefore thinking here can be "moral" in a different way—that is, certain, well-known, and well-accepted, tied to the rather more seventeenth-century idea of "moral" as "sentiment," as disciplined affect. Again, the point is that the anthropological truth claim is made at the confluence of these two senses.

We have visited this confluence in relation to one axis of moral economy, that of testimony and trust. Another such axis is curiosity and novelty. I know no better way to underline the centrality of this axis in our scholarly life than to focus for a moment on the commonplace descriptor "interesting." Now, "interesting" can be used in several ways. First, it can be a bare minimum descriptor—a way of saying, without really saying so, that a book, a talk, or a seminar wasn't all that interesting, not a dismissal but an assessment of minimum acceptability. Second—and this is its core, I would say—it is a way asking for more. Very often when one scholar is describing a project to another the other says, "That is [so] interesting" at the first pause. Another comment may prove disruptive: "Interesting" is about a novelty/curiosity matrix— about the inherent virtue of particular kinds of empirical investigations in the social sciences. It is not simply saying, "Aha! That is a worthy epistemological object!" but saying that the subject is worthy of further work—hence its value to students and those beginning projects as a preliminary interlocution. But of course the idea of "interest" has its own limits. "Interesting" is well and good, and so is "interested" as in "I am interested in the LTTE" or even "I am interested in violence." But having an "interest," as in financial reward, would of course be transgressive of the discipline of our epistemological ethics. What if that "interested" translated into an alliance with a violent group, one that was engaged in killing and bombing, which by its logic were morally justifiable? How far can interest go? My point is this: the word itself maps out a terrain of disciplined affect, marking both possibilities and limits, inciting to further work, and warning of excess.

Moral economies, then, are tenuous, perhaps far more than we commonly think and rather more so in relation to "violence" taken as an anthropological object. Consider, for example, the possibility that Cohen, Geertz's informant of 1968, who recalled events from 1912, was speaking not about stealing sheep but about violence—that Geertz's conversation with Cohen circulated around a violation, torture perhaps, and, in its aftermath, the enunciation of pain.

Let me be clear here that I am not claiming that an anthropology of pain or one of violence is impossible because the object is unknowable. Nor am I arguing that words have to spoken by an informant for an ethnography to be written. Far from it: my reflections on the problem of pain should have underlined the opposite; anthropological work can begin when a person is constituted by his or her inability to enunciate pain. But configuring that enunciation can be complex: I am suggesting that the interpretations, imaginings, and interest(s) we bring to our disciplinary knowledge production in the face of "violence" may well struggle at the limits of particular moral economies.

Final Thoughts

I return, finally, to my seminar at the Eastern University. I have suggested, invoking Chatterjee's reflections on a far more important event that he was part of, that I recognized for myself a duality of location that I inhabited at that moment. Having reflected at length on the problem of the tortured person in anthropological disciplinarity, let me attempt pull the last threads of my thoughts together. My seminar that day was on nationalism—that is to say, the canonical literature on nationalism. And certainly it seems to me that if we were engaged in an exercise of canon building and teaching Anderson, whatever one's disagreements with him, would have to be accounted for. But for the members of my audience this was not the case, and not because they were fundamentally anti-intellectual but because of their location in the political field of nationalism. As contributors to nationalist thought, they sought to set aside the very idea of an imagined community, for in the register of Tamil nationalist thought, as I understand it, the collective burden of experienced pain is central. Sri Lankan Tamil nationalist thought has for some time now been about enormous pain and the resultant suffering.

The question I want my readers to consider is this: Would I be able to work with and within the disciplinary epistemological ethic I have outlined if I were to commence fieldwork in this context and world? My problem would be the apprehension of pain. Would I be able to maintain the controlled web of affect that I have argued is crucial to the government of the anthropological self? Would anyone?

To counter what appears to be a common, insidious misunderstanding of my concerns that has appeared as this chapter has been reviewed, let me clarify one more time that I am not advocating a "Tamil anthropology" as opposed to an American anthropology, nor am I making a simple argument of cultural relativism. Rather, the question I have raised is how anthropological knowledge about what is taken to be "culture" is acquired. Therefore, such a straightforward opposition is antithetical to my analysis. My opposition is the anthropologist and the critical nationalist or national and their respective epistemological practices. These are both subject positions that I inhabit, and I have attempted to delineate that inhabitation to the best of my ability.

Cultural anthropologists know by doing fieldwork; of this many of them are certain. Can a critical nationalist or a national "do fieldwork" and claim the truth of that knowledge within anthropological disciplinarity, American or some other? To do so as a national who lives and works with and against a tradition of nationalist thought would surely be to constitute that epistemological practice within a political field that may be oppositional, contingent, and shifting, characterized by relationships of alliance and enmity and, certainly, high stakes and danger.

Can the fragile epistemological ethics of cultural anthropology that I have described in relation to the problem of pain survive this challenge?

Notes

1. The name is imaginary.

2. I tried to imagine this in fiction soon afterward (see Jeganathan 1989, 2004).

3. Taylor's essay "The Person" is a bridge, by way of reflections on and location in relation to Mauss, between an earlier (1981) and a later (1995) treatment of the subject.

4. Scott's work is, I think it is fair to say, influenced by Asad's (1993) important critique of anthropology, which has, of course, informed my own specific account here. Although written in a slightly different register, Herzfeld (1987) would be a parallel example.

5. I take Narayan (1996) to be an example of such an account, of which there is a wide variety. Weston (1997) is a more recent and sophisticated formulation.

6. As Alison Wylie's remarks on my work at the symposium have made me even more acutely aware, there are stakes here in one's overarching philosophical orientation to the sciences. On the one hand, this essay is not envisaged in any way as a contribution to that philosophical debate, but if it were to be located there in broad terms it would sit with Helen Longino's (2001) call for the navigation of the two poles of social constitution and rationality in the epistemology of science.

7. I am grateful to David Scott for bringing this essay to my attention.

Situational Ethics and Engaged Practice: The Case of Archaeology in Africa

Martin Hall

C an there be standards of practice that guide or regulate work in anthropology?

On the one hand, most anthropological practice is now imbued, in one way or another, with the epistemology of postmodernism and affected by the epistemology of relativity. Modernist concepts such as generalized laws of behavior and objective truths have been discounted in favor of a larger meta-theory—that there can be no general principles of knowledge. In one sense ethical codes and concepts of morality are anathema, relics from the grand theories of modernism. At the same time, though, postmodernism seems profoundly ethical, insisting on the equivalence of all social contexts and exposing the "othering" that is anthropology's burden.

On the other hand, anthropology and its subdisciplines are increasingly involved in giving professional advice. As public institutions such as state-funded universities and museums have become more commercially oriented, disciplines such as archaeology have joined a broad family of professional consultants that includes psychology, cultural resource management, environmental impact analysis, geology, and the earth and life sciences in general. Such professionalization invariably tends toward codes of practice as gatekeeping devices and because customers require a measure of value for money.

This paradox is resolved by looking at the more general pattern. Models such as Arjun Appadurai's study of global flows of resources, people, and information (996), Manuel Castells's "network society" (1996, 1997, 1998) and Hardt and Negri's "empire" (2000) show the ligaments of a new order in which the decentered networks that challenged the ordered world of modernism have been turned to the advantage of international capital. Hardt and Negri argue that post-modernist theories misrecognize the "enemy" by opposing a form of modernism that is already redundant: "What if a new paradigm of power, a postmodern sovereignty, has come to replace the modern paradigm and rule through differential hierarchies of the hybrid and fragmentary subjectivities that these theorists celebrate? In this case, modern forms of sovereignty would no longer be at issue, and the postmodernist and postcolonialist strategies that appear to be liberatory would not challenge but in fact coincide with and even unwittingly reinforce the new strategies of rule" (Hardt and Negri 2000:138). From this perspective, the radical agenda of postmodernism, the decline in state expenditure on disinterested research, and the increasing import-ance of professional ethics of practice are part of the same package.

Given this, is the debate about ethics redundant? Clearly not—the issues raised are complex and are intertwined with the politics of the realignment of forms of domination and resistance that have character-ized the past decade. As Michel Foucault (building in turn on Nietzsche) showed, all social behavior is penetrated by power, taking the form of multiple relations that are "immanent in the sphere in which they operate and which constitute their own organisation" (Foucault 1980: 92). In its turn, power always includes the possibility of resistance, "for if there were no possibility of resistance. . . there would be no relations of power" (Foucault, in Bernauer and Rasmussen 1988:12). In an analysis that, strikingly, prefigured the shift in global politics after September 2001, Hardt and Negri showed how the new global flows of the network society generate countercurrents of opposition, resistance, and rejection. Now, forms of resistance that invoke ethical positions are evident: new forms of fundamentalism that evoke religious princi-ples against global market culture, the fluid networks of anticapitalist and anarchist groups that have paralyzed cities such as Seattle, Prague, Gothenburg, and London, and the multiple public spheres seen by Nancy Fraser (1997) as characteristic of "postsocialist" society.

It is therefore worth looking at some of the issues raised by this contemporary scenario from the perspective of the periphery of the new networks of power and resources. Castells has shown how, in the network society flows of information, capital, and people (through both elite and mass migration) create new centers of power and new peripheries of exclusion. Given that such centers of power are defined as nodes that control transactions in information and financial and cultural capital (particularly in the "world cities" of the West and North) and are dominated by the professional elites of the service economy, it follows that issues of ethics may be different at the center and at the periphery. Concepts such as "transcendental ethics" and "truth" may be anathema in some circles, schooled in the tradition of the revolt against modernism. But, as Hardt and Negri (2000:155) point out, forms of resistance may reject postmodernism and valorize absolute principles: "in the context of state terror and mystification, clinging to the primacy of the concept of truth can be a powerful and necessary form of resistance."

Similarly, the rejection of concepts such as absolute values, ethics, and codes of practice presumes strong secular traditions and institutions that serve as a consensus for principles of social justice. As Achille Mbembe has pointed out, Western notions of civil society rest on constructing, legitimizing, and resolving disputes in the public domain. But this in turn depends on the existence of autonomous institutions that are intermediaries between the state and society: "There can be no civil society without places and spaces where ideas of autonomy, representation, and pluralism can publicly crystallize, and where juridical subjects enjoying rights and capable of freeing themselves from the arbitrariness of both state and primary group (kin, tribe, etc.) can come into being" (2001:39). Because colonial regimes countered the formation of such autonomous institutions at every turn, the "post-colony" is a "song of shadows": "disconnections, superimpositions, colours, costumes, gestures and appearances, sounds and rhythms, ellipses, hyperboles, parables, misconnections, and imagined, remembered, and forgotten things, bits of spaces, syncopes, intervals, moments of enthusiasm and impetuous voices" (2001:242).

Land Rights

A case in point: South Africa has a sophisticated constitution, an independent judiciary and constitutional court, and diverse legislation directed at national reconstruction. However, the public institutions of South Africa's new civil society are less than a decade old and are not yet buttressed by established conventions that promote social justice. In September 2000 the communities of Lekkersing, Eksteenfontein, Kuboes and Sandrift—together known as the Richtersveld—turned to the postapartheid legislation to claim the restitution of land that had been annexed under the British colonial administration of 1847. In March 2001 their claim was rejected because it was unclear to the Land Claims Court that "aboriginal title" was established as a right in the South African constitution and because the court understood land restitution to apply only to cases after 1913 and cases in which communities had been removed in terms of apartheid legislation such as the Group Areas Act.

What makes the Richtersveld case pertinent here is that the claim was opposed by the South African government, which owns the land in question through the state-owned diamond mining company, Alexcor. Although the case was briefly reported (Geldenhuys 2001), there was no effective public pressure on behalf of the Richtersveld Nama community, which will find it difficult if not impossible to assemble the resources to contest the issue on appeal. As is well established, such aboriginal title claims may often depend heavily on anthropological and archaeological testimony and the readiness of anthropologists and archaeologists to act in the public interest according to a "transcendental ethics" that rests on a sense of abstract social justice. Although well-developed civil institutions may serve this purpose, allowing anthropologists to step back from advocacy, in South Africa there is not yet such a tradition of public advocacy. Who, then, is to speak for these small rural communities in the face of a government with an overwhelming electoral majority and a multinational diamond mining company?

A second case adds a further dimension. Two years earlier, the Khomani community was granted a large tract of state-owned land in and immediately south of the Kalahari Gemsbok National Park in South Africa's Northern Province. Here the government's logic for the settlement agreement was continuity with the past. One of the reasons for the promulgation of the park in 1931 had been to help the San people maintain their "hunter-gatherer way of life." This, though, had not been honored, and the 1999 settlement agreement represented a return to the original undertaking. Land restitution to the Khomani was conditional on the land's being managed as a conservation area consistent with the goals of the national park.

Passing over the implication that the South African government is prepared to honor aboriginal rights to state land only when they contribute to its own revenue generation, what is relevant here is the style of public discourse. The Richtersveld community, unsuccessful in its claim for land given over to the thoroughly modern business of diamond mining, was reported as thoroughly modern in its disappointment and anger. Here is Richtersveld municipal councillor Willem Cloete: "We are shocked about this finding. Our community's evidence and our legal teams were so good. But we will test this result in the highest court." And secretary of the Richtersveld Community and Landowners' Association Willem Louw: "The land claim has motivated our people to stand together. We did not expect our legitimate claim to be rejected like this. We have been done an injustice when our land was taken, and we wont just accept this ruling" (*Legal Brief* 2001; Geldenhuys 2001).

In contrast, the success of the Khomani community in its claim to be part of the ecology of the Kalahari Gemsbok National Park is reported as the "coming in from the cold" of "South Africa's oldest people" in an event marked by rain in the Kalahari, "a celestial sign fit for a significant milestone" (*Independent Online* 1999). In a ceremony to mark the land settlement held on March 21, 1999, at a game lodge, then-Deputy President Thabo Mbeki addressed the Khomani in a premodern style consistent with their standing as representatives of an earlier age:

> We shall mend the broken strings of the distant past so that our dreams can take root. For the stories of the Khoe and the San have told us that this dream is too big for one person to hold. It is a dream that must be dreamed collectively, by all the people. It is by that acting together, by that dreaming together, by mending the broken strings that tore us apart in the past that we shall all of us produce a better life for you who have been the worst victims of oppression. It is now my place to say: Here is your land. Take it, look after it and thrive.

This incident is one small instance of a general trope in which South Africa is "heritage." Representations of ancient hunter-gatherers and their art and customs, tribal life, and the colonial past are woven together with images of game parks, wilderness areas, scenery, and beaches to form an attractive destination for those weary of the pressures of life in the "world cities" of the North (a destination made all the more attractive through the discount of an ever-cheaper local currency). This is a manifestation of the new network society, with its complex interdependencies between center and periphery and the material value of cultural capital if it is deployed to best advantage. But such discourse is also an instance of a trope long identified as problematic in anthropology—"spatialized time," in which distancing devices are used to deny "coevalness." "There is," in Fabian's (1983:31) words, "a persistent and systematic tendency to place the referent(s) of anthropology in a Time other than the present of the producer of anthropological discourse."

Ethics at the Margins

My approach to issues of ethics at the margins of the network society will be through the lens of archaeological practice in parts of Africa. Anthropology in Africa takes ethical issues to their limits: the moral claims of colonization and enlightenment and the subsequent castigation of such positions as the epitome of unethical practice, the extremes of apartheid and the case for a "militant anthropology" (Scheper-Hughes 1995), the rise of new nation-states built around historical identities and subsequent collapses into economic disaster, dictatorship, war, or genocide, the diaspora of African intellectuals to European and North American universities, the infinite needs of education, health care, and other social services, against which claims for resources for anthropological research appear obscene. Against this, Africa has a historical identity of unrivaled depth that includes the origins of both humanity and anatomically modern humans, the longest known tradition of art, which poses complexities of interpretation beyond the conceptual capabilities of Europe's languages, the independent domestication of plants and animals in several centers, and the development of complex societies along the Nile that connected equatorial Africa to the Mediterranean, early urban civilizations in West and southern Africa, and syncretic African/Arab cultures along the length of the east coast (Hall 1996).

These complexities were captured in the London Royal Academy's exhibition *Africa: The Art of a Continent* and its opening. There were more than eight hundred objects, ranging from southern Africa to the Mediterranean and from five thousand years ago to the present—a celebration of "the fertile contribution to the visual culture of the world from the whole of this vast and infinitely various continent" (Phillips 1995:20). "Never before has there been gathered such a rich and vast array of African art-objects and artefacts from such a broad time span. And rarely has any exhibition embraced the artistic treasures of the whole of Africa, from Egypt to Ife to Great Zimbabwe" (West 1995:9). Despite such accolades, Simon Jenkins (1995) of the *Times* wrote:

> On Monday night I put on my best suit and attacked the African art show, talk of the town at the Royal Academy. I was immediately stumped. Outside were a dozen prancing Zulu war drummers, skimpily clad in raffia

briefs, beaming and whooping at the passing guests. The guests had no idea how to react. Were these renegade militants, satirising the white man's image of Africa? Or were they one of the exhibits, "performance art" courtesy of the Bank of Ulundi? Should we throw coloured beads, or raise a fist in salute? Ambassadorial limousines cruised the forecourt menacingly, as if about to spew AK47s and mow us all down.

For Jenkins and others who share his viewpoint, Africa has been used up. Having inspired Napoleon and droves of adventurers after him to plunder the Nile Valley, the British to raid Benin for its bronzes, and the Belgians to strip the Congo for King Leopold II's collections, Africa has no "art" that can satisfy British taste (Hall 1996, 2001a).

The contradiction here resides in place—Africa as the "source of life" and the "heart of darkness"—but also in the sense of time. The purpose of *Africa: The Art of a Continent* is to present Africa "as it really is," stripped of the influence of the outside world. Nothing that is syncretic or cosmopolitan, nothing that dilutes the strong streams of Africa's "authentic" artistic traditions will be allowed into the show (Phillips 1995). The consequence is the depiction of a continent frozen in an "ethnographic present," a relative chronology in which the absolute dates of objects in the show vary widely from place to place but the time horizon is always before Europe's "influence." African cultures can be seen to affect one another but not to be influenced from or to exert influence beyond the continent's periphery. Africa is a continent in a glass jar, an unearthed spectacle at which the Academy's visitors can gaze in wonder (Hall 1996, 2001a). Africa is the "timeless continent": Joseph Conrad's *Heart of Darkness*, the apocalyptic encounter of civilization and its nemesis (Achebe 1988). It is Karl Jung's "collective unconscious," the unchanging baseline of the human psyche (Jung 1973), and Karen Blixen's *Out of Africa* (1954), the herds of antelope sweeping across the Serengeti. But at the same time, Africa is the continent of origins: the precolonial cities of Great Zimbabwe and Jenne-jeno, mathematics, architecture and astronomy in early Egypt, animal husbandry and crop cultivation, artistic representation. Above all else, it is the continent in which humanity itself originated and the continent that, in the popular consciousness of the North and West, now stands for humanity's decline.

In seeking to connect the legacy of archaeological practice that has contributed to this controversial archive with the contemporary debate about ethics and the moralities of anthropological inquiry, I will follow Pels (1999) and trace major strands through the major archaeological approaches in the continent over the past two centuries. However, in contrast to Pels I see these approaches not as a "prehistory" but as coeval moralities that together give definition to the contemporary state of archaeology and its options for the future. Thus archaeology in Africa is founded on the moral justifications for colonialism—anthropology's seminal problem and the source of an enduring sense of ambiguity and shame. This provided sharp focus for the second trope—the ethics of nationalism and national construction that defined Africa's political culture in the second half of the past century. In parallel again, with roots in the earliest expeditions and well-developed branches in today's archaeology, is the epistemology and ethics of science: an obligation to pursue "truth" irrespective of context or consequence.

Ideas of Africa

What was to become "Africa" started as a set of rumors and assumptions in religious and popular early modern tales, manuscripts, and early books (Hall 2000). *Mandeville's Travels*, available in every major European language by the end of the fourteenth century, claimed Africa for parahuman inhabitants that "go completely naked" and "eat human flesh more gladly than any other" (Moseley 1983:127–128). Ideas about Africa were closely associated with heat and suffering. For Dante, burning sand signified the doom of Sodom and Gomorrah, and "Libya's sand" was associated with the serpents and "breeds so strange beside" in the Seventh Chasm of the Eighth Circle (Sayers 1949:160). These vague shapes took specific form as mapmaking progressed. Descriptive fragments were brought together in early travel accounts and influenced early medieval maps and charts, while the cartography of the continent was given clearer form from the closing years of the fifteenth century with the first Portuguese voyages of discovery (Boxer 1965; Crone 1968).

This creation of Africa from the periphery extended steadily into the interior, following the lines of rivers and other routes. On the way, new observations were made and trophies collected, yielding in time to the systematic procedures of collecting and classifying that are the distinctive mark of the discipline of archaeology (Hall 2000). At the same time, Africa was segmented into colonial divisions with boundaries that followed lines of latitude and longitude or major topographic features, reflecting the histories of disputes between European powers.

The first part of the continent to gain an archaeology was Egypt, following Napoleon's invasion in 1798 and the description of Egyptian antiquities published in the *Description de l'Egypte* between 1809 and

1813 (Fagan 1977). "The whole Expedition is a fascinating turning point in European attitudes to the East. In many ways the elaborate surveys, maps and drawings, and the stealing of objects and cultural monuments to embellish France, was an early example of the standard pattern of studying and objectifying through scientific enquiry that became a hallmark of European imperialism" (Bernal 1991:184). Similarly, collections of artifacts were made from the early years of colonial possession and settlement in other areas and were based on the same premises that inspired archaeologists in nineteenth-century Europe (Hall 2001a). Some of the earliest descriptions of African antiquities outside Egypt came from Senegal in 1851 (de Barros 1990) and from the Eastern Cape, South Africa, where Thomas Holden Bowker made a collection in 1858 (Deacon 1990). The first known collections from East Africa came somewhat later, in 1893 (Robertshaw 1990).

African archaeology, then, was founded in two concepts that were, to an extent, intertwined. The first of these was an obsession with the exotic—a fascination with the "underworld" that defined European medievalist perceptions of existence beyond its own known surfaces and continued into the era of European colonial expansion as a rich band of popular consciousness. The second was the concept of scientific discovery, collection, and classification held in common with the origins of the discipline in Europe, North America, and other parts of the world.

Can we understand these founding concepts as ethical—as practice directed by a set of moral values held in higher regard than the contingencies of the moment? As with critiques of colonialism in general, it has become axiomatic that early African exploration and archaeology were both consequences and agents of Europe's colonial interests (Trigger 1990; Robertshaw 1990). But, in the framework of an inquiry about ethics, there is a risk of anachronism in leaving interpretation at this level. Many early archaeologists of Africa would have believed both that Europe had a moral obligation to bring a higher order of civilization to Africa and that their fieldwork would reveal the truth of human origins and histories through such evidence as stone tool typologies and sequences and art and artifact collections brought back to European museums for study, preservation, and display.

There can be few better examples of this colonial value system and of the contingent relationship between ethical values and politics identified by Pels (1999) than Cecil John Rhodes's motivation in combining the colonization of Mashonaland (later Rhodesia and Zimbabwe) with the sponsorship of excavations at Great Zimbabwe

(Garlake 1973; Hall 1995). In this Rhodes could claim to be establishing a historical truth (extending the patchy biblical account of the Queen of Sheba with modern archaeological evidence) and furthering a set of moral values (Europe's obligation to bring a higher order of society to Africa, still trapped in an earlier stage of social evolution). And, because Mashonaland was (in Rhodes's view, not generally shared in London) a source of land and mineral wealth of particular importance to the British Empire, the requirements of truth and morality served to "mask" politics in precisely the manner seen by Pels as the key to the "ethical triad" of anthropological practice.

In 1891 the first archaeological expedition to Great Zimbabwe left England under Rhodes's patronage and with the support of the Royal Geographic Society and the British Association for the Advancement of Science. Theodore Bent, the leader of the expedition, saw evidence in the stars. "It is remarkable that only stars of the northern hemisphere seem to have been observed at Zimbabwe. . . . This, of course, points to a northern origin for the people" (1969:174). This early civilization was overrun by the dark forces of barbarism; the ancestors of the "Karanga," whose past, "like all Kaffir combinations," was a story of "a hopeless state of disintegration" and who were little more than animals, to be classed together with "a tribe of baboons," "more closely allied to one another than they are to the race of white men, who are now appropriating the territory of both" (1969:33, 43).

However, it is one thing to recognize the contingencies of truth, morality, and material advantage and quite another to manage these interrelationships effectively. In the event, the requirements of truth claims escaped from the net of political control. Work by Bent and particularly by his successor, the notorious R. N. Hall, was sufficiently careless and cavalier to attract a backlash from the British Association, which sent first David Randall-MacIver and then, some years later, Gertrude Caton-Thompson, to investigate the site (Garlake 1973; Hall 1996). Caton-Thompson had in-depth knowledge of Egyptian archaeology and brought a fierce empiricism to the Zimbabwe controversy, basing her interpretations on a close reading of stratigraphy and the relative chronology of key assemblages. She has been widely celebrated as a pioneer of modern archaeological methods in sub-Saharan Africa, and in her 1931 monograph on Great Zimbabwe she asserted that she had "no germ of preconceived ideas as to the ruins' origin and age," was "unconcerned with speculations," and was "unencumbered by a priori hypotheses as to who might have done what, who sacrificed to the morning star, and who worshipped the new moon." These, she declared, were "subjects which have no place at all in the earlier chapters of archaeological research, and which lead, unless firmly tethered by chronological data, to wildernesses of deductive error" (Caton-Thompson 1931:2).

New Nationalisms

Africa may have seemed secure for continuing exploration in the colonial style when Caton-Thompson traveled to Great Zimbabwe in 1929, but in the years that followed nationalist movements grew across the continent, leading to the creation of nation-states from former colonial territories. Nationalists, whether opposing colonial regimes from the bush or seeking to consolidate postindependence identities, needed to find unifying historical themes that encouraged national pride and countered colonial narratives asserting that Africa had no past worthy of being called "history" with a sense of the richness of Africa's past (Hall 1996).

In West Africa "Negritude" writers stressed the superiority of African culture, with its mystical connections with the past and with the land, over the corrupt materialism of Europe. This was most prominently expressed in the work of the Senegalese intellectual Cheikh Anta Diop. Diop argued that there had been a close relationship between black Africa and ancient Egypt. He stressed the achievements of Egyptian civilization and argued that the ancient Egyptians had been black and that the Nile Valley was the point of origin for African people ranging from the Fulani to the Zulu. He used archaeological evidence to trace migration routes, arguing, for instance, that the "burial mounds" of the inland Niger Delta were West African versions of the pyramids (Diop 1979; Holl 1990). Subsequently, a distinctive brand of archaeology developed in the region. This work has remained closely connected to issues of national consciousness and ethnic identity, and writing has stressed the continuities between the past and the present, often providing a "charter" for the present day that is given authority by reference to the past (Hall 1996; Holl 1990).

The significance of a "grassroots consciousness" of the importance of the past and the way in which excitement about the past could lie hidden beneath colonial rule is well shown in Raymond Asombang's account of the museum assembled by Peter Shinwin Atanga at Akum, a few kilometers from Bameda in Cameroon. A farmer and bookshop keeper, Atanga started a private museum collection in the late 1940s. He saw the purpose of his collection as "teaching the past to posterity and providing material for research for Cameroonians, Africans and people of all races" (Asombang 1990). An example of the value given to archaeology after independence comes from Mozambique. Before 1975 there had been little widely shared interest in Mozambique's precolonial past. Independence brought a major drive to establish a history for the new nation that stressed origins deep in the past rather than its servile status to a colonial power. This was linked with a particular emphasis on public education. In 1977 a new Serviço Nacional de Museus e Antiguidades was set up with education goals on a national scale and a department of archaeology was established at the Universidade Eduardo Mondlane in Maputo. Apart from conducting research and teaching, staff concentrated on producing textbooks for schools and taught *agentes de cultura* at the secondary school level. Despite a protracted civil war, the number of known archaeological sites doubled in the first decade of independence (Sinclair et al. 1993:429).

Turning archaeology around in this way required the transformation of cultural institutions such as museums and universities. Raymond Asombang points out that, for many people, museums were inescapably part of the colonial legacy: "There is no denying the fact that the museum in its current form and structure is an alien institution in Africa. It was introduced by the colonial master. Despite arguments to the contrary, it is generally believed that the intention was to collect and preserve the culture of the colonized peoples." But acceptance that museums had a new role introduced new tensions. Should national museums stress cultural unity, seeking to smooth over historical differences in the interest of a perception of the future? Or should they mirror cultural diversity, protecting minority traditions from being lost from memory (Asombang 1990)?

When considered against the triad of truth claims, morality, and politics, African nationalist archaeology shows a revealing contrast with the colonial archaeology so well demonstrated in Rhodes's project for Great Zimbabwe. Whereas colonial archaeology, in common with many other archaeologies, masks its politics behind claims for truth and morality, African nationalist archaeology has tended to make its political agenda explicit, taking as an a priori condition the project of national reconstruction and seeking to use the evidence for the past as a means to develop national identity. This has been possible because its politics and moral baseline are independent—the injustices of colonialism and the imperative of national consciousness as a means of liberation. As a result, and rather than being categorized with nationalist movements in other parts of the world, African nationalist archaeology has been valorized as progressive and anticolonial.

Archaeology in South Africa

These brief impressions of colonial and nationalist archaeological practice in Africa have shown how the play between the discovery of truth, ethics, and politics has shaped strands within the broader discourse of anthropological inquiry. Consequently, it is not surprising that the practice of archaeology in South Africa should be different again. Apartheid legislation that followed the National Party's acquisition of power in 1948 took precedents of colonial control, underpinned them with a pervasive religious morality, and established a society organized by race and privilege that persisted long after similar systems of ethics had been discredited in other parts of the world and after all other African colonial regimes had been replaced by forms of majority rule (Hall 1984, 1988, 1990).

Because apartheid almost exclusively restricted the profession of archaeology to South Africans who were classified as white, archaeologists working in South Africa were denied both a domestic field of support and connections with the rest of the continent. In this situation, archaeologists' strongest connections were with North America and Europe. Given the increasing pressure against engagement with South Africa from the early 1980s onwards, these foreign partnerships were dominated by those who were interested in archaeological science and in theories and approaches such as structuralism and logical positivism that denied or played down the role of the politics of the present in the interpretation of the past. The niche for white South African archaeologists in the complex ecology of apartheid was that of apolitical practitioners working for a higher goal (science) in a living laboratory with abundant possibilities. This was most strongly expressed in Botswana in 1984, when the Southern African Association of Archaeologists failed to pass a resolution condemning apartheid, causing Zimbabwean and Mozambican archaeologists to withdraw from the organization and preparing the ground for a formal academic boycott of South African archaeology two years later.

South African archaeology's predominant interest in the truth value of the "archaeological record" is reflected in a well-developed tradition of archaeological science (with departments of archaeology located in the science divisions of their universities), a set of values that favors primary fieldwork over other forms of inquiry, and an interest in systems of classification. Of course, these are also characteristic of archaeological practice in other parts of the world, but in South Africa they are thrown into relief by the absence of counterbalancing intellectual strands. With the exception of rock-art studies, postprocessual archaeology is poorly developed. With the exception of specialized units, there is little interest in making the results of archaeological inquiry widely available. And, what is particularly significant given that written records rarely go back more than four hundred years, there is only the weakest of links with either social anthropology or history. Archaeology as it is practiced and written in South Africa has long been divorced from the interests of the large majority of South Africans and largely remains so a decade after the fall of the apartheid state.

The style of South African archaeology can again be illustrated by returning to that icon of southern Africa's past, Great Zimbabwe. Following Caton-Thompson's fieldwork in 1929, there was little research here until the late 1950s and early 1960s, when the availability of the technique of radiocarbon dating allowed the contentious issue of chronology to be largely resolved to the satisfaction of professional archaeologists (if not to many others). During Zimbabwe's war of liberation the site was available only to Rhodesian security forces and guerrilla fighters and became an important symbol of nationalism. But, following Zimbabwe's independence in 1980, Great Zimbabwe again became generally accessible and the key element in a broad, structuralist interpretation of the last five hundred years of a large swath of South Africa's Iron Age (Hall 1987).

This strong tradition in recent South African archaeological writing can be illustrated by taking a closer look at one key text—Thomas Huffman's *Snakes and Crocodiles* (1996). In Huffman's interpretation, Great Zimbabwe's central stone architecture, from the overall design of the stone walling to the smallest detail of decoration, is drawn into a schema that, in turn, rests on a "cognitive structure" that spans the best part of a millennium. This is set within an explicitly scientific ethic. What is important, Huffman writes, is "the relevance and success of the overall interpretation compared to other alternatives. The hypothesis based on the least dubious assumptions, covering the most data and with the greatest coherence and predictive potential is superior" (8). He sees in this and other sites a "Zimbabwe Pattern," a cultural system in which a sacred leader and a small number of officials lived secluded in an elevated enclosure, close by an area reserved for the leader's younger wives and for national rituals. Other wives lived in a separate residential area with an initiation center, and commoners were housed in a protective circle surrounding this elite area (13). Buildings, the use of symbols, and settlement design were integrated with social relations in a tightly welded unity, the essence of what it was and is to be Shona.

Making such symbolic interpretations—what Huffman calls "cognitive archaeology"—is a particular challenge to archaeological method. All the evidence was made prior to direct written description and beyond the reach of present-day oral histories. Consequently, Huffman's approach stands on two pillars—the utility of a normative theory of the human mind and the reconstruction of a direct ethnography stretching back from his own informants to the Portuguese in the early sixteenth century. Thus the Zimbabwe Pattern can be expressed—and is indeed represented—as a diagrammatic map of the Shona mind. Secular and sacred, private and public, front and back, and east and west are opposed along the dimension of life forces. First and second, male and female, senior and junior, and older and younger give their paired expression to the intersecting dimension of status. Wives and court, guards and musicians, and king and followers intersect again on the dimension of security. Huffman uses these "underlying principles of organisation" (1996:113) as the framework for understanding the expression of cognitive structure in Shona ethnography and the architecture and symbolism of settlements. For example, geometric designs in the stonework are read as representing the crocodile, the snake, and the ritual pool of water and, in terms of the generalized cognitive structure, as symbolizing the dimensions of life forces, status, and security. In turn, each of these key designs is seen to have both male and female forms, adding a further layer of complexity to the mental template.

On the basis of this argument for Shona "sameness" (Huffman 1996: 6) through four centuries of travelers' tales, ethnographic accounts, and recorded oral histories, Huffman matches details of the archaeological sites that fall into the same time period with details from the written record on the basis of what he describes as a "straightforward premise" (8):

> Since social and settlement organizations are different aspects of the same thing and products of the same view of the world, a continuity in settlement pattern is evidence for a continuity in social organization and world-view. Methodologically, therefore, where there is identity or at least no crucial difference between settlement patterns in the ethnographical present and archaeological past, we can infer identity in world-view and social organisation.

It is not merely that social meaning can be read from the archaeological evidence—the well-established practice of ethnographic analogy—but that settlement patterns themselves restrict the things that people can do in the places where they live; Huffman sees them as "permitting" and "making possible" a "limited range of behavior" (103). The Shona are, to turn a cliché, where they live; their cognitive structures do not allow them to step outside the boundaries of their dimensions of thought and binary-coded reading of the world.

For archaeology this is a useful premise, because it means that the bare traces of a long-abandoned village can be read with the same confidence as a rich ethnographic monograph. Rather than being subsidiary to historical and ethnographic texts, archaeological evidence becomes equal or superior, allowing, where necessary, ethnographic sources to be modified to fit the archaeological evidence: "Once general principles are extracted, archaeological data provide the historical context in which to judge ethnographic detail. Thus, there is a reciprocal relationship between archaeology and ethnology" (Huffman 1996:213).

Structuralism, as practiced at Great Zimbabwe, in the interpretation of many other Iron Age sites in South Africa, and in South African historical archaeology, can be seen as the apogee of scientific method, offering a series of generalized laws of human behavior, organized systematically and brought together as a "cognitive pattern," from which the meaning of partially preserved archaeological traces can be read. Used in this way, structuralist interpretations also deny history. To argue recursively between an ethnography that is based on an assumption of continuity and equivalence and an archaeology that preserves only the imprint of the richness and variety of the ways in which people lived is to invite circularity: this social custom elucidates an aspect of the archaeology, while that feature of the settlement pattern justifies the relevance of the ethnography. *Snakes and Crocodiles* consigns "the Shona" to timeless entrapment in a cognitive structure that has allowed no significant change over almost a millennium.

Beyond Ethics?

If we understand ethics as appealing to absolute principles to define conventions of behavior, then we can discern a number of distinct strands that have served to define the practice of archaeology in Africa: first, the ethics of the civilizing mission: the obligation to bring light to the "dark continent": second, the ethics of liberation, nationalist histories in support of the universal right to self-determination; third, the ethics of science, the pursuit of truth for its own sake, irrespective of political context or implication. The focus here, though, is *"beyond ethics"* and the morality of the "boundaries of the public and the professional," and this takes me back to the contemporary framework of the network society. What are the implications of these different ethical positions for practice today and for the relationship between practitioners and the people of the Richtersveld, the =Khomani, and all those others for whom the politics of their history is a matter of vital contemporary concern?

Although these ethical systems are to an extent sequential, they are also coterminous. The strong identification of South African archaeology with the absolutes of science can be seen as a refuge from an archaeology of nationalism to which South African archaeologists, themselves victims of the consequences of apartheid, had no access. In consequence, these ran as parallel ethical systems from the early 1960s on. At the same time, the concept of the West's civilizing mission to Africa, despite adaptations to fit more general moralities, has continued relentlessly. Its contemporary roots are anthropology's fascination with the Kalahari San, crystallized in Lee and DeVore's (1968) *Man the Hunter.* Despite trenchant critiques such as Wilmsen's (1989) *Land Filled with Flies* and good evidence for complex historical interactions between Khoe and Bantu-speakers in southern Africa that span centuries, for many the "hunter-gatherers" of the subcontinent are living fossils and an image of their own prehistory, now lost in the mists of time. This is the trope that accounts for the different reactions to the land claims of the Richtersveld and Khomani communities. In facing up to a diamond company, the people of the Richtersveld are everyday losers whose fate is regrettable but commonplace. In negotiating with the National Parks Board for a place within a conservation zone, the Khomani are a success story, demonstrating the continuity of the wilderness idea of Africa, and a model of sustainable development. As such, they are best addressed in the archaic language of another age: "We shall mend the broken strings of the distant past so that our dreams can take root."

That Thabo Mbeki should have chosen the Kalahari Gemsbok settlement agreement as a public opportunity is no quirk of individual sentiment. Similarly, the Khomani settlement is no unique case; there have been similar settlements to land claims in the northern part of the Kruger National Park and in Kwa-Zulu Natal, lauded as models for more widespread "sustainable development." One of the most pervasive features of the network society is the redistribution of resources and opportunities. Global electronic networks—Castells's "space of flows"—enable both the concentration of financial resources and high-level expertise in the "world cities" of the North and the West and the marketing of specific regional attributes in a global shopping mall. Africa has long been known for its wildlife and its exotic people, art, and memorabilia, and this trade value continues to grow with the global entertainment and leisure industry that thrives on the ease with which images can be distributed and worldwide travel for the affluent.

This sort of marketing is hardly surprising. In the global flows of Internet commerce, any African sector must emphasize its particularly local characteristics if it is to gain any competitive edge. In the mid-1990s South Africa's nascent online commodity marketing showed this trend. Web sites emphasized the ethnic and the exotic. SA Arts and Crafts, for example, was promoted as "a place for you to make all your ethnic and hand-created purchases via the Internet" (http://www.sacrafts.co.za). The Great African Emporium took a similar line, inviting the digital shopper to "step inside our oasis, and discover the wonders of Africa. Here you can sample and buy some of the exotic goods on offer. Hang up your pith helmet and step up to the counter." Merchants included African Legacies, offering fabrics, wooden key racks, and wooden puzzles "to bring a touch of Africa to your mantlepiece and coffee table, and South African Bears, featuring a golliwog and a range of teddy bears (http://www.emporium.co.za). A more recent example is Authentic Africa (http://www.authenticafrica.com), based in New York and Philadelphia, which offers "unique regional and tribal handcrafted objets d'art" with "a genuine ceremonial or daily use background" and a "flexible return policy" to ensure customer satisfaction. Authentic Africa's online showroom includes masks, spears, clubs, shields, fetishes, exotic animal skins, tribal music CDs, and dolls, together representing "the culture and craftsmanship of Angola to Zaire, from Ashanti to Zulu." Customers are warned to expect "markings or scrapes" on their purchases and should "rest assured that this is because it is in its original condition and was actually used in its related function" (Hall 2001b).

An enduring landmark in South Africa's virtual world—and offering a similar exoticism—is the Internet safari offered by Mala Mala, an exclusive private game reserve deep in the eastern lowveld. The design of this now-veteran web site captures the circle of representation that links the oldest images of the continent with their repetition via the latest media. A series of sepia-tinted maps recalls the discovery of untamed wilderness. First, a click of the mouse brings a map of Africa in the style of the seventeenth century—"Discover the untamed soul of Africa." A further keystroke takes the explorer closer in, with a map of southern Africa that places Mala Mala close to the fifteenth-century empire of the Monomatapa while also showing the present-day cities of Pretoria and Johannesburg. The next screen—Mala Mala itself—is accompanied by a quote from Sir Thomas Browne: "We carry within us the wonders we seek without us: there is all Africa and her prodigies in us." Finally, the web site provides details of how to make a reservation and offers the download of a free screen saver: "Why settle for any old screen saver when you can go wild with the sights and sounds of the African bush?" (http://www.malamala.com).

Thus the rise of the network society and the "information revolution" offers a rehabilitation of anthropology's original sin—the distancing of the exotic through devices that use space and time to draw a boundary between the civilized and primitive worlds (Fabian 1983). Through new technical devices—the collapse of time and space in virtual reality—Africa is made exotic through being readily accessible but always different. The thread of continuity with nineteenth-century social evolutionism was maintained through interpretive traditions such as structuralism's eternal presence in innate cognitive orders and through public discourse such as that of the Royal Academy's *Africa: The Art of a Continent*. Mala Mala uses the web's aesthetics to bring Sir Thomas Browne, an ancient landscape, and modern cities and airports onto the same surface. Land settlements with Africa's "oldest people" and other rural communities are an inevitable positioning that follows from this emerging order, because this is where the possibilities lie for revenues from the ever-expanding market in exotic tourism and its myriad of spin-off industries.

What set of general principles will guide these new terms of engagement? As is so often the case, Disney's imagineers have pointed the way. Florida's Disney Animal Kingdom presents Africa after colonialism and via the gateway of Harambane, an East African town claimed as "incredibly authentic" and seemingly a combination of Arab, Portuguese, and British colonial pasts. The Animal Kingdom's voices, though, are African, presiding over the ruins of colonialism, running crafts and safari businesses, and combating poachers. This theme is developed in the Pangani Forest Exploration Trail, imagined as a training school and sanctuary, a "joint effort by the citizens of Harambe and international conservation groups" under the direction of "Dr. K. Kulunda." The conservation school theme introduces people into the story in the form of "cultural representatives," such as the South African student Mamvelase from

Germiston, who states authoritatively that hippos can stay under water for five minutes without breathing. At the exit, there is a message from Dr. Kulunda: "To our esteemed visitors, thank you for joining us here today in the beautiful Pangani Forest. The staff and students hope that you have found here a renewed appreciation for all the animals of our wild Africa. It is only through our concerted efforts and commitment that we can hope to save these precious animals for future generations. Asante sana—thank you."

Dr. Kulunda and his cultural representatives position the visitor with the postcolonial citizens of Harambe and the international conservation organizations that are determined to save Africa's wildlife. This ethical identification is developed further in the Animal Kingdom's second major attraction, the Kilimanjaro Safari. This is set in the Harambe Wildlife Reserve, which the visitor is asked to imagine was established in the 1970s. Videos introduce the visitor to the animals, and the warden—a local citizen of Harambe—asks for help in combating poachers, whose destruction of the wildlife is illustrated by video. As the visitors rattle through the park, splashing through streams and navigating rickety bridges, benign antelopes, giraffes, and elephants watch from their appointed positions and Warden Wilson Matua directs the driver via a crackling radio link in a chase after an elephant-poaching gang.

Disney Animal Kingdom has appropriated the position of indigenous wildlife conservation after periods of colonial rule and turned this into moral theater and entertainment. Its postcolonial conservation and antipoaching themes draw visitors into the ethical project of its animal curators, helping to justify the visitors' expenditure. At the same time, it is made clear that this is all theater, presented by a "cast" that includes the animals. A third African attraction is a train journey. The Eastern Star Railway leaves "Africa" from Harambe Station, taking its passengers "backstage" to the Conservation Station. On the way, the line passes the animal houses where the conductor ("Crystal—all the way from South Africa") tells the passengers that the animals return each night and receive the "best care possible"; the animals are actors as well. The Conservation Station is dedicated to animal well-being: "Through field conservation efforts, emerging rescue programs, scientific studies, and public education efforts in the United States and other countries, Disney's Animal Kingdom cast are helping to save wildlife for the future." And at the end of the day, it's all good fun, best captured every afternoon in Mickey's Jammin' Jungle Parade, in which the newcomers in the Animal Kingdom are joined by the stars of The Lion King and the veterans of the Magic Kingdom, including the Mouse himself.

Situational Ethics

The morality-as-entertainment offered by Disney Animal Kingdom may be a caricature of the complex relations that define the new world of the network society, but there can be little doubt that, in the new flows of cultural capital and in the global diasporas that service new economic forms, identities have new saliences and that the past—and with it, archaeology—is invoked in new ways. Appadurai (1996:15) has termed this "culturalism—"the deliberate, strategic, and populist mobilization of cultural material." In this situation, "the past is not now a land to return to in a simple politics of memory. It has become a synchronic warehouse of cultural scenarios, a kind of temporal central casting, to which recourse can be taken as appropriate, depending on the movie to be made, the scene to be enacted, the hostages to be rescued" (1996:30).

And, of course, this is not all Disney, or all Africa. Yugoslavia's wars of disintegration were fought in the name of cultural affiliations and their archaeologies, whether Croatia's medieval Catholicism, Serbia's visceral attachment to the monasteries and churches of a long-established Orthodox Christianity, or Bosnia's Islamic histories (Hall 2001c). Thus in 1992 Serbian forces attacked Sarajevo's Oriental Institute with phosphorous grenades, weapons designed to maximize damage by fire. The entire holdings were destroyed, including 5,263 bound manuscripts in Arabic, Persian, Turkish, Hebrew, and Serbo-Croatian-Bosnian in Arabic script, as well as tens of thousands of Ottoman-era documents (Riedlmayer 1998). Later that same summer it was the turn of the National Library, known for the richness and diversity of its archive and preserving the record of centuries of Serb, Croat, and Muslim interaction. Hundreds of incendiary rockets were fired from Serbian artillery in the hills surrounding the city, followed by machine gun and mortar fire to deter people from rescuing the books and manuscripts: "black, sooty, still hot butterflies—books and papers aflame, the library's treasure—were flying around and falling over distant parts of the city" (Lovrenovic 1994).

What ethics are appropriate for this contemporary network society, with all its crosscutting complexity? What principles are appropriate for the practice of archaeology in Africa (and particularly—because it is the context from which I write—in South Africa), now and in the future?

Although Hardt and Negri's point that "clinging to the primacy of the concept of truth can be a powerful and necessary form of resistance" (2000:155) still stands, it is also clear that simple dichotomies between relative and absolute knowledge are misrepresentations that serve as distractions. As Donna Haraway showed some time ago, claims that all knowledge is socially constructed lead to "a kind of epistemological electro-shock therapy which, far from ushering us into the high stakes tables of the game of contesting public truths, lays us out on the table with self-induced multiple personality disorder" (1991:186). The issue was—and is—how to get the benefits of new knowledge, critique, and ethics in the same frame: "how to have simultaneously an account of radical historical contingency for all knowledge claims and knowing subjects, a critical practice for recognizing our own 'semiotic technologies' for making meanings, and a no-nonsense commitment to faithful accounts of a 'real' world, one that can be partially shared and friendly to earth-wide projects of finite freedom, adequate material abundance, modest meaning in suffering, and limited happiness" (187). Bruno Latour develops Haraway's position further through a close anthropological reading of science-in-action. For Latour, questions of whether "reality exists" or whether scientific knowledge is "absolute" are irrelevant. The purpose of "science studies" is to assist science in "sorting out the 'cosmos' from an 'unruly shambles'" by developing a "politics of things" (Latour 1999:22).

In considering the knowledge claims of the social sciences, Bent Flyvbjerg has argued that all effective inquiry will be contextualized and, consequently, that appropriate ethics will be situational. Flyvbjerg argues that social behavior is context-specific: "the problem in the study of human activity is that every attempt at a context-free definition of an action, that is, a definition based on abstract rules or laws, will not necessarily accord with the pragmatic way an action is defined by the actors in a concrete social situation" (2001:42). His response is to develop Aristotle's concept of phronesis—practical wisdom—to include power. Building on the tradition of Nietzsche and following Foucault and Bourdieu, Flyvbjerg argues that social behavior is always penetrated by power.

What are the implications of this position for the ethics of practice? Because such research is always shaped by context, researchers necessarily position themselves, in one way or another, in relation to one or more reference groups within the social context they are studying. This is evident in the overview of archaeological practice in Africa. With the wisdom of hindsight, we can see clearly how early archaeology was aligned with the reference group of explorers and colonial administrators, whether Napoleon's generals who directed the exploration of Egypt, social evolutionists who believed in Europe's civilizing mission

in Africa, or district commissioners who believed that orderly categorization and scientific reports underpinned effective rule. We can also see
how the nationalist archaeologies of the mid-twentieth century were
aligned with the objectives of independence movements and newly
independent governments—how interpretations such as Cheikh Anta
Diop's argument for the southern diffusion of Egyptian civilization met
the needs of postcolonial administrators attempting to build the
instruments of civil society. More controversially, because it is a past
that is still upon us, it can be argued that South Africa's dominant
paradigm of archaeology-as-science appealed to a reference group of
white academics caught between the opposing forces of a racist state,
which they rejected, and black nationalism, to which they could not
easily affiliate.

If one accepts the case for situational ethics and the inevitable
alignment between the researcher and one or more reference groups
within the society that is being studied, then it follows that ethical
research will recognize the nexus of knowledge, power, and politics and
declare its alignments explicitly. Again, this can be related specifically
to the history of archaeology in Africa.

In rejecting a motion condemning apartheid at its Botswana meeting
in 1984, the Southern African Association of Archaeologists was not
saying that it supported the apartheid state. Rather, its South African
and U.S. members were arguing that politics has no place in the pursuit
of knowledge and therefore the resolution was unethical. Situational
ethics turns this argument on its head. In failing to acknowledge that
the creation of new knowledge in South African archaeology was the
result of a play of interests and resources with political consequences,
those opposing the motion were obfuscating the issue through an
indefensible claim for context-free, absolute ways of knowing about the
past; it was their position that was unethical. Ethical research requires
an explicit consciousness of the role of power: "Who gains, and who
loses? Through what kinds of power relations? And is it desirable to do
so? Of what kind of power relations are those asking these questions
themselves a part?" (Flyvbjerg 2001:131).

Recognizing the role of power and politics in research is, then, central
to an appropriate ethics. Such recognition also allows an appropriate
position with regard to empirical evidence. Archaeology is a practical
discipline in which fieldwork and the demonstrated ability to work with
"hard evidence" are particularly valorized, a tradition that is further
complicated by gender. A concern for politics and social context has
often been caricatured as "soft" and "feminine," the recourse of those

who do not have the endurance for excavations and prolonged data analysis.

But once we see (as Haraway, Latour, and others have shown) that the dichotomy between "reality" and "relativity" is an artificial construct, the requirement for situational ethics leads naturally into a requirement for ethics in assembling and managing evidence. This is because, as Flyvbjerg has shown, every interpretation in contextualized research must be based on claims of validity that are built up from the rationality of the detailed empirical data. Such validity claims are arguments that stand until better, empirically based arguments are developed. The objective of such work (and therefore its "morality," although Flyvbjerg does not use the term) is to increase "the capacity of individuals, organizations, and society to think and act in value-rational terms" (Flyvbjerg 2001:130). In other words, because situational ethics requires that research be explicitly located in a social context, it is not enough to satisfy oneself (the "sovereign mind" or "brain-in-a-vat" of the Cartesian and Kantian traditions of absolute knowledge [Latour 1999]) or one's professional colleagues. Reference groups must also be satisfied and persuaded through interpretation and argument that is based on the rationality of evidence.

In making the connection with reference groups, "situational archaeologists" need to be particularly conscious of the insidious qualities of time. In the Cartesian tradition of archaeology-as-science, time is seen as an external dimension; along with space, time is an axis of a graph on which archaeological observations are plotted. But time is a more complicated concept than this allows. As Fabian (1983) has shown, the denial of coevalness was one of anthropology's founding strategies, and, as this overview of archaeological practice has shown, this same denial has persisted to the present day. An ethical practice for the network society needs to recognize the importance of "intersubjective time" (Fabian 1983), allowing histories to interrelate rather than freezing "cultures" into "ages" or ethnically labeled boxes in the style of *Africa: The Art of a Continent.*

Understanding the role of empirical evidence sheds light on one of the stranger aspects of archaeological practice in southern Africa. Since 1994, when South Africa gained a postapartheid constitution and a representative government, the general interest in archaeology has declined. Student demand has fallen off, and university departments have closed. Museum budgets have been cut, and resources available for new fieldwork are at an all-time low. Many archaeologists have been surprised and shocked by this reversal, having expected the opposite, given that archaeology is the only route into precolonial black history. There is a stark contrast with earlier times that seems, at first glance, bizarre. Thus, when Gertrude Caton-Thompson presented the results of her fieldwork at Great Zimbabwe at a conference in Johannesburg in 1931, her report was headline news not only in the Transvaal but also a thousand miles to the south in Cape Town. Ian Smith's successionist Rhodesia of the 1960s and 1970s was sufficiently concerned to preserve the "white civilization" line of interpretation that Rhodes had initiated that the security forces took action against archaeologists who disagreed. But when this history of the role of evidence is set within its context, the paradox is solved. Caton-Thompson's reference group was politically and economically dominant and demanded to see and debate the evidence. Today South African archaeology, which eschewed the politics of context and is an overwhelmingly white discipline, has a reference group made up largely of its own practitioners.

But how should an appropriate reference group be identified? Flyvbjerg leaves this question open. For him the primary ethical imperatives are recognizing that research is contextual in the first place and then seeking to increase a society's internal capacity for "value-ethics" over contingent "instrumental-ethics." But in social contexts such as Africa's, where social and economic differentiation is far more acute than in the West and the North and where choices of research priority may be literally a matter of life and death, such an approach is incomplete.

Here it is helpful to combine Haraway's earlier formulation with Nancy Fraser's work on the "postsocialist position." In considering an appropriate agenda for feminist inquiry, Haraway proposes "a doctrine of embodied objectivity." This involves "seeing" from the perspective of the "subjugated" not because people who are oppressed are "innocent" but because "in principle they are least likely to allow denial of the critical and interpretative core of all knowledge. . . . 'subjugated' standpoints are preferred because they seem to promise more adequate, sustained, objective, transforming accounts of the world" (1991:191). For her part, Fraser is concerned with social justice and the reconnection of political economy and the "symbolic order." This project necessarily requires an ethical position from which forms of injustice are identified—a position that Fraser opens up by developing Habermas's concept of a public sphere, understood as "a theater in modern societies in which political participation is enacted through the medium of talk": "something like Habermas's idea of the public sphere is indispensable to critical social theory and to democratic political practice . . . no attempt to understand the limits of actually existing late-capitalist democracy can succeed without in some way or another making use of it" (1997:70–71). Fraser argues that Habermas's founding concept needs elaboration and modification, allowing for a "plurality of competing publics" and, in particular, "subaltern counterpublics" where subordinate groups develop counterdiscourses that formulate "oppositional interpretations" of "identities, interests and needs" (1997:81).

Taken together, Haraway's and Fraser's conceptualizations identify both the criteria for an appropriate positioning for an ethical, contextualized research and the channels in which this engagement can take place in the network society. In this view, anthropologists—and archaeologists—are not all-knowing experts who defend their rights as a privileged professional caste. Nor can they be divorced from the context in which they work; their contextualization is inevitable, if often unrecognized. Consequently, the issue is not whether the concept of ethics is still relevant—whether the practice of archaeology in Africa can be "beyond ethics." The issue is rather to make the ethics of practice explicit, empowering, in David Harvey's (2000b) phrase, "insurgent architects" who can contribute to the competing publics and "counterpublics" that serve to challenge and limit the hegemony of dominant interests in our network society.

Part 3

Exemplars and Warnings

A Science of the Gray: Malthus, Marx, and the Ethics of Studying Crop Biotechnology

Glenn Davis Stone

"Crop biotechnology" encompasses a wide range of technologies, but most of the vexing ethical issues concern the technology of genetic modification (genetic engineering, recombinant DNA). In genetic modification the scientist usually isolates and removes genes from one or more organisms (virus, bacterium, plant, or animal), recombines them in a gene construct, and then introduces them into a target organism. The target organism is then a genetically modified organism.

My first engagement with genetically modified agriculture was when I bought a Flavr Savr tomato—the first genetically modified organism marketed in the United States—at a Manhattan greengrocer's in 1995. The connection between this tomato (engineered to rot slowly) and my research activity (then focused on conflict, population, and agricultural change in Nigeria) seemed remote. Yet by 2000 I was not only conducting field research on genetically modified crops but taking a leave from university teaching to participate in the modification of crops. This change in research focus confronted me with a set of ethical problems I had never faced in my previous work on the social aspects of nonindustrial agricultural systems. In fact, it was partly stimulated by ethical issues: as much as anything else, it was the biotech industry's ethical self-justifications that led me to take up this research. Crop biotechnology took a remarkable turn in the late 1990s, when the collapse of its market in the United Kingdom and continental Europe was followed by a corporate media campaign claiming an ethical high ground by promising to feed the Third World. Claims by anti–genetic modification activists also gravitated toward ethical grounds for blocking the technology from the Third World (and elsewhere, for that matter). As an anthropologist who studied food production in the Third World, I recognized that both sides suffered from a studiously blinkered perspective on the topic. Whatever weaknesses anthropology may have as a discipline, one of its strengths is the holistic perspective it can offer on such topics, and, given the importance of the biotechnology debate, I had difficulty justifying remaining on the sidelines. Yet entering this arena as an anthropological researcher posed its own set of ethical questions, which I conceive as a case of contested *ethical platforms*.

Crop biotechnology lies at the intersection of a remarkably wide set of important concerns, and it can be (and is being) condoned or condemned on widely varying grounds. Biotech discourse is aptly described as "a patch quilt of neighborly and competing factions" (Visvanathan and Parmar 2002:2715). But from the jungle of arguments, claims, and predictions emerge a few key positions that we may call ethical platforms—rationales for prioritizing or privileging concerns, "big-picture" meta-arguments that often appeal to high-level implicit propositions. My concern in this chapter is with the interplay among ethical platforms: the proponents' case, based on neo-Malthusian claims by industry and allies, an opposing case, based on issues in political economy (best developed by Marxist writers), and the responsibilities of an anthropologist entering such contested terrain.

The Proponents' Ethical Platform: Biotech Neo-Malthusianism

Pioneering experiments in genetic modification began in the early 1970s, and by 1983 plants were being genetically modified (Lurquin 2001; Charles 2001). The first commercial genetically modified product sold in the United States was the tomato mentioned above, and by 1996 genetically modified cotton, soy, and maize seed had begun to penetrate American farming while genetically modified ingredients were spreading throughout the American food supply. Soon after this, genetically modified crops encountered disastrous opposition in Europe and particularly in Britain. The main resistance was triggered not by the first genetically modified food in British stores (tomato paste, clearly labeled, which sold well) but by the arrival of American genetically modified soya, which went into countless processed food products. Various reasons for the subsequent British aversion to genetic modification have been cited, including different attitudes toward government regulation, a stronger and more mainstream green movement, and exquisitely bad timing in relation to the mad cow disease scandal. It did not help that the corporation behind the soya (and also the world leader in crop biotechnology) was Monsanto, a bête noire of the European green movement. In 1997 the smoldering opposition to genetically modified products burst into flame, and by 1998 British grocery chains were removing genetically modified products from their shelves (Purdue 2000; Lambrecht 2001; Charles 2001; Levidow 1999; Stone 2002a).

The closing of European markets did much more than hurt U.S. exports. The European backlash also provided—and continues to provide—inspiration and support to the opposition to genetically modified organisms worldwide. The collapse of the European market put Monsanto and the biotechnology industry on notice about the precariousness of the entire enterprise and the urgency of winning over a suspicious and potentially hostile public. Monsanto reacted with a didactic media campaign in Britain, the spectacular failure of which left the company's director of communications out of work and its CEO apologizing to a Greenpeace convention.

One of the themes of Monsanto's "Let The Harvest Begin" campaign was the need for crop biotechnology to feed the hungry in developing countries. In 2000 Monsanto and six other biotech firms jointly formed the Council for Biotechnology Information (CBI), a public relations consortium with an initial war chest of $250 million (Lambrecht 2001:9) for TV and newspaper ads, web sites, and even coloring books. From the outset, the driving theme was the promise of and need for genetically modified crops in developing countries. This was hardly an obvious issue to campaign on, since over 99 percent of the acreage devoted to genetically modified crops were in the United States, Canada, and Argentina as of 1999 (and the number is still over 95 percent).[1] But it was an issue that the CBI partners could agree on (whereas insecticide reduction was not—some of the biotech companies were still in that business), and it seemed to resonate reasonably well with the American public (if somewhat less so with the Europeans).

Genetic engineers were interested in the developing world not only for its rhetorical value. By 1999, genetically modified crops were available to farmers in China, Mexico, and South Africa, test plots were growing in India, and *Science* published an article entitled "Crop Engineering Goes South" (Moffat 1999). Actually, the crop leading genetic modification into the south was not a subsistence crop but cotton, and while cotton farmers did offer interesting fodder for the public relations mill (Stone 2002b), the industry campaign focused mainly on the malnourished masses.

The CBI campaign was also provided with a very timely poster child in the form of "Golden Rice," which appeared on the cover of *Time* in July 2000 as a plant that "could save a million kids a year." Developed as part of the Rockefeller Foundation's Asia Rice Initiative, Golden Rice was a prototype that contained genes for producing beta carotene in the endosperm. Its aim was to mitigate vitamin-A-deficiency blindness in poor children on rice-based diets. The CBI soon flooded the U.S. television and print media with ads touting Golden Rice. Although the corporate sector had refused to fund development of Golden Rice (Potrykus 2000), it was not long before the industry had apparently spent more advertising it than Rockefeller had spent developing it (much to Rockefeller's dissatisfaction [see Brown 2001]).

This rhetorical move south was a response to an increasingly polarized public debate in which negative biotech coverage was just reaching its peak in the United Kingdom (Gaskell et al. 2003). Its intent was to establish for the biotech debate an ethical platform based on a neo-Malthusian dogma tailored to the situation (Kleinman and Kloppenburg 1991). Variants on Malthus's doctrine have had a long history of surges in Western popular and intellectual culture; these neo-Malthusianisms have differed through the years, reflecting their times and often having major impacts on public opinion and policy (Ross 1998). The particular variety of neo-Malthusianism holding sway at the time (particularly in North America) did not suit biotechnology's public relations problem: it focused on environmental security problems rather than hunger. Filling the political space left by the collapse of the Soviet Union and the cold war paradigm, "environmental security neo-Malthusianism" emphasized conflicts and societal breakdown as results of resource scarcity ultimately driven by overpopulation (Peluso and Watts 2001)[2] The biotechnology industry and its academic allies, backed by a media budget such as no previous neo-Malthusianism had enjoyed, refocused attention on the crude balance between mouths and mouthfuls, much as had Paul Ehrlich's (1968) neo-Malthusianism of the late 1960s and 1970s. However, this "biotech neo-Malthusianism" parted with Ehrlich's in touting agricultural technology as a solution. It has come to assume a dominant role in the debate and has become a predictable mantra at the opening of presentations advocating genetically modified crops. It can be decomposed into several dogmas, concerning demography, agriculture, and investment (for a different analysis specifically of Monsanto's discourse, see Kleinman and Kloppenburg 1991).

1. *Demography*. The primary dogma is that the various problems posed by biotechnology are trumped by the specter of population outstripping food supply. This follows Malthus's explicit argument that unchecked population increases geometrically while subsistence increases arithmetically ([1798] 1959:5).[3] Prominent biotechnologists have claimed demographic trends to be heading toward "Malthus's worst predictions" (Martina McGloughlin, in *Hotwired* 1997). Yet in some ways Malthusian doctrine has been turned on its head. Malthus's primary concern with the British poor is replaced by the focus on hunger in an overpopulated Third World; there is no mention of the class distinctions that preoccupied Malthus and certainly no mention of the thirty-five million food-insecure people in the United States, the world's leading producer of genetically modified crops (Nord, Andrews, and Carlson 2003).

Biotech neo-Malthusianism routinely presents assured projections of future population levels, reflecting popular notions sufficiently entrenched that no plus-or-minus factor or source seems to be needed. Indeed, the causal link between population and famine often goes unstated: trained to perceive the world as a place of food shortages rather than surpluses, the public readily makes the causal link between population growth and malnourishment when provided with numbers of hungry.

2. *Agricultural growth*. Biotech neo-Malthusianism depicts existing agriculture as already maximized, with further increases generally being impossible without biotechnology. This is a remarkable reversion to Malthus's late-eighteenth-century understanding of agricultural inelasticity. Malthus was writing before the era of rapid technological change in agriculture and before any comparative research on means of raising output by increasing labor and material inputs. He offered only this rudimentary acknowledgment of what today we would call agricultural intensification and raising of producer prices ([1798] 1959:33):

> Premiums might be given for turning up fresh land, and if possible encouragements held out to agriculture above manufactures, and to tillage above grazing. Every endeavour should be used to weaken and destroy all those institutions relating to corporations, apprenticeships, etc., which cause the labours of agriculture to be worse paid than the labours of trade and manufactures.

However, he saw such steps only as "palliatives" because of the absolute impossibility, from the fixed laws of our nature, of removing the pressure of want from the lower classes of society (25–35). Biotech neo-Malthusianism also stresses agricultural inelasticity, but not as an inevitability: it depicts production as expandable by (and only by) technological means. For instance, in "Without Biotechnology, We'll Starve," the director of an industry-supported university biotechnology program warned that "the human population continues to grow, while arable land is a finite quantity. So unless we will accept starvation or placing parks and the Amazon Basin under the plow, there really is no alternative to applying biotechnology to agriculture" (McGloughlin 1999:164). This position resonates well enough with popular notions that Senator Christopher Bond read it into the *Congressional Record*, in remarks immediately republished on Monsanto's web site.

These two dogmas are combined in the claim that only through biotechnology can starvation be averted in less developed countries (Thomson 2000):

> The recent debate over biotechnology foods is a luxury well-fed people of the industrialized world can afford. But in developing nations, where the population is soaring while the supply of farmland shrinks, people are grappling with a much thornier—and higher-stakes—dilemma. Unless they can grow more food on less land they will starve. . . . Biotechnology crops are safe and nutritious and offer perhaps the only hope for producing enough food for a growing world population.

3. *Incentives to capital.* A key feature in biotech neo-Malthusianism is the explicitly capitalist veneer it adds to the model of overcoming overpopulation through technology. It holds that corporate investment is vital to the scientific and technological advances needed for agricultural growth; strong incentives to capital are needed to feed the poor. This argument has featured in other struggles over proprietary rights in agriculture, such as the disputes surrounding the 1970 Plant Variety Protection Act (Kloppenburg 1988:131). Malthus would never have made such an argument, not just because it militated against the feeding of the poor but because his writing predated the expansion of agrarian capitalism (Wood 2000). But stressing the need for agricultural investment to feed developing countries is important because of the high levels of investment required by biotechnology and because industry has been put on the defensive by publicity surrounding gene-use restriction technologies (GURTs): nicknamed "Terminator" by genetic modification opponents, these are technologies for creating sterile seeds.[4] Although reviled by various parties that support and even practice genetic modification for developing countries (including the

Rockefeller Foundation and the network of international agricultural research labs), it is staunchly defended by biotech neo-Malthusians (Weiss 1999):

> Supporters see in Terminator a possible solution to Third World hunger and poverty, which could become more widespread in coming years as populations expand and farmlands are lost. "The rhetoric has been extremely alarmist without looking at the whole situation," [the U.S. Department of Agriculture (USDA) developer of the technology, Mel Oliver] said. Henry Shands, assistant administrator for gene resources at the USDA's ARS [Agricultural Research Service], said foreign farmers need to recognize that biotech companies are not going to export their best-engineered varieties to parts of the world where patent protection is weak unless they can be assured farmers won't resell or replant harvested seeds. [GURTs], he and others said, will give poor farmers access to better seeds.

Asserting Ethical Priorities

In the 1970s, Paul Ehrlich used to cut off critics who sought to raise other issues in response to his demographic catastrophism by saying, "There are other problems, but if you don't solve this one you won't be around to solve the others." Biotech neo-Malthusianism is used in the same way: to put the biotechnology issue on an emergency footing that diminishes objections based on longer-range and more synthetic criteria. For instance, the head of an industry-backed foundation recently lashed out at genetic modification critics: "To turn a blind eye to 40,000 people starving to death every day is a moral outrage. . . . We have an ethical commitment not to lose time in implementing transgenic technology" (Macilwain 1999:342).

Senator Bond, from biotech-heavy Missouri, exemplifies how neo-Malthusian ethics can be used to demean critics (2000:S61):

> Let me emphasize this critical point. The issue of risk is not one-dimensional. Yes, we must understand and evaluate the relative risk to a Monarch Butterfly larvae. . . . But there is another risk. That risk is that naysayers and the protectionists succeed in their goals to kill biotechnology and condemn the world's children to unnecessary blindness, malnutrition, sickness and environmental degradation.

Similarly, the Washington Legal Foundation (2002) writes, "So why is it that so many professional activist groups and special interest radicals have no appetite for genetically enhanced foods? How can they attack dramatic technological advances that could end world hunger?"

The theme is sounded most indignantly by the Kenyan biotechnologist Florence Wambugu, who asserts: "The biggest risk in Africa is doing nothing. I appreciate ethical concerns, but anything that doesn't help feed our children is unethical" (Butler 1999). The academic biotechnologist C. S. Prakash (2000) writes that "anti-technology activists accuse corporations of 'playing God' by genetically improving crops, but it is these so-called environmentalists who are really playing God, not with genes but with the lives of poor and hungry people." Critical opposition is even branded as crime. One biotech executive said, "We're talking about the food security of the world. . . . When people talk about crimes against humanity—wouldn't it be a crime if political narcissism delayed things to the point where there were major food shortages in the Third World?" (Raymond Rodriguez, quoted in Charles 2001:262). Ingo Potrykus (of Golden Rice fame) announced at the 2000 World Food Prize conference that Golden Rice critics were potentially guilty of murder.

The primary target of this invective may be professional activists, but the relevance to social science research on genetically modified crops is obvious. This ethical platform demands that objections to the central role of corporations in developing the technology be outweighed by considerations of raising food output in the Third World and, indeed, that that role be embraced.

Biotech neo-Malthusianism is, of course, by no means the only rationale for promoting genetically modified crops (cases are also made on the basis of free trade and environmental advantages, for instance). I have isolated it here because it offers the most developed and influential ethical argument for crop genetic modification and because it directly concerns issues that an agrarian anthropologist may be obliged to confront. In now turning to the biotechnology opposition, one finds a welter of perspectives, including several that are based in part on ethics. However, given my starting point—the agrarian anthropologist's ethical position entering this arena—I will examine only the position that offers a well-developed ethical platform, which is, moreover, a platform that directly contradicts the tenets of biotech neo-Malthusianism.

An Opposing Ethical Platform: Political Economy of Agriculture

There is in social science an important and diametrically opposed ethical platform based on issues in political economy. Its application specifically to biotechnology may be less developed, but its underlying logic is well known. It maintains that considerations of raising food output in the Third World are trumped by considerations of the central role of biotechnology in expanding the role of corporations. It is not necessarily Marxist, although the relevant ideas have been best developed within the Marxist tradition. This began with Marx himself in discussions of agricultural technology as a mechanism of capitalist penetration ([1858]:527–528):

> If agriculture rests on scientific activities—if it requires machinery, chemical fertilizer acquired through exchange, seeds from distant countries, etc., and if rural, patriarchal manufacture has already vanished . . . then the [products of external trade] appear as *needs* of agriculture. . . . Agriculture no longer finds the natural conditions of its own production within itself, naturally, arisen, spontaneous, and ready-to-hand, but these exist as an industry separate from it. . . . This pulling away of natural ground from the foundations of every industry . . . is the tendency of capital.

Agriculture has long posed difficulties to this capitalist penetration (Mann and Dickinson 1978), and the "pulling away of natural ground" has occurred only in grudging stages. A key step in the process was the advent of nonreplantable hybrid seeds (Kloppenburg 1988; Lewontin and Berlan 1986); another was the flood of cheap nitrogen fertilizer following World War II that ended integrated crop-stock production (Foster and Magdoff 2000). Today, as biotechnology firms use genetic modification to render seeds sterile and make natural properties dependent on chemical inputs (the so-called Terminator and Traitor technologies), Marx's general point remains highly relevant, indeed prescient.

Given the vituperativeness of the debates, I should note that my concern here is with arguments for opposing genetically modified crops, not on their advocates' political leanings. The political inspirations of the various opponents vary widely. Moreover, charges of "Marxist " are used in North America to discredit genetic modification opponents. Vandana Shiva is attacked as Marxist by various conservative groups in the United States (for example, Georgetown College Republicans 2002); Greenpeace founder Patrick Moore, who later switched allegiances, disparages Greenpeace as having filled up with pro-Soviet Marxists after the end of the cold war (Elvin 1997).

Whatever the opponents' politics, the theory that crop genetic modification is driven not by food supply, environment, or farmers but by the needs of capital to commodify the "natural ground" of agricultural production fits some of the history of this technology well. Soon after the first experiments in recombinant DNA, it began to emerge that this technology would open the door to capital's claiming proprietary rights over the basic productive force of genes.[5] Despite the profound economic, political, and ethical questions involved, the United States saw little debate on or public appreciation of the advent of gene patenting. Remarkably, it was never formally decided that genes should be patentable in the United States; it was a latent result of decisions on other matters made before any plant had been genetically modified. Yet genetic modification was pivotal in the advent of gene patenting, and this warrants a closer look because of its relevance to the ethical platform being considered.

"Products of nature" are ineligible for utility patents by long-established principle in American law, but exceptions have been allowed for "artificially purified forms."[6] As early as an 1873 case involving Louis Pasteur, the patent office granted a patent on "yeast, free from organic germs of disease, as an article of manufacture," and in 1910–11 patents were granted on purified forms of adrenaline, aspirin, and calcium carbide (Gipstein 2003). This would seem, however, to have little to do with ownership of plants or genes. Such purified variants of natural substances were patentable only if the difference in purity rendered the product "for every practical purpose a new thing" (Golden 2001:125). Even the 1952 Patent Act, which famously declared "anything under the sun that is made by man" to be patentable, would seem to leave natural genes immune.

Proprietary rights over breeder-developed plants came not from utility patents but from plant patents (provided by the Plant Protection Act of 1930) and certificates (from the Plant Variety Protection Act of 1970); these rights pertained to whole plants that had not existed previously in nature, and they had various limitations that utility patents lacked (Hamilton 1993). But with genetic modification came the need to rethink what an invented organism was. In the early 1970s the General Electric biologist Ananda Chakrabarty used early methods of genetic modification to transform a bacterium so that it would degrade crude oil. The patent office allowed the claim on his method of transferring genes but not his claim on the bacterium itself, which was deemed to be a product of nature. In 1980 this was overturned in *Diamond v. Chakrabarty*.[7] Burger's (1980:2208) majority opinion (in a five-to-four decision) held that the genetically modified microorganism was patentable because it "is not a hitherto unknown natural phenomenon, but a nonnaturally occurring manufacture or composition of matter—a product of human ingenuity."

This ruling took on particular significance because the "purification exception" had just been extended to biological products. In the 1979 *Bergy* decision, the Court of Customs and Patent Appeals held that a particular pure bacterial culture was a "product of a microbiologist" rather than a product of nature (Golden 2001). This made into law the position of the patent office first expressed in the Pasteur patent, and it did so just in time for the law to be applied to DNA sequences. The combined result of the *Bergy* and *Chakrabarty* rulings was to render the "product of nature" doctrine "effectively toothless, because biotechnology by nature involves isolating and replicating biological materials to produce 'unnatural' levels of purity" (Golden 2001:127). Before a DNA gene can be transferred or altered, it must be isolated and cloned, which leaves it in an artificially purified form eligible for patenting. As Golden (2001:127–128) puts it, "with respect to biotechnology, the century-old 'purification exception' tends to swallow the rule."

This established the right to exclusive control over a fundamental productive force, and biotech corporations promptly began a period of explosive growth and frenzied patenting of genes. In some cases, genes were actually invented—examples are the Flavr-Savr antisense PG gene and Monsanto's synthesized Bt gene (Martineau 2001; Charles 2001)— but most patented genes were merely located and purified. The process has been likened to the gold rush (Rai 2000) or the Oklahoma Land Run, as in this description by Jerry Caulder, who left Monsanto to form Mycogen (Charles 2001:48):

> Like the early U.S. railroads, which made their profits selling land rather than by carrying passengers or freight, Caulder decided the near-term profits in agricultural biotechnology lay in intellectual real estate. "My strategy was simple," Caulder says. "Let's find as many genes as we can and patent them. We'd jump ahead and build intellectual property." Caulder saw the early competition in biotechnology as a kind of Oklahoma Land Run, a race for property rights.

Yet the analogy between genes and plots is deceptive. Plots of land are unique, and ownership of one does not keep a different buyer from owning another; a forty-niner gained exclusive rights only to gold on his claim, not to gold on other similar land or to gold itself. In contrast, U.S. patent #5,352,605 applies to the biotechnological use of every CaVM 35S promoter in every strand of DNA in every country where the patent is recognized. In sum (Golden 2001:130–131):

what might have seemed to be entrenched doctrines of patent law prior to 1980 have shown remarkable flexibility in the face of the biotechnology industry's craving for expansive intellectual property rights. The patentability of most basic biotechnological products is now well established, and supposedly central requirements such as utility and nonobviousness have often merely nibbled at the margins of patentability's broad realm.

Gene patenting in the United States was quickly followed by a push to internationalize such proprietary rights. In the 1994 Uruguay Round of the General Agreement on Tariffs and Trade, which established the World Trade Organization, 137 countries agreed to move toward harmonizing intellectual property rights by adopting patent or other sui generis protection for plants. Signers included India and several other developing countries that were to become crucial in the debate on biotechnology.

This ethical platform, then, argues that the package of genetic modification and privatized gene rights is the latest stage in the capitalist penetration of agriculture, an enormously transformative stage that is being exported to the Third World (Kloppenburg 1988; Lappé and Bailey 1998; Lewontin 2000). It further recognizes the devastating effects of capitalization of agriculture in industrialized countries, including the elimination of most farmers; indeed, Hobsbawm marks the disappearance of peasantries as the signal social transformation of the past half-century (1994:289). Large numbers of peasant farmers may still be on the land in the Third World, but the continuation of peasantries would be threatened by the specter of U.S.-style farm concentration (Magdoff, Foster, and Buttel 2000). If one accepts these threats to farmers as more credible than famine from absolute food shortages, could this not impel one to prioritize the impeding of the technology over a quixotically "objective" research agenda that could generate fodder for the biotech media machine? After all, the lead item in the American Anthropological Association's Code of Ethics is "Anthropological researchers have primary ethical obligations to the people, species, and materials they study and to the people with whom they work. These obligations can supersede the goal of seeking new knowledge."

The problem is that it is only after seeking objective knowledge that the anthropologist can even begin an informed assessment of the relative threats of the courses of action recommended by the competing ethical platforms. What the two ethical platforms appear to have in common is an overriding commitment to an ethical black-and-white. Both are intended to delegitimate an examination of the grays.

Prejudicial, Your Honor

The two ethical platforms do more than simply make a case for or against biotech; they inveigh against detailed scrutiny of biotechnology's various potential impacts on the grounds that such considerations would threaten larger ethical imperatives with ultimately trivial impediments. Each challenges the validity of an objective-as-possible investigation of the effects of genetically modified crops in developing countries: research findings, even if "accurate," may have broader harmful effects that outweigh the value of the information made public. For example, the ecologist Allison Snow has suffered withering criticism from the biotech neo-Malthusian perspective for finding that outcrossing transgenes could confer adaptive advantage on wild sunflowers: "it is unknown how many [Africans] starved to death" as a result of her work, fumed biologist Neal Stewart in a major biotechnology journal (2003:353).[8] Again, Altieri has criticized my attempt to analyze fallacies on both sides of the biotech debate, arguing that anthropologists should know that "technical choices are simultaneously political choices," that they should criticize technologies "pursued without concern for the environment or social displacement," and that "as long as researchers attempt to maintain political 'neutrality' their research will always serve those who are in a position to dictate the research agenda"; he goes on to link production of knowledge in international agricultural research to the demise of struggles over land and water (2002:619).

I agree with the premise of both ethical platforms that there may be information or lines of inquiry that are like the evidence that is excluded from a trial as prejudicial: they should be avoided because their probative value is exceeded by the potential damage to an analysis of larger issues. The problem here is how one knows a priori what environmental or social effects genetic modification in general or any particular use of it will have. Genetic modification is a highly variable and rapidly evolving technology, and an ethical platform would have to be overpoweringly compelling to justify overriding an attempt at a "neutral" analysis. My assessment, as I became involved in the issue, was that neither platform was compelling to this extent and, indeed, that both were seriously flawed.

Biotech neo-Malthusianism's first dogma (population outstripping food supply) has been a very poor fit in a world where famine is commonplace and absolute food shortages are rare. Although this has been argued by numerous writers (Sen 1981, 1993; Lappé, Collins, and Rosset 1998; Altieri, Rosset, and Thrupp 1998; Altieri and Rosset 1999; among others), it makes biotech neo-Malthusians apoplectic (Prakash 2000):

> Critics of biotechnology invoke the trite argument that the shortage of food is caused by unequal distribution. There's plenty of food, they declare; we just need to distribute it evenly. That's like saying there is plenty of money in the world so let's just solve the problem of poverty in Ethiopia by redistributing the wealth of Switzerland (or maybe the United Kingdom, where the heir to the throne is particularly opposed to companies "playing God" with biotechnology).

Yet the surplus is not only in wealthy Switzerland or Britain but also in Prakash's native India, which is home to a plurality of the world's hungry and also tens of millions of tons of grain above the desired level in the national buffer stocks (Stone 2002a). We might consider that what is a moral outrage is not depriving the hungry of genetic modification technology but using the hungry in the corporate media to justify genetically modified products *without specifically addressing how genetic modification will feed them.* India reminds us that simply boosting production, however beneficial to corporations selling the inputs and seed, may be less than beneficial to the hungry.

The second dogma, that the Third World needs to avert famine through new technology, is largely inconsistent with my own experience with Third World agricultural systems. The heavily subsidized search for ever-increasing yields is better suited to industrial agribusiness interests than to the Third World. It gives little weight to the needs of producers where inputs are unreliable, since the market dependably provides purchased inputs (and credit to buy them) and the government provides lavish relief payments when rains fail. Richards (1997), for example, shows that the more "advanced" breeding of the Green Revolution has much less to offer African rice farmers than "Farmer First" conventional breeding oriented toward reliability under actual field conditions.

The third dogma is likewise dubious in the context of the Third World; indeed, there is ample reason to believe that the intersection of institutional interests and the patenting regime will stultify pro-poor public research. The 1980 Bayh-Dole Act allowed government-funded research results to be patented and commercialized. Thus government-funded discoveries with promise for developing countries are patented and licensed to corporations rather than becoming public goods. Genetic modification always involves multiple patented technologies, and this promotes corporate consolidation to develop patent portfolios (DeVries and Toenniessen 2001). Since public-sector research has no such portfolio, this has disastrous consequences for the same malnourished populations used as an ethical justification for biotechnology (De Vries and Toenniessen 2001:73):

> Leading academic researchers are interested in research competitiveness. They readily sign research MTA's[9] to keep competitive but are then restricted from further transferring their research products. Their universities now have "technology transfer offices" where the incentives are to maximize [intellectual property (IP)] royalty income, often by granting exclusive licenses. The net result is that improved plant materials produced by academic scientist-inventors are highly IP-encumbered and commercially useful only to a big company having an IP portfolio large enough to cover most of the IP constraints. The international agricultural research system does not have such an IP portfolio and as a consequence the traditional flow of materials through the system is breaking down, particularly at the point where useful new technologies and improved plant materials flow from public sector researchers in developed countries to international centres and national crop improvement programmes in developing countries. Africa, in particular, is being short changed of the benefits of biotechnology.

But the anti-biotech ethical platform sketched above has its own problems in the real world, and just as its strongest theoretical rationale comes from Marxist writing, it also inherits serious problems from the Marxist programs for action. Marx maintained that capitalism, along with its attendant social makeups, governmental forms, and ideologies, should and would change; the whole package, integrally related, would decompose, perhaps even without intervention. Early Marxists bifurcated into camps of critical Marxists, who aimed to mobilize a proletarian revolution, and scientific Marxists, who took the evolution of political forms to be preordained (Gouldner 1980). The evolutionary Zeitgeist left little room in either camp for serious consideration of mitigating the effects of capitalism; indeed, some writers looked forward to a worsening of conditions for the working classes to precipitate the systemic overhaul Marx had predicted.

Marx's analysis of capitalism may have been right on the money, but his model of political-economic evolution has fared poorly. Since the failure of the envisioned evolution beyond capitalism, his writings have lost relevance as a program for changing the world.[10] Like capitalism, crop genetic modification is not going away: it is very big business, it has become a fundamental tool in biological research, and it is taught in all major research universities in the United States and practiced in virtually every country with a developed scientific infrastructure. There is little chance of killing it. As an activist against genetic modification per se, a researcher sacrifices not only the ability to investigate the range of effects it may have but also the ability to influence how it is developed. This is the key problem running through the uncomfortable overlap between scholarship and activism; witness the interchange in *Hungry for Profit* (Magdoff, Foster, and Buttel 2000), an analysis of the capitalist transformation of food production, which includes an upbeat survey of sustainable alternatives to corporate farming (Henderson 2000). This chapter evoked an editors' italicized afterword suggesting that such activities might be no more than a "minor irritant to corporate dominance of the food system" because actual reform would require "complete transformation of society."

The implication that sustainable agricultural programs are a waste of time echoes the scientific Marxist position that social improvements are mere palliatives. This is an odd corner for researchers ethically committed to the welfare of Third World farmers to have painted themselves into—opposing potentially beneficial agricultural strategies or technologies because they might impede a complete transformation of the agricultural system. If the complete transformation never comes, one has relinquished the ability to mitigate the excesses of the extant system. And since the complete transformation of crop biotechnology (putting the genie back in the bottle) seems impossible, I see my ethical obligation to Third World farmers (and also my professional obligation as a researcher) as investigating how various plant transformations and institutional arrangements might actually affect Third World agriculture and society without predisposing the research toward supporting or opposing biotechnology. This approach, explicitly designed to counter the assigning of black-and-white ethical values to biotechnology itself, is a science of the gray.

Science of the Gray

A principal aim of an anthropologist's study of the gray of biotechnology is to probe the enormous diversity within the biotechnology project. My analysis of fallacies in both sides of the debate has highlighted the illusion of biotechnology as a unified project by biotechnology's most strident proponents and opponents alike (Stone 2002a). Both sides employ a strategy of blurring distinctions between corporate and public biotechnology: industry wants to take credit for pro-poor technologies from nonprofit labs, and opponents want to tar all biotechnology with the "corporate takeover" brush. It is true that the borders of the two sectors overlap, but there remain differences that are crucial to the Third World. This is why I spent the fall of 2000 on leave from teaching, working as an apprentice (and participant-observing) at the International Laboratory for Tropical Agricultural Biotechnology (ILTAB), a public-sector biotechnology lab engaged in genetic modification of crops for the Third World poor housed in the Donald Danforth Plant Science Center in St. Louis. My training and participant-observation were sponsored by a National Science Foundation Scholar's Award for Methodological Training in Cultural Anthropology. They combined hands-on experience in genetic modification of crops with observations of the interaction between considerations of biology, intellectual property, and Third World agriculture.

An analysis of ILTAB's work is a classic gray subject. ILTAB is part of a center that, while legally nonprofit, is very much part of the American biotechnology establishment. It is located across the street from Monsanto, receives support from Monsanto, affords Monsanto opportunities for image-burnishing announcements, and potentially provides genetic modification technologies that Monsanto may commercialize. It also patents and profits from the licensing of biotechnologies. At the same time, my involvement at ILTAB has convinced me that its work stands a very good chance of benefiting farmers in some situations in the Third World. I arrived at this position only after considering likely broader impacts of specific crop modifications. I have described the two examples of nutritionally enhanced cassava and apomixis, specifically addressing the question why these interventions, in contrast to most genetically modified crops now available, may actually improve food security (Stone 2002a). These crop modifications are, however, still years off, and ILTAB is further along with another genetically modified cassava that may offer dramatic advantages to African farmers. A rapidly spreading gemini virus is devastating East African cassava, and whereas conventional breeding has been incapable of providing resistant strains, ILTAB has achieved viral resistance through genetic modification. The cassava is (as of this writing) being tested in Kenya. From an anthropological perspective, the matter goes far beyond the agronomy; it includes the nature of local economies (cassava can be used both for sale and subsistence), labor scheduling (cassava is particularly flexible vis-à-vis labor demands), and control over means of production (cassava is vegetatively propagated and so not amenable to corporate control).

Although success for ILTAB's genetically modified cassava would predictably be used as proof of biotech neo-Malthusianism, particularly its first two dogmas, this misses the point. This would not be a case of population outpacing food supply but one of a problem of declining production that happens to be solvable by genetic modification. Regarding the third dogma, it would be more accurate to say that the cassava has been developed in spite of corporate control over biotechnologies, since ILTAB has had to avoid incorporating some technologies into crops because of (usually corporate) patent encumbrances.

Gray issues have also been instrumental in my choice of field research sites. My principal ethnographic focus in biotechnology research is now in Warangal District of Andhra Pradesh, India. India is the most hotly contested battleground for genetically modified crops in the Third World, and Warangal in particular was the site of an epidemic of suicides by cotton farmers in 1998 (Reddy and Rao 1998). The suicides coincided with field trials of India's first genetically modified crop, a cotton, and galvanized a resistance movement that destroyed many of the plots. Both the biotech firms (Monsanto and Mahyco) and green critics (in particular Vandana Shiva) used the suicides in their rhetoric (Stone 2002b). The two sides offered a stark choice of causes for the suicides: American bollworms, in Monsanto's view, or multinational-driven globalization, according to Shiva. Equally stark was the contrast in their views of the likely results of selling genetically modified cotton: Monsanto claimed that it would prevent suicides, Shiva that it would cause more.

Of course, specifying causality in the complex affairs of society is an exercise in holding variables constant. Suicides are "caused" not just by either American bollworms or globalization but by a dozen insect pests, by pesticide resistance and the high cost of pesticides, by the ready availability of means for suicide (the pesticides themselves), by vendors' usurious lending practices and their draconian collection tactics, by unscrupulous seed salesmen and a weak regulatory system that fails to protect farmers from bogus seed, by the boom in the cotton market and government campaigns enticing farmers into risky practices, by the large number of small and marginal farmers, by the dropping water tables combined with the preponderance of thirsty cotton varieties, by the cost and unpredictability of hitting water in a bore well, by government payments to suicides' families, by alcohol abuse, and by a long list of other general and specific factors. Rather than championing a cause that serves one's own interests at the expense of a richer understanding of the situation at hand, my ethnographic science of the gray reaches for a more systemic and synthetic analysis of the sociocultural context into which genetically modified crops are being introduced.

This has led, so far, to an analysis of "agricultural deskilling" among cotton farmers in Warangal (Stone 2004). Deskilling is a concept from the Marxist literature (Braverman 1974); it originally referred to factories, but activists in Andhra Pradesh have charged that farmers would be deskilled by genetically modified cotton (Harwick 2000). In contrast, the biotech companies involved and other biotech proponents who have taken an interest in the Indian case have argued that the region's severe agricultural insect problems need to be solved by the latest market-driven technology. Agricultural skilling and deskilling are partly social processes, and they offer a good example of the need for the sort of synthetic perspective that is anthropology's strength. In this case, my analysis showed how and why farmers have already been partly "deskilled" in cotton (but not rice) cultivation. However, the first two years of Bt cotton planting have already brought qualitatively new disruptions in the skilling process and left farmers increasingly susceptible to paid lobbying by both green and industry sources.

The science of the gray is emphatically not an attempt to forge a middle ground in the biotech debate. Indeed, it has tended to arrive at a ground quite apart from industry of green orthodoxy (Stone 2002a). It has also attracted vigorous criticism from both sides on ethical grounds. It often seems a fairly lonely enterprise; there are few anthropologists asking discriminating questions from the perspective of Third World farmers (one other is Tripp [2001]). At the same time, it can also seem to place one in the company of farmers whose lives may undergo significant and subtle changes with new technologies and who would surely want to know that questions have been asked before they were answered.

Acknowledgments

For insights into topics discussed in this chapter I am grateful to Richard Fox, Charles McManis, and Nigel Taylor, although any errors in fact or interpretation are mine alone. Laboratory training in crop biotechnology was supported by the National Science Foundation under Grant No. 0078396 (Scholar's Award for Methodological Training in Cultural Anthropology); research on biotechnology and agriculture in Andhra Pradesh is supported by the National Science Foundation under Grant No. 0314404.

Notes

1. Data are from the International Service for the Acquisition of Agri-Biotech Applications (ISAAA) (James 2000). The ISAAA categorizes Argentina as a "developing" rather than an "industrialized" country, which is potentially misleading given that Argentina's transgenic crops are herbicide-resistant soybeans on mega-farms averaging 500 ha in size (Qaim and Traxler 2004).

2. The lead popularizer of this school of thought was the journalist Robert Kaplan, whose lurid essay "The Coming Anarchy" (1994) quickly found its way onto high government officials' desks; the leading academic proponent was Thomas Homer-Dixon (1994).

3. The demographic argument was in part theoretical, drawing on Malthus's consideration of the "passion between the sexes" ([1798] 1959:4); it was also empirical, the demography of colonial America providing the main case study. In all social classes growth may be slowed somewhat by anti-natalist "preventive checks," but "the lowest orders of society" (25) are characterized by "positive checks" of misery and vice, since "the lower classes . . . are disabled from giving the proper food and attention to their children" (22). . . . "The positive check to population, by which I mean the check that represses an increase which is already begun, is confined chiefly, though not perhaps solely, to the lowest orders of society" (25).

4. In 1998 the U.S. Department of Agriculture (USDA) was awarded a joint patent with the cotton seed company Delta Pine & Land for the first GURT. A GURT would oblige farmers to rebuy seed each year rather then replanting. In some crops, the nonreplantability that the seed industry craves is built in. The classic example is hybrid maize, which is produced by crossing inbred lines of this normally outbreeding plant; segregation causes a drop in yield in the F2 generation. Several other crops, notably soybeans, are not sold as hybrids, and genetically modified seeds could be replanted; biotech companies have to combat this through contracts with farmers. The "Terminator" patent was a public relations windfall for genetic modification opponents and was used to direct international attention to its threat to Third World farmers (Steinbrecher and Mooney 1998). Industry (and the USDA) avowed that the technology would actually benefit less developed countries by attracting investment into crop development, but the issue was enough of a public relations problem that Monsanto promised not to use the technology and never acquired Delta Pine & Land as it had intended. (Although media attention continues to be focused on this one patent, 14 have been issued, and some have been field-tested [RAFI 2001]).

5. The industry seeking to control this force has, perhaps not surprisingly, offered misdirection on this point. In 2000 Monsanto's director of public affairs

wrote that "a quarter of a century ago, Monsanto Co. scientists presented their senior managers with a dilemma: We could continue to discover new chemicals to be sprayed on crops . . . or we could chart the then-unknown waters of biotechnology and potentially help farmers grow healthy, safe food for more people and better protect the environment. . . . To travel [the biotechnology] path would be an enormous shift for Monsanto. . . . We made some choices at Monsanto 25 years ago based on information that led us to believe that biotechnology held the promise for a better way of growing food" (Foster 2000). The year 1975, mentioned three times in short piece, coincides with key advances in the laboratory, but it actually was in 1980 that Monsanto began building its biotechnology division (see Charles 2001). This was the time that gene patenting was established.

6. The "products of nature" doctrine is a part of the Supreme Court's long struggle to distinguish between an "invention" and a mere "discovery"—a distinction made necessary by the fact that the U.S. Constitution creates an ambiguous power in Congress to secure to "Inventors" the exclusive right to their "Discoveries." In case law the classic statement of this principal came in a 1889 case in which a patent was denied on a plant fiber that "nature had intended to be equally for the use of all men" (Ex parte Latimer, 1889 Dec. Comm'r Pat. 123, Comm'r Patents 1889). The principle was reaffirmed in 1948, when the Supreme Court invalidated a patent for a mixed bacterial culture on the grounds that the invention amounted to "no more than the discovery of some of the handiwork of nature . . . part of the storehouse of knowledge of all men" (*Funk Brothers Seed Co. v. Kalo Inoculant Co.*, 333 U.S. 127 (1948)). Even the Supreme Court's 1980 *Chakrabarty* decision affirmed that the "laws of nature, physical phenomena, and abstract ideas" are unpatentable, as is "a new plant found in the wild" (Burger 1980:2208).

7. Diamond was the commissioner of patents.

8. Strictly speaking, Stewart's criticism concerned Snow's having allowed "premature release" of her findings on gene flow, but this was patently not the real issue; in fact, Stewart himself had just allowed the "premature release" of his own results, which reflected positively on genetically modified crops (Adam 2003), and Snow's research was already in press in a major scientific journal (Snow et al. 2003).

9. A material transfer agreement is a contract permitting a researcher to use a patented technology under specific conditions, which invariably include the researcher's not having the right to sell or distribute any inventions arising from that use.

10. "Overthrow capitalism and replace it with something nice," read a plaintive sign at the 2001 May Day demonstration at King's Cross in London.

The Morality of Exhibiting Indians

Craig Howe

The circumstances by which a middle-aged Indian man was incorporated into an anthropology museum as a living exhibit, died in one of the museum's exhibit rooms, and then was dissected and had his brain removed for scientific study provide a compelling case for examining the morality of exhibiting Indians. That man, of course, is known by the single name "Ishi." He walked into the white world at Oroville, California, on August 29, 1911, after all his relatives had been systematically murdered by bounty hunters and everyone he had known was gone. Believed to be the last living person of his tribe, Ishi lived in the Museum of Anthropology on Parnassus Heights in San Francisco, where he served as janitor, cultural informant, and living museum exhibit until he passed on to the next world in an emptied exhibit room around noon on March 25, 1916.

On the day before Ishi died, his good friend and director of the museum Alfred Kroeber wrote from New York City to his colleague and the museum's curator Edward Gifford. Keenly aware that he probably would not see Ishi alive again, Kroeber conveyed his wishes should Ishi pass away in his absence (Kroeber 1961:234):

> Please stand by our contingently made outline of action, and insist on it as my personal wish. There is no objection to a case (death mask). I do not, however, see that an autopsy would lead to anything of consequence, but would resolve itself into a general dissection. Please shut down on it. As to disposal of the body, I must ask you as my personal representative to yield nothing at all under any circumstances. If there is any talk about the interests of science, say for me that science can go to hell. We propose to stand by our friends.

Six days later, Gifford replied to Kroeber by return mail (Kroeber 1961:235):

I took the stand which you asked me to take some time ago: namely that he [Ishi] have a Christian burial like any other friend. The only departures from your request were that a simple autopsy was performed and that the brain was preserved. The matter was not entirely in my hands—in short what happened amounts to a compromise between science and sentiment with myself on the side of sentiment.

The excesses and atrocities committed by anthropologists and others against Indians and Indian communities are inescapable. The exhibition of Indians by non-Indians started at least as early as 1493, when the six survivors from "the Indies" that Christopher Columbus had kidnapped were paraded nearly naked through the streets of Barcelona to the astonishment of the locals (Koning 1991).The Columbian legacy, now 510 years old and counting, is by many accounts genocidal. The atrocities committed by Columbus, those under his command, and those who followed him are legion. In the name of God or science, in the pursuit of glory or gold, and in the service of imperialism or manifest destiny, the bodies and beliefs of the Indian peoples of the Western Hemisphere, along with their possessions and their lands, were plundered and debased. And a substantial portion of the American Indian collections hoarded in museums is made up of that tainted bounty. Therefore, when a museum decides to exhibit some of its American Indian collection, issues related to this legacy often arise. Such is the case for the National Museum of the American Indian, which is in the process of developing the inaugural exhibits for its soon-to-be-built museum in Washington, D.C.

The National Museum of the American Indian

The National Museum of the American Indian (NMAI) was established in 1989, when President George H. W. Bush signed its enabling legislation. With a stroke of his pen, the Smithsonian Institution acquired the unparalleled collection of photographs, art works, archives and artifacts that George Gustav Heye had compiled over a period of sixty years (Force 1999). The collection began with the purchase of a deerskin shirt in 1897. At that time Heye was an assistant superintendent of construction for a railroad company in what is now Arizona. He had just graduated from the School of Mines of Columbia College with a degree in electrical engineering. One of the foremen he supervised was a Navajo man, and from that man's wife Heye purchased the deerskin shirt. It was then that the collecting bug bit him, and for the rest of his life he devoted his energy and finances to amassing a collection of American Indian materials representing hundreds of cultural traditions indigenous to the Western Hemisphere and spanning thousands of years. He hired anthropologists, archaeologists, and enthusiastic collectors to conduct fieldwork and buying expeditions, and he purchased extant collections in the United States and abroad. Heye bought everything—not just what others considered objects of high art but ordinary and utilitarian artifacts as well—and he bought in bulk.[1] He died in 1957 at the age of eighty-two, leaving as his legacy a renowned collection of American Indian materials known as the Museum of the American Indian, Heye Foundation, which now constitutes the backbone of the NMAI.

The NMAI's enabling legislation stated that the "Indian human remains and Indian funerary objects in the possession or control of the Smithsonian Institution" were to be inventoried and identified "in consultation and cooperation with traditional Indian religious leaders and government officials of Indian tribes" (Pub. L. 101–185, Sec. 11, November 28, 1989, 103 Stat. 1343).[2] These two distinct constituencies within Indian communities are representative of separate and unique roots of tribal sovereignty. On the one hand, an Indian tribe "is simply a group of Indians that is recognized as constituting a distinct and historically continuous political entity for at least some governmental purposes" (Canby 1988:4). Because the lands within what is now the United States of America were occupied and controlled by tribal peoples and the European immigrants could not or would not totally eradicate those tribal peoples, the United States government obtained lands through a process that it judged to be internationally justifiable. Its phenomenally successful (from the viewpoint of nontribal peoples) acquisition of tribal lands was carried out through treaties and treaty substitutes that often reserved and set aside lands for the "use, possession, and benefit" (Pevar 1992:19) of a tribe. The reserved lands, or reservations, were "intended to establish homelands for the tribes, islands of tribalism largely free from interference by non-Indians or future state governments" (Wilkinson 1987:14). The establishment and perpetuation of a tribe's reservation normally ensured that the tribe was officially recognized as such by the federal government. Tribes, then, are political entities that interact on a government-to-government basis with the federal government and that exercise decision-making authority within legally described parcels of land. Under this definition, tribal sovereignty rests on legal and political principles.

There is, however, a nonpolitical definition of tribal sovereignty that is not the product of negotiated settlements involving European-derived concepts, though it is evident in those agreements. "At almost every treaty . . . the concern of the Indians was the preservation of the people" (Deloria and Lytle 1984:8), a concern that certainly preceded the arrival of Europeans in the Western Hemisphere. According to Deloria and Lytle (1984:8):

> The idea of the people is primarily a religious conception, and with most American Indian tribes it begins somewhere in the primordial mists. In that time the people were gathered together but did not yet see themselves as a distinct people. A holy man had a dream or a vision; quasi-mythological figures of cosmic importance revealed themselves, or in some other manner the people were instructed. They were given ceremonies and rituals that enabled them to find their place on the continent. Quite often they were given prophecies that informed them of the historical journey ahead. In some instances the people were told to migrate until a special place was revealed; in the interim, as with the Hebrews wandering in the deserts of Sinai, the older generation, which had lost faith, and the cynics and skeptics in the group would be eliminated until the people were strong enough to receive the message.

We see here an interrelationship between community, land, and religion: "When lands and peoples are both chosen and matched together in a cosmic plan, the attachment to the land by the people becomes something extraordinary and involves a sense of identity and corresponding feeling of responsibility" (Deloria 1992a:31–32). Viewed in this light, tribal communities are "guided by internal prophetic instructions rather than external political and economic events" (32). Consequently, "the idea of peoplehood transcends the contemporary political organizations and speaks to generations of people, people past and people yet to come" (Deloria and Lytle 1984:242). Tribes, then, are spiritual associations with a moral responsibility to continue fulfilling the original instructions given them. Those original instructions constitute the inherent spiritual sovereignty of tribal communities.

Though representations from both the political and the spiritual foundations of tribal sovereignty were written into the inventory and identification requirements of the National Museum of the American Indian Act, the NMAI sometimes circumvented tribal representation by hiring Indians to assist with these tasks and to determine "traditional care" policies for the collection. Instead of being vested in individuals elected to political office or trained in tribal traditions, decision-making authority was thereby imposed upon or usurped by employees who were or claimed to be biologically Indian. Without at least one of the foundations of tribal sovereignty as the basis for their decision making, such individuals ended up codifying pan-Indian and non-Indian generalizations into the identification and care of tribal collections by basing their decisions on personal feelings and private philosophies. Sometimes the museum itself accepted object identifications and collections restrictions that a visiting Indian requested, whether or not that person was appointed to represent his or her tribal community in these matters. Indiscriminate acceptance and incorporation of information in this and other ways resulted in policies and procedures that were not tribally generated or sanctioned. Tribal sovereignty is grounded in the exercise of decision-making authority by the proper representatives of specific tribes, and, whether or not individuals and the museum saw it as such, the incorporation of pan-Indian and non-Indian policies and procedures related to identification and care of the collection was a direct attack on tribal sovereignty.

In addition to the repatriation of Indian human remains and the cultural property of Indians and Indian tribes, the NMAI's enabling legislation also stated that the museum was to "collect, preserve, and exhibit Native American objects of artistic, historical, literary, anthropological, and scientific interest" (Pub. L. 101–185, Sec. 3, November 28, 1989, 103 Stat. 1336). According to its official mission statement,

The National Museum of the American Indian shall recognize and affirm to Native communities and the non-Native public the historical and contemporary culture and cultural achievements of the Natives of the Western Hemisphere by advancing—in consultation, collaboration, and cooperation with Natives—knowledge and understanding of Native cultures, including art, history, and language, and by recognizing the museum's special responsibility, through innovative public programming, research and collections, to protect, support, and enhance the development, maintenance, and perpetuation of Native culture and community.

Embedded in its mission statement are three identifiable "publics": the NMAI itself, its non-Native visitors, and the Indian communities of the Western Hemisphere. The central positioning of this latter public is pivotal in distinguishing the NMAI from other museums. As discussed above, the sovereignty of Indian communities rests on both political and spiritual foundations, and therefore the idea of consulting, collaborating, and cooperating with Indian communities is a complex undertaking, but promoting the "development, maintenance, and perpetuation" of those communities is a moral obligation unparalleled in the history of museums. The typical model of developing Indian exhibitions parallels the way the NMAI conducted its collection inventory and identification and developed its traditional care policies. The model revolves around the relationship between a museum and an Indian consultant or employee who acts as an interpreter between the museum and the consultant's tribe or Indian tribes in general, similar to Ishi's role in the Museum of Anthropology. Consultations are usually conducted at the museum and are structured by a contractual relationship that fulfills the museum's desire to elicit "the Indian voice" during the process of developing exhibitions while at the same time maintaining its institutional control over that process. The NMAI's "special responsibility" is to transcend these past practices by collaborating with Indian communities not only to develop exhibits but to do so in a way that protects, supports, and enhances those communities.

In the spring of 1997 the NMAI produced, in conjunction with an outside consulting firm, conceptual designs and draft narrative walk-throughs for its inaugural exhibits. Years of work and substantial resources were devoted to this effort. Before advancing to content and design development, however, the designs were vetted by past and present NMAI trustees, university-based academics, and community-based Indians. My involvement with the NMAI began when I accepted an invitation to participate in the academic vetting workshop. The response from all three groups was overwhelmingly negative. In spite of the NMAI's rhetoric of being dedicated to a "fresh . . . approach to museum exhibition" and its insistence "that the authentic Native voice and perspective guide all our policies, including, of course, our exhibition philosophy" (NMAI 2000:7), the designs were widely felt to be neither different from nor better than the exhibitions that mainstream museums were mounting.[4] The NMAI's insistence on the participation of paid Indian consultants predictably did not produce a Native exhibition philosophy or fulfill the museum's mission to collaborate with tribal communities. The museum's attempt to develop a Native exhibition philosophy through "consultation, collaboration, and cooperation" with Native individuals from across the Western Hemisphere failed because philosophy is not dependent on or inherent in an individual's biological or genetic makeup. Rather than seize the opportunity to chart a new route to tribal sovereignty through the choppy waters of community collaborations, the NMAI resorted to the calm and familiar course of consultation and found itself adrift in conventional Indian exhibits without a Native philosophy.

Native Exhibition Philosophies

There are at least four types of exhibition philosophies that may theoretically fall under a Native label. The first type is a philosophy founded entirely upon the principles of a particular tribe. A Lakota philosophy, for example, might be called Lakotaism and would appropriately be employed for a Lakota exhibit but not for an exhibit of Crow or any other tribal or nontribal materials. The second type is founded upon a limited set of principles that are present in the vast majority—if not all—of tribe-specific philosophies. This type is called tribalism and is appropriate for exhibits that incorporate multiple tribes but wish to differentiate each from the others while simultaneously avoiding nontribal principles. Intertribalism is a third Native philosophy, and it draws from or combines two or more tribe-specific philosophies. Whereas it and the first two types rest to varying degrees on Native principles, the fourth type is a philosophy based on non-Native principles that are asserted to be Native. This type is called Indianism, and it is founded on stereotypical beliefs and attitudes asserted to be true about all Indians. It is therefore inappropriate for exhibits other than those that aspire to examine racism and similar manifestations of "othering" by the dominant culture.

The conceptual designs and draft narrative walk-throughs for the inaugural exhibits were based on an inarticulate combination of intertribalism, Indianism, and non-Native philosophies. In response to the vetting meetings, I was hired by the NMAI to undertake the daunting task of redesigning the three proposed exhibits by incorporating tribal communities in fundamentally new ways and by structuring the exhibits in a manner that resonated with those communities and facilitated the expression of their unique experiences, beliefs, and knowledge. Tribalism was my choice of a Native philosophy to guide our work. It has four dimensions. The spatial dimension encompasses an understanding that tribal peoples and their lands are intimately interconnected and conceptually inseparable. The social dimension relates land and identity to the concept of "peoplehood," a unique community identity differentiated from those of other tribes and from individual Indian persons. The spiritual dimension guides the relationships between tribal communities and their lands. These community-specific spiritual instructions embody the moral and ethical standards by which tribe members conduct their interactions not only with the land but also with each other and with outsiders. Lastly, the experiential dimension recognizes that tribal communities are perpetuating ongoing relationships with their higher spiritual powers today and will do so for the foreseeable future. These dimensions of tribal sovereignty were translated into principles—locality, community, viewpoint, and vitality—that informed the conceptual development of the new exhibitions. These principles were then reordered hierarchically and a fifth one—Native voice—was added. They were then paired with assertions that crystallized the attitude of the exhibits—Community: *Our tribes are sovereign nations*; Locality: *This is Indian land*; Vitality: *We are here now*; Viewpoint: *We see things differently*; and Voice: *These are our stories*. Finally, each of the principles was operationalized in the context of the exhibition as follows:

Community: *Our tribes are sovereign nations*. This principle stressed that Native rights and issues are community-based and that as sovereign entities tribal communities possess unique rights and inherent powers. Its foci were the Native nations indigenous to the Western Hemisphere.

Locality: *This is Indian land*. This principle showed the interrelationship between geographical landscape, spiritual tradition, and community identity. It focused on particular places and their inextricable relationships to indigenous spiritual traditions of the Western Hemisphere.

Vitality: *We are here now*. This principle presented Native cultures as living cultures that continue through space and time. It focused on continuities within Native communities today.

Viewpoint: *We see things differently*. This principle developed interpretations from interdisciplinary viewpoints, but with indigenous worldviews always central. Its foci were Native philosophical systems, their distinct worldviews, and the Native languages that transmit this information.

Voice: *These are our stories*. This principle incorporated stories from multiple and divergent perspectives but with Native voices always central. It focused on Native individuals and their personal stories.

These principles were posited as the overarching philosophy for reconceptualizing the three exhibits. Foremost among them was the principle of community, which is the foundation of tribal sovereignty. The next three principles subsumed community, even though each focused on another dimension of tribalism. The fifth principle, conversely, had its roots in individualism and therefore linked the past processes of Indian consultations, in which Native voice was intended goal, and the new Native exhibition philosophy, in which Native voices were merely one way of presenting personal stories and were conceptually less important than the community-based principles of tribalism.

The three exhibits originally envisioned were reconceived as a single exhibition with three interrelated galleries—Our Universes, Our Peoples, and Our Lives—that focused on tribal philosophies, tribal histories, and tribal identities, respectively. Then an overarching statement was written that clearly situated the galleries within the dimensions of tribalism:

> Our tribal ancestors are the mentors, curators, developers and designers of this exhibition. As Native individuals, they were born onto these lands, lived their lives within these lands, and their bones are mingled with the soils of these lands. Though countless generations of Native individuals lived and died, from time immemorial their communities have persisted. Each community forged an intimate and complex relationship with their environment that was articulated in their unique philosophical system. These systems provided principles for comprehending their universes: how their worlds were ordered, how those orders are maintained, their origins and their destinies. Many of these communities thrived and survive today, but others were wiped out in one way or another. Throughout their existences, these communities experienced important events that shaped their identities as distinct peoples. Just as each community's philosophical system is unique, so too is the list of events that constitute their history. As such, the identities of the indigenous communities of this hemisphere, from the tip of Tierra del Fuego to the Arctic Circle and beyond, were rooted in this land philosophically and experientially. Similarly, our tribal ancestors expressed their identities through the way they lived their daily lives. To do things in a good way was to conduct one's life within the philosophical framework of one's community, and individuals aspired to this ethical ideal. An individual's identity, therefore, was determined primarily by the community to which he or she belonged, secondly by one's roles and responsibilities as a member of that community and thirdly by one's personality. Since non-Indians arrived and began their quest to possess these lands, a collective "Indian" identity has also arisen. Like a braid of hair, individual identity and community history is woven together with a philosophical system that gives tribally specific meanings to both. This tripartite braid is the link between our ancestors, their communities and this exhibition.

With the philosophy of both the exhibition and the galleries firmly rooted in tribalism, tribal sovereignty was incorporated into the plan by dividing decision-making authority with regard to content and design between the NMAI and the Indian communities. The three galleries were to share a conceptual structure with five components: an introduction, hemispheric commonalities, tribal exhibits, linkage nodes between the commonalities and two or more tribal exhibits, and a conclusion. The tribal exhibits component was the most important conceptually and in terms of the amount of floor area assigned to it. Tribe-specific exhibits were conceived of as modules that would systematically rotate in and out of the galleries. These might be developed in Indian communities, rotate into the NMAI galleries for exhibition, and then, after being digitized, archived, and made available to visitors digitally both in the museum and on the Internet, rotate out as traveling exhibits. Indian communities were to control the content and design of this component, whereas the content and design of the other four components would be controlled by the NMAI.

A unique concept was then developed for each of the galleries that established criteria for selecting and grouping appropriate communities to be presented in each gallery's tribal exhibits. The tribal history gallery, Our Peoples, which will serve as the case study for the remainder of this discussion, was to be organized along a pathway that represented a north-south axis spanning the Western Hemisphere. Six places were situated in spatial relation to one another along the axis, each functioning as a linkage node for three tribal history exhibits. Any community whose remembered past included one of those places, regardless of where the community members now lived, was eligible to have its tribal history presented in one of the three exhibits linked to that place. This was intended to provide a Native way of organizing the histories of multiple tribes without resorting to the conventional culture areas, themes, or timelines of mainstream museums. The tribal histories themselves were reconceived as event-centered rather than narrative-driven. They were made up of twelve to sixteen important events that living tribe members or their ancestors had experienced. These events spanned the period from the first appearance of tribe members on this earth to an omega event at the end of time, and they were expected to be epitomizing events that crystallized the community's values and beliefs or in some fundamental way shaped its identity. The gallery entrance, located just north of the center of the axis, was to be an experiential representation of the Choctaw emergence onto this earth through an opening in a small mound in what is now Georgia. Its central inland position along the north-south axis was intended to provide an alternative to the coastal starting points of Indian histories that begin with the arrival of non-Indians—such as Columbus—on the shores of the Western Hemisphere.

In the spring of 1999 the museum selected from the list of eligible tribes a short list for the eighteen tribal history exhibits. The selection of tribes was based on a number of factors, including hemispheric location, museum collections, staff expertise, and the desire to have different tribes represented in each of the three galleries. For each tribe selected, the museum conducted background research on tribal history, developed a preliminary list of epitomizing events, compiled a tribal bibliography and an inventory of museum resources from and about that tribe, and identified potential academic scholars—persons who had conducted extensive research on the history of that tribe, knew the location and general holdings of repositories with tribal materials, and had personal contact with tribe members. The scholar was to review the preliminary materials that the museum produced and nominate a number of tribal liaison candidates for the exhibit. A tribal liaison candidate was a tribe member who lived in the community, spoke both the tribal language and English, was knowledgeable about community protocol, and was comfortable taking on a leadership role in developing the exhibit. The liaison was to serve as the museum's primary contact in each community and work closely with museum staff all the way to opening day and beyond.

Before initiating contact with academic scholars, tribal liaisons, or Indian communities, a workshop was convened in late spring 1999 during which the philosophy and conceptual framework of this gallery, its draft narrative walk-through, and the methodology outlined below were vetted by a select group of "big thinkers" from outside the museum. The four individuals invited were highly respected by their peers in the field of Indian history and had demonstrated a capacity to rethink the conventional philosophies and methodologies of Indian exhibitions. Collectively, they were Indian and non-Indian; they were widely published and highly educated and had extensive experience living and working in tribal communities. Only after they had approved its philosophy, concepts, and methodology was the plan for the gallery vetted within the NMAI itself. Though individuals and even departments disagreed to some extent on certain aspects of the gallery and of the exhibition in general, it was imperative that the NMAI as an institution commit to the gallery's philosophy, concepts, and methodology before initiating contact with the tribal communities. This was a critical point because the process of developing the gallery entailed moral and ethical commitments on the part of all participating partners.

A central purpose of this chapter is to discuss those commitments and examine whether they are being honored.

The methodology for developing the eighteen tribal history exhibits was directly linked to the philosophy and concepts of the Our Peoples gallery and grew out of previous experiences with collaborative projects involving Indian communities. The initial methodological model divided the development of a tribal history exhibit into five phases, each represented by an important meeting between tribal and museum representatives. The location of these meetings alternated between the two partners; the first, third, and fifth were in the community and the second and fourth at the NMAI. The extensive community fieldwork and documentary research that went into developing each exhibit began well before the phase 1 meeting and continued through to phase 5.

In phase 1, NMAI staff traveled to the tribal community, and in a public meeting organized by the tribal liaison the community was invited to create its history exhibit within the philosophical, conceptual, and methodological framework adopted for the gallery. If the community chose to work within the gallery's dictates, tribe members were selected to serve as community representatives throughout the developmental process. These individuals, along with the tribal liaison, were primarily responsible for finalizing their community's epitomizing events and for selecting the objects, photographs, and other media through which the events would be presented. They and the tribal liaison traveled to the museum for the phase 2 meeting, a workshop lasting three or four days. The community representatives and tribal liaison were shown all of the materials from and about their community that were in the NMAI's possession, including objects, photographs, and archival documents. These were the primary materials from which they selected items to illustrate their chosen epitomizing events. Before returning to their community, the representatives and the liaison met with the exhibit designer to discuss the epitomizing events, the selected materials, and ideas for presenting their tribal history. On the basis of these conversations, the designer began work on their exhibit.

At the phase 3 meeting the exhibit's schematic design was presented to the community, and tribe members examined the results of the phase 2 workshop and had an opportunity to comment on that work and to suggest revisions. Feedback from this meeting was incorporated into the exhibit design and was reviewed by the tribal liaison at the phase 4 meeting, held at the NMAI. This meeting was attended by the eighteen liaisons, who reviewed the designs of their communities' exhibits and examined how the other communities were presenting their histories. This was an opportunity for these individuals to network with each other and to see how the eighteen tribal histories were linked to the six geographic places presented in the gallery. By this point in the process, the design of the gallery's four NMAI components had been completed. The tribal history exhibits, however, were still at a stage where suggestions from the tribal liaisons could be incorporated into their final design, which was then taken back to the community for the phase 5 meeting. At this third public meeting, to which the entire community was again invited, the tribal history exhibit was presented and the community was asked for its approval. Once the community had approved it, the exhibit's design was finalized. If any changes to the exhibit were later undertaken by the NMAI or the designer, staff members were to return again to the community for another approval.

The philosophical, conceptual, and methodological framework presented above articulated the rights and responsibilities of the NMAI and the tribal communities. The NMAI was to be responsible for developing an overarching philosophy and conceptual framework for the gallery that was neither museum-specific nor tribe-specific. It was also to be responsible for identifying all items in its collections pertaining to the collaborating communities, for sharing this information with those communities, and for funding the processes of developing and presenting each tribal history. The NMAI had the right, within the framework, to develop the other four components of the gallery in its own way, and the tribal communities had the right to choose whether to participate in the process. If they chose to collaborate, they had the right to be treated as sovereign nations, to have preeminent authority—within the framework—over the design and content of their history exhibits, and to retain all intellectual and cultural property rights to the information shared knowingly and unknowingly with NMAI staff. Tribal communities were responsible for making the history exhibits uniquely theirs by participating fully in the process of identifying and then sharing accounts of the important events they or their ancestors had experienced that had fundamentally shaped their identities.

Late in the summer of 1999 the curatorial department of the NMAI started phase 1 of this process by inviting the Seminole Tribe of Florida to collaborate in developing a Seminole history exhibit. The Seminoles and the other Indian tribes that were invited to participate in developing their own history exhibits unanimously accepted. A wide spectrum of community members participated in and expressed enthusiasm for the iterative process outlined above, partly because it respected their knowledge and decision-making abilities but also, one suspects, because it established an ongoing relationship between the community and the NMAI. The museum promised to not come into their community and appropriate what it needed and then go away and do with that information what it wanted. Rather, it committed itself to an ongoing collaboration with community members, a partnership wherein communities exerted a considerable amount of decision-making authority with regard to their tribal histories. Working within the established framework, community members were to decide which events to present, what information to share about each event, who within their community would share the information, which objects and images to use to illustrate the events, and even the shape and design of the space within which their history would be exhibited. They were promised the opportunity to tell their own histories from their own perspectives using their own words.

Moral and Ethical Obligations

Like so many other promises made by outsiders, the NMAI's promises to the Indian communities were broken when it was convenient to do so. After the museum had obtained a trove of information from extensive fieldwork in the tribal communities, a small cadre of staff decided to dismantle the philosophical, conceptual, and methodological framework for the gallery that had been vetted by all parties and was still in effect.

Instead of an intellectual and philosophical foundation rooted in tribalism, the premise on which the gallery is now being developed is that its primary target audience is children and youth and that its unique contribution to exhibit theory and practice is incorporation of "the Native voice." This notion, of course, is not new. The advent of children's museums in the 1960s led to the emergence and professionalization of exhibit developers whose role was to make the often dense label copy written by curators accessible to the target audience—that is to say, to children. Therefore, the shift toward a target audience of children and youth suggests that exhibit developers are wielding greater authority in developing the Our Peoples gallery. As their influence increases, we can expect to see a greater emphasis on technology, fewer artifact labels with fewer words on them, an aversion to both exhibit theory and artifact research, and an increase in strategies to minimize the influence of tribal communities. The predictable justification for these changes is that exhibits need to be more experiential, that visitors will not read long labels, that the average museumgoer will spend only a relatively brief amount of time in the gallery, and that community members do not know how to communicate to their exhibit audience.

Conceptually, the gallery now has a thematic organization that squeezes each tribal exhibit into one preassigned category and then groups three or four tribal exhibits under one of three themes— "Survival," "Land," or "Freedom." For example, under "Freedom" there are four tribal exhibits, each linked to a different category: Blackfeet, Forced Culture Change; Ka'apor, Inequality; Chiricahua Apache, Control; Kiowa, Economy. The geographic sequence of these four tribes—Montana, Brazil, New Mexico, and Oklahoma, respectively—is indicative of the aspatial organization of the gallery. Instead of entering the gallery at a particular place and at the beginning of Choctaw time, visitors will now enter through an exhibit entitled "What is History?" and segue into a large area labeled "America Changes Everything." Next, visitors will encounter three tribal exhibits grouped under the "Survival" theme. The three preassigned categories, one for each tribal exhibit, are "Violence," "Invasion," and "Diaspora." America Changes Everything is spatially more important than tribal histories, since all visitors must pass through it and it is larger than any tribal exhibit. The focus of the gallery has changed from event-centered tribal histories that are geographically linked and arranged to a thematically organized narrative history of Indian-white relations in which tribes are used as exemplars of preassigned categories arbitrarily grouped under one of three themes considered important by the NMAI.

The methodology for developing the Our Peoples gallery also changed in fundamental ways. The fieldwork was discontinued, and the vetted framework for the gallery was abandoned. Tribal communities that were collaborating with the museum were not consulted; it was only after all the changes had been implemented that efforts were made to inform the partner communities and individuals. Furthermore, the decision-making authority over their own history exhibits that had been promised to those communities and individuals was revoked.

The result of this systemic countermand is a gallery design that embodies nontribal and even antitribal philosophies, concepts, and methodologies. The NMAI's efforts to be a different kind of museum depended in large part on how it was going to interact with tribal communities and individuals in developing exhibitions. Developing tribal history exhibits in collaboration with Indian communities proved to be a complex undertaking that necessarily reduced the control that individuals and departments within the NMAI had conventionally exercised. It is not surprising, therefore, that the staunchest opposition to this new, collaborative, community-based process came from within the museum itself.[5] This intramuseum conflict evokes the postmortem handling of Ishi's body.

In the letter that Gifford wrote Kroeber after Ishi's death it is revealed that there had been a compromise between science and sentiment regarding the treatment of Ishi's body. On the sentiment side were Gifford and Kroeber, asking that no autopsy be performed. On the other side were colleagues who, in pursuit of science, dissected Ishi's body and extracted his brain. This morbid behavior not only contradicted the wishes of Kroeber and Gifford but also was contrary to Ishi's own wishes and his tribal beliefs. Because his knowledge and expertise had proved invaluable to its research program and institutional stature, the museum had accommodated Ishi as long as he lived, but on his death it abandoned its commitments to him in the name of science. Seven months later, in a letter to Aleš Hrdlička, head of the physical anthropology department of the Smithsonian Institution, Kroeber himself capitulated to the scientific enterprise by reneging on his promise to stand by his friend: "I find that at Ishi's death last spring his brain was removed and preserved. There is no one here who can put it to scientific use. If you wish it, I shall be glad to deposit it in the National Museum Collection" (Thomas 2000:221).[6]

History is replete with good intentions gone awry, and the fact that the NMAI is a federal institution in Washington, D.C., only magnifies the memories of the historical legacy of treaties and promises made by the federal government to Indian communities in the utmost good faith only to be unilaterally abandoned by the government with devastating effects to those communities. In spite of this trail of broken treaties, it is tempting to propose that in the development of a tribal history exhibit the relationship between the NMAI and the tribal community be governed by a treaty. Treaties are the products of negotiations and between the federal government and Indian tribes, and they are critical documents that bear directly on the legal and political identities of Indian tribes. Moreover, breach of a treaty could be cause for adjudication. A treaty-like document spelling out the rights and responsibilities of the two parties might therefore encourage both to fulfill their obligations. With history as our guide, however, we should not expect the government or the NMAI to honor the terms of any treaty.

Whereas treaties constitute the political foundation of tribal sovereignty, the original instructions given to communities by their higher powers constitute tribal sovereignty's spiritual foundation. Tribal histories are not merely histories of tribes; they are intimately bound up with indigenous spiritual traditions. To tell the history of their tribe, members inevitably begin with the appearance of their ancestors on this earth, and some share what the end of time on this earth will be like for their people. Thus tribal history in this context stretches from the beginning of time to the end of time, and the stories about those two points in time rest firmly within what many people would categorize as a spiritual tradition.

Because tribal spiritual traditions are ongoing and efficacious, it was imperative that the process of developing tribal history exhibits respect those traditions. Tribalism is a Native exhibition philosophy that recognizes and reaffirms tribal sovereignty. Its four dimensions constituted an explicit set of moral criteria for governing the negotiations between the NMAI and tribal communities that was positioned above the ethics of the NMAI and the individual tribes. Its purpose was to operationalize the museum's published intention of developing an innovative approach to creating exhibitions guided by "authentic Native voice[s] and perspective[s]" so as to "protect, support, and enhance the development, maintenance, and perpetuation of Native culture[s] and communit[ies]." The success of this endeavor, however, depended on a commitment from the NMAI to forgo its absolute control over every aspect of the exhibition process. It was a moral and ethical decision that the NMAI had to make, and initially the museum did promise tribal communities control over history exhibits. But once it had extracted all the information it needed from them, it revoked those promises and returned to its conventional exhibition process, much as the Museum of Anthropology did after Ishi died. The Museum of Anthropology, however, was cutting its commitments to a dead man, while the NMAI was revoking its commitments to tribal communities and Indian individuals who are very much alive.

The revocation of these was not merely a reversion to a conventional way of developing Indian exhibits but a moral and ethical breach. Tribal sovereignty is the foundation that differentiates American Indians from all other so-called minority groups not only in the United States but in the entire Western Hemisphere. That sovereignty predates the arrival of non-Indians and in the United States has been recognized by the Supreme Court. The authentic integration of tribalism into exhibits requires a radical restructuring of the process of developing those exhibits. Exhibits that embody tribalism cannot be created within the conventional organizational structure and processes of the NMAI. If the

NMAI truly wishes to realize its mission and vision, then it must strive for something beyond novel exhibits and empty rhetoric. It has a moral and ethical obligation to do so, and from Parnassus Heights to inside the beltway Indian individuals and tribal communities anxiously await its fulfillment of that obligation.

Acknowledgments

I thank the friends and colleagues who read and commented on drafts of this paper, including Harvey Markowitz and LeAnne Howe.

Notes

1. The Museum of the American Indian, Heye Foundation, described its mission in 1929 as follows: "This Museum occupies a unique position among institutions, in that its sole aim is to gather and to preserve for students everything useful in illustrating and elucidating the anthropology of the aborigines of the Western Hemisphere, and to disseminate by means of its publications the knowledge thereby gained" (1929:3).

2. The National Museum of the American Indian Act, passed by Congress on November 28, 1989, contains the following findings: (1) "by order of the Surgeon General of the Army, approximately 4,000 Indian human remains from battlefields and burial sites were sent to the Army Medical Museum and were later transferred to the Smithsonian Institution"; (2) "through archaeological excavations, individual donations, and museum donations, the Smithsonian Institution has acquired approximately 14,000 additional Indian human remains"; and (3) these human remains "have long been a matter of concern for many Indian tribes . . . which are determined to provide an appropriate resting place for their ancestors" (Pub. L. 101–185, Sec. 2, November 28, 1989, 103 Stat. 1336). Passage of the act established the legal requirement that the Smithsonian Institution return to tribal communities not only ancestral remains but also associated and unassociated funerary objects. The Native American Graves Protection and Repatriation Act extended this legal requirement to all institutions that receive federal funds. It also identified two more categories of cultural property to be returned to tribal communities: sacred objects and objects of cultural patrimony. However, institutions holding American Indian cultural property and Indian human remains that do not receive federal moneys

are exempt from the requirement to return such objects and remains, even if legitimate requests are made by appropriate Indian tribes and individuals.

3. The mission statement was accessed at http://americanindian.si.edu/subpage.cfm?subpage=press&second=mission on April 19, 2004.

4. The three exhibitions—The Native Universe, Stories of the People, and Living in the Native Universe—were conceived of as chronologically ordered. The Native Universe focused on the prehistoric past, predictably focusing on "civilizations" such as the Inca and the Maya. Stories of the People focused on the historic past from first contact with Columbus to the Pequot casino in Connecticut. Living in the Native Universe focused on current conversations with contemporary Indians regarding their perceptions of personal identity. The three exhibition titles were all singular, suggesting that there was but one Native universe and one Native people. Further, the history exhibition began with the appearance of Columbus, a non-Indian, thereby suggesting that tribal histories are the product of interactions with nontribal peoples.

5. This frustrating phenomenon was manifested in many forms and was initially mitigated to some extent by having "big thinkers" from outside the museum evaluate the philosophical, conceptual, and methodological bases of the exhibition early in the process. But the "big thinkers" remained outside consultants and therefore lacked the authority to cause the museum to fulfill its commitments.

6. Ishi's brain was shipped from San Francisco to Washington, D.C., in January 1917 and stored—supposedly never used for scientific purposes—at the Smithsonian Institution until it was returned upon request under the provisions of the National Museum of the American Indian Act to the Redding Rancheria and Pit River Tribes for burial in the traditional homelands of Ishi's ancestors in May 1999.

Documenting Ethics

Don Brenneis

In a recent meeting of the Committee on Educational Policy at the University of California, Santa Cruz (UCSC), one of my colleagues presented proposed new requirements for a major in computer engineering. In a section on how students could be dropped from the major, the proposal stated that being found guilty of academic dishonesty in one course could lead to disqualification and that two such findings would certainly do so. When a committee member asked him about these rules, he responded that the department wanted to produce "ethical graduates." Along with the committee's discovery that no other program at Santa Cruz had such a requirement and its approval of the proposal, my colleague's comment speaks to the intersection of scientific and educational bureaucracies with ethical issues. What are the characteristics of an ethical person or of ethical behavior? Are they defined in terms of positive, specific behavior or in terms of the absence of negatively valued action? What are the responsibilities of institutions with regard to ethical education and to the monitoring and supervision of their members' behavior? What kinds of measures are appropriate and effective for such monitoring, how and when should they be applied, and what are their consequences? And how do broader political and regulatory processes shape the ways in which institutions and their members act?

This chapter approaches these big issues through a brief examination of small and routine practices. I will be discussing some aspects of the ways in which institutional review boards, the usually local committees that review research involving human subjects, conduct their reviews of specific projects. The materials at the heart of this chapter are documentary ones in the quite literal sense; they include both the *IRB*

Guidebook of the Office for Human Research Protection of the U.S. Department of Health and Human Services (OHRP 2000) and the informational materials and forms provided by my university's Committee for the Protection of Human Subjects. These are, in Richard Harper's (1998) term, "mundane" documents, and they engender routine responses both from those filling them out and from later readers. They also link histories of broad policy making and detailed planning with decisions shaping the course of scholarly and scientific knowledge and of the lives of researchers and their research subjects. Such documents are born in the work of staff and the recommendations of committees, circulate among and are animated by individual researchers, and go on to figure centrally in the decisions made at institutional review board meetings. At the same time, they and their consequences remain, in large part because of their very ordinariness, analytically invisible.

Local institutional review boards constitute a critical nexus in the shaping of research ethics across many disciplines. It is through their deliberations that policy is converted into practice and may be modified and reworked. The anticipation of review may shape the design of research and, indeed, the range of topics considered feasible. Further, what is highlighted in the review process and what is left unaddressed are critical and consequential issues for government, institutions, researchers, and the subjects such regulatory practices are designed to protect. While institutional review boards are local, they operate within a very complex framework of federal and state regulations and agencies.

Relationships between local institutional review boards and federal agencies are now at a particularly critical juncture. Historically there has been considerable heterogeneity of federal rules concerning the protection of human subjects, with many offices initially developing their own rules and ethical review linked directly to the funding source. Most agencies now participate in what is called the Common Rule, with the responsibility for assessing individual and institutional compliance resting with the specific relevant agency; most campus institutional review boards operate within the Common Rule framework. While earlier ethical review was generally linked to federal research support, the mandate of institutional review boards now covers the whole gamut of institutionally based research (including, on campuses, undergraduate class work).

In December 2000 the National Bioethics Advisory Commission (NBAC) proposed a major reworking and consolidation of federal human-subjects review and oversight practices, calling for the creation of a single federal office, the National Office of Human Research Oversight, to deal with "policy development, including rulemaking, and interpretation; education; research review; monitoring; enforcement; and accountability" (NBAC 1999: recommendation 2.2). The commission further suggested the development of accreditation standards for institutions and certification for individuals, whether researchers or institutional review board members. The NBAC recommendations have been the subject of numerous hearings and have drawn considerable criticism, especially for their extension of biomedical research models to the entire range of research involving human subjects. Whatever the outcome of the present process, it seems clear that the ethical dimensions of research with human subjects will increasingly become a matter of bureaucratic attention both for the federal government directly and for its local, accredited institutional review panels. And, judging from the NBAC recommendations and related materials, it also seems clear that the standards and practices employed will become increasingly standardized and routine.

My purpose here is not to address these proposed changes but to try to capture something of the present situation, one in which federal agencies provide not regulations but guidance for local institutional review boards and in which there is considerable variation from campus to campus in the way policy is put into practice.

My strategy is a comparative one. I will present some of the findings from a long-term ethnographic project on how federal research funding panels do their work—how grant proposals are read, evaluated, discussed, and dealt with. I will then turn to some of the more striking features of the documents mentioned above and conclude with some comparative observations considering grant review and ethical review practices, as well as some suggestions for further research. The comparison of research funding committees with institutional review boards is warranted because, despite their differences in focus, the two kinds of review are both arenas in which managerial and assessment practices have been extended into the academic world. Both have something in common with what Power (1994, 1997), Strathern (1997), and others refer to in the British context as "audit culture," a situation in which models of auditing, a financial practice, have penetrated first into systems of broader managerial evaluation and then into organizations of quite disparate types, including academic ones. One of Power's insights on audit—or, more broadly, assessment—practices is particularly relevant here. He argues that even in its most traditional role in business, "the knowledge base of the financial audit process is fundamentally obscure" (Power 1997:30). Auditors necessarily rely on partial measures as if they captured entire truths, developing proxies or other kinds of indicators that are taken somehow to map the fiscal well-being of an organization. What financial auditors "know" is inherently obscure and partial, but they act upon it as if it provided a full, adequate, and explicit account. And the strategies that audits develop for pursuing such indicators are taken as broadly applicable to a range of financial situations and only rarely reexamined. With the extension of financial audit practices as a strategy for ensuring accountability in broader administrative activity, the "knowledge base" issue becomes even trickier as techniques are adapted to assess increasingly complex kinds of phenomena.

Marilyn Strathern makes a related argument along these lines: that audit procedures encourage the generation of too much information of a particular, decontextualized type, as they make "transferable skills an objective . . . reduc[ing] what makes a skill work, its embeddedness" (1997:14). She makes the compelling suggestion that what is needed is not the development of such transferable (and inherently partial) skills but "the very ability to embed oneself in diverse contexts . . . that can only be learned one context at a time."

Both Power's point about the partial nature of selected indicators and Strathern's concerns about decontextualized, overgeneralized information are directly relevant to institutional practices of research and ethical review. What kinds of proxies might we take as indexing the scientific promise of a proposed study or the balance of risk to subjects and possible benefits? How might the development of general criteria obscure or efface the particularities of specific research proposals, whether with an eye to their scholarly merit or to their consequences for participants? And, perhaps most important, are these difficulties inevitable in the bureaucratization of such assessment practices? The subsequent discussion is intended to provide a provocation (and perhaps to suggest some questions) for further discussion rather than any definitive answers.

Documenting Promise

This brief discussion represents a small part of a broader project, a language-focused ethnographic study of the research grant proposal and other funding applications as important genres of academic writing and of the reading practices and events through which such proposals are evaluated. My principal methodology has been that of participant turned observer (with the informed and invaluable help of program officers and fellow panelists and the benefit of many years of service on various funding panels). At the core of the broader work is the understanding that, for many of us at least, before we can write culture, we must write money. What strategies, rhetorical as well as methodological, do applicants draw upon, how are their proposals read and evaluated, and how, over time, do readers and writers jointly shape not only what is written and funded but what is taken to constitute good scholarship? Texts and talk about texts are inextricably intertwined over time in the research funding process, with a range of documents—proposals, recommendations, evaluations—providing the critical connective tissue.

Harper's (1998:3) notion of a document's "career" is instructive here. What kinds of "doings with documents" recurrently take place within an institution, and how do the documents both derive from and help constitute the work of that institution? An exemplary document in this regard is the National Science Foundation (NSF) proposal review form that is used by panel members and external, ad hoc reviewers to evaluate grant proposals. This form is sent to each reader along with the proposal and solicits both an overall rating (ranging from "excellent" to "poor") and a summary statement assessing the proposed research in terms of particular criteria. Completed forms then figure centrally in discussions at panel meetings, where they are sometimes circulated beforehand, sometimes read whole or in part, and sometimes, in the case of responses by external reviewers, presented, commented upon, and reframed by designated lead panel members. Such evaluations do not directly determine the outcome of panel deliberations but play a critical if varying role in the conversations. They are also provided as feedback to applicants when requested.

Two notable changes took place in the review forms during the 1990s. First, the criteria for evaluation were changed. Prior to 1997, four criteria had to be taken into account by reviewers: researcher competence (often referred to as the "threshold component," that is, the explicitly most heavily weighted element), the intrinsic merit of the research, its utility or relevance, and its potential contribution to the infrastructure of science and technology. In 1997 these were replaced by two criteria: the intellectual merit of the proposed activity and the activity's broader impacts. There is no longer an explicit threshold criterion, and the relative weighting of the two criteria may vary depending upon the reviewer's, the panel's, and the program officer's judgment. This change followed more than five years of study, consultation, retreats, circulated reports, and collegial and "stakeholder" responses. This activity stemmed from several quite varied sources: concerns with fairness in the peer review process, questions about the value of basic research in a time of reduced federal resources, an increasing emphasis on transparency and accountability in bureaucratic practice, Vice President Al Gore's task force on governmental reorganization, and the development of a strategic plan by the NSF in 1995. The reasons for the change in criteria are not, however, explained in the materials sent to reviewers; the new criteria are merely there, along with short paragraphs suggesting issues that might be considered under each rubric.

Second, the title of the narrative material accompanying the form was changed from "Information for Reviewers" to "Instructions for Reviewers." The work of the group developing the new criteria and forms focused directly on how best to elicit the most useful, comprehensible, and comparable information and how to bridge the gap between institutional intentions and requirements and individual respondents' private criteria. Not only must there be greater clarity as to what is desired by NSF; participants need to learn how to respond appropriately and to discipline themselves to act upon that learning. The shift from "information" to "instructions" and the concomitant increased specificity as to how evaluations must be justified and supported all point to a much greater concern for controlling and standardizing responses not in content per se but with regard to the kinds of issues that must be addressed and the terms in which proposals can be compared.

At the National Institutes of Health (NIH), a similar concern for disciplined response was striking in a 1996 report on the rating of grant applications. Central for the NIH committee was the issue of reliability, defined in terms of the extent to which a rating was a "quantitative representation of scientific merit and . . . not representing any other property of the application" (NIH 1996:iv). The notion of interrater reliability was salient here: there is a phenomenon out there, "scientific merit," and the role of scoring systems should be to enable reviewers to attend directly, solely, and accurately to that phenomenon in the instance of any particular proposal. Under this assumption, one would expect consistency across multiple evaluations of the same proposal. Obtaining reliable data for decision making requires guidance, carefully designed criteria, and considerable restraint. Reviewers and panelists must be educated and must shape their readings and responses appropriately.

One way in which such reader education is accomplished is through the use of a range of framing documents—program descriptions, explicit evaluative criteria, and the like. Such documents assume a critical secondary role, however, as panelists are always faced with more promising research projects than can be funded and so frequently turn to these framing documents to find programmatic or procedural ways of reducing the field of contenders. Such texts are taken very seriously and often quite literally. Panel discussions are often shared interpretive exercises, with as much focus on the "real" meanings of such documents and the fit between specific proposals and such meanings as on the proposals themselves. And what is highlighted in the framing documents, as well as, perhaps more important, what is not specifically addressed, shapes these discussions profoundly.

I have written elsewhere at length about the nature of panel discussions (Brenneis 1994, 1999). Four features are worth reiterating here, however. First, the outcomes of panel discussions are recommendations, not final decisions. Panels advise program officers, who then make their own, often binding recommendations to supervisors and staff committees. While a panel discussion may lead to a ranked list of proposals, the content of the commentary may prove more important than this formal outcome. Second, funding discussions of this sort, while usually attending to each proposal in its own terms, are also always comparative. Slowly a field of stronger and weaker, more and less promising candidates emerges. While the terms of evaluation are taken at one level to reflect the intrinsic merit of each proposal, they always end up being deployed in a shifting field of relative rankings. Third, comparability is a major concern; notions of fairness make the ability to weigh proposals against each other within the same framework crucial. Finally, this process is one of "peer review" in two senses: participants are at the same time reviewing the work of peers (or aspiring peers) and negotiating being peers with each other. In contrast to my early assumption that panel discussions would be marked by angry debate and strategic intransigence, the prevailing tone of the meetings I participated in was of amiable mutual deference. The more extreme opinions expressed were almost always made relatively safe through the use of humor or indirection, and individual panelists rarely went out on a limb or stayed there very long if they did. In this kind of communicative context, we always funded very good proposals indeed, but particularly innovative ones—those that might have produced fairly ardent disagreement and that might well have been "incomparable" with others—were often tabled for later discussion and rarely received such discussion.

Documenting Ethics

Local campus-based institutional review boards are made up primarily of academic members but usually include representatives of the nonacademic community as well. At UCSC, a campus without a medical school and on which the great bulk of research involving human subjects is in the social rather than natural sciences, the institutional review board includes primarily social scientists; a physician from the campus clinic participates, as does as a staff member of the Office of Sponsored Projects (OSP) and a minister from the community.

Individuals and groups proposing research involving human subjects, including unfunded and course-related student research, must apply to the board for review. Consideration can take many forms and lead to various outcomes depending on the nature of the research proposed. Proposed research may be defined as exempt from review under certain clearly defined circumstances. The requirement for formal, written informed consent may be waived if the board determines that the research proposed poses no or minimal risk to participants. Review may be expedited, or a full review may be required. For class-related research, a faculty member can apply for a blanket waiver for all the students who will be participating. The application documents often serve as starting points for discussion between the applicant and the board's chair and are subject, in a way in which research proposals are not, to ongoing revision and reworking. In part this has to do with an understanding that board review is an educational as well as a regulatory process. At UCSC research proposed to the institutional review board often receives either a waiver of informed consent or expedited review; at campuses with medical schools full review is more frequently demanded of applicants not only from medicine but from other disciplines.

The framing documents involved are particularly important. They define the terms in which board evaluation takes place, and they tend to be made up of highly detailed and at times quasi-legal definitions. They also provide flow charts and other guides to the board's decision making. The *IRB Guidebook* is a significant resource for institutional boards and, secondarily, individual applicants, representing as it does general Department of Health and Human Services policy. It begins with a crucial statement: "It is hoped that the Guidebook will provide precisely what its title is intended to denote: guidance. *The Guidebook does not itself constitute regulations but rather has been prepared for the convenience and reference of IRB members and administrators*" (OHRP

2001:I.1). While a complex web of regulations underlies the advice given in the guidebook, it assumes principled autonomy on the part of local boards.

After outlining the broad administrative and regulatory framework of human-subject protection, the *Guidebook* turns to basic review. Central to the discussion is a consideration of risk/benefit analysis, perhaps the key feature of institutional review board assessment and decision making. As the introduction notes, "risks to research subjects posed by participation in research should be justified by the anticipated benefits to the subjects or to society" (OHRP 2001:III.1). The text defines "benefit," "minimal risk," and "risk." "Benefit," for example, means "[a] valued or desired outcome; an advantage," and such advantage can be either the research subject's or that of society, including the generation of significant new knowledge. "Minimal risk" is defined as the situation in which "the probability and magnitude of harm or discomfort anticipated in the proposed research are not greater, in and of themselves, than those encountered in everyday life or during the performance of routine physical or psychological examinations or texts" (OHRP 2001:III.1). The notion of "minimal risk" is particularly important in that it is one of the conditions under which the informed-consent requirement may be waived.

Discussion then moves to a detailed consideration of the kinds of issues that must be taken into account in weighing potential gains against potential risk. Risks are not solely physical; potential psychological, social, and economic harms must also be contemplated. A central responsibility of the institutional review board (OHRP 2001:III.4) is to

> obtain complete information regarding experimental design and the scientific rationale ... underlying the proposed research, and the statistical basis for the structure of the investigation. IRBs should analyze the beneficial and harmful effects anticipated in the research. ... [A] way for IRBs to meet this responsibility is to assess whether the research design will yield useful data. When the sample size is too small to yield valid conclusions or a hypothesis inadequately formulated, subjects may be exposed to risk without sufficient justification.

A subsequent chapter focuses solely on questions of research design, including a discussion of research methodology in science (OHRP 2001:IV.2), so that board members can effectively consider potential benefits.

The *Guidebook* also provides case studies, short glossaries of relevant terms, exegeses of statutes as appropriate, and "points to consider." Again, it does not mandate institutional review board behavior but provides a well-worked out framework within which boards are encouraged to think and act. This framework matters both in what it explicitly highlights and in what is never mentioned. For example, much of the discussion of scientific merit is quite appropriate for biomedical research but unlikely to capture the value of ethnographic methodologies, whether in anthropology or in other fields, and a board guided solely by this document would have no explicit examination of the scientific merit of qualitative research to help guide its deliberations—an omission with potentially serious consequences for social scientists.

A second framing document, also from the OHRP, is *Human Subject Regulation Decision Charts*, a set of flow charts that clarify how boards can systematically make three determinations: "a) If the definition of "human subject" at Section 46.102(f) [of the Code of Federal Regulations] [is] met; b) If the research [is] exempt in accordance with Section 46.101(b)(4); and c) If the Institutional Review Board [may] employ Section 46.116(d) to waive informed consent or alter informed consent elements" (OHRP 1998:1–3). Significantly for anthropologists, the third flow chart suggests that informed consent may be waived for much ethnographic research provided that particular conditions are met.

A third kind of framing document, one that is probably the most salient for individual researchers, is the guidelines of the local board, in this instance those of UCSC's Committee for Protection of Human Subjects (OSP 2000). In comparison with the guidelines discussed above, the local materials are considerably more regulatory and less narrative in form, with no exemplary cases and little connective prose. Much of the language is taken directly from federal materials or systemwide University of California policies. Reading these admittedly draft guidelines—essentially a long list of regulations—is an even more daunting experience than studying the federal guidelines. The local guidelines do make clear, however, that consultation with the board chair, committee members, or its staff representative is strongly encouraged, something that their rather technical nature may well make necessary. And it is also clear that the actual practices of the board are, while quite thoughtfully considered, considerably less formal than the policies outlined in the document. The guidelines web site provides links to the necessary documents as well: the "Registration Form for Exempt Research," the "UCSC Protocol for a Project Involving the Use of Human Subjects," a statement of the documentation required for inviting subjects to participate and for getting their informed consent, and a sample consent form. My impression is that the guidelines are not directly linked to the forms; it is not entirely clear which forms are appropriate or necessary for what purposes, and the range of possible actions that the board may take is not fully spelled out. There is, for example, no discussion of expedited review, nor is there a clear explanation of how the board makes decisions on waivers of informed consent.

Some Initial Comparisons

There are two broad areas of difference between reviews of research proposals and reviews of human-subjects proposals. The first has to do with the nature of the task. For the research funding panel, while the adjectives available for rating each proposal (for example, "excellent") can be understood in absolute terms, the judgments are always necessarily comparative, and final recommendations rarely map onto simple semantic categories. Whatever the language used, proposals are always evaluated vis-à-vis each other. Panelists always work with a sense of far more good proposals than can be funded and often search for procedural or programmatic reasons to limit the field. As the demands of competitive ranking place a premium on the comparability and therefore the transparency of the proposals, some projects may be excluded from serious comparison because, however interesting, they are seen as the apples to everyone else's oranges. For a variety of reasons, making decisions on the basis of scientific merit within a large pool of good proposals is particularly difficult.

By contrast, the discussions of institutional review boards are not comparatively framed. There is no upper limit on the number of projects that can be approved. Proposals are judged on a case-by-case basis with the guidance of policy statements, definitions, flow charts, and the like. Where relative judgment enters into the board's deliberations is in the weighing of risks and benefits. This difference between ranking vis-à-vis competitive proposals and measuring against a shared standard should lead to real differences in the conduct and texture of panel discussions.

Second, the view that reviewers' evaluations should to the extent possible be consistent, reflecting the shared assessment of the scholarly merit of the proposed research to some extent informs the panel's reading and discussion practices. It has also helped shape the shift from information to instruction in the materials provided to reviewers. Something akin to a high degree of interrater reliability is being sought.

Perhaps the interactional decorum characteristic of many panel meet-ings derives as much from this desire as from a shared concern for working together as peers.

In the case of human-subjects review, however, both the composition of the boards, incorporating as they do lay as well as institutional actors, and the provision of guidelines appear to underline a view that ethical discussions should reflect a range of interests and possible positions within broad limits and should and will assume specific to their local and institutional contexts. Under such conditions disagreement or at least productive discussion of how particular cases match up against general principles is perhaps to be expected.

A particularly complex situation may arise when an institutional review board takes seriously, as many must, the suggestion that an evaluation of scientific merit should be part of its deliberations over relative risks and benefits. Here a committee established for one purpose—and one marked in many ways by the nonspecialist nature of its membership and procedures—is asked to assume another role, one for which it may be ill suited and that involves quite different styles of conversation, argument, and deliberation. This is in fact a major point of contention in the commentary on the NBAC's draft proposals (see, for example, Levine 2001) because they foreground the review of scholarly merit.

Roads Not Taken

A marked feature of evaluation and audit procedures is their inevitable partiality. They always rely upon partial measures, indicators based on part of the phenomenon in question; they are also often partial in reflecting the interests and concerns of the assessors. The choice of proxies—measurable variables by which broader practices and conse-quences may be tracked—often reflects considerable care but also draws directly upon the assessors' assumptions of where value can best be found. At the same time, the use of such proxies always necessarily excludes a wide range of other features the consideration of which may well be required for a comprehensive assessment.

In thinking about how institutional review boards operate, an analogy to printmaking may be helpful. The effect of a print certainly depends in large part on the direct traces of ink left on paper by the block or stone. Its visual effect, however, also relies on negative space, the space created where the printmaker did not work. The remaining "blank" paper is anything but empty; it takes form from and in turn shapes the created image. What is not considered in the institutional review process may figure directly in the ethical implications and complexity of any particular project. The adoption of the Common Rule, the NBAC recommendations for transforming it, and local institutional procedures raise certain critical issues. While, for example, most current critiques of the NBAC-proposed changes argue that they are too global, they suffer at the same time, although perhaps in less evident ways, from being too focused. They obscure considerations and concerns that, for a fuller view of ethical practice, should be brought explicitly onto the page.

It is clear, for example, that for many cultural anthropologists the critical question is *how* research is conducted. For archaeologists, in contrast, in large part because of ongoing negotiations with "most likely descendants" and other concerned lay communities, local and other, the critical questions have to do with the ethics of representation, knowledge dissemination, and entitlement: Whose story is the research product to tell, to whom, and for what purposes? Attention to local audiences and interlocutors in planning publications, exhibits, and site materials is central: Who has a legitimate interest in the findings, and how might that interest be most effectively served? Despite the lack of fit between the NBAC recommendations and the methods and values of cultural anthropologists, there is at least some agreement on where the problems lie. Issues central to archaeology, however, are not addressed directly by either current review board practice or the proposed changes. The biomedical analogy is even more loosely articulated vis-à-vis archaeology; it is likely, however, to be no less constraining in the future.[1]

In a recent paper responding to the NBAC proposals and examining the protection of participants in nonmedical research, Philip Rubin, Director of Behavioral and Cognitive Sciences at NSF, lists a number of points to consider in contemplating new forms of regulation. His first point is most relevant here: "It would be useful to *conduct research and gather data on the human research protection process*" (2001:3). I hope that this exploratory essay will suggest that such research is critical and potentially consequential. One hopes, as my Santa Cruz colleague does, for ethical researchers (and graduates). The kinds of institutional policies and practices for ethical assessment developed over the past fifty years and even more rapidly being transformed at present demand thoughtful, thorough, and broad-gauged consideration. Such inquiry also requires attention to the crucial ethical issues for which proxies are not provided and that remain largely invisible.

Acknowledgment

I thank Lynn Meskell and Peter Pels for including me in the conversations in which this volume is rooted. The intellectual exhilaration, amiability, and challenge of our discussions were remarkable; I thank all my fellow participants. I very much appreciate the Wenner-Gren Foundation's support of the symposium, and especially the work of Laurie Obbink, Mary Beth Moss, Marisa Lazzari, and Richard Fox in making the event and this volume possible. I also thank Marilyn Strathern and colleagues in Santa Cruz for their lively response when I presented this paper in a departmental colloquium.

Note

1. These comments reflect both general conversation in the symposium and more intense discussion with Lynn Meskell, Ian Lilley, and Faye Ginsburg, to whom I am deeply indebted. That discussion has provoked thinking about the "life history" of a research project and the different kinds of ethical concerns and opportunities that different stages in that life history present; I am currently working on an essay examining these questions.

Solid Histories for Fragile Nations: Archaeology as Cultural Patrimony

Rosemary A. Joyce

C opan, the only site in Honduras listed as a cultural property on the UNESCO World Heritage List, is located within a few miles of the border that separates Honduras and Guatemala, but the road leading from Copan to Guatemala is notorious for its poor condition. The call issued by the National Geographic Society in 1988 to improve this road as part of a proposed "Ruta Maya" that would reunite the sites of ruins of cities of the Maya Classic period (ca. AD 250–850) might consequently be seen as an unequivocally positive move (Garrett 1989:436). In fact, however, the call to improve roads and facilitate border crossings for international tourists ignored local, national, and regional social, economic and political realities that have kept this stretch of road more a ruin than the carefully restored buildings of the ancient archaeological site itself. Copan Ruinas, as a "place in history" (Herzfeld 1991), is a site of contestation, and archaeologists, as participants in the production of the contemporary material reality of the Copan Valley, are faced with formidable challenges to ethical practice.

In the pages that follow I describe a series of episodes in the debate within Honduras concerning how to manage the physical remains of pre-Hispanic habitation at Copan and elsewhere in the country as a focus for raising a number of issues. I first consider the complexity of archaeological stakeholding, a topic made current by the revision of the code of ethics of the Society for American Archaeology (SAA), the professional organization with the broadest cross-section of members in the United States (Lynott and Wylie 1995a; Lynott 1997). Through an extended consideration of debates about the management of Copan as a UNESCO World Heritage site, I explore the complexity that anthropological archaeologists face in reaching judgments about how to act as advocates in situations where their scientific expertise may be invoked as a resource. Finally, juxtaposing the case of Copan with the treatment accorded my own current research site, Puerto Escondido, I consider the compelling influence exercised by monumentality on ideas of significance, preservation, and cultural heritage that archaeologists explicitly or implicitly engage with.

Stakeholders in the Honduran Past

Contemporary archaeology is deeply embroiled in debate over a change from a language of rights to one of responsibilities. In the United States this transformation is signified vividly by shifts in the understanding of the central concept of archaeological stewardship (Lynott and Wylie 1995b; Wylie 1996:183–187; 1999:330–331). The new concept of stewardship that has emerged here owes much to repatriation initiatives (for example, Bray 2001; Bray and Killion 1994; Swidler et al. 1997; Watkins 2000). Repatriation has forced substantial reflection on ethics within the archaeological community, including debate about steward-ship and stakeholding (Wylie 1992, 1996; Joyce 2002). But diverse interests in archaeology were seen as posing ethical issues for archaeologists long before repatriation became a legal and political reality.

Along with most writers on the multiple interests in archaeology in the past twenty years, I deliberately use the term "stakeholding" here rather than adopt any of the other terms that might be used for the engagements of people with archaeology. The parties in the kinds of events I describe below do not simply speak for and from specific positions; they do not simply represent their interests or provide their interpretations. In fact, they have and argue for stakes in ambiguous situations regarding material remains. Even if they do not directly benefit from the economic exploitation of archaeological sites, they will find their lives affected by what is made of them and will often benefit or suffer materially. The power of the language of stakeholding, in my view, is that it forces us to acknowledge that political and economic interests, including those of archaeologists, are at risk in the situations I describe (Joyce 2002).

Mark Raab (1984:57) posed the question "Whose interests are at stake?" in private-sector archaeology and proceeded to identify three stakeholding positions: those of the archaeologist-as-researcher, the client, and the public. Raab's analysis placed archaeologists in the position of control, "balancing and harmonizing" different interests. Writing in the same volume, Paul Healy (1984) conceived of a much more complex set of stakeholders from his standpoint as an archaeologist operating in Central America. While not pretending to be comprehensive (Healy 1984:124), his survey of stakeholding positions is a model illustrating how things change if the question is not what interests archaeologists need to mediate but what responsibilities they may acquire through the privilege of conducting research. Healy identifies ethical responsibilities to host governments, scholars, and the public in host countries and, under the covering term "culture resource management," in the areas of site preservation, private collecting, and international trafficking in antiquities.

Wylie (1996:162–166; 1999:325–327) shows that a concern with preserving archaeological sites has been central to the way U.S. archaeologists have approached ethics. The idea that archaeology should be aimed at preserving material remains of past peoples, conserving them as a resource for future research on human pasts, has been central to the development of successive SAA ethics codes (Lynott and Wylie 1995a:30–31). The rapid pace of site destruction in the contemporary world has given site preservation additional urgency. A second pressure for a preservation ethic comes from the prospect that new methodologies will allow future researchers to extract different information from archaeological materials (Wylie 1999:326). The emphasis on preservation in previous SAA ethics guidelines was justified only by the consequences for academic researchers, by implication constituting archaeologists as specially privileged (Wylie 1996:180–183). Academic archaeologists have based their claim to authority on special access to the mechanisms of science and a preference for the scientific mode of knowing over other procedures (156–162). The end result was that earlier codes of ethics assumed that archaeologists were specially situated to act as "stewards," implicitly having the final say in the disposition of material traces of past human activity (Wylie 1999:329; compare Deloria 1992b:595; McGuire 1992:817).

Wylie (1996; 1999:331) argues that the contemporary understanding of stewardship embodied in the revised SAA principles of ethics requires the admission that archaeologists do *not* occupy a special position of greater detachment that warrants the reservation of decision making to them. This reframing of the archaeologist's position as one of joint stewardship (Brown 1998:205) should encourage archaeologists to work with other stakeholders to develop shared decision making concerning the materials on which archaeological practice depends. The new SAA principles of ethics position archaeologists not as disinterested judges but as interested stakeholders.

Since archaeologists have interests, they can also have conflicts of interest in situations in which decisions will affect their access to the sources of knowledge production or change the status gained through the control of knowledge production (Joyce 2002). Archaeologists, having had to cede their claim of unique authority to make decisions or to arbitrate when negotiation reaches an impasse, must be continually engaged in dialogue with other stakeholders. The diversity of parties that can present themselves or be presented as stakeholders cannot be delimited, leaving archaeologists with no way of evading responsibility for any broader effects of their actions. Stakeholders cannot be identified in advance; they emerge in action. Increasingly, archaeological stakeholding is emergent in new contexts created by regulatory agencies, whether local, national, or international. This is the position in which I found myself in Honduras in 1997 and 2001.

Managing Archaeological Knowledge

In July 1997 the director of the Honduran Institute for Anthropology and History requested that I prolong my stay in Honduras after my field season in order to attend a meeting to be held at Copan, a form of service covered by the terms of the contract allowing me to conduct research in the country. The agenda for the meeting I attended was, on the surface, simple. Participants were to consider a proposal by archaeologists working at the site to replace the Hieroglyphic Stairway on Structure 26 with a copy and move the original into a newly created museum to prevent further damage to it (see Fash et al. 1996; Fash and Fash 1997). Arguably, the Hieroglyphic Stairway is one of the main reasons Copan is a UNESCO World Heritage site today.

Copan, explored during the mid- to late nineteenth century, was one of the earliest reported scientifically excavated Maya sites (Stephens 1841; Maudslay 1889; Gordon 1896, 1902). It served as the source of monuments and inscriptions for the first seriation of Maya sculpture (Spinden 1913) and contributed much of the pottery for the initial definition of Classic Maya polychrome style (Vaillant 1927). As the UNESCO citation listing it as a UNESCO World Heritage site in 1980 stresses, a case can even be made for its having been one of the first Classic Maya sites seen by Europeans: "Discovered in 1570 by Diego García de Palacios, the ruins of Copán, one of the most important sites of Mayan civilization, were not excavated until the 19th century. Its citadel and imposing public squares characterize its three main stages of development, before the city was abandoned in the early 10th century" (UNESCO 2001d).

The designation of Copan as a UNESCO World Heritage site was based on its meeting specific criteria, fulfilling a "test of authenticity," and having "adequate legal and/or traditional protection and management mechanisms" to ensure its conservation (UNESCO 2001b). Copan was cited as "an outstanding example of a type of building or architectural or technological ensemble or landscape which illustrates (a) significant stage(s) in human history" and is "directly or tangibly associated with events or living traditions, with ideas, or with beliefs, with artistic and literary works of outstanding universal significance." Its recognition as a UNESCO World Heritage site created a context in which multiple stakeholders had to negotiate their interests in Copan. The archaeological stake in delineating historical events and adjudicating their significance is juxtaposed with other stakes: those of national institutions charged with managing the site and conservation professionals who have the expertise to judge whether reconstruction "is carried out on the basis of complete and detailed documentation on the original and to no extent on conjecture" (UNESCO 2001b).

The archaeological stake in Copan and particularly the Hieroglyphic Stairway places greatest emphasis on the contribution of the sculptures to the identification of events in dynastic history at the site. Often described as the longest continuous Classic Maya inscription that has been preserved, the stairway was one of the monuments recorded during the late nineteenth-century florescence of Maya archaeology. The majority of the carved stones that make up the stairway were encountered out of order in the 1890s (Gordon 1902). What tourists see today was restored by archaeologists in the mid-twentieth century, before the modern study of Maya writing, and consequently the sculptures were reassembled out of what today is believed to be the correct order (Fash et al. 1992; Stuart 1992). One large section of the stairway was removed by the archaeologists who worked at Copan in the 1890s and taken to Harvard University's Peabody Museum, in full compliance with the legal requirements of the agreements under which the researchers worked at the time (Gordon 1902). This was a spur to revision of Honduran antiquities legislation to prevent future investigators from removing such materials (Agurcia Fasquelle 1984). The gap left in the stairway has been the subject of repeated public comment in Honduran newspapers, and calls for the repatriation of the original sculpture are repeatedly made.

The priority of research at Copan made it a particularly potent symbol for the new nation of Honduras in the late nineteenth century (Euraque 1998; Joyce 2003). Honduras, homeland of Francisco Morazán, the leader of the Central American republic, could represent itself as the source of legitimacy for Central American nationalism, and Copan, located in Honduras, could be taken as the origin of Classic Maya civilization. The valorization of Copan was reinforced by the activities of archaeologists who emphasized signs of Classic Maya culture over the diversity represented by most sites elsewhere in the country (Euraque 1998; compare Joyce 1993). Other sites had produced no carved stone monumental texts. Texts were central to the concerns of international archaeologists because writing and calendrical records were used as evidence for the civilized status of the Maya. That civilized status was critical to archaeologists in U.S. institutions seeking an equivalent in the Americas to classical antiquity in order to bolster their status (Hinsley 1985:69–72).

Stakeholders in Copan, 1997–98

For all parties engaged in the practice of archaeology in Honduras, Copan's Hieroglyphic Stairway has a charged status. An icon of the Honduran nation and of world heritage, a sign of Maya "civilization," it is fundamental to the realization of touristic desires for experiences of the right kind (Mortensen 2001a, 2001b; compare Brown 1999; Castañeda 1996; Hervik 1998). The stakes were high when the first meeting of "experts" was convened in July 1997. Participating "experts" included Honduran and North American archaeologists working both at Copan and elsewhere in the country and conservation professionals, some engaged actively in site preservation in the Maya lowlands and others with less direct experience on Maya sites but broader knowledge of cultural heritage and preservation issues. Representatives of a number of agencies with formal interests in the site, notably the Honduran Institute of Anthropology and History, the Honduran Tourism Institute, and UNESCO, were also present.

At the outset, it was not entirely clear what the purpose of the assembly was, whether to act as an advisory group, to listen and provide reactions to those charged with making ultimate decisions about the site, or to function as a decision-making body. The outcomes reached were later represented as decisions made by the "experts," who were characterized as having warded off possible actions feared by the Institute of Anthropology and History (*La Prensa de Honduras,* July 22,

1997). It is not that the legal lines of authority were at all murky: the Honduran constitution empowers the institute to manage the national patrimony of archaeological and historical sites and movable goods (*Ley del patrimonio cultural* 1984; Agurcia Fasquelle 1984; Hasemann 1986; Herrera 1995). UNESCO World Heritage site designation does not override local authority; its documents stress the consensual effect of joining a "community" (UNESCO 2001a):

> The overarching benefit of joining the World Heritage Convention is that of belonging to an international community of appreciation and concern for unique, universally significant properties that embody a world of outstanding examples of cultural diversity and natural wealth. The States Parties to the Convention, by joining hands to protect and cherish the world's natural and cultural heritage, express a shared commitment to preserving our legacy for future generations.

In principle, the UNESCO program expresses a global commitment to assisting local authorities in managing designated properties, but "it is the State Parties' responsibility to provide adequate protection and management for their sites." In theory, UNESCO designation has limited direct funding implications, since only about US$3 million is provided annually for World Heritage Fund grants throughout the world. Over the period from 1980 to 1998, Honduras received approximately US$125,000 for Copan in direct funding as a UNESCO World Heritage site (UNESCO 2001c). In effect, UNESCO World Heritage site designation can establish priorities for local administrations, which must direct resources and efforts toward the preservation of their piece of global cultural capital. Newspaper reports in June 2001 cited an expenditure of almost US$1 million for preservation of Copan in that year alone (*La Nación de Honduras*, June 6, 2001).[2] Designation as a UNESCO World Heritage site may well serve to establish priorities and to shift funding away from other possible goals without extensive deliberation or obvious decision making.

The Honduran Institute of Anthropology and History would be obliged to direct much of its efforts to the management of Copan even without UNESCO World Heritage designation simply because the site is viewed as critical to the economic development of tourism. The Honduran Ministry of Tourism reported that income from tourism rose from US$195 million in 1999 to US$240 million in 2000 and was expected to rise an additional 15 percent in 2001 (*La Prensa de Panama*, July 22, 2001).[3] About 17 percent of the 410,000 tourists to Honduras in 2000 visited Copan, potentially accounting for approximately US$40 million in tourism income. Projections for tourist development suggest that with more promotion this total could rise to over US$500 million. Such projections affect the evaluation of the stake that the Honduran government has in Copan.

This interest is not unrelated to the stake archaeologists have developed in the site because of the strong emphasis that tourist development places on the authenticity and value of the Classic Maya culture, which in turn is justified through archaeological knowledge. In contrast to Mexico, Guatemala, or Belize, Honduras cannot count on a large number of archaeological sites identified with the Classic Maya to attract longer-term visitors. The location of Copan so close to the Guatemalan border has operationally made tourism to Copan an add-on for travelers staying primarily in Guatemala. The lopsided tourist development that makes Copan an oasis of First World amenities, including destination restaurants, resorts, and Internet cafes, in a country with inadequate water, electrical power, and other basic services is the most obvious sign of the virtual annexation of Copan to Maya tourism emanating from Guatemala.

But interests in the authenticity of Copan are not limited to the international tourists for whom it is an appendage of Guatemala. It is no accident that it was through takeovers of Copan that Chorti Maya people called for negotiation of indigenous land rights (Joyce 2003; Mortensen 2001b). In October 1998, thousands of Chorti Maya occupied Copan and brought tourism to a standstill to dramatize land claims and issues of indigenous rights not only for themselves but for a coalition of indigenous groups.[4] The loss of tourism income from the two-week takeover, which happened in the off-season for tourism, was estimated at around US$500,000. The economics and symbolism of the action and a very real sense of stakeholding in both the archaeological site and movable archaeological property were consciously articulated by indigenous protestors. José Rufino Pérez is quoted (*Out There News*)[5] as saying, "This is a sacred place. That's why we have a right to the benefits that come in, because all the revenue goes to the government and the people have no resources." Similarly, *La Prensa de Honduras* (October 22, 1998)[6] quotes José Ernesto Suchite as follows: "We aren't going to go until the government also approves 25 percent of the income from the ruins, participation and administration as indigenous people, and not to send archaeological pieces out of the country."

It is likely that few present at the table in summer 1997 imagined that such events lay in the near future, but the central position of Copan

as a national symbol and an important location of Honduran participation in global processes was quite clear. The issues debated at the
meeting were, in contrast, surprisingly limited.[7] Initial discussions
involved whether sufficient data existed to justify the risk of damage
inherent in removing the stairway from the site and what the benefits
would be for scholars and visitors to the site in replacing the original
with a copy. As discussion continued, it became clear that there were
distinct understandings of what would constitute a positive visitor
experience at Copan and what Copan's significance was at different
scales. These discussions exposed differences in the stakes of archaeologists and others at the table.

The archaeological proposal was supported by evidence of deterioration in the legibility of incised texts since the late 1970s, when modern
archaeology began to be practiced at the site, but once the suggestion
of replacing the deteriorating original with a replica was raised the issue
became what the replica would be. Would it show the stairway's state
of preservation at the time of removal or its condition before the recent
dramatic erosion? If the latter, would there be any reason not to provide
details long lost but documented in casts and photographs dating from
the earliest nineteenth-century research? If missing details were to be
restored, might it not be worth considering adding details that contemporary specialists in Maya writing have been able to reconstruct,
even if these were not visible in any preserved record?[8]

The proposal to remove the monument from the site drew strong
reactions from other participants. A representative of the Honduran
Institute of Tourism spoke eloquently in favor of the view that the
authenticity of the site would be compromised by such a change.
Implicit in her comments was an understanding of the value of the site
as a place whose history of deterioration was part of its significance. A
representative of an international museum elucidated this implicit
argument, suggesting that once the original stones were removed and
replicas created there would be no reason in theory to visit Copan itself:
replicas could be sited anywhere in the world, allowing a remote
experience of the essence of the site. This was presented not as a positive
vision of democratization of access (in the manner of naïve "virtual
reality" claims for computer-generated imagery) but as a dystopic vision
of a future impoverished by a loss of the sense of the real. This speaker
explicitly argued that he would prefer a decaying original to a pristine
replica because the marks of historical change were part of what made
the site significant as human cultural heritage. Along with several other
speakers, he expressed doubt that the currently accepted understanding

by specialists of the order and details of the original text would stand the test of time. He encouraged the use of virtual representation for experimentation with reordering the text quite apart from the physical management of the site.

The divide that opened between archaeologists and nonarchaeologists demonstrated very different understandings of what made Copan a significant place. The archaeologists treated the site and its monuments as data for scientific analysis, resulting in documentation of the historical development of the ancient Maya kingdom recorded in the monuments. The information contained in the Hieroglyphic Stairway could be enhanced by removing the eroded original sculpture from the site and replacing it with a replica in which details had been filled in by employing specialist knowledge. Many nonarchaeologists present viewed the site instead as a location whose attractions were grounded not in the degree to which correct historical knowledge could be gained from the sculptures but in something else. This something else was partly the evidence that the ruins provided of the persistence of products of human labor through time and partly the experience of being at a site of past human activity. In neither case would the experience be enhanced by the replacement of the original stone by a replica.

The meeting ended with a call for detailed study of the condition of the stairway and the monitoring of environmental conditions by conservation professionals. The conservation professionals present at the meeting, representing multiple institutions, constituted another distinct stakeholding group. Their contributions to the discussion emphasized an ideal of minimal intervention and a commitment to gathering data over a long period before making any decision. Whereas the archaeologists and nonarchaeologists who directly debated the proposal for a replica differed in seeing the site either as information or as a historic place, the conservation professionals were most closely engaged with the monument as a material object. The emergence of a call for detailed conservation studies, endorsed by all present, reflected the framing of the meeting as an examination of a proposal to deal with problems and exploit opportunities of one specific sculpture. This very narrow emphasis is the more apparent when this meeting is juxtaposed with a meeting in September 2001 billed as the "second meeting of experts in conservation of the Copan Archaeological Park."

"Expert" Stakeholders as Managers, 2001

The second meeting retrospectively positioned the original session as having been a general consideration of the conservation of Copan by a group of experts, taking the outcome of that meeting as its character. But the agenda of this meeting had very little to do with conservation of the park, and the returning "experts" were presented with a very different task that further exposed the fault lines of differences among stakeholders. A handout for the second meeting listed its general objectives: (1) assembly of specialists in conservation to evaluate the progress of the conservation projects generated since 1997, (2) official presentation of the management plan for the Copan Archaeological Park for 2001–10, and (3) presentation and analysis of experiences in conservation projects in the Central American region.[9] Six specific objectives followed, five having to do with reports on conservation or preservation issues of specific components of the site. The last called for "review and analysis of the proposals of the programs of management of cultural and natural resources, public use, and operations of the Copan Archaeological Park."

This initial charge substantially broadened the acknowledged array of stakeholders in the life of the archaeological site. It positioned the site in a context entirely absent from the first meeting, with its dual perspectives of local debates about Copan and global concerns about a UNESCO World Heritage site. This new context was that of the geopolitical region, signaled by the inclusion of discussion completely unrelated to Copan as the third general objective. In the press, the director of the Honduran Institute of Anthropology and History presented Copan as an example and "pilot center" for the region (*La Prensa de Panama*, September 30, 2001).[10] The expansion to this level, intermediate between the local and the global, was a strategic move that framed problems experienced in Honduras as less the product of unique circumstances needing local solutions than the outcome of global processes. Other countries in Central America have been grappling with their own issues of management of archaeological sites and movable property that threaten to overwhelm local resources while tying national archaeological institutions into the demands of global tourism and nation building (see Joyce 2003; de Lugan 1994, 2000). But in the event, the time allocated for this portion of the program was drastically cut in order to allow participants to visit the site itself, reemphasizing the degree to which the monuments of Copan continued to exercise their overwhelming gravitational pull.

Perhaps most significant in terms of newly acknowledged stakeholders was the explicit mention of the public, albeit limited to a reference to "public use" of the site. The dramatic intervention of the indigenous public in the life of the site in October 1998 might have been expected to form part of the context of the meeting, particularly since the site had been occupied once again in September 2000. Government agreement to meet the Chorti Maya's demands for land had split the local community over different understandings of costs and benefits of these land transactions and of the authenticity of the claimants (Chenier, Sherwood, and Robertson 1999; Mortensen 2001b). Into this volatile situation the proposed plan introduced another set of claims on local land emanating from expectations of international agencies concerned with cultural preservation and of global tourism. Archaeological remains are widely distributed in the Copan Valley, and therefore the proposals of the management plan (such as reforestation projects) will affect most people living in the area (Lena Mortensen, personal communication, September 2001).[11]

No one who could be readily identified as a member of the general public was in fact present at the meeting, and here the appeal to expertise was presumably key. The management plan for Copan that was presented, an update of the initial plan formulated shortly after the site attained UNESCO World Heritage status (IHAH 1984), is a document required by UNESCO. It was prepared by an international consulting body with substantial experience in the management of natural parks (Mortensen 2001a). The principal architects of the plan were not archaeologists but wildlife conservation specialists relying for archaeological understanding on the advice of those working at the site. The plan covered, in a broad fashion, issues ranging from the physical location of visitor facilities to the establishment of priorities for research and conservation. In each of its sections it specified levels of staffing that would require the creation of new positions and, as the plan directly stated, increased funding of the site by the Honduran government.

The "experts" engaged in this meeting were asked to review specific sections of the plan and suggest improvements. In fact, what ensued was a series of critiques in which each set of experts found fault with the scope and specifics of the document from the standpoint of the stake each held in the archaeological materials. If there was any consensus it was that the management plan, in which months of effort had been invested, was fundamentally flawed. The critical positions were so varied that it should have been difficult to discern any commonality, but in fact three distinct critiques grounded in different understandings of archaeological significance and ethical responsibilities emerged. These critiques highlight the ambiguous position of archaeologists as stakeholders in emergent ethical debates.

First, a number of archaeologists engaged closely with the site objected to the plan's prioritization of needs. Those involved in the detailed study of the Hieroglyphic Stairway noted that its stabilization was given a very low priority. Others working at Copan suggested that the management plan would make difficult the kinds of intensive subsurface work in which they were engaged, which had produced unparalleled information about the early dynastic history of the site. An archaeologist who specialized in the study of ceramics drew attention to the fact that the guidelines for the restoration of pottery disqualified vessels from the earliest (and thus potentially archaeologically most critical) phases. Unifying these diverse claims, which on one level were expressions of the archaeologists' individual investments, was a shared understanding that archaeological materials are significant only through an interpretive lens provided by the specialist. As emerged in the first meeting, for the archaeologists the site was a source of information, and they wanted its management to maximize— or at least not make impossible—the production of new information.

Conservation professionals were equally convinced that the plan for management of the site was ill-conceived. At times they complained about the same items: one conservation specialist argued that the guidelines for the restoration of pottery vessels would set her field back a hundred years. Her example of the problem, however, was distinct: the day-to-day life of ordinary people would not be illustrated if vessels for reconstruction were selected primarily for their artistic value as the protocol proposed. The conservation specialists working to monitor the Hieroglyphic Stairway agreed with the archaeologists that the monument required a higher priority while continuing to dissent from revised proposals for construction of a physical replica. Because their studies had shown that deterioration of the monument was no longer rapid, they were prepared to see the eroded monument remain in place. They offered their highly precise digital model of the stairway as an adequate substitute for any physical replica, the cost of which (estimated in the millions of dollars) would divert resources from other potential uses. In effect, the conservation professionals took seriously the framing of the archaeological stake as the information the monument could provide, and this left the archaeologists in a weaker position to argue for a stake in the specific materiality of the monument.

A third critical position was expressed by anthropologists from Honduras, some trained as archaeologists and others as ethnographers. They objected to the framing of the site as important primarily to a global audience of tourists. They objected to the lack of attention to local education and the failure to place the site in the wider context of the archaeology and history of the country as a whole. These objections to the management plan were echoed by foreign archaeologists working outside Copan, myself included. As I tried to explain, Copan could not be considered as simply a collection of major buildings. The institute's responsibility for the site in fact encompassed all the historical and pre-Hispanic traces of human activity. By law, it was required to intervene when any trace of historic or ancient human activity was affected. The plan, as written, would not require intervention in the event of disturbance of a site lacking Late Classic Maya cut-stone architecture, even if that site were an example of the earliest occupation of the region or of a unique colonial settlement. The definition of what constituted the protected site would not encompass recovery of buried remains of the more perishable houses of the majority of the population that supported the elites of central Copan. The proposed interpretive frameworks for the site placed it only in relation to an artificial, synthetic concept of the "Maya world" (compare Brown 1999; van den Berghe 1995). It left undeveloped and unaddressed multiple indigenous histories that are a central concern for Honduran scholars interpreting the country's cultural patrimony (for example, Agurcia Fasquelle 1984; Cruz Sandoval 1997; Euraque 1998; Hasemann, Lara Pinto, and Cruz Sandoval 1996; Rivas 1993; compare Joyce 2003; Mortensen and Pyburn 2000).

From Analysis to Practice: The Ethical Dilemma

As was the case with the first meeting, the role of the participants in the September 2001 meeting was never clear, although press reports after the fact again stated that the "experts" had made the final decisions (see, for example, *El Tiempo*, September 30, 2001).[12] Those in attendance acted as stakeholders, took the opportunity offered them to evaluate the proposed management plan, and rejected it, but that rejection had no force. Their expertise was being invoked as a form of authority that could be separated from their overall judgment of the management plan. The consultants asked those objecting to the document to provide specific alternative language for the sections offered as examples of bad practice or objectionable priorities, even when the issue was restated as a fundamental objection to the entire proposal.

For the authors of the management plan, it would appear, the materiality of Copan was less relevant than it was for other stakeholders. As one consultant said, most visitors to Tikal, a UNESCO World Heritage site in Guatemala, were interested in bird-watching in the forest reserve, not in the archaeology of that monumental Classic Maya center. A proposal in the draft management plan for Copan to reforest sections of the valley made sense as directed at such global stakeholders. It seemed discordant with a goal of interpreting the experience of the Copan Valley at the peak of settlement in the eighth century AD, when, according to archaeological data, the area was completely deforested (Abrams and Rue 1988). Interest in interpreted archaeological sites was, the consultant assured me, confined to a small group of atypical visitors. That such sites might be significant in the historical consciousness of local people was something he admitted, but it could not be the basis for operating a national park, which needed to bring in sufficient tourist income to support preservation activities.

The meeting of experts might best be seen as a piece of political theater in which archaeologists (and conservation professionals) played the role of the white-coated specialist on a television commercial for an over-the-counter cold remedy. In that situation, where does an ethical course of action lie for the archaeologist? There were, as was pointed out at the meeting, many other uses that could be found for the funding proposed for replacing the stairway. Copan, reduced in the course of the planning process to its most showy remains, no longer merely exercised a strong gravitational pull: it seemed to threaten to collapse inward, drawing with it immense financial resources and human efforts and erasing all the complexity of its social context.

The Monumental and the Trace

What are the ethical alternatives for an archaeologist trapped in the management plan, where contributing language or refusing to do so both imply consent to its fundamental assumptions? My own pragmatic resolution of the contradiction drew on my experiences in other contexts in archaeological practice in Honduras. Here I provide a brief account of that experience and its implications for the model of ethical archaeological practice briefly summarized above.

The archaeological work in which I was engaged in 1997, when I received my first summons to join the deliberations over the management of Copan, was taking place about three hours' drive east of Copan, in the lower Ulua River valley. Today this is the center of Honduras's agricultural and manufacturing development, with the rapidly growing city of San Pedro Sula as its hub. The area around San Pedro was the center of some of the first Spanish efforts at colonization but was rapidly marginalized in colonial Honduras (Pastor Fasquelle 1989). In the late nineteenth century the north coast of Honduras became the center of new agricultural development and business interests and multinational immigration (Euraque 1996; Gonzalez 1992; Pastor Fasquelle 1989).

In the town of La Lima, east of San Pedro, what became the United Fruit Company established its headquarters and converted much of the eight hundred square miles of the valley into plantations (Argueta 1989; Euraque 1996). Beginning in the 1970s, some land formerly under company control was converted to private ownership or to communal land grants. During this dynamic moment the Honduran Institute of Anthropology and History, in anticipation of the need to implement archaeological cultural resource management established its first formal presence in the valley. In 1979 it initiated an inventory of the archaeological sites in the valley, as part of which I conducted field research from 1979 to 1983. In the 1990s I joined a collaborative project with a research design that allowed my codirector and me to act as an extension of the institute, conducting more extensive archaeological excavations at selected sites than its limited resources would allow.

While we identified over five hundred sites in our initial survey, those under greatest threat of destruction made up a discrete, spatially limited subset located in the center of the valley. The institute has generally been successful in negotiating preservation of at least part of sites with visible surface architecture through the redesign of development projects to leave green spaces around these visible mounds. Sites that appear only as low earthen rises formed by the deposit of successive years of primarily domestic activities have been much more vulnerable to bulldozing to make way for *maquilas*. The situation is quite clear on the ground: the image of significant archaeological sites has been firmly set by Copan and, more specifically, by a small proportion of the physical remains at that location. Our research design emphasized the information that the less impressive sites could provide for understanding everyday, small-scale practices in a region where archaeological remains are open to an interpretation challenging evolutionary assumptions about the inevitability of sociopolitical centralization (Daviss 1997).

I have felt confident that my choice to structure my research around the reality of site destruction was ethically sound. In direct response to the SAA principles, this decision has allowed me to refrain from excavation of unthreatened sites and respond to the interests of other stakeholders, represented initially by the institute, for whom the threatened sites are a common good. But it has also put me in a position not unlike that described by Richard Wilk (1999), who found his research being used in ways destructive to the interests of the people he studied. Wilk suggests that part of the problem came from his initial acceptance of terms that framed his research in ways conducive to its use against particular stakeholders. He takes himself to task for not having examined the implications of concepts of group identity and continuity that have been used against local interests.

In much the same way, I often find myself forced to engage in the evaluation of the archaeological sites in which I have research interests in terms that poorly serve either my stake or that of Honduran people who are not directly engaged in cultural heritage management. When one site we were asked to investigate yielded previously undocumented traces of very early village life (Joyce and Henderson 2001), we were faced with trying to shift or expand the previously negotiated green space from an area with massive stone construction. Rather than operating, as I would have liked to, as a stakeholder negotiating interests with other stakeholders, I was required by my expertise in interpretation to insist that these material traces were significant and urgently in need of preservation. As the director of the institute, a historian, commented when we showed her the best evidence, simply a line of whiter soil, of buildings at Puerto Escondido dating before 1000 BC, "You archaeologists; you tell us these things and we simply have to trust you." Clearly, despite her acceptance of our assurances and her support of subsequent efforts at site preservation, what we were demonstrating was less than convincing as evidence of significance. One of the main obstacles to making our point through a less asymmetric exchange was the image of significance that my own discipline, reinforced by international agencies and global tourism, had constructed.

Two other contexts of archaeological practice converged at Puerto Escondido to reframe the question of ethical practice there for me. In 1993 I had collaborated in the curation of archaeological galleries for a public museum of archaeology and history that opened in San Pedro Sula in January 1994. The museum rapidly became a central cultural institution in the city and, drawing twenty thousand visitors a year, had raised awareness of the long history of human occupation in the region that is, for the most part, architecturally invisible. Puerto Escondido was in fact originally reported, voluntarily, when bulldozing operations exposed the buried site. The museum sponsored public talks about archaeology in general and the site in particular. Increased interest in archaeology overall led to news media attention, culminating in summer 2000 in coverage by Honduran newspapers, radio, and television and by CNN en Español.

Press coverage began with the assumption that there must be something important here or North Americans would not be spending time at the site. The first reporter to visit the site came unannounced, prepared to broadcast live radio coverage of our excavation of a Late Classic burial. Excavating burials was not a goal of our research but had proved unavoidable because of the nature of the site, where a Late Classic hamlet had been built on the remains of the much earlier village. Since the Classic inhabitants of the region regularly buried their dead below house floors, it was impossible to avoid excavating burials in household sites, and it was in fact the disturbance of human remains that had attracted the attention of the bulldozer operators who reported the site. There have to date been no stated objections to the excavation of burials from Honduran indigenous groups, whose concerns about archaeology have centered more on the accessibility of knowledge about the past and the institute's effectiveness in safeguarding archaeological properties. Nonetheless, here, as elsewhere, the decision to excavate human remains was potentially highly charged. Archaeological excavation of burials elsewhere in Honduras has been interpreted as recovery of "disappeared" persons from the 1980s (Patricia Urban, personal communication, 2000). Following a change of government after elections in fall 2001, a new director of the institute would be appointed who would serve only through August 2002. In conversations with foreign archaeologists he expressed reservations based on Christian religious beliefs about burial excavation and especially curation of burial remains (Julia Hendon, personal communication, 2002). Both as part of a general commitment to teaching students to respect the humanity of those whose burials we must disturb and with the possibility of such negative public perceptions in mind, I was not happy at the prospect of press sensationalization of the excavation of this burial.

Nor was I entirely at liberty to speak to the press. Since the institute requires that all press coverage take place through it or with its prior written authorization, this visit precipitated a crisis. We dispatched someone to the regional office of the institute while I attempted to explain the delay to the reporter. It did not go well; stories about bureaucratic cover-ups are a staple of the Honduran media, and the institute had come under criticism for a variety of actions, including sending archaeological properties out of the country, where one item had been lost or stolen in transit. By undertaking to explain what we were doing off air while waiting for a representative of the institute, I managed to defuse the situation. The institute departed from its preferred practice of not publicizing archaeological work until after its completion and called a press conference for the remaining media outlets in San Pedro. By the time these reporters arrived in the field, the human remains were no longer visible, and I was able to substitute the story line of Honduras's earliest village for that of ghoulish finds of dead bodies. My authority stood me in good stead as reporter after reporter filmed a patch of bleached-out clay to illustrate my assertion that here were the remains of the earliest known house in Honduras and, indeed, all of Central America. The circle was closed when reporters for CNN, interviewing the director of the institute, asked if the site was being preserved, prompting the visit on which she expressed the ambivalent trust she felt compelled to place in us.

The press coverage of the site produced none of the negative outcomes that the institute had feared. It perhaps had the effect of increasing the turnout for the public talk at the museum scheduled for near the end of the field season. There we repeated our representation of the site to the local community as a material sign of the past integration of the valley into social networks extending from northern South America to Mexico. Given the colonial history of the valley, the audience for the talk could assert neither the direct continuity with that past nor the maintenance of stable cultural traditions that Wilk (1999) notes are problematic side effects of anthropological practice in the region. As one of the effects of the museum, our work is no longer subject to representation as the exploration of an essentialized "Maya" past in the manner critiqued by Anne Pyburn (1998a, 1998b). In fact, it has become implicated in the partly self-conscious formation of a multicultural past congruent with a contemporary reformulation of Honduras as a nation of many ethnicities (Joyce 2003).

Local Honduran stakeholders have less interest in constructing a claim of indigenous identity than in advancing the idea of a multi-rooted Honduran identity. A public intellectual involved in the museum (Rodolfo Pastor Fasquelle, quoted in England and Anderson 1998:3), commenting on Afrocentric claims by Honduran Garifuna, has been quoted as saying,

> One cannot invent oneself according to one's whim or preference. To try to pass as African is just as questionable for a Garifuna as it would be for [then President] Carlos Roberto Reina to dress like a Lenca or for me to presume to be a Briton or a Pech Indian just because I have these ancestors. Like all other Hondurans, the Garifuna are mestizos.

This alternative vision of national identity inspires just as much interest in the cultural patrimony as more romantic notions of cultural essentialism. Archaeological knowledge occupies a much more crucial position in mediating the construction of a shared Honduran past by local stakeholders who claim no special access to that past. Participation by Honduran mestizos in constructing interpretations of archaeological materials in the form of temporary exhibits, publications, and conference presentations both draws on the expertise of foreign archaeologists and assumes that expertise to be contestable. Here, finally, at the site of the museum, I can locate something that experientially feels like fully ethical practice, in which my own stake is something I can legitimately advocate in a position of situated authority and decentered power.

Acknowledgments

I thank Lynn M. Meskell, Peter Pels, and Richard Fox for inviting me to participate in the symposium leading to this volume. My understanding of ethical issues in archaeology has been immeasurably enriched by discussions with my colleague K. Anne Pyburn that have contributed to shaping my decisions about practice. My great debt to Alison Wylie should be clear from the in-text citations, but I reiterate here my respect for the clarity of her arguments concerning these issues and the influence she has had on my thought and writing. The symposium gave me the opportunity to benefit from the interventions of three extraordinary discussants, Faye Ginsburg, Ian Lilley, and Susan Lindee, and I regret that their more coherent perspectives are not represented here in place of my beginning steps. Lena Mortensen has been a generous interlocutor on terrain that is more truly her own, and I thank her for her stimulating comments.

Notes

1. http://www.laprensahn.com/natarc/9707/n22002.htm.
2. http://www.nacion.com/ESTACION21/2001/junio/06/arqueo.html.
3. http://mensual.prensa.com/mensual/contenido/2001/07/22/hoy/negocios/200601.html.
4. This discussion is based on newspaper articles concerning these events obtained from the Agence France Presse news service. Related coverage can be

found at http://www.honduras.com/thisweek/archive/98-10-23.html and http://www.laprensahn.com/natarc/9810/n24001.htm.

5. http://www.megastories.com/mitch/map/copan.htm.

6. http://www.laprensahn.com/natarc/9810/n22001.htm.

7. My report of the issues debated is based on my own notes of the proceedings. These took place in Spanish, and thus none of the words used here are quotes—they are paraphrases. Where the rhetoric of particular points struck me, I recorded the original Spanish precisely. Because I was providing my notes as a source for a colleague in attendance who did not speak Spanish, they are a more complete transcript than would otherwise be the case, and I draw on them extensively here.

8. The last option, of course, would violate the UNESCO World Heritage rules, a point made at the meeting by the UNESCO representative.

9. The original documents I cite here and in the following discussion were all in Spanish unless otherwise noted. The translations are my own.

10. http://mensual.prensa.com/mensual/contenido/2001/09/30/hoy/revista/276422.html.

11. This topic is one of the ethnographer Lena Mortensen's concerns in an ongoing study of the relationship between archaeology and local communities at Copan (Mortensen 2001a, 2001b). Mortensen participated in a number of planning activities, including the September 2001 meeting, and her work provides a nuanced discussion of these issues.

12. http://www.tiempo.hn/edicante/2001/septiembre/30%20septiembre/nacion~1/nacional.htm.

References

AAA (American Anthropological Association). 2001a. New AAA task force on indigenous peoples. *Anthropology News* 42(7):13.

———. 2001b. Update on human research oversight proposals. *Anthropology News* 42(7):21.

Abrams, Elliot M., and David J. Rue.1988. Causes and consequences of deforestation among the prehistoric Maya. *Human Ecology* 16:377–395.

Achebe, Chinua. 1988. *Hopes and impediments: Selected essays 1965–1987*. London: Heinemann.

Adam, David. 2003. Transgenic crop trial's gene flow turns weeds into wimps. *Nature* 421:462.

Agurcia Fasquelle, Ricardo. 1984. Depredación del patrimonio cultural en Honduras, el caso de la arqueología. *Yaxkin* 7:83–96.

Albert, Bruce, ed. 2001. *Research and ethics: The Yanomami case, Brazilian contributions to the* Darkness in El Dorado *controversy*. Documentos Yanomami 2. Brasilia/Boa Vista: CCPY/Pró-Yanomami.

Allen, G. 1999. Modern biological determinism: The Violence Initiative, the Human Genome Project, and the new eugenics. In *The practices of human genetics,* edited by M. Fortun and E. Mendelsohn, 1–23. London: Kluwer.

Almond, B. 1991. Rights. In *A companion to ethics,* edited by Peter Singer, 259–269. Oxford: Blackwell.

Altieri, Miguel A. 2002. Comment on Both sides now; Fallacies in the genetic-modification wars, implications for developing countries, and anthropological perspectives, by Glenn Davis Stone. *Current Anthropology* 43:619–620.

Altieri, Miguel A., and Peter Rosset. 1999. Ten reasons why biotechnology will not ensure food security, protect the environment, and reduce poverty in the developing world. *AgBioForum* 2(3 & 4):163–174.

Altieri, Miguel A., P. Rosset, and L. A. Thrupp. 1998.*The potential of agroecology to combat hunger in the developing world.* 2020 Brief 55. Washington, D.C.: International Food Policy Research Institute.

Anderson, Benedict. 1984. *Imagined communities: Reflections on the origins and spread of nationalism.* London: Verso.

Anderson, W. 2000. The possession of kuru: Medical science and biocolonial exchange. *Comparative Studies in Society and History* 42:713–744.

Andreski, Stanislaw. 1973. *Social sciences as sorcery.* Harmondsworth: Penguin.

Apel, Karl-Otto. 1999. The problem of justice in a multicultural society: The response of discourse ethics. In *Questioning ethics: Contemporary debates in philosophy,* edited by Richard Kearney and Mark Dooley. London and New York: Routledge.

Appadurai, Arjun. 1990. Disjuncture and difference in the global cultural economy. In *Global culture: Nationalism, globalization, and modernity,* edited by M. Featherstone, 295–310. London: Sage Publications.

———. 1996. *Modernity at large: Cultural dimensions of globalization.* Minneapolis: University of Minnesota Press.

Argueta, Mario R. 1989. *Bananos y política: Samuel Zemurray y la Cuyamel Fruit Company en Honduras.* Colección Realidad Nacional 27. Tegucigalpa: Editorial Universitaria.

ASA (Association of Social Anthropologists of the Commonwealth). 1987. *Association of Social Anthropologists of the Commonwealth: Ethical guidelines for good practice.* n.p.

Asad, Talal. 1993. *Genealogies of religion.* Baltimore: Johns Hopkins University Press.

———. 1994. Ethnographic representation, statistics, and modern power. *Social Research* 61:55–88.

———. 1997. On torture, or cruel, inhuman, and degrading treatment. In *Social suffering,* edited by Arthur Kleinman, Veena Das, and Margaret Lock. Berkeley: University of California Press.

Asombang, Raymond N. 1990. Museums and African identity: The museum in Cameroon—a critique. *West African Journal of Archaeology* 20:188–198.

Attwood, Bain, and John Arnold, eds. 1992. *Power, knowledge, and Aborigines.* Bundoora: La Trobe University Press.

Avise, John C. 1998. *The genetic gods: Evolution and belief in human affairs.* Cambridge: Harvard University Press.

Aziz, Heba. 1995. Understanding attacks on tourists in Egypt. *Tourism Management* 16:91–95.

Barth, Fredrik. 1974. On responsibility and humanity: Calling a colleague to account. *Current Anthropology* 15:100–102.

Baudrillard, Jean. 1994. *Simulacra and simulation.* Translated by S. F. Glaser. Ann Arbor: University of Michigan Press.

Bauman, Zygmunt. 1993. *Postmodern ethics.* Oxford: Blackwell.

Begley, Sharon. 2000. Into the heart of darkness. *Newsweek,* November 27.

Behe, Michael J. 1996. *Darwin's black box: The biochemical challenge to evolution.* New York: Free Press.

Bender, Susan J., and George S. Smith, eds. 2000. *Teaching archaeology in the twenty-first century.* Washington, D.C.: Society for American Archaeology.

Bent, J. Theodore. [1895] 1969. *The ruined cities of Mashonaland.* Bulawayo: Books of Rhodesia.

Bernal, Martin. 1991. *Black Athena: The Afroasiatic roots of classical civilization.* Vol.1. *The fabrication of ancient Greece: 1785–1985.* London: Vintage.

Bernauer, James, and David Rasmussen, eds. 1988. *The final Foucault.* Cambridge: MIT Press.

Berreman, Gerald D. 1962. *Behind many masks: Ethnography and impression management in a Himalayan village.* Ithaca: Society for Applied Anthropology.

———. 1991. Ethics versus "realism" in anthropology. In *Ethics and the profession of anthropology: Dialogue for a new era,* edited by Carolyn Fluehr-Lobban, 36–71. Philadelphia: University of Pennsylvania Press.

Biella, Peter. 2000. Visual anthropology in the Plague Year. *Anthropology News* 41(9):5–6.

Blixen, Karen. 1954. *Out of Africa.* London: Penguin.

Blok, Anton. 1962. A note on ethics and logic. *Sociologische Gids* 19:294–298.

Blundell, Geoff 1998. Rand, rock art, and resources: Tourism and our indigenous heritage. *Rock Art* 4–6:15–16.

Bond, Christopher. 2000. The benefits and politics of biotechnology: In front of the U.S. Senate. *Congressional Record,* January 26, S58–S63.

Boniface, P., and P. J. Fowler. 1993. *Heritage and tourism in "the global village."* London: Routledge.

Bourdieu, Pierre. 1977. *Outline of a theory of practice.* Translated by R. Nice. Cambridge: Cambridge University Press.

Boxer, C. R. 1965. *The Dutch seaborne empire, 1600–1800.* London: Hutchinson.

Braverman, Harry. 1974. *Labour and monopoly capital: The degradation of work in the twentieth century.* New York and London: Monthly Review Press.

Bray, Tamara L., ed. 2001. *The future of the past: Archaeologists, Native Americans, and repatriation.* New York: Garland.

Bray, Tamara L., and Thomas W. Killion, eds. 1994. *Reckoning with the dead: The Larsen Bay repatriation and the Smithsonian Institution.* Washington, D.C.: Smithsonian Institution Press.

Brenneis, Donald. 1994. Discourse and discipline at the National Research Council: A bureaucratic Bildungsroman. *Cultural Anthropology* 9(1):23–36.

——. 1999. New lexicon, old language: Negotiating the "global" at the National Science Foundation. In *Critical anthropology now: Unexpected contexts, shifting constituencies, changing agendas,* edited by George F. Marcus, 123–146. Santa Fe: School of American Research Press.

Briggs, Charles L., and Clara E. Mantini-Briggs. 2001. Review of *Darkness in El Dorado,* by Patrick Tierney. *Current Anthropology* 42:269–271.

Brown, Chris. 1999. Universal human rights: A critique. In *Human rights in global politics,* edited by Tim Dunne and Nicholas Wheller. Cambridge: Cambridge University Press.

Brodie, Neil, Jennifer Doole, and Colin Renfrew, eds. 2001. *Trade in illicit antiquities: The destruction of the world's archaeological heritage.* Cambridge: McDonald Institute for Archaeological Research.

Brown, Denise Fay. 1999. Mayas and tourists in the Maya world. *Human Organization* 58:295–304.

Brown, Michael F. 1998. Can culture be copyrighted? *Current Anthropology* 39:193–222.

Brown, Paul. 2000. Scientist "killed Amazonian Indians to test race theory." *The Guardian,* September 26.

——. 2001. GM rice promoters "have gone too far." *Guardian* (London), February 10.

Buckle, S. 1991. Natural law. In *A companion to ethics,* edited by Peter Singer, 161–174. Oxford: Blackwell.

Burger, Warren. 1980. Opinion in *Diamond v. Chakrabarty. Supreme Court Reporter* 100A, 447 US 303, 2205–2214.

Butler, Declan. 1999. Biotech industry seeks "honest brokers." *Nature* 398:360.

Byrne, Dennis. 2004. Messages to Manila. In I. Macfarlane, R. Paton, and M.J. Mountain (eds) *Many exchanges: Archaeology, history, community and the work of Isabel McBryde.* Canberra: Aboriginal History Inc.

———. 2003b. Nervous landscapes: Race and space in Australia. *Journal of Social Archaeology* 3:169–193.

Canby, William, Jr. 1988. *American Indian Law*. St. Paul: West.

Cantwell, Anne-Marie, Eva Friedlander, and Madeleine Tramm, eds. 2001. *Ethics and anthropology: Facing future issues in human biology, globalism, and cultural property*. New York: Annals of the New York Academy of Sciences.

Carneiro da Cunha, Maria Manuela. 1989. Letter to the editor/the AAA Committee on Ethics. *Anthropology News* 30(1):3.

Carrither, Michael, Steven Collins, and Steven Lukes. 1985. *The category of the person*. Cambridge: Cambridge University Press.

Castañeda, Quetzil. 1996. *In the museum of Maya culture: Touring Chichén Itzá*. Minneapolis: University of Minnesota Press.

Castells, Manuel. 1996. *The information age: Economy, society, and culture*. Vol.1. *The rise of the network society*. Oxford: Blackwell.

———. 1997. *The information age: economy, society, and culture*. Vol. 2. *The power of identity*. Oxford: Blackwell.

———. 1998. *The information age: Economy, society, and culture*. Vol. 3. *End of millennium*. Oxford: Blackwell.

Caton-Thompson, Gertrude. 1931. *The Zimbabwe culture: Ruins and reactions*. Oxford: Clarendon Press.

Cavalli-Sforza, L. L., P. Menozzi, and P. A. Piazza. 1995. *The history and geography of human genes*. Princeton: Princeton University Press.

Cavalli-Sforza, L. L., A. C. Wilson, C. R. Cantor, R. M. Cook-Deegan, and M.-C.King. 1991. Call for a worldwide survey of human genetic diversity: A vanishing opportunity for the Human Genome Project. *Genomics* 11:490–491.

Cavell, Stanley. 1997. Comments on Veena Das' essay. In *Social suffering*, edited by Arthur Kleinman, Veena Das, and Margaret Lock. Berkeley: University of California Press.

Chagnon, Napoleon. 1989. Letter. *Anthropology News* 30(1):3, 24.

———. 2000. Letter. Time, September 22. http://www.anth.ucsb.edu/chagnon2.html (accessed September 25, 2000).

Chalk, Rosemary, Mark S. Frankel, and Sallie B. Chafer.1980. *Professional ethics activities in the scientific and engineering societies*. Washington, D.C.: American Association for the Advancement of Science.

Chambers, Erve, ed. 1997. *Tourism and culture: An applied perspective*. Albany: State University of New York Press.

Champe, J. L., D. S. Byers, C. Evans, A. K. Guthe, H. W. Hamilton, E. B. Jelks, C. W. Meighan, S. Olafson, G. S. Quimby, W. Smith, and F. Wendorf. 1961. Four statements for archaeology. *American Antiquity* 27:137–139.

Charles, Daniel. 2001. *Lords of the harvest: Biotech, big money, and the future of food*. Cambridge: Perseus.

Chatterjee, Partha. 1997. Talking about our modernity in two languages. In *A possible India: Essays in political criticism*. Delhi: Oxford University Press.

Chatters, James C. 2001. *Ancient encounters: Kennewick Man and the first Americans*. New York: Simon and Schuster.

Chenier, Jacqueline, Stephen Sherwood, and Tahnee Robertson. 1999. Copan: Collaboration for identity, equity, and sustainability. In *Cultivating peace: Conflict and collaboration in natural resource management*, edited by Daniel Buckles. Ottawa: IDRC/World Bank.

Chomsky, Noam. 1967. The responsibility of intellectuals. In *American power and the new Mandarins*. New York: Pantheon.

Clark, Geoff A. 1996. NAGPRA and the demon-haunted world. *Society for American Archaeology Bulletin* 14(5):3, 15(2):4.

——.1998. NAGPRA, the conflict between science and religion, and political consequences. *Society for American Archaeology Bulletin* 16(5):22, 24–25.

Clifford, James, and George Marcus, eds. 1986. *Writing culture: The politics and poetics of ethnography*. Berkeley: University of California Press.

Colwell-Chanthaphonh, Chip. 2003a. Dismembering/disremembering the Buddhas: Renderings on the Internet during the Afghan purge of the past. *Journal of Social Archaeology* 3:75–98.

——. 2003b. Signs in place: Native American perspectives of the past in the San Pedro Valley of southeastern Arizona. *Kiva* 69:5–29.

Colwell-Chanthaphonh, Chip, and T. J. Ferguson, 2004. Virtue ethics and the practice of history: Native Americans and archaeologist along the San Pedro Valley of Arizona. *Journal of Social Archaeology* 4.

Comaroff, Jean, and John Comaroff. 1992. Ethnography and the historical imagination. In *Ethnography and the historical imagination*, edited by John and Jean Comaroff, 3–48. Boulder: Westview Press.

Comaroff, John, and Simon Roberts. 1981. *Rules and processes: The cultural logic of dispute in an African context*. Chicago: University of Chicago Press.

Coon, Carleton S. 1962. *The origin of races*. New York: Knopf.

Coroñil, Fernando. 2001a. Review of *Darkness in El Dorado*, by Patrick Tierney. *Current Anthropology* 42:265–256.

——. 2001b. Science-ethics-power: The production of knowledge and indigenous peoples. *Journal of the International Institute, University of Michigan* 9 (1):6–7, 26–27.

Crick, Malcolm. 1994. *Resplendent sites, discordant voices: Sri Lankans and international tourism.* Chur: Harwood Academic Publishers.

Crone, G. R. 1968. *Maps and their makers.* London: Hutchinson.

Cruz Sandoval, Fernando. 1997. Indian land conflict has roots that run historically deep. *Honduras This Week,* June 16. http://www.marrder. com/htw/jun97/editorial.htm (accessed January 10, 2002).

Cunningham, H. 1997. Colonial encounters in post-colonial contexts. *Critique of Anthropology* 18:205–233.

Dalton, Rex. 2000. Anthropologists in turmoil over allegations of misconduct. *Nature,* November 23, 391.

D'Andrade, Roy. 1995. Moral models in anthropology. *Current Anthropology* 36:399–408.

Daniel, Valentine. 1996. *Charred lullabies.* Princeton: Princeton University Press.

Das, Veena. 1997. Language and body: Transactions in the construction of pain. In *Social suffering,* edited by Arthur Kleinman, Veena Das, and Margaret Lock. Berkeley: University of California Press.

Daston, Lorraine. 1995. The moral economy of science. In *Constructing knowledge in the history of science,* edited by Arnold Thackeray, 3–24. Osiris 10.

Daston, Lorraine, and Katherine Park. 1995. *Wonders and the orders of nature: 1150–1750.* London: Zone.

Davis, Hester A., Jeffrey H. Altschul, Judith Bense, Elizabeth Brumfiel, Shereen Lerner, James J. Miller, Vincas P. Steponaitis, and Joe Watkins. 1999. Teaching archaeology in the 21st century: Thought on undergraduate education. *Society for American Archaeology Bulletin* 17(2):8–22.

Daviss, Bennett. 1997. Simple art of survival. *New Scientist* 154(2086):38–41.

Dawkins, Richard. 1995. *River out of Eden: A Darwinian view of life.* New York: Basic Books.

Deacon, Jeanette. 1990. Weaving the fabric of Stone Age research in Southern Africa. In *A history of African archaeology,* edited by Peter Robertshaw, 39–58. London: James Currey.

Dear, Peter. 1995. *Discipline and experience: The mathematical way in the scientific revolution.* Chicago: University of Chicago Press.

de Barros, P. 1990. Changing paradigms, goals, and methods in the archaeology of Francophone West Africa. In *A history of African archaeology,* edited by Peter Robertshaw, 155–172. London: James Currey.

de Duve, Christian. 2002. *Life evolving: Molecules, mind, and meaning.* New York: Oxford University Press.

de Lugan, Robin. 1994. Everything is coming up Maya! Archaeology, tourism, and identity in El Salvador, Central America. Undergraduate senior honors thesis in anthropology, University of California, Berkeley.

———. 2000. *Indigenismo:* Interests, motives, and government practice. Paper presented at the Twenty-third International Congress of the Latin American Studies Association, Miami.

Deloria, Vine, Jr. 1992a. American Indians. In *Multiculturalism in the United States,* edited by J. D. Buenker and L. A. Ratner, 31–52. New York: Greenwood Press.

———. 1992b. Indians, archaeologists, and the future. *American Antiquity* 57:559–566.

Deloria, Vine, Jr., and Clifford M. Lytle. 1984. *The nations within.* New York: Pantheon Books.

Dembski, William A. 2002. *No free lunch: Why specified complexity cannot be purchased without intelligence.* Lanham: Rowman and Littlefield.

De Munck, Victor. 2001. Science dehumanizing? *Anthropology News* 42(4):3.

Denning, Kathryn E. 1999. On archaeology and alterity. Ph.D. diss., University of Sheffield.

Derrida, Jacques. 1976. *Of grammatology.* Translated by G. C. Spivak. Baltimore: Johns Hopkins University Press.

Derrida, Jacques, et al. 1999. Hospitality, justice, and responsibility: A dialogue with Jacques Derrida. In *Questioning ethics: Contemporary debates in philosophy,* edited by Richard Kearney and Mark Dooley. London and New York: Routledge.

Desmond, Adrian. 1997. *Huxley: From devil's disciple to evolution's high priest.* Reading, Mass.: Addison-Wesley.

DeVries, Joseph, and Gary Toenniessen. 2001. *Securing the harvest: Biotechnology, breeding, and seed systems for African crops.* New York: CABI International.

Diop, Cheikh Anta. 1979. *Nations nègres et culture.* Paris: Présence Africaine.

Dixon, Roland B. 1913. Some aspects of North American archaeology. *American Anthropologist* 15:549–566.

Dolgin, J. L. 2001. Ideologies of discrimination: Personhood and the "genetic group." *Studies in the History and Philosophy of Biology and Biomedical Sciences* 32:705–721.

Dongoske, Kurt E., Mark Aldenderfer, and Karen Doehner eds. 2000. *Working together: Native Americans and archaeologists.* Washington, D.C.: Society for American Archaeology.

Dorsey, G. A. 1900. The Department of Anthropology of the Field

Columbian Museum: A review of six years. *American Anthropologist* 2:247–265.

Dowson, Thomas. 1994. Re-production and consumption: The use of rock art imagery in Southern Africa today. In *Miscast: Negotiating the presence of the Bushmen,* edited by Pippa Skotnes, 315–321. Cape Town: University of Cape Town Press.

Duster, T. 2003. Medicine and people of color. *San Francisco Chronicle,* March 17.

Economist. 1997. Bloodbath at Luxor. November 20.

Edensor, Tim. 1998. *Tourists at the Taj: Performance and meaning at a symbolic site.* New York: Routledge.

EDTF (El Dorado Task Force). 2003. *El Dorado Task Force final report.* 2 vols. http://www.aaanet.org.edtf/final (accessed August 10, 2003).

Ehrlich, Paul R. 1968. *The population bomb.* New York: Ballantine Books.

El-Din, M. S. 1999. Plain talk. *Al-Ahram Weekly Online.* http://www/weekly.ahram.org.

Elia, Ricardo J. 1995. Conservators and unprovenanced objects: Preserving the cultural heritage of servicing the antiquities trade? In *Antiquities trade or betrayed: Legal, ethical, and conservational issues,* edited by K. W. Tubb, 244–255. London: Archetype.

———. 1997. Looting, collecting, and the destruction of archaeological resources. *Nonrenewable Resources* 6:85–98.

Ellis, Walter. 1997. In the name of Allah. *Sunday Times,* November 23.

El Saadawi, Nawal. 1997. *The Nawal El Saadawi reader.* New York: Zed Books.

Elvin, John. 1997. Greenpeace: A green activist changes colors. *Insight on the News,* October 20. http://www.insightmag.com/news/1997/10/20/Nation/Greenpeace.A.Green.Activist.Changes.Colors-211809.shtml.

England, Sarah, and Mark Anderson. 1998. Authentic African culture in Honduras? Afro-Central Americans challenge Honduran Indo-Hispanic mestizaje. Paper prepared for presentation at the Twenty-first International Congress of the Latin American Studies Association, Chicago.

Eshleman, J. A., R. Malhi, and D. G. Smith. 2003. Mitochondrial DNA studies of Native Americans: Conceptions and misconceptions of the population prehistory of the Americas. *Evolutionary Anthropology* 12:7–18.

Euraque, Darío A. 1996. *Reinterpreting the Banana Republic: Region and state in Honduras, 1870–1972.* Chapel Hill: University of North Carolina Press.

———. 1998. Antropólogos, arqueólogos, imperialismo y la mayanización de Honduras: 1890–1940. *Yaxkin* 17:85–101.

Evans-Pritchard, E. E. 1940. *The Nuer.* Oxford: Oxford University Press.

Fabian, Johannes. 1971. Language, history, and anthropology. *Philosophy of the Social Sciences* 1:19–47.

———. 1979. Rule and process: Thoughts on ethnography as communication. *Philosophy of the Social Sciences* 9:1–26.

———. 1983. *Time and the other: How anthropology makes its object.* New York: Columbia University Press.

———. 1991. Dilemmas of critical anthropology. In *Constructing knowledge: Authority and critique in social science,* edited by Lorraine Nencel and Peter Pels, 180–202. London: Sage Publications.

Fagan, Brian M. 1977. *The rape of the Nile: Tomb robbers, tourists, and archaeologists in Egypt.* London: Macdonald and Jane.

———. 1993. The arrogant archaeologist. *Archaeology* 46:4–16.

Fahim, H. M. 2001. European travelers in Egypt. In *Travellers in Egypt,* edited by Paul Starkey and Janet Starkey, 7–11. London: Tauris Parke.

Fash, William L., Ricardo Agurcia Fasquelle, Barbara W. Fash, and Rudy Larios Villalta. 1996. The future of the Maya past: The convergence of conservation and restoration. In *Eighth Palenque Round Table, 1993,* edited by Martha J. Macri and Jan McHargue, 203–211. San Francisco: Pre-Columbian Art Research Institute.

Fash, William L., and Barbara W. Fash. 1997. Investing in the past to build a better future: The Copán Sculpture Museum in Honduras, Central America. *Cultural Survival Quarterly* 21(1):47–51.

Fash, William L., Richard V. Williamson, Carlos Rudy Larios, and Joel Palka. 1992. The Hieroglyphic Stairway and its ancestors: Investigations of Copan Structure 10L-26. *Ancient Mesoamerica* 3:105–115.

Ferguson, T. J. 1990. NHPA: Changing the role of Native Americans in the archaeological study of the past. *Society for American Archaeology Bulletin* 17(1):33–37.

———. 1996. Native Americans and the practice of archaeology. *Annual Review of Anthropology* 25:63–79.

Fluehr-Lobban, Carolyn, ed. 1991. *Ethics and the profession of anthropology: Dialogue for a new era.* Philadelphia: University of Pennsylvania Press.

———. 1994. Informed consent in anthropological research: We are not exempt. *Human Organization* 53(1):1–10.

Flyvbjerg, Bent. 2001. *Making social science matter: Why social inquiry fails and how it can succeed again.* Cambridge: Cambridge University Press.

Force, Roland. 1999. *Politics and the Museum of the American Indian.* Honolulu: Mechas Press.

Forsman, Leonard A. 1997. Straddling the current: A view from the bridge over clear salt water. In *Native Americans and archaeologists*, edited by Nina Swidler, Kurt E. Dongoske, Roger Anyon, and Alan S. Downer, 105–111. Walnut Creek: AltaMira Press.

Foster, John B., and Fred Magdoff. 2000. Liebig, Marx, and the depletion of soil fertility: Relevance for today's agriculture. In *Hungry for profit: The agribusiness threat to farmers, food, and the environment*, edited by Fred Magdoff, John B. Foster, and F. H. Buttel, 43–60. New York: Monthly Review Press.

Foster, Scarlett Lee. 2000. Counterpoint: Biotechnology has been subjected to thousands of lab and field tests. *St. Louis Post-Dispatch*, May 20.

Fotiadis, Michalis. 1993. Regions of the imagination: Archaeologists, local people, and the archaeological record in fieldwork, Greece. *Journal of European Archaeology* 1:151–170.

Foucault, Michel. 1980. *The history of sexuality*. New York: Vintage.

———. 1982. Discourse on language. In *The archaeology of knowledge*. New York: Pantheon.

———. 1988. Technologies of the self. In *Technologies of the self: A seminar with Michel Foucault*, edited by L. H. Martin, H. Gutman, and P. H. Hutton. Amherst: University of Massachusetts Press.

Fox, Richard G., ed. 1991a. *Recapturing anthropology: Working in the present*. Santa Fe: School of American Research Press.

———. 1991b. Introduction: Working in the present. In *Recapturing anthropology: Working in the present*, edited by Richard G. Fox, 1–16. Santa Fe: School of American Research Press.

Franklin, A., and M. Crang. 2001. The trouble with tourism and travel theory? *Tourist Studies* 1:5–22.

Fraser, Nancy. 1997. *Justice interruptus: Critical reflections on the "post-socialist" condition*. New York: Routledge.

Freed, S. A., R. S. Freed, and L. Williamson. 1988. Capitalist philanthropy and Russian revolutionaries: The Jesup North Pacific Expedition 1897–1902. *American Anthropologist* 90:7–24.

Gamboni, D. 2001. World heritage: Shield or target? *Conservation: The Getty Conservation Institute Newsletter* 16:5–11.

Garlake, Peter S. 1973. *Great Zimbabwe*. London: Thames and Hudson.

Garrett, Wilbur E. 1989. La Ruta Maya. *National Geographic* 176:424–479.

Gaskell, George, Nick Allum, Martin Bauer, Jonathan Jackson, Susan Howard, and Nicola Lindsey. 2003. Climate change for biotechnology? UK public opinion 1991–2002. *AgBioForum* 6 (1&2):55–67. http://www.agbioforum.org/v6n12/v6n12a12-gaskell.htm.

Geldenhuys, H. 2001. Court rejects Richtersveld claim. *Cape Times,* March 23.

Georgetown College Republicans. 2002. Marxist Vandana Shiva speaks on campus. http://ky.collegerepublicans.org/georgetown/Marxist .html 4/25/2002.

Ghasarian, Christian. 1997. Ethique et anthropologie aux Etats Unis. Paper presented at the workshop "Questions d'éthique en anthropologie sociale," Association Professionelle des Rechercheurs en Anthropologie Sociale, Paris, October 22.

Gipstein, Richard Seth. 2003. The isolation and purification exception to the general unpatentability of products of nature. *Columbia Science and Technology Law Review* 2 (January 15). http://www.stlr.org/ cite.cgi?volume=4&article=2.

Golden, John M. 2001. Biotechnology, technology policy, and patentability: Natural products and invention in the American system. *Emory Law Journal* 50:101–191.

Goldstein, Lynne. 1992. The potential for future relationships between archaeologists and Native Americans. In *Quandaries and quests: Visions of archaeology's future,* edited by LuAnn Wandsnider, 59–71. Center for Archaeological Investigations, Southern Illinois University, Occasional Paper 20.

González, Nancie L. 1988. *Sojourners of the Caribbean: Ethnogenesis and ethnohistory of the Garifuna.* Urbana: University of Illinois Press.

———. 1992. *Dollar, dove, and eagle: One hundred years of Palestinian migration to Honduras.* Ann Arbor: University of Michigan Press.

Goodin, R. E. 1991. Utility and the good. In *A companion to ethics,* edited by Peter Singer, 241–248. Oxford: Blackwell.

Goodman, A. 2000. Why genes don't count for racial differences in health. *American Journal of Public Health* 90:1699–1701.

Gordon, George Byron. 1896. *Prehistoric ruins of Copan, Honduras: A preliminary report of the explorations by the museum, 1891–1895.* Peabody Museum Memoirs 1(1). Cambridge: Peabody Museum of American Archaeology and Ethnology, Harvard University.

———. 1902. *The Hieroglyphic Stairway, Ruins of Copan: Report on explorations by the museum.* Peabody Museum Memoirs 1(6). Cambridge: Peabody Museum of American Archaeology and Ethnology, Harvard University.

Gouldner, Alvin W. 1980. *The two Marxisms: Contradictions and anomalies in the development of theory.* London: Macmillan.

Greely, H. T. 1997. Proposed model ethical protocol for collecting DNA samples. *Houston Law Review* 34:1431–1473.

——. 1998. Legal, ethical, and social issues in human genome research. *Annual Review of Anthropology* 27:473–502.

Green, Ernestene L., ed. 1984. *Ethics and values in archaeology.* New York: Free Press.

Greenberg, Joseph H., Christy G. Turner II, and Stephen L. Zegura. 1986. The settlement of the Americas: A comparison of the linguistic, dental, and genetic evidence. *Current Anthropology* 27:477–497.

Greenblatt, Stephen. 1999. The touch of the real. In *The fate of culture: Geertz and beyond,* edited by Sherry Ortner. Berkeley: University of California Press.

Guillaumin, Colette. 1991. Race and discourse. In *Race, discourse, and power in France,* edited by Maxim Silverman. Aldershot: Avebury.

Gupta, Akhil, and James Ferguson. 1997. *Anthropological locations: Boundaries and grounds of a field science.* Berkeley: University of California Press.

Hall, Martin. 1984. The burden of tribalism: The social context of southern African Iron Age studies. *American Antiquity* 49:455–467.

——. 1987. *The changing past: Farmers, kings, and traders in Southern Africa, 200–1860.* Cape Town: David Philip.

——. 1988. Archaeology under apartheid. *Archaeology* 41(6):62–64.

——. 1990. "Hidden history": Iron Age archaeology in Southern Africa. In *A history of African archaeology,* edited by Peter Robertshaw, 59–77. London: James Currey.

——. 1995. Great Zimbabwe and the lost city: The cultural colonization of the South African past. In *Theory in archaeology: A world perspective,* edited by Peter J. Ucko, 28–45. London: Routledge.

——. 1996. *Archaeology Africa.* Cape Town: David Philip.

——. 2000. *An archaeology of the modern world.* London: Routledge.

——. 2001a. Timeless time: Africa in the world. In *Archaeology: The widening debate,* edited by B. Cunliffe, W. Davies, and C. Renfrew. London: British Academy.

——. 2001b. Straylight, Mala Mala, Pink Frikkie, Blekgelexy, and Rumba Kali @Africa. The net: New apprentices and old masters. *Mots Pluriels* 18 (August).

——. 2002. Blackbirds and black butterflies. *Refiguring the archive,* edited by Carolyn Hamilton, Verne Harris, Jane Taylor, Michael Pickover, Graeme Reid, and Razia Saleh, 333–361. Cape Town: David Philip.

Hamer, Dean H., and Peter Copeland. 1998. *Living with our genes.* New York: Doubleday.

Hamer, D., S. Hu, V. L. Magnuson, N. Hu, and A. M. L. Pattatucci.1993. A linkage between DNA markers on the X chromosome and male sexual orientation. *Science* 261:321–327.

Hames, Raymond. 2001. Review of *Darkness in El Dorado*, by Patrick Tierney. *Current Anthropology* 42:271–272.

Hamilton, Neil D. 1993. Who owns dinner? Evolving legal mechanisms for ownership of plant genetic resources. *Tulsa Law Journal* 28:587–657.

Hannerz, Ulf. 2003. Macro-scenarios: Anthropology and the debate over contemporary and future worlds. *Social Anthropology* 11:169–187.

Haraway, Donna. 1991. *Simians, cyborgs, and women: The reinvention of nature*. London: Free Association Books.

Hardt, Michael, and Antonio Negri. 2000. *Empire*. Cambridge: Harvard University Press.

Harper, Richard. 1998. *Inside the IMF: An ethnography of documents, technology, and organizational action*. San Diego: Academic Press.

Harry, D., and J. Marks. 1999. Human population genetics versus the HGDP: Comment on the paper by Resnick. *Politics and the Life Sciences* 19:303–305.

Harvey, David. 2000a. *Spaces of hope*. Edinburgh: Edinburgh University Press.

——. 2000b. Cosmopolitanism and the banality of geographical evils. *Public Culture* 12:529–564.

Harwick, Hugh. 2000. Guilty as charged. *Ecologist* 30(7):52–53.

Hasemann, George, Gloria Lara Pinto, and Fernando Cruz Sandoval. 1996. *Indios de Centroamerica*. Madrid: Editorial MAPFRE.

Hasemann, George. 1986. Acercamiento a los principios de la salvaguardia del patrimonio construido en América Latina. *Yaxkin* 9:77–91.

Hawthorn, Geoffrey. 1976. *Enlightenment and despair: A history of sociology*. Cambridge: Cambridge University Press.

Healy, Paul F. 1984. Archaeology abroad: Ethical considerations of fieldwork in foreign countries. In *Ethics and values in archaeology*, edited by Ernestene L. Green, 123–132. New York: Free Press.

Henderson, Elizabeth. 2000. Rebuilding local food systems from the grassroots up. In *Hungry for profit: The agribusiness threat to farmers, food, and the environment*, edited by Fred Magdoff, John B. Foster, and F. H. Buttel, 175–188. New York: Monthly Review Press.

Herbert, David T., ed. 1995. *Heritage, tourism and society*. London: Mansell.

Herrera, Rossibel. 1995. Patrimonio cultural mueble: Su situación actual. *Yaxkin* 13:92–100.

Herscher, E., and F. P. McManamon. 2000. Public education and outreach: The obligation to educate. In *Ethics in American archaeology*, edited by Mark J. Lynott and Alison Wylie. Washington, D.C.: Society for American Archaeology.

Hervik, Peter. 1998. The mysterious Maya of *National Geographic. Journal of Latin American Anthropology* 4:166–197.

Herzfeld, Michael. 1987. Romanticism and Hellenism. In *Anthropology through the looking-glass*. Cambridge: Cambridge University Press.

———. 1991. *A place in history: Social and monumental time in a Cretan town*. Princeton: Princeton University Press.

Hewett, Edgar L. 1908. The groundwork of American archaeology. *American Anthropologist*, n.s.,10:591–595.

Hill, Jane. 2000. Getting out the real story. *Anthropology News* 41(8):5.

Hinsley, Curtis. 1985. From shell heaps to stelae: Early anthropology at the Peabody Museum. In *Objects and others: Essays on museums and material culture*, edited by George W. Stocking Jr., 49–74. History of Anthropology 3. Madison: University of Wisconsin Press.

Hobsbawm, Eric. 1994. *The age of extremes: A history of the world, 1914–1991*. New York: Pantheon Books.

Hochschild, Adam. 1999. *King Leopold's ghost: A story of greed, terror, and heroism in colonial Africa*. London: Macmillan.

Hodder, Ian. 1998. The past and passion and play: Çatalhöyük as a site of conflict in the construction of multiple pasts. In *Archaeology under fire: Nationalism, politics, and heritage in the Eastern Mediterranean and the Middle East*, edited by Lynn M. Meskell, 124–139. London: Routledge.

Hofstadter, Richard. 1967. *The paranoid style in American politics and other essays*. New York: Vintage Books.

Holl, Augustin. 1990. West African archaeology: Colonialism and nationalism. In *A history of African archaeology*, edited by Peter Robertshaw, 296–308. London: James Currey.

Homer-Dixon, Thomas. 1994. Environmental scarcities and violent conflict: Evidence from cases. *International Security* 19:5–40.

Hooton, Earnest A. 1939. *The American criminal: An anthropological study*. Vol. 1. *The native white criminal of native parentage*. Cambridge: Harvard University Press.

Hotwired. 1997. Biotech: A healer or hazard? January 3–22. http://hotwired.wired.com/braintennis/97/02/index0a.html.

Hrdlička, Aleš. 1914. Physical anthropology in America: An historical sketch. *American Anthropologist* 16:507–554.

Huband, M. 2001. *Egypt: Regional leader and global player, a market for the 21st century*. London: Euromoney Books.

Huffman, Thomas N. 1996. *Snakes and crocodiles: Power and symbolism in ancient Zimbabwe*. Johannesburg: Witwatersrand University Press.

Hufford, Mary. 1994. Introduction: Rethinking the cultural mission. In *Conserving culture: A new discourse on heritage,* edited by Mary Hufford, 1–11. Urbana: University of Illinois Press.

Hurtado, A. M., K. Hill, H. Kaplan, and J. Lancaster. 2001. Disease among indigenous South Americans. *Anthropology News* 42(2):5–6.

Huxley, Thomas H. 1892. Science and morals. In *Essays upon some controverted questions.* London: Macmillan.

Hymes, Dell. 1964. Introduction: Toward ethnographies of communication. In *The ethnography of communication,* edited by John J. Gumperz and Dell Hymes, 1–34. American Anthropologist 66(6), pt. 2.

Ignatieff, Michael. 1978. *A just measure of pain: The penitentiary in the Industrial Revolution, 1750–1850.* New York: Pantheon.

IHAH (Instituto Hondureño de Antropología e Historia). 1984. *Monumento nacional Ruinas de Copan, plan de manejo y desarrollo: Resumen.* Tegucigalpa.

Independent Online. 1999. San people. http://www.iol.co.za.

Jacobs, Jane M. 1996. *Edge of empire: Postcolonialism and the city.* London: Routledge.

Jackson, F. 2001. The Human Genome Project and the African American community: Race, diversity, and American science. In *The Human Genome Project and minority communities: Ethical, social, and political dilemmas,* edited by R. A. Zilinskas and P. J. Balint, 35–52. Westport: Praeger.

Jackson, J. J., Jr. 2001. "In ways unacademical": The reception of Carleton S. Coon's *The Origin of Races. Journal of the History of Biology* 34:247–285.

James, Clive. 2000. *Global status of commercialized transgenic crops: 1999.* Ithaca: ISAAA.

Janke, T. 1998. *Our culture—our future: Report on Australian indigenous cultural and intellectual property rights.* Surrey Hills: Australian Institute of Aboriginal and Torres Strait Islander Studies and the Aboriginal and Torres Strait Islander Commission.

Jeganathan, Pradeep. 1989. Train from Batticoloa. *The Thatched Patio* 53.
———. 2004. The train from Batticoloa. In *At the water's edge.* New York: South Focus.

Jenkins, Simon. 1995. Out of Africa and out of context. Why is the Royal Academy using artefacts of African life to adorn walls that have hung Rembrandt and Titian? *Times,* October 7.
———. 1997. Hysteria calls the shots. *Times,* November 19.

Jenner, P., and C. Smith. 1993. *Tourism in the Mediterranean.* London: Economist Intelligence Unit.

Johnson, Elden. 1973. Professional responsibilities and the American Indian. *American Antiquity* 38:129–130.

Johnson, Phillip E. 1998. *Objections sustained: Subversive essays on evolution, law, and culture.* Downer's Grove, Ill.: InterVarsity Press.

Joyce, Rosemary A. 1993. The construction of the Mesoamerican frontier and the Mayoid image of Honduran polychromes. In *Reinterpreting prehistory of Central America,* edited by Mark Miller Graham, 51–101. Niwot: University Press of Colorado.

———. 2002. Academic freedom, stewardship, and cultural heritage: Weighing the interests of stakeholders in crafting repatriation approaches. In *The dead and their possessions: Repatriation in principle, policy and practice,* edited by Cressida Fforde, Jane Hubert, Paul Turnbull, 99–107. London: Routledge.

———. 2003. Archaeology and nation building: A view from Central America. In *The politics of archaeology and identity in a global context,* edited by Susan Kane, 79–100. Archaeological Institute of America Colloquia and Conference Papers 7.

Joyce, Rosemary A., and John S. Henderson. 2001. Beginnings of village life in eastern Mesoamerica. *Latin American Antiquity* 12:5–24.

Juengst, E. T. 1998. Groups as gatekeepers to genomic research: Conceptually confusing, morally hazardous, and practically useless. *Kennedy Institute of Ethics Journal* 8:183–200.

Jung, Carl C. 1973. *Memories, dreams, reflections.* London: Random House.

Kahn, Joel S. 1995. *Culture, multiculture, postculture.* London: Sage Publications.

———. 2001a. *Modernity and exclusion.* London: Sage Publications.

———. 2001b. Anthropology and modernity. *Current Anthropology* 42:651–680.

Kaplan, Robert D. 1994. The coming anarchy: How scarcity, crime, overpopulation, and disease are rapidly destroying the social fabric of our planet. *Atlantic Monthly,* February, 44–76.

Karafet, T. M., S. L. Zegura, O. Posukh, L. Osipova, A. Bergen, J. Long, D. Goldman, W. Klitz, S. Harihara, P. de Knijff, V. Wiebe, R. C. Griffiths, A. R. Templeton, and M. F. Hammer. 1999. Ancestral Asian sources of New World Y-chromosome founder haplotypes. *American Journal of Human Genetics* 64:817–831.

Kaufman, J., and S. Hall. 2003. The slavery hypertension hypothesis: Dissemination and appeal of a modern race theory. *Epidemiology and Society* 14:111–126.

Kennedy, Michael D. 2001. The Yanomamo and the global university. *Journal of the International Institute, University of Michigan* 91:7.

Kidd, J. R., K. K. Kidd, and K. M. Weiss. 1993. Forum: Human genome diversity initiative. *Human Biology* 65:1–6.

Killion, T., W. Sturtevant, D. Stanford, and D. Hunt. 1999. The facts about Ishi's brain. *Anthropology News* 40(6):9.

Kipling, Rudyard. 1893. *Barrack room ballads and other verses.* 6th ed. London: Methuen.

Kirshenblatt-Gimblett, Barbara. 1998. *Destination culture: Tourism, museums, and heritage.* Berkeley: University of California Press.

Kitcher, Philip. 2001. *Science, truth, and democracy.* Oxford: Oxford University Press.

Kleinman, Daniel Lee, and Jack Kloppenburg Jr. 1991. Aiming for the discursive high ground: Monsanto and the biotechnology controversy. *Sociological Forum* 6:427–447.

Klockars, C. B. 1979. Dirty hands and deviant subjects. In *Deviance and decency: The ethics of research with human subjects,* edited by C. B. Klockars and F. W. O'Connor. London: Sage Publications.

Kloppenburg, Jack Ralph, Jr. 1988. *First the seed: The political economy of plant biotechnology, 1492–2000.* Cambridge: Cambridge University Press.

Kluckhohn, Clyde. 1939. The place of theory in anthropological studies. *Philosophy of Science* 6:328–344.

Kohl, Philip L., and Clare Fawcett, eds. 1995. *Nationalism, politics, and the practice of archaeology.* Cambridge: Cambridge University Press.

Kolman, C., N. Sambuughin, and E. Bermingham. 1996. Mitochondrial DNA analysis of Mongolian populations and implications for the origin of New World founders. *Genetics* 142:1321–1334.

Koning, Hans. 1991. *Columbus: His enterprise.* New York: Monthly Review Press.

Kroeber, Theodora. 1961. *Ishi in two worlds.* Berkeley: University of California Press.

Kuklick, Henrika, and Robert Kohler, eds. 1996. *Science in the field.* Osiris 11, special issue.

Lambrecht, Bill. 2001. *Dinner at the New Gene Cafe.* New York: St. Martin's Press.

Lamphere, Louise. 2003. The perils and prospects for an engaged anthropology: A view from the United States. *Social Anthropology* 11:153–168.

Landau, Misia. 1991. *Narratives of human evolution.* New Haven: Yale University Press.

Lanfant, Marie-Françoise, John B. Allcock, and Edward M. Bruner, eds. 1995. *International tourism: Identity and change.* London: Sage Publications.

Lappé, Frances Moore, Joseph Collins, and Peter Rosset.1998. *World hunger: 12 myths*. New York: Grove Press.

Lappé, Marc, and Britt Bailey. 1998. *Against the grain: Biotechnology and the corporate takeover of your food*. Monroe, Maine: Common Courage Press.

Latour, Bruno. 1993. *We have never been modern*. Cambridge: MIT Press.

——. 1999. *Pandora's hope: Essays on the reality of science studies*. Cambridge: Harvard University Press.

Latour, Bruno, and Steven Woolgar. 1979. *Laboratory life: The construction of scientific facts*. Princeton: Princeton University Press.

Lawler, A. 2003. Impending war stokes battle over fate of Iraqi antiquities. *Science* 299:643.

Lee, Richard B., and Irven DeVore, eds. 1968. *Man the hunter*. Chicago: Aldine.

Le Fleur, C. A. 2001. Resolutions as agreed by official and associate delegates to the National Khoisan Consultative Conference on Khoisan diversity in national unity. http://www.und.ac.za/und/ccms/anthropology (accessed April 2003).

Legal Brief. 2001. Richtersveld community loses fight for land, March 23.

Levidow, Les.1999. Regulating Bt maize in the United States and Europe: A scientific-cultural comparison. *Environment* 41(10):10–22.

Levine, Felice. 2001. Written testimony submitted on behalf of the Consortium of Social Sciences Associations in cooperation with the American Sociological Association to the Committee on Assessing the System for Protecting Human Research Subjects, the Institute of Medicine, the National Academies. http://www.cossa.org/humanparticipants.html.

Levy, Janet. 1993. Anthropological ethics, the PPR, and the CoE: Thoughts from the frontline. *Anthropology News* 35(2):1, 5.

Lewontin, R. C. 2000. The maturing of capitalist agriculture: Farmer as proletarian. In *Hungry for profit: The agribusiness threat to farmers, food, and the environment*, edited by Fred Magdoff, John B. Foster, and F. H. Buttel, 93–106. New York: Monthly Review Press.

Lewontin, R. C., and Jean-Pierre Berlan. 1986. Technology, research, and the penetration of capital: The case of U.S. agriculture. *Monthly Review* 38(3):21–34.

Ley del patrimonio cultural de la nación. 1984. *Yaxkin* 7:123–139.

Lilley, Ian, ed. 2000a. *Native title and the transformation of archaeology in the postcolonial world*. Oceania Monographs 50. Sydney: University of Sydney.

———. 2000b. Professional attitudes to indigenous interests in the native title era: Settler societies compared. In *Native title and the transformation of archaeology in the postcolonial world*, edited by Ian Lilley, 99–119. Oceania Monographs 50. Sydney: University of Sydney.

Lilley, Ian, and M. Williams. n.d. Archaeological and indigenous significance: A view from Australia. In *Heritage of value, archaeology of renown: Reshaping archaeological assessment and significance*, edited by C. Mathers, T. Darvill, and B. Little. Gainesville: University of Florida Press.

Lindee, Susan. 2001. Review of *Darkness in El Dorado*, by Patrick Tierney. *Current Anthropology* 42:272–274.

Lipe, William D. 1974. A conservation model for American archaeology. *The Kiva* 39:213–245.

———. 1996. In defense of digging: Archaeological preservation as a means, not an end. *CRM Magazine* 19(7):23–27.

Logan, G., and M. P. Leone. 1997. Tourism with race in mind: Annapolis, Maryland, examines its African-American past through collaborative research. In *Tourism and culture: An applied perspective*, edited by Erve Chambers, 129–146. Albany: State University of New York Press.

Longino, Helen. 2002. *The fate of knowledge*. Princeton: Princeton University Press.

Lovrenovic, Ivan. 1994. The hatred of memory: In Sarajevo, burned books and murdered pictures. *New York Times*, May 28.

Lurquin, Paul F. 2001. *The green phoenix: A history of genetically modified plants*. New York: Columbia University Press.

Lynott, Mark J. 1997. Ethical principles and archaeological practice: Development of an ethics policy. *American Antiquity* 62:589–599.

Lynott, Mark J., and Alison Wylie, eds. 1995a. *Ethics in American archaeology: Challenges for the 1990s*. Washington, D.C.: Society for American Archaeology.

———, eds. 1995b. Stewardship: The central principle for archaeological ethics. In *Ethics in American archaeology: Challenges for the 1990s*, edited by Mark J. Lynott and Alison Wylie, 28–32. Washington, D.C.: Society for American Archaeology.

MacCannell, Dean. 1992. *Empty meeting grounds: The tourist papers*. London: Routledge.

———. 2000. Cultural tourism. *Conservation: The Getty Conservation Institute Newsletter* 15:24–27.

———. 2001. Tourist agency. *Tourist Studies* 1:23–37.

McGimsey, Charles R. 1995. Standards, ethics, and archaeology: A brief history. In *Ethics in American archaeology: Challenges for the 1990s*, edited by Mark J. Lynott and Alison Wylie, 11–13. Washington, D.C.: Society for American Archaeology.

McGimsey, Charles R., and Hester A. Davis, eds.1977. *The management of archaeological resources: The Airlie House report.* Washington, D.C.: Society for American Archaeology.

McGloughlin, Martina. 1999. Ten reasons why biotechnology will be important to the developing world. *AgBioForum* 2(3&4):163–174. http://www.agbioforum.org.

McGuire, Randall. 1992. Archaeology and the First Americans. *American Anthropologist* 94:816–836.

Macilwain, Colin. 1999. Access issues may determine whether agri-biotech will help the world's poor. *Nature* 402:341–345.

MacIntyre, Alasdair. 1984. *After virtue.* 2d ed. Notre Dame: University of Notre Dame Press.

———. 1993. Ethical dilemmas: Notes from outside the field. *Anthropology News* 34(7):5–6.

Magdoff, Fred, John B. Foster, and F. H. Buttel, eds. 2000. *Hungry for profit: The agribusiness threat to farmers, food, and the environment.* New York: Monthly Review Press.

Malinowski, Bronislaw. 1922. *Argonauts of the Western Pacific.* London: Routledge.

———. [1926] 1972. *Crime and custom in savage society.* Totowa: Littlefield, Adams.

———. [1922] 1972. *Argonauts of the Western Pacific.* Prospect Heights: Waveland Press.

Malthus, Thomas R. [1798] 1959. *Population: The first essay.* Ann Arbor: University of Michigan Press.

Mann, Susan, and James Dickinson. 1978. Obstacles to the development of capitalist agriculture. *Journal of Peasant Studies* 5:466–481.

Marcus, George. 1986. Contemporary problems of ethnography in the modern world system. In *Writing culture: The poetics and politics of ethnography,* edited by James Clifford and George Marcus, 165–193. Berkeley: University of California Press.

Marcus, George, and Michael Fischer. 1986. *Anthropology as cultural critique: An experimental moment in the human sciences.* Chicago: University of Chicago Press.

Marks, Jonathan. 1999. They saved Ishi's brain! *Anthropology News* 40(4):22.

———. 2000. Human biodiversity as a central theme of biological anthropology: Then and now. *Kroeber Anthropological Society Papers* 84:1–10.

———. 2002. "We're going to tell those people who they really are": Science and relatedness. In *Relative values: Reconfiguring kinship studies,* edited by Sarah Franklin and Susan McKinnon, 355–383. Durham, N.C.: Duke University Press.

———. 2003. *What it means to be 98% chimpanzee.* Berkeley: University of California Press.

Martineau, Belinda. 2001. *First fruit: The creation of the Flavr Savr™ tomato and the birth of genetically engineered food.* New York: McGraw-Hill.

Marx, Karl. [1858] 1973. *Grundrisse: Foundations of the critique of political economy.* New York: Vintage Books.

Massad, Joseph A. 2001. *Colonial effects.* New York: Columbia University Press.

Maudslay, Alfred P. 1889. Archaeology volume 1, preface, introduction: Copan. In *Biologia central-americana,* edited by F. Ducane Godman and Osbert Salvin. London: Published for the editors by R. H. Porter and Dulau & Co.

Mbembe, Achille. 2001. *On the postcolony.* Berkeley: University of California Press.

Mead, Margaret, and Rhoda Métraux, eds. 1953. *The study of culture at a distance.* Chicago: University of Chicago Press.

Meehan, B. 1995. Aboriginal views on the management of rock art sites in Australia. In *Perceiving rock art: Social and political perspectives,* edited by Knor Helskog and Bjornar Olsen, 295–316. Oslo: Institute for Comparative Research in Human Culture.

Mehta, Uday. [1990] 1997. Liberal strategies of exclusion. In *Tensions of empire: Colonial cultures in a bourgeois world,* edited by Frederick Cooper and Ann Stoler. Berkeley: University of California Press.

Menget, Patrick. 1996. Ethique et anthropologie. In *Dictionnaire d'éthique et de philosophie moral,* edited by M. Canto-Sperber and A. Fagot-Lagean. Paris: Presses Universitaires de France.

Merriwether, A., F. Rothhammer, and R. E. Ferrell. 1995. Distribution of the four founding lineage haplotypes in Native Americans suggests a single wave of migration for the New World. *American Journal of Physical Anthropology* 98:411–430.

Meskell, Lynn M., ed. 1998. *Archaeology under fire: Nationalism, politics, and heritage in the Eastern Mediterranean and the Middle East.* London: Routledge.

——. 2001. The practice and politics of archaeology in Egypt. In *Ethics and anthropology: Facing future issues in human biology, globalism, and cultural property*, edited by Anne-Marie Cantwell, Eva Friedlander, and Madeleine Tramm, 146–169.

——. 2002a. The intersection of identity and politics in archaeology. *Annual Review of Anthropology* 31:279–301.

——. 2002b. Negative heritage and past mastering in archaeology. *Anthropological Quarterly* 75:557–574.

Messenger, Phyllis Mauch, ed. 1999. *The ethics of collecting cultural property.* Albuquerque: University of New Mexico Press.

Miller, D. W. 2000. Scholars fear that alleged misdeeds by Amazon anthropologists will taint entire discipline. *Chronicle of Higher Education,* September 20.

Mitchell, Timothy. 2002. *Rule of experts: Egypt, techno-politics, modernity.* Berkeley: University of California Press.

Moffat, Anne Simon. 1999. Crop engineering goes South. *Science* 285:370–371.

Morris, C. 1997. Indigenous intellectual property rights: The responsibilities of maintaining the oldest continuous culture in the world. *Indigenous Law Bulletin* 19. http://www.austlii.edu.au/au/journals/ILB/1997/19.html (accessed April 2003).

Mortensen, Lena. 2001a. Ancient Maya, *Mundo Maya,* Hotel Maya: Managing the future and past at Copan. Paper presented at the Sixty-first Annual Meeting of the Society for Applied Anthropology, Mérida.

——. 2001b. Las dinámicas locales de un patrimonio global: Arqueoturismo en Copán, Honduras. *Mesoamérica* 22(43):103–134.

Mortensen, Lena, and K. Anne Pyburn. 2000. The future of the past: The development potential of archaeological settlement patterns. Paper presented at the Annual Meeting of the Society for American Archaeology, Philadelphia.

Moseley, C. W. R. D., ed. 1983. *The travels of Sir John Mandeville.* Harmondsworth: Penguin.

Moser, S., D. Glazier, S. Ballard, J. Phillips, L. N. el Nemer, M. S. Mousa, S. Richardson, A. Conner, and M. Seymour. 2002. Transforming archaeology through practice: Strategies for collaborative archaeology and the Community Archaeology Project at Quseir, Egypt. *World Archaeology* 34:220–248.

Mowaljarlai, D., P. Vinnicombe, G. K. Ward, and C. Chippindale. 1988. Repainting of images on rock in Australia and the maintenance of Aboriginal culture. *Antiquity* 62:690–696.

Müller-Hill, Benno. 1988. *Murderous science*. New York: Oxford University Press.

Murphy, M. 1997. Lure of ancient capital of the pharaohs. *Times*, October 19.

Museum of the American Indian. 1929. Indian Notes and Monographs 36.

Nader, Laura. 1970. From anguish to exultation. In *Women in the field*, edited by Peggy Golde. Chicago: Aldine.

Narayan, Kirin. 1997. How native is a native anthropologist? *American Anthropologist* 95(3):19–34.

Narayan Swamy, M. R. 2001. *Tigers of Lanka: From boys to guerrillas*. Delhi: Konark.

National Institutes of Health. 1996. *Report on the rating of grant applications*. Bethesda.

National Museum of the American Indian. 2002. *The changing presentation of the American Indian*. Washington, D.C.: Smithsonian Institution/Seattle: University of Washington Press.

National Research Council. 1997. *Evaluating human genetic diversity*. Washington, D. C.: National Academy Press.

NBAC (National Bioethics Advisory Committee). 1999. *Ethical and policy issues in research involving human participants: NBAC recommendations*. Washington, D.C.

Nicholas, George P. 2000. Archaeology, education, and the Secwepemc. In *Working together: Native Americans and archaeologists*, edited by Kurt E. Dongoske, Mark Aldenderfer, and Karen Doehner, 155–164. Washington, D.C.: Society for American Archaeology.

Nord, Mark, Margaret Andrews, and Steven Carlson. 2003. *Household food security in the United States, 2002*. Food Assistance and Nutrition Research Report (FANRR35). Washington, D.C.: USDA Economic Research Service. http://www.ers.usda.gov/publications/fanrr35/.

Nugent, Stephen. 2001. Anthropology and public culture; The Yanomami, science, and ethics. *Anthropology Today* 173:10–14.

Numbers, Ronald L. 1992. *The creationists*. New York: Knopf.

Odermatt, P. 1996. Built heritage and the politics of representation: Local reactions to the appropriation of the monumental past in Sardinia. *Archaeological Dialogues* 3:95–136.

OHRP (Office for Human Research Protections). 1998. *Human subject regulations decision charts*. Washington, D.C.: U.S. Department of Health and Human Services. http://ohrp.osophs.dhhs.gov/human subjects/guidance/decisioncharts.html.

——. 2001. *IRB guidebook*. Washington, D.C.: U.S. Department of Health and Human Services. http://ohrp.osophs.dhhs.gov/irb_guidebook.html.

OSP (Office of Sponsored Projects), University of California, Santa Cruz. 2000. *Draft guidelines of the Committee for Protection of Human Subjects, UCSC Institutional Review Board*. http://www.ucsc.edu/osp/hsirb.html.

Pagden, Anthony. 1995. *Lords of all the world: Ideologies of empire in Spain, Britain, and France, c. 1500–c. 1800*. New Haven and London: Yale University Press.

——. 1998. The genesis of "governance" and Enlightenment conceptions of the cosmopolitan world order. *International Social Science Journal* 50(155):7–15.

Passmore, John. 1974. *Man's responsibility for nature*. New York: Scribner.

Pastor Fasquelle, Rodolfo. 1989 *Biografía de San Pedro Sula: 1536–1954*. San Pedro Sula: DIMA.

Pels, Peter. 1994. National codes of ethics and European anthropology: A call for cooperation and exchange. *EASA Newsletter* 13:9–10.

——. 1999. Professions of duplexity: A prehistory of ethical codes in anthropology. *Current Anthropology* 40:101–136.

——. 2000. The trickster's dilemma: Ethics and the technologies of the anthropological self. In *Audit cultures: Anthropological studies in accountability, ethics, and the academy*, edited by Marilyn Strathern, 135–172. London and New York: Routledge.

——. 2001a. Letter. *Anthropology News*.

——. 2001b. Review of *Darkness in El Dorado*, by Patrick Tierney. *Current Anthropology* 42:268–269.

Pels, Peter, and Oscar Salemink. 1999. Introduction: Locating the colonial subjects of anthropology. In *Colonial subjects: Essays in the practical history of anthropology*, edited by Peter Pels and Oscar Salemink, 1–52. Ann Arbor: University of Michigan Press.

Peluso, Nancy Lee, and Michael Watts. 2001. Violent environments. In *Violent environments*, edited by Nancy Lee Peluso and Michael Watts, 3–38. Ithaca: Cornell University Press.

Pevar, Stephen. 1992. *The rights of Indians and tribes*. Carbondale and Edwardsville: Southern Illinois University Press.

Phillips, Tom. 1995. Introduction. In *Africa: The art of a continent*, edited by Tom Phillips, 11–20. London: Royal Academy of Arts.

Politis, Gustavo. 2001. On archaeological praxis, gender bias, and indigenous peoples in South America. *Journal of Social Archaeology* 1:90–107.

Potrykus, Ingo. 2000. The "Golden Rice" tale. *AgBioWorld,* November 25. http://www.agbioworld.org/biotech_info/topics/goldenrice/tale.html.

Power, Michael. 1994. *The audit explosion.* London: Demos.

———. 1997. *The audit society: Rituals of verification.* Oxford: Oxford University Press.

Prakash, C. S. 2000. Genetically engineered crops can feed the world! *21st Century Science and Technology Magazine,* Summer. http://21st centurysciencetech.com/articles/biotech.html#Royalty.

Preston, D. 1997. The lost man. *The New Yorker,* June 16, 70–78, 80–81.

Price, David. 2000a. Anthropologists as spies. *The Nation,* November 20.

———. 2000b. The AAA and the CIA. *Anthropology News* 41(8):13–14.

Purdue, Derrick A. 2000. *Anti-genetiX: The emergence of the anti-GM movement.* Aldershot: Ashgate.

Pyburn, K. Anne. 1998a. Consuming the Maya. *Dialectical Anthropology* 23:111–129.

———. 1998b. Opening the door to Xibalba: The construction of Maya history. *Indiana Journal of Hispanic Literatures* 13:125–130.

Pyburn, K. Anne, and Richard Wilk. 2000. Responsible archaeology is applied anthropology. In *Ethics in American archaeology,* edited by Mark J. Lynott and Alison Wylie. Washington, D.C.: Society for American Archaeology.

Qaim, M., and G. Traxler. 2004. Roundup Ready soybeans in Argentina: Farm level and aggregate welfare effects. *Agricultural Economics* 40. In press.

Raab, L. Mark. 1984. Achieving professionalism through ethical fragmentation: Warnings from client-oriented archaeology. In *Ethics and values in archaeology.* Edited by Ernestene L. Green, 51–61. New York: Free Press.

Rabinow, Paul. 1997. Introduction: The history of systems of thought. In *Ethics, subjectivity, and truth: Essential works of Foucault,* vol. 1, edited by Paul Rabinow, xi–xlii. New York: New Press.

RAFI (Rural Advancement Foundation International). 2001. *2001, A seed Odyssey: RAFI's annual update on Terminator and Traitor technology.* RAFI Communiqué, April 11. http://www.etcgroup.org/documents/com_2001.pdf.

Rai, Arti. 2000. Addressing the patent gold rush: The role of deference to PTO patent denials. *Washington University Journal of Law and Policy* 2:199–227.

Ramos, Alcida Rita. 1987. Reflecting on the Yanomami: Ethnographic images and the pursuit of the exotic. *Cultural Anthropology* 2:284–304.

———. 2001a. Review of *Darkness in El Dorado*, by Patrick Tierney. *Current Anthropology* 42:274–276.

———. 2001b. About ethics in ethnographic research. *Journal of the International Institute, University of Michigan* 9(1):7.

Rawls, John. 1971. *A theory of justice.* Cambridge: Harvard University Press.

Reddy, A. Sudarshan, and Venkateshwar Rao, eds. 1998. The gathering agrarian crisis: Farmers' suicides in Warangal District (A.P.), India. http://www.artsci.wustl.edu/~stone/suicide.html.

Reid, Donald. M. 1985. Indigenous Egyptology: The decolonization of a profession? *Journal of the American Oriental Society* 105:233–246.

Reiss, A. J., Jr. 1979. Governmental regulation of scientific inquiry: Some paradoxical consequences. In *Deviance and decency: The ethics of research with human subjects,* edited by C. B. Klockars and F. W. O'Connor. London: Sage Publications.

Renfrew, Colin. 2000. *Loot, legitimacy, and ownership: The ethical crisis in archaeology.* London: Duckworth.

Rice, G., C. Anderson, N. Risch, and G. Ebers. 1999. Male homosexuality: Absence of linkage to microsatellite markers at Xq28. *Science* 284:665–667.

Richards, Paul. 1997. Toward an African Green Revolution? An anthropology of rice research in Sierra Leone. In *The ecology of practice: Studies of food crop production in sub-Saharan West Africa,* edited by A. Endre Nyerges, 201–252. Amsterdam: Gordon and Breach.

Riedlmayer, Andras. 1998. Fighting the destruction of memory: A call for an ingathering of Bosnian manuscripts. http://www.applicom.com/manu/ingather.htm.

Risch, N., E. Burchard, E. Ziv, and H. Tang. 2002. Categorization of humans in biomedical research: Genes, race, and disease. *Genome Biology* 3:2007.1–2007.12.

Ritchie, Mark Andrew. 2001. False murder charges letter. *Anthropology News* 42(4):3.

Rivas, Ramon D. 1993. *Pueblos indígenas y garífuna de Honduras.* Tegucigalpa: Editorial Guaymuras.

Robertshaw, Peter. 1990. The development of archaeology in East Africa. In *A history of African archaeology,* edited by Peter Robertshaw, 78–94. London: James Currey.

Robison, Richard, ed.1996. *Politics and economics in the twenty-first century: Is there an Asian model?* Pacific Review 9(3).

Rojek, Chris, and John Urry, eds. 1997. *Touring cultures: Transformations of travel and theory.* London: Routledge.

Rorty, Richard. 1991. *Objectivity, relativism, and truth.* Cambridge: Cambridge University Press.

Rosaldo, Renato. 1993. Grief and a head-hunter's rage. In *Culture and truth: The remaking of social analysis.* Boston: Beacon Press.

Rosenberg, N. A., J. K. Pritchard, J. L. Weber, H. M. Cann, K. K. Kidd, L. A. Zhivotovsky, and M. W. Feldman. 2002. Genetic structure of human populations. *Science* 298:2181–2185.

Ross, Eric B. 1998. *The Malthus factor: Population, poverty, and politics in capitalist development.* London: Zed Books.

Rubin, Philip. 1998. The protection of participants in non-medical research. Paper presented at the OHRP/USC National Human Subjects Protections Education Workshop, Long Beach, Calif.

Rushdie, Salman. 1998. Comment: It's human nature. *The Guardian,* December 3.

Rushton, J. Philippe. 1995. *Race, evolution, and behavior: A life-history approach.* New Brunswick: Transaction.

SAA (Society for American Archaeology). [1977] 1995. By-laws. In *Archaeologists of the Americas: 1995 membership directory,* 17–25. Washington, D.C.: Society for American Archaeology.

———. 1996. Principles of archaeological ethics. *American Antiquity* 61:451–452.

Sahlins, Marshall. 2000. Guilty not as charged. *Washington Post,* December 10.

Said, Edward W. [1978] 1985. *Orientalism.* Harmondsworth: Penguin.

———. 1989. Representing the colonized: Anthropology's interlocutors. *Critical Inquiry* 75:205–225.

Sayers, Dorothy L., ed. 1949. *The comedy of Dante Alighieri the Florentine.* Cantica 1. *Hell.* Harmondsworth: Penguin.

Scham, Sandra A. 1998. Mediating nationalism and archaeology: A matter of trust? *American Anthropologist* 100:301–308.

Scham, Sandra A., and Adel Yahya. 2003. Heritage and reconciliation. *Journal of Social Archaeology* 3:399–416.

Scheper-Hughes, Nancy. 1995. The primacy of the ethical: Propositions for a militant anthropology. *Current Anthropology* 36:409–420.

———. 1996. Theft of life. *Anthropology Today* 12:3–11.

Schepers, Emile. 2001. Uncertainty and naiveté. *Anthropology News* 42(3):3.

Schmitt, Carl. 1996 1932. *The concept of the political.* Chicago: University of Chicago Press.

Scholte, Bob. [1969] 1974. Toward a reflexive and critical anthropology. In *Reinventing anthropology,* edited by Dell Hymes, 430–457. New York: Vintage Books.

Schouten, F. 1995. Heritage as historical reality. In *Heritage, tourism, and society,* edited by David T. Herbert, 21–31. New York: Mansell.

Scott, David. 1994. *Formations of ritual.* Minneapolis: University of Minnesota Press.

Scott, James C. 1985. *Weapons of the weak: Everyday forms of peasant resistance.* New Haven and London: Yale University Press.

Sen, Amartya. 1981. *Poverty and famines.* Oxford: Clarendon.

——. 1993. The economics of life and death. *Scientific American,* May, 40–47.

Sennott, C. M. 1997. Egyptian tourist attack leaves 71 dead: Government puts blame on Islamic militants. *Boston Globe,* November 18.

Shaffer, Simon. 1994. Self-evidence. In *Questions of evidence: Proof, practice, and persuasion across the disciplines,* edited by James Chandler, Arlond I. Davidson, and Harry Harootunian, 56–91. Chicago and London: University of Chicago Press.

Shapin, Steven. 1994. *A social history of truth: Civility and science in seventeenth-century England.* Chicago: University of Chicago Press.

Shea, Christopher. 2000. Don't talk to humans: The crackdown on social science research. *The New Republic Online* 106 (accessed September 25, 2000).

Shepherd, Nick. 2003. "When the hand that holds the trowel is black . . .": Disciplinary practices of self-representation and the issue of "native" labour in archaeology. *Journal of Social Archaeology* 3:334–351.

Shore, Cris, and Susan Wright. 1997. *Anthropology of policy: Critical perspectives on governance and power.* London and New York: Routledge.

Shore, Cris, and Susan Wright. 1999. Audit culture and anthropology: Neo-liberalism in British higher education. *Journal of the Royal Anthropological Institute* 5:557–575.

——. 2000. Coercive accountability: The rise of audit culture in higher education. In *Audit culture. Anthropological studies in accountability, ethics, and the academy,* edited by Marilyn Strathern, 57–89. London and New York: Routledge.

Simpson, Caroline. 2000. Modern Qurna: Pieces of an historical jigsaw. Paper presented at the Theban Necropolis Colloquium, British Museum, London.

——. 2001. Qurna discovery on the move. *Theban Panoramas' News* 4:1–3.

Simpson, George Gaylord. 1949. *The meaning of evolution.* New Haven: Yale University Press.

Sinclair, Paul, Innocent Pikirayi, et al. 1993. Urban trajectories on the Zimbabwean plateau. In *The archaeology of Africa: Food, metals, and towns*, edited by Thurstan Shaw, Paul Sinclair, B. W. Andah, and A. Okpoko, 705–731. London: Routledge.

Skotnes, Pippa, ed. 1996. *Miscast: Negotiating the presence of the Bushmen.* Cape Town: University of Cape Town Press.

Slyomovics, Susan. 1989. Cross-cultural dress and tourist performance in Egypt. *Performing Arts Journal* 33–34:139–150.

Smith, Elizabeth A. 1999. "Primitive other" or "our distant ancestors"? Nubian identity in tourism in Egypt. M.A. thesis, New York University.

Smith, Linda Tuhiwai. 1999. *Decolonizing methodologies.* London: Zed Books.

Snow, A. A., D. Pilson, L. H. Rieseberg, M. J. Paulsen, N. Pleskac, M. R. Reagon, D. E. Wolf, and S. M. Selbo. 2003. A Bt transgene reduces herbivory and enhances fecundity in wild sunflowers. *Ecological Applications* 13:279–286.

SOPA (Society of Professional Archaeologists).1991.Code of ethics. In *Guide to the Society of Professional Archaeologists*, 7–11. n.p.

Spector, Janet D. 2000. Collaboration at Inyan Ceyaka Atonwan (Village at the Rapids). In *Working together: Native Americans and archaeologists*, edited by Kurt E. Dongoske, Mark Aldenderfer, and Karen Doehner, 133–138. Washington, D.C.: Society for American Archaeology.

Spinden, Herbert J. 1913. *A study of Maya art, its subject matter and historical development.* Peabody Museum Memoirs 6. Cambridge: Peabody Museum of American Archaeology and Ethnology, Harvard University.

Sponsel, Leslie. 2002. On reflections on *Darkness in El Dorado. Current Anthropology* 43:149–150.

Stanton, William. 1960. *The leopard's spots: Scientific attitudes toward race in America, 1815–59.* Chicago: University of Chicago Press.

Stark, Miriam T. 1992. Where the money goes: Current trends in archaeological funding. In *Quandaries and quests: Visions of archaeology's future*, edited by L. Wandsnider, 41–58. Carbondale: Center for Archaeological Investigations, Southern Illinois University.

Starn, Orin. 2004. *Ishi's brain: In search of American's last "wild" Indian.* New York: W. W. Norton.

Steinbrecher, Ricarda A., and Pat Roy Mooney. 1998. Terminator technology: The threat to world food security. *Ecologist* 28:276–279.

Stephens, John Lloyd. 1841. *Incidents of travel in Central America, Chiapas, and Yucatan.* London: John Murray.

Stewart, C. Neal, Jr. 2003. Press before paper: When media and science collide. *Nature Biotechnology* 21:353–354.

Stocking, George W., ed. 1983. *Observers observed: Essays on ethnographic fieldwork.* Madison: University of Wisconsin Press.

Stocking, George W. 1995. Delimiting anthropology: Historical reflections on the boundaries of a boundless discipline. *Social Research* 62(4).

Stolcke, Verena. 1995. Talking culture: New boundaries, new rhetorics of exclusion in Europe. *Current Anthropology* 36:1–24.

Stoll, David. 2001a. Science attacks Amazon tribe. *The New Republic,* March 19, 34–39.

——. 2001b. The altar boy and the anthropologist. *Anthropology News* 42(4):6.

Stone, Glenn Davis. 2002a. Both sides now: Fallacies in the genetic-modification wars, implications for developing countries, and anthropological perspectives. *Current Anthropology* 43:611–630.

——. 2002b. Biotechnology and suicide in India. *Anthropology News* 43(5):5.

——. 2004. Biotechnology and the political ecology of information in India. *Human Organization* 63:

Strathern, Marilyn. 1997. From improvement to enhancement: An anthropological comment on the audit culture. Founder's Memorial Lecture, Girton College, Cambridge.

——, ed. 2000a. *Audit culture: Anthropological studies in accountability, ethics, and the academy.* London and New York: Routledge.

——. 2000b. Accountability and ethnography. In *Audit cultures: Anthropological studies in accountability, ethics, and the academy,* edited by Marilyn Strathern. London and New York: Routledge.

——. 2000c. New accountabilities. In *Audit cultures: Anthropological studies in accountability, ethics, and the academy,* edited by Marilyn Strathern. London and New York: Routledge.

Stuart, David. 1992. Hieroglyphs and archaeology at Copan. *Ancient Mesoamerica* 3:169–184.

Subramanian, S. 1995. The story in our genes. *Time,* January 16, 54–55.

Swain, J. 1997. Terror at the Temple. *Sunday Times,* November 23.

Swidler, Nina, Kurt Dongoske, Roger Anyon, and Alan Downer, eds. 1997. *Native Americans and archaeologists: Stepping stones to common ground.* Walnut Creek: AltaMira Press.

Szathmary, Emöke. 1993. MtDNA and the peopling of the Americas. *American Journal of Human Genetics* 62:1153–1170.

Tagueiff, Pierre-André, ed. 1992. *Face au racisme.* Vol. 2. *Analyses, hypothèses, perspectives.* Paris: La Découverte.

Tatomir, Joanna. 2001. Can scientists be trusted? *Anthropology News* 42(5):3.

Taylor, Charles. 1981. The concept of the person. In *Philosophical papers*, vol. 1. Cambridge: Cambridge University Press.

——. 1989. *Sources of the self: The making of the modern identity*. Cambridge: Cambridge University Press.

——. 1995. *Sources of the self*. Chicago: University of Chicago Press.

——. 2001. Two theories of modernity. In *Alternative modernities*, edited by D. P. Gaonkar, 172–196. Durham: Duke University Press.

Teilhard de Chardin, Pierre. 1959. *The phenomenon of man*. New York: Harper and Row.

Thomas, David Hurst. 2000. *Skull wars: Kennewick man, archaeology, and the battle for Native American identity*. New York: Basic Books.

Thomson, Jennifer. 2000. The poor need biotechnology. *Chicago Tribune*, July 27.

Tierney, Patrick. 2000a. The fierce anthropologist. *The New Yorker*, October 9, 50–61.

——. 2000b. *Darkness in El Dorado: How scientists and journalists devastated the Amazon*. New York and London: W. W. Norton.

Tobias, Philip V. 2002. Saartje Baartman: Her life, her remains, and the negotiations for their repatriation from France to South Africa. *South African Journal of Science* 98:107–110.

Tomaselli, K. G. 1999. Encounters in the Kalahari: A revisionist history. *Visual Anthropology* 12:2–3.

Tooby, John. 2000a. Jungle fever. *Hey, Wait a Minute: Slate Archives*. http://slate.msn.com/HeyWait/00-12-24/HeyWait.asp (accessed November 24, 2000).

——. 2000b. Witchcraft accusations in anthropology. *Anthropology News* 41(9):8.

Torroni, A., J. Neel, R. Barrantes, T. Schurr, and D. Wallace. 1994. Mitochondrial DNA "clock" for the Amerinds and its implications for timing their entry into North America. *Proceedings of the National Academy of Sciences, U.S.A.* 91:1158–1162.

Toumey, Christopher P. 1994. *God's own scientists: Creationists in a secular world*. New Brunswick: Rutgers University Press.

Travel Industry World Yearbook. 1998–1999. *Egypt*. New York: Child and Waters.

Trigger, Bruce G. 1984. Alternative archaeologies: Nationalist, colonialist, imperialist. *Man* 19:355–370.

——. 1989. *A history of archaeological thought*. Cambridge: Cambridge University Press.

——. 1990. The history of African archaeology in world perspective. In *A history of African archaeology*, edited by Peter Robertshaw, 309–319. London: James Currey.

Tripp, Robert. 2001. "Twixt cup and lip": Biotechnology and resource-poor farmers. *Nature Biotechnology* 19(2):93.

Tully, James. 1995. *Strange multiplicity: Constitutionalism in an age of diversity.* Cambridge: Cambridge University Press.

Turnbull, Colin. 1973. *The mountain people.* New York: Simon and Schuster.

Turner, Terence. 2000. Letter to Samuel Katz, September 29. http://www.egroups.com/message/evolutiuonary-psychology/7470 (accessed November 24, 2000).

———. 1997. Human rights, human difference. In *Universal human rights versus cultural relativity,* edited by Terence Turner and Carole Nagengast, 273–291. Journal of Anthropological Research 53(3).

UNESCO. 2001a. Benefits of ratification. http://www.unesco.org/whc/kit-ratification.htm#debut (accessed January 10, 2001).

———. 2001b. Criteria for inclusion of cultural properties in the World Heritage List. http://www.unesco.org/whc/opgulist.htm#para23 (accessed January 10, 2001).

———. 2001c. Honduras. http://www.unesco.org/whc/sp/hon.htm (accessed January 10, 2001).

———. 2001d. Maya site of Copan. UNESCO World Heritage List. http://www.unesco.org/whc/sites/129.htm (accessed January 10, 2001).

University of Michigan. 2000. University of Michigan report pts. 1–3 on the ongoing investigations of the Neel-Chagnon allegations.

———. 2001. Statement from the Office of the Provost, May 29. *Journal of the International Institute, University of Michigan* 9(1):6.

Vaillant, George C. 1927. The chronological significance of Maya ceramics. Ph. D. diss., Harvard University.

Urry, John. 1990. *The tourist gaze.* London: Sage Publications.

———. 1995. *Consuming places.* London: Sage Publications.

van den Berghe, Pierre L. 1995. Marketing Mayas: Ethnic tourism promotion in Mexico. *Annals of Tourism Research* 22:568–588.

van der Hoeven, Rutger. 2000. Stammenstrijd onder antropologen. *Trouw,* October 20.

van der Spek, Kees. 1998. Dead mountain versus living community: The Theban Necropolis as cultural landscape. In *Proceedings of the Third International Seminar Forum UNESCO: University and Heritage,* edited by W. S. Logan, C. Long, and J. Martin, 176–182. Melbourne: Deakin University Press.

van Meijl, Toon. 2000a. Modern morals in postmodernity: A critical reflection on professional codes of ethics. *Cultural Dynamics* 121:65–81.

——. 2000b. The politics of ethnography in New Zealand. In *Ethnographic artifacts: Challenges to a reflexive anthropology,* edited by S. J. Jaarsma and M. A. Rohatynskyj, 86–103. Honolulu: University of Hawai'I Press.

Vergano, Dan. 2000. Anthropologists to air violent Amazon dispute. *USA Today,* November 16.

Verrips, Jojada. 2003. Dr. Jekyll and Mr. Hyde: Modern medicine between magic and science. In *Magic and modernity: Interfaces of revelation and concealment,* edited by Birgit Meyer and Peter Pels, 223–240. Stanford: Stanford University Press.

Visvanathan, Shiv, and Chandrika Parmar. 2002. A biotechnology story: Notes from India. *Political and Economic Weekly,* July 6, 2714–2724.

Vitelli, Karen D. 1984. The international traffic in antiquities: Archaeological ethics and the archaeologists' responsibility. In *Ethics and values in archaeology,* edited by Ernestene L. Green, 143–155. New York: Free Press.

——, ed. 1996. *Archaeological ethics.* Walnut Creek: AltaMira Press.

Wade, N. 2002. Gene study identifies 5 main human populations. *New York Times,* December 20.

Wagner, Peter. 1999. The resistance that modernity constantly provokes: Europe, America, and social theory. *Thesis Eleven* 58:35–58.

Washington Legal Foundation. 2002. Fight hunger, not biotechnology. January 22. http://www.wlf.org/communicating/advocacy/hunger. htm.

Watkins, Joe. 1999. Conflicting codes: Professional, ethical, and legal obligations in archaeology. *Science and Engineering Ethics* 5:337–346.

——. 2000. *Indigenous archaeology: American Indian values and scientific practice.* Walnut Creek: AltaMira Press.

Weber, Max. 1958. Science as a vocation. In *From Max Weber: Essays in sociology,* edited by H. H. Gerth and C. Wright Mills, 129–158. New York: Oxford University Press.

Weiss, Rick. 1999. Sowing dependency or uprooting hunger? *Washington Post,* February 8.

Welchman, Jennifer. 1999. The virtues of stewardship. *Environmental Ethics* 21:412–423.

West, Cornel. 1995. Preface. In *Africa: The art of a continent,* edited by Tom Phillips, 9–10. London: Royal Academy of Arts.

Weston, Kath. 1997. Virtual anthropologist. In *Anthropological locations: Boundaries and grounds,* edited by Akhil Gupta and James Ferguson. Berkeley: University of California Press.

White, Hayden. 1978. *Tropics of discourse.* Baltimore: Johns Hopkins University Press.

Whittaker, J. 2000. Old brains and modern sentiments. *Anthropology News* 41(8):4.

Wildesen, L. E. 1984. The search for an ethic in archaeology. In *Ethics and values in archaeology,* edited by Ernestene L. Green, 3–12. New York: Free Press.

Wilford, John Noble, and Simon Romero. 2000. Book seeks to indict anthropologists who studied Brazil Indians. *New York Times,* September 28.

Wilk, Richard R. 1999. Whose forest? whose land? whose ruins? Ethics and conservation. *Science and Engineering Ethics* 5:367–374.

Wilk, Richard R., and K. Anne Pyburn. 1998. Archaeological ethics. In *Encyclopedia of applied ethics,* vol. 1, 197–207.

Wilkinson, Charles. 1987. *American Indians, time, and the law.* New Haven: Yale University Press.

Williams, Raymond. 1977. *Marxism and literature.* Oxford: Oxford University Press.

Wilmsen, Edwin N. 1989. *Land filled with flies: A political economy of the Kalahari.*

Wilson, E. O. 1998. *Consilience.* New York: Knopf.

Wilson, Jeyaratnam. 2000. *S. J. Chelvanayakam and the crisis of Sri Lankan Tamil nationalism, 1947–77: A political biography.* London: Hurst.

Wissler, Clark. 1917. The new archaeology. *American Museum Journal* 17:100–101.

Wittgenstein, Ludwig. 1958. *Philosophical investigations.* London: Blackwell.

Wolf, Eric.1994. Perilous ideas: Race, culture, people. *Current Anthropology* 35:1–12.

Wolfe, Patrick. 1999. White man's flour: The politics and poetics of an anthropological discovery. In *Colonial subjects: Essays on the practical history of anthropology,* edited by Peter Pels and Otto Salemink, 196–240. Ann Arbor: University of Michigan Press.

Wood, Allan W. 1999. *Kant's ethical thought.* Cambridge: Cambridge University Press.

Wood, Ellen M. 2000. The agrarian origins of capitalism. In *Hungry for profit: The agribusiness threat to farmers, food, and the environment,* edited by Fred Magdoff, John B. Foster, and F. H. Buttel, 23–41. New York: Monthly Review Press.

Wood, M. 1998. The use of the pharaonic past in modern Egyptian nationalism. *Journal of the American Research Center in Egypt* 35:179–196

Woodiwiss, Anthony. 1998. *Globalisation, human rights, and labour law in Pacific Asia.*

Wylie, Alison. 1992. Rethinking the Quincentennial: Consequences for past and present. *American Antiquity* 57:591–594.

———. 1996. Ethical dilemmas in archaeological practice: Looting, repatriation, stewardship, and the (trans)formation of disciplinary identity. *Perspectives on Science* 4:154–194.

———. 1999. Science, conservation, and stewardship: Evolving codes of conduct in archaeology. *Science and Engineering Ethics* 5:319–336.

———. 2000. Rethinking unity as a working hypothesis for philosophy of science: How archaeologists exploit the disunity of science. *Perspectives on Science* 7:293–317.

———. 2002. *Thinking from things: Essays in the philosophy of archaeology.* Berkeley: University of California Press.

Zalewski, Daniel. 2000. Anthropology enters the age of cannibalism. *New York Times*, October 8.

Zimmerman, Larry J. 1995. Regaining our nerve: Ethics, values, and the transformation of archaeology. In *Ethics in American archaeology: Challenges for the 1990s*, edited by Mark J. Lynott and Alison Wylie, 64–67. Washington, D.C.: Society for American Archaeology.

Zimmerman, Larry J., Karen D. Vitelli, and Julie Hollowell-Zimmer, eds. 2003. *Ethical issues in archaeology.* Walnut Creek: AltaMira Press.

Index